中国故事丛书

Understanding Modern China Series

（Editor-in-Chief：Feng Jun）

冯 俊◎主编

中国治理新方略

China's New Strategies for Governing the Country
By Feng Jun，et al

冯 俊◎主编

人民出版社

总　序

　　中国国家的制度安排是怎样的？中国共产党为什么能够长期执政并带领全中国人民不断从胜利走向胜利？中国共产党执政的"秘诀"有哪些？中国的发展道路是什么？中国现阶段有哪些重大战略？中国下一步发展向何处去？中国经济为什么能够快速发展？诸如此类的问题，都是国际社会尤其是外国政党政要来华访问时思考和询问的问题。为了回答这些问题，让读者了解一个真实的中国和中国共产党，我们组织编写了《"中国故事"丛书》（以下简称《丛书》），作为介绍中国共产党，介绍中国发展道路、发展理论和发展经验的基本材料。

　　《丛书》以党的十八大以来习近平总书记提出的治国理政新理念新思想新战略为指导，着力体现"中国梦"的发展愿景和"两个一百年"的奋斗目标，着力体现协调推进"五位一体"的总体布局和统筹推进"四个全面"的战略布局，着力体现把握、适应和引领中国经济发展的新常态和贯彻落实"五大发展理念"，着力体现"一带一路"、京津冀协调发展、长江经济带等三大经济发展战略，在占有大量鲜活案例和经验的基础上,讲好中国故事,传播中国声音,分析中国问题,提供中国方案。

在编写过程中,《丛书》还努力注意把握好以下四个方面:一是在全面介绍中国改革开放以来取得的成就经验的基础上,注重阐释党的十八大以来全面深化改革的新举措、经济发展的新思路、对外工作的新理念等;二是在展示中国经济社会发展成果的同时,着重分析取得这些成果的原因、背后的运行逻辑、演进的过程;三是坚持问题导向、需求导向,不求大而全,不求系统完整,从国外受众需求出发,有针对性地释疑解惑;四是既讲中国"从何处来",更讲中国"向何处去",一方面引导读者了解认识中国历史发展进程,另一方面注重讲清楚中国如何把握过去、现在和未来的有机统一,继承与创新的有机结合,规划设计未来发展走向。

《丛书》在中共中央对外联络部的指导下,由中国浦东干部学院组织编写。

中共中央对外联络部(简称中联部)是中国共产党负责对外工作的职能部门。目前,中国共产党同世界上160多个国家和地区的600多个政党和政治组织有着不同形式的联系和交往,其中既有左翼政党,也有右翼政党;既有执政党,也有在野党。中国共产党的对外工作是党的事业的一条重要战线,也是国家总体外交的重要组成部分,其工作目标是通过政党交往促进国家与国家、人民与人民之间的了解与沟通。

中国浦东干部学院(CELAP)是中国国家级干部学院,作为中国开展国际合作培训交流的窗口,自2005年3月创立以来,坚持国际性、时代性、开放性的办学特色,大力开展国际合作培训,培训对象包括外国政党政要、企业高管、高级专家等各类国际领导人才。截至2015年年底,已经培训了来自130个国家和地区的学员6000余名,获得了培训国家和地区以及参训学员的广泛认可和普遍好评。

基于国外学员学习的需要,中国浦东干部学院于2012年年初启动《丛书》编写工作,历经 4 年的打磨精炼,数易其稿,于 2015 年年底定稿。《丛书》首批推出 10 册,分别是《中国治理新方略》、《中国共产党党的建设》、《中国经济改革与开发区建设》、《中国政府架构与基本公共服务》、《中国城镇化》、《中国农业与农村发展》、《中国外交与和平发展》、《中国干部选拔任用》、《中国干部教育》、《中国改革开放的"排头兵"——上海》。丛书的作者主要来自中国浦东干部学院,此外还有上海市政府发展研究中心、上海国际问题研究院、杭州城市学研究中心的领导和专家。

《丛书》以中英文对照方式出版,英文翻译主要由上海外国语大学的资深教授主持,深致谢忱! 人民出版社对《丛书》的出版予以大力支持,在编写和翻译过程中提出了诸多建设性意见,一并表示感谢!

编写供国外学员学习培训的系列化教材,在国内尚属首次。作为一种新的探索和尝试,难免有所疏漏、错谬,敬请指正。

《中国故事丛书》编写委员会

2016 年 9 月

中国故事
Modern China

目 录

导　论

2012年11月,中国共产党第十八次全国代表大会召开,选举了以习近平为总书记的新一届党中央,为中国的发展确立了新的目标,中国的治国理政又有了新的方略,中国的历史也随之翻开了新的一页。

在第十八次全国代表大会上,中国共产党作为执政党提出了中国未来发展的"两个一百年"的奋斗目标。大家知道,中国共产党是1921年成立的,到2020年前后就是建党100年,中华人民共和国是1949年成立的,到2050年前后就是成立100年。中国共产党领导全国人民取得了新民主主义革命的胜利,成立了新中国,实现了民族的独立、人民的解放,中国共产党成为执政党,选择走上了社会主义的道路。中国在1978年实行了改革开放,走中国特色社会主义的道路,30多年的改革开放使国家走向了富强,人民过上了幸福生活。连续30多年的经济高速增长,使中国成了世界上第二大经济体。今后中国该怎么发展呢? 肯定还是要沿着中国特色社会主义的道路走下去。"只要我们胸怀理想、坚定信念,不动摇、不懈怠、不折腾,顽强奋斗、艰苦奋斗、不懈奋斗,就一定能在中国共产党成立一百年时全面建成小康社会,就一定能在新中国成立一百年时建成富强民主文明和谐的社会主义现代化国家。全党要坚定这样的道路自信、理论自信、制度自信!"①

(一) 全面建成小康社会

"全面建成小康社会"是第一个"一百年目标"。"小康社会"的概念最早是由邓小平提出来的。1979 年 12 月 6 日,邓小平在会见当时的日本首相大平正芳时,他第一次提出了"小康"概念以及在 20 世纪末达到"小康社会"的构想。1982 年党的十二大正式引用了这一概念,并把它作为 20 世纪末的战略目标。1997 年,江泽民同志在党的十五大报告中提出"建设小康社会"的历史新任务。2002 年党的十六大提出了到 2020 年全面建设小康社会的奋斗目标。2007 年党的十七大报告提出,确保到 2020 年实现全面建设小康社会的奋斗目标,并提出了经济、政治、文化、社会、生态文明等五个方面的要求。到党的十八大报告提出确保到 2020 年全面建成小康社会。在中国传统文化中"小康"只是形容殷实、富足,是一个相对概念,但是建设"小康社会"还是有具体的量的指标的,以经济指标为例,党的十六大提出国内生产总值到 2020 年力争比 2000 年翻两番,党的十七大继续沿用了这一指标,但更强调发展的协调性,要实现经济又好又快发展。党的十八大提出了"两个翻一番",即国内生产总值比 2010 年翻一番,城乡居民人均收入比 2010 年翻一番。除经济的指标外,还有社会主义民主、道德、文化、社会事业以及环境保护等方面发展的要求等。

---

① 胡锦涛:《坚定不移沿着中国特色社会主义道路前进,为全面建成小康社会而奋斗》,人民出版社 2012 年版。

党的十八大提出在 2020 年"全面建成小康社会"，核心就在"全面"。这个"全面"，体现在覆盖的人群是全面的，它是不分地域的全面小康，是不让一个人掉队的全面小康，把 13 亿多人全部带入全面小康。这个"全面"，也体现在涉及的领域是全面的，经济、政治、社会、文化和生态文明建设"五位一体"总体布局。是"干部清正、政府清廉、政治清明"，"找到全社会意愿和要求的最大公约数"的全面小康；是"破除城乡二元结构，建设农民幸福生活的美好家园"的全面小康；是"国家物质力量和精神力量都增强，全国各族人民物质生活和精神生活都改善"的全面小康；是"望得见山、看得见水、记得住乡愁"的全面小康；等等。全面建成小康社会是处于引领地位的战略目标。

2020 年要全面建成小康社会，只剩下五年的时间了，这是一个近期目标，那么再过三十年即 2050 年前后，中国发展成什么样子呢？那就是要沿着中国特色社会主义道路继续走下去，"中国特色社会主义道路，就是在中国共产党领导下，立足基本国情，以经济建设为中心，坚持四项基本原则，坚持改革开放，解放和发展社会生产力，建设社会主义市场经济、社会主义民主政治、社会主义先进文化、社会主义和谐社会、社会主义生态文明，促进人的全面发展，逐步实现全体人民共同富裕，建设富强民主文明和谐的社会主义现代化国家"[①]。建设"富强、民主、文明、和谐的社会主义现代化国家"，这个国家要促进人的全面发展，逐步实现全体人民共同富裕。这就是 2050 年前后实现的第二个"一百年"的目标，也就是实现"中华民族伟大复兴的中国梦"。

（二）"中国梦"

为实现"两个一百年"的目标和任务，需要一个核心概念来阐述，也需要有一面精神旗帜来激励人民的志气，激发社会的正能量。2012

[①]　胡锦涛：《坚定不移沿着中国特色社会主义道路前进，为全面建成小康社会而奋斗》，人民出版社 2012 年版。

年11月29日，习近平总书记等党和国家领导人参观《复兴之路》展览，他在面对媒体发表的即兴讲话中提出了"中国梦"的概念，后来他在不同的场合丰富了"中国梦"的内涵。"中国梦"的内涵是"国家富强，民族振兴，人民幸福"。实现中华民族伟大复兴，是中华民族近代以来最伟大的梦想。中国梦是人民的梦，是民族的梦，是每一个家庭的梦，也是每一个人的梦，"中国梦"要让人民共享人生出彩、梦想成真的机会，要倾听人民呼声、回应人民期待。人民对美好生活的期待就是我们的奋斗目标。要实现"中国梦"就要走中国道路，弘扬中国精神，凝集中国力量。"中国梦"和世界各国人民的梦也是相通的。全面建成小康社会是实现中华民族伟大复兴的重要里程碑。"中国已经进入全面建成小康社会的决定性阶段。实现这个目标是实现中华民族伟大复兴中国梦的关键一步。""中国梦"的提出，既生动形象又富有感召力，是凝聚全社会的"最大公约数"，成为中国共产党带领全国各族人民共同奋斗的时代主题。"中国梦"是中国共产党召开第十八次全国代表大会以来习近平同志所提出的重要指导思想和重要执政理念。

（三）"五位一体"的总体布局

在党的十八大报告中提出了中国特色社会主义"五位一体"的总体布局，即建设中国特色社会主义要经济建设、政治建设、文化建设、社会建设和生态文明建设一起抓。要"建设社会主义市场经济、社会主义民主政治、社会主义先进文化、社会主义和谐社会、社会主义生态文明"。经济建设的重点是"加快完善社会主义市场经济体制和加快转变经济发展方式"，政治建设的重点是"坚持走中国特色社会主义政治发展道路和推进政治体制改革"，文化建设的重点是"建设社会主义文化强国，加强社会主义核心价值体系建设"，社会建设的重点是"改善民生和创新社会管理"，生态文明建设的重点是"节约资源、保护环境，推进绿色发展，循环发展，低碳发展，建设美丽中国"。建设中国特色社会主义这五个方面缺一不可，"五位一体"。而要完成中国特色社会主义这项伟大的事业,离不开中国共产党的领导,党的领导是中国特色社会主义建立和发展的保障,因此,上面的"五位一体"还应该加一,那就是加上党的建设。

(四)"四个全面"的战略布局

2012年11月党的十八大报告提出"全面建成小康社会";党的十八大以来,以习近平同志为核心的党中央提出了"两个一百年"奋斗目标和"实现中华民族伟大复兴的中国梦";2013年11月党的十八届三中全会提出了"全面深化改革",并且第一次将全面深化改革的总目标确定为"完善和发展中国特色社会主义制度、推进国家治理体系和治理能力现代化";2014年10月中国共产党十八届四中全会召开,提出"全面依法治国",并将全面依法治国的总目标确定为"建设中国特色社会主义法治体系,建设社会主义法治国家";2014年12月13—14日,习近平在江苏省视察时第一次提出"全面从严治党",并且把"全面从严治党"和前面提到的三个全面放在一起讲,确立了"四个全面"的战略布局。"四个全面"是坚持和发展中国特色社会主义道路、理论、制度的战略抓手。

这"四个全面",是从我国发展现实需要中得出来的,是从人民群众的热切期待中得出来的,是为推动解决我们面临的突出矛盾和问题提出来的,立足治国理政全局,抓住改革发展稳定关键,统领中国发展总纲,确立了新形势下党和国家各项工作的战略方向、重点领域、主攻目标。习近平总书记坚持问题导向和科学思维,以当代中国共产党人的全局视野和战略眼光,坚定中国自信、立足中国实际、总结中国经验、针对中国难题,提出"四个全面"战略布局。"四个全面"相辅相成、相互促进、相得益彰。"四个全面",既有目标又有举措,既有全局又有重点,每一个"全面"都具有重大战略意义。"全面建成小康社会"是战略目标,其他三个全面是战略举措。"全面深化改革"和"全面依法治国"是"姊妹篇",形成"鸟之两翼、车之双轮"。"全面从严治党",锻造我们事业更加坚强的领导核心,是政治保障。四者不是简单的并列关系,而是有机联系、相互贯通的顶层设计,建成小康社会、焕发改革精神、增强法治观念、落实从严治党,"四个全面"勾绘出社会主义中国的未来图景。

(五) 五大发展理念

2015年10月26—29日,在北京举行了中国共产党第十八届中央委员会第五次全体会议,会议主要是研究中国未来五年即2016—2020年中国经济社会的发展,审议通过了《中共中央关于制定国民经济和社会发展第十三个五年规划的建议》。"十三五"时期是全面建成小康社会决胜阶段,党的十八届五中全会最突出的贡献和亮点是提出了创新、协调、绿色、开放、共享五大发展理念。"这五大发展理念,是'十三五'乃至更长时期我国发展思路、发展方向、发展着力点的集中体现,也是改革开放30多年来我国发展经验的集中体现,反映出我们党对我国发展规律的新认识"[1]。五大发展理念丰富和发展了中国共产党关于发展的思想理论,是对科学发展观的新突破、新发展,是对以习近平同志为核心的党中央治国理政新理念新思想新战略的概括和总结。

首先,五大发展理念把创新放在前所未有的重要的位置。"坚持创新发展,必须把创新摆在国家发展全局的核心位置,不断推进理论创新、制度创新、科技创新、文化创新等各方面创新,让创新贯穿党和国家一切工作,让创新在全社会蔚然成风。"[2]党的十六大以后,我们党提出"要始终把改革创新贯彻到治国理政各个环节","提高自主创新能力,建设创新型国家"。党的十八大提出了创新驱动发展战略,"把改革贯穿于经济社会发展各个领域各个环节,以改革促创新发展"。而到党

---

[1] 习近平《关于〈中共中央关于制定国民经济和社会发展第十三个五年规划的建议〉的说明》。

[2] 《中共中央关于制定国民经济和社会发展第十三个五年规划的建议》(2015年10月29日中国共产党第十八届中央委员会第五次全体会议通过)。

的十八届五中全会,则把创新看作是"引领发展的第一动力",要求"必须把创新摆在国家发展全局的核心位置"。把创新放在前所未有的重要位置,这既是时代发展的要求,也是发展理念和发展思路的重要调整。讲创新并不单纯是指科技创新,而是包含"理论创新、制度创新、科技创新、文化创新"等各方面的创新。创新中第一位的是理论创新,"四个全面"战略布局是理论创新,"五大发展理念"是理论创新,理论是先导,是灵魂,是总开关,有了新理论的引领,发展方向就明了,路径就清晰;其次是制度创新,国家治理体系和治理能力的现代化既是全面深化改革的总目标,也是最大的制度创新,制度创新为其他创新提供保障;科技创新是关键,是最有活力的创新,要推动大众创业,万众创新,要推动新技术、新业态、新产业的形成;文化创新这里是指广义的文化,既指各种文化艺术形式,文化事业、文化产业的创新,还应该包括社会主义核心价值观和精神文化、政治文化和道德文化等领域的创新。"让创新贯穿党和国家一切工作,让创新在全社会蔚然成风"。这是对科学发展观的一大突破。

第二,五大发展理念更加注重协调发展的整体性。"坚持协调发展,必须牢牢把握中国特色社会主义事业总体布局,正确处理发展中的重大关系,重点促进城乡区域协调发展,促进经济社会协调发展,促进新型工业化、信息化、城镇化、农业现代化同步发展,在增强国家硬实力的同时注重提升国家软实力,不断增强发展整体性。"①协调发展的理念除了讲"推动区域协调发展、推动城乡协调发展""新型工业化、信息化、城镇化和农业现代化同步发展"外,新提出来要"推动物质文明和精神文明协调发展""推动经济建设和国防建设融合发展",使协调的范围更大更广了,这才是真正的"全面协调",整体的协调,而不仅仅是经济领域的协调。第一次把精神文明建设也纳入协调发展的范围,真正体现了物质文明和精神文明两手抓,两手都要硬。"两个文明"协调

---

① 《中共中央关于制定国民经济和社会发展第十三个五年规划的建议》(2015 年 10 月 29 日中国共产党第十八届中央委员会第五次全体会议通过)。

发展是坚持和发展中国特色社会主义的必然要求,也是全面建成小康社会的基本内容。

第三,五大发展理念更加强化人和自然和谐共生的绿色发展。"坚持绿色发展,必须坚持节约资源和保护环境的基本国策,坚持可持续发展,坚定走生产发展、生活富裕、生态良好的文明发展道路,加快建设资源节约型、环境友好型社会,形成人与自然和谐发展现代化建设新格局,推进美丽中国建设,为全球生态安全作出新贡献。"①应该使绿色发展成为一种生产方式和生活方式,一种社会风尚。"绿色发展"和科学发展观中讲的"可持续"是对应的,但是比"可持续"的含义更丰富了,除了"推动低碳循环发展、全面节约和高效利用能源、加大环境治理力度、筑牢生态安全屏障"之外,还要"坚持绿色富国,绿色惠民,为人民提供更多优质生态产品,推动形成绿色发展方式和生活方式,协同推进人民富裕,国家富强,中国美丽"。和以往相比,更加突出了人与自然和谐共生的理念,更加强调主体功能区概念,还要建设美丽中国。

第四,五大发展理念突出了开放发展。"坚持开放发展,必须顺应我国经济深度融入世界经济的趋势,奉行互利共赢的开放战略,发展更高层次的开放型经济,积极参与全球经济治理和公共产品供给,提高我国在全球经济治理中的制度性话语权,构建广泛的利益共同体。"②改革开放已经三十多年了,在本世纪初我们就提出来实施"引进来"和"走出去"相结合的对外开放战略。党的十八大以来,开放的局面也发生了很大的变化,过去开放更注重的是"引进来",是接受世界政治经济的秩序,是利用别人的舞台宣传自己、展示自己;今天我们更多的是要"走出去",要自己搭建国际合作的舞台,建设政治经济的新秩序,例如"一带一路"的倡议,亚洲基础设施投资银行、丝路基金和自贸区的建设等。开放发展要求在新的形势下,顺应我国经济深度融入世界经

---

① 《中共中央关于制定国民经济和社会发展第十三个五年规划的建议》(2015 年 10 月 29 日中国共产党第十八届中央委员会第五次全体会议通过)。

② 《中共中央关于制定国民经济和社会发展第十三个五年规划的建议》(2015 年 10 月 29 日中国共产党第十八届中央委员会第五次全体会议通过)。

济的趋势,坚持统筹国际国内两个大局,发展更高层次的开放型经济,完善对外开放战略布局,形成对外开放新体制,打造陆海内外联动、东西双向开放的全面开放的新格局,利用好国际国内两种资源和两个市场。积极参与全球经济治理,提高我们在国际规则制定中的话语权,构建广泛的利益共同体。中国已经是世界上第二大经济体,要体现出我们是一个负责任的大国,要积极承担国际责任和义务。开放发展理念是在新的国际环境下对开放的新审视、新思考,是对科学发展观的新发展。

第五,五大发展理念强调了共享发展。"坚持共享发展,必须坚持发展为了人民、发展依靠人民、发展成果由人民共享,作出更有效的制度安排,使全体人民在共建共享发展中有更多获得感,增强发展动力,增进人民团结,朝着共同富裕方向稳步前进。"①改革开放三十多年了,原来重视发展速度与效率、效益,现在越来越重视民生,越来越强调公平正义。党的十六大以后,我们提出了要坚持"共同建设、公共享有"的原则,形成"社会和谐人人有责,和谐社会人人共享"的局面。共享发展体现出了人民性和以人为本,要"人人参与,人人尽力,人人享有",把人民群众的根本利益作为出发点和落脚点,人民群众的期盼就是我们努力的方向。党的十八届五中全会提出的共享发展的最大特点是民生导向、公平导向,例如缩小收入差距,坚持居民收入增长和经济增长同步,劳动报酬提高和劳动生产率提高同步;要实施脱贫攻坚工程,精准扶贫,精准脱贫;积极应对人口的老龄化,建设多层次的养老服务体系,增加养老服务和产品供给;推进健康中国建设,实施食品安全战略;促进人口均衡发展,全面实施一对夫妇可生育两个孩子政策。这些都是亮点,体现出新意,都是新发展。

发展是时代的主题和世界各国的共同追求。"五大发展理念"是发展理论的与时俱进,体现了思维方式、思维方法的变革,其中包含了

---

① 《中共中央关于制定国民经济和社会发展第十三个五年规划的建议》(2015 年 10 月 29 日中国共产党第十八届中央委员会第五次全体会议通过)。

辩证思维、系统思维、底线思维等思维方式方法的综合运用。

以习近平同志为核心的党中央领导中国人民实现"两个一百年"的奋斗目标，"全面建成小康社会"，实现中华民族伟大复兴的"中国梦"；把握中国特色社会主义建设"五位一体"的总体布局；协调推进"四个全面"的战略布局；贯彻落实"五大发展理念"。这些关键词凝练地概括了在习近平的领导下中国治国理政新方略的核心内容。

本书由冯俊担任主编，导论由冯俊撰写，第一章由何立胜撰写，第二章由王友明撰写，第三章由刘哲昕撰写，第四章由胡涵锦撰写，第五章由黄力之撰写，第六章由于洪生撰写，第七章由燕乃玲撰写，第八章由刘靖北撰写。

一、引领经济新常态

"我国发展仍处于重要战略机遇期,我们要增强信心,从当前我国经济发展的阶段性特征出发,适应新常态,保持战略上的平常心态。在战术上要高度重视和防范各种风险,早作谋划,未雨绸缪,及时采取应对措施,尽可能减少其负面影响。"——习近平在河南考察时的讲话(2014年5月)①

---

① 《习近平在河南考察时强调深化改革发挥优势创新思路统筹兼顾,确保经济持续健康发展社会和谐稳定》,《人民日报》2014年5月11日。

（一）经济新常态：如何打造中国经济升级版

"新常态"的字面含义，所谓"新"异于"旧质"，"常态"是时常持续呈现的状态。经济新常态是不同于过度依赖要素、投资驱动，偏重粗放高速增长的经济状态，是指增长速度变化、结构趋向优化、动力向创新转化、体制改革深化并将持续较长时间的一种经济运行状态。步入经济新常态，表明中国经济进入了一个新阶段，这是一种趋势性、内生性的经济运行状态。关于经济新常态的特征，正如习近平总书记指出："新常态下，我国经济发展表现出速度变化、结构优化、动力转换三大特点，增长速度要从高速转向中高速；发展方式要从规模速度型转向质量效率型，经济结构调整要从增量扩能为主转向调整存量、做优增量并举，发展动力要从主要依靠资源和低成本劳动力等要素投入转向创新驱动。这些变化不依人的意志为转移，是我国经济发展阶段性特征的必然要求。"①

1. 从高速增长转为中高速增长，是经济新常态的基本特征

就直观而言，中国经济处于增速换挡期，从高速增长转向中高速增长，从长期保持在 10% 左右的高速增长转为 7% 左右的增长，这是经济新常态的为人熟悉的表征。因为随着劳动力、资源、土地等要素资源成本或价格的上升，无论是环境因素约束性导致的环境压力加大，还是资源消耗、市场约束因素，都无法支撑那么高的增长速度，或难以承受过高的增长速度，使得那种仅仅依靠要素投入、外延扩张、投资驱动的经济发展方式已难以为继。在经济新常态下，中国经济增长速度虽然有所下降，但经济增长要"在提高发展平衡性、包容性、可持续性的基础上，到二〇二〇年国内生产总值和城乡居民人均收入比二〇一〇年翻一番"。②

---

① 习近平：《关于〈中共中央关于制定国民经济和社会发展第十三个五年规划的建议〉的说明》，新华网，2015 年 11 月 3 日。
② 《中共中央关于制定国民经济和社会发展第十三个五年规划的建议》，新华网，2015 年 11 月 3 日。

在全球范围内仍然是最具活力的国家,依然是世界经济增长的龙头。中国要实现"两个一百年"的宏伟蓝图,到 2020 年全面建成小康社会,以 2010 年的 GDP 进行测算,只要能保持 7% 的增长速度,之后即使每十年降一个点,即:2020—2030 年按 6%,2030—2040 年按 5%,2040—2050 年按 4%,其结果是 2030 年与美国相当,2050 年中国经济的整体规模将超越美国,成为美国的 1.34 倍。正如习近平在 2015 年博鳌论坛演讲中所指出的那样:"我们看中国经济,不能只看增长率,中国经济体量不断增大,现在增长 7% 左右的经济增量已相当可观,聚集的动能是过去两位数的增长都达不到的。"①

2. 经济新常态是实实在在没有水分的增长

合适的经济增长速度,一是看多大规模上的速度;二是看增长的质量,增长的效率,这是关键。改革开放以来,在我国经济快速增长过程中,一些地方、一些领域出现了"唯 GDP 或国内生产总值"、片面追求经济增长速度的问题。目前我们遇到的资源过度开发问题、环境污染严重问题、经济结构不合理问题等,都与此密切相关。对此,习近平总书记反复强调,要全面认识持续健康发展和生产总值增长的关系,不要简单以国内生产总值增长率论英雄。不简单以国内生产总值增长率论英雄,是我国经济发展到现阶段的必然要求。经过三十多年高速发展,我国已成为世界第二大经济体,这么大的块头、这么大的底数,再追求两位数的快速发展是不现实的。而且资源、环境的承载能力,也不容许我们再盲目追求这样的高速度。此外,解决高速发展过程中积累下的诸多深层次矛盾和问题,也需要把增速调整到合适的"挡位",留下余地和空间,确保经济行稳致远。

中国经济经过三十多年的高速增长,经济总量、基数已经很大,每增长一个百分点所代表的增量不可小看。据统计,2014 年,国内生产

① 《习近平主席在海南博鳌亚洲论坛 2015 年年会上的主旨演讲(全文)》,新华网,2015 年 3 月 29 日。

总值达到 63.6 万亿多元(现价,下同),按汇率折算,迈上 10 万亿美元的大台阶,占世界经济份额 13.3%,一年增量相当于一个中等发达国家的经济总量;人均国内生产总值 7594 美元,按世界银行标准,居中高收入国家中等水平,城乡居民人均可支配收入分别为 2.9 万元和 1.1 万元。2014 年中国的经济总量较 2013 年多出了 8665 亿美元,意味着目前中国经济一年所实现的增量,比 1996 年全年的总量还高出约 57 亿美元。从横向看,比土耳其 2013 年的经济总量还要多 275 亿美元,而后者是当今全球排名第 17 位的经济体,如将 2014 年与 2007 年进行一番比较就明白了,2014 年 7.4%的增速尽管是中国经济进入新世纪以来增速最低值,但每增长一个百分点所对应的 GDP 新增量高达 1171 亿美元,是 2007 年的两倍多。如在产业结构变动的前提下,2014 年 GDP 每增长一个百分点,能带动约 180 万人就业,以 2014 年的经济增速目标计算,新经济增量就约达 5 万多亿元,约相当于 1994 年全年的经济总量。2013 年以来,中国第三产业(服务业)增加值占 GDP 比重均超过了第二产业,而一些发达国家服务业已占 GDP 的 80%以上,步入经济新常态,中国服务业比重上升将是长期趋势。在速度换挡期,中国经济既要走出高速增长的困境,又要保持合理的增长速度,让经济运行长期处于合理空间,保持经济中高速增长和迈向增长的中高端水平,既有可能,也很必要,合理的增长速度,既不能过高,也不能过低。那么什么速度是合适的呢?"到 2020 年翻一番,按照居民收入增长和经济增长同步的要求,'十三五'时期经济年均增长至少也要达到 6.5%。经济保持中高速增长,有利于改善民生,让人民群众更加切实感受到全面建成小康社会的成果。"①经济增速过低会带来系列衍生问题,累及结构调整、就业保障、民生改善和社会稳定,如果速度过快下降甚至失速性下降,也会造成政府财政收入减少,进而导致公共开支减少、社会失业率陡然上升、居民收入增速剧烈下滑,从而超出了社会的可承受

---

① 习近平:《关于〈中共中央关于制定国民经济和社会发展第十三个五年规划的建议〉的说明》,新华网,2015 年 11 月 3 日。

度。因此,不简单以国内生产总值增长率论英雄,并不是说不重视经济增长,而是要追求有效益、有质量、可持续的经济发展。中国经济增长的速度要与全面建成小康社会的目标相衔接,与经济总量扩大、结构升级的要求相适应,符合客观实际,符合经济发展规律,要充分考虑稳增长、调结构的双重需要,充分考虑充分就业,收入稳定增长的要求。总之,新常态下的经济增长,是产业结构动态平衡的增长,是民众福利的实际增长,是区域协调发展的增长,是质量与效益统一的增长,是节能环保的增长,是实实在在没有水分的增长。也正如习近平总书记在2013 年 12 月中央经济工作会议上强调:"我们要的是实实在在、没有水分的速度,是民生改善、就业比较充分的速度,是劳动生产率同步提高、经济活力增强、结构调整有成效的速度,是经济发展质量和效益得到提高又不会带来后遗症的速度。"是可持续的增长,着力在转变经济发展方式、优化经济结构、改善生态环境、提高发展质量和效益中实现经济增长。

3. 结构优化是经济新常态的内在特点

结构优化要求"主要经济指标平衡协调,发展空间格局得到优化,投资效率和企业效率明显上升,工业化和信息化融合发展水平进一步提高,产业迈向中高端水平,先进制造业加快发展,新产业新业态不断成长,服务业比重进一步上升,消费对经济增长贡献明显加大。户籍人口城镇化率加快提高。农业现代化取得明显进展。迈进创新型国家和人才强国行列。"①改革开放以来,中国经济增长取得了举世瞩目的成就,中国经济发展的模式、道路也为世界认可。虽然粗放式的经济增长模式与我们新兴经济体、发展中国家的比较优势、后工业化国家有着一致性,并在一定时期支撑了我国经济的持续快速增长,但在一定程度上带来了重要的结构性缺陷和矛盾,使得经济发展方式粗放、贸易条件恶化、能源资源和环境压力很大,甚至是难以为继。如经济增长过度依赖

---

① 《习近平在中央经济工作会议上发表重要讲话》,新华网,2013 年 12 月 13 日。

投资扩张,全球分工中过度依赖加工制造环节和加工贸易,竞争战略过度依赖成本价格,而产业链和价值链中研发设计、营销、品牌和供应链管理等高附加值环节缺失,即经济增长中的"三个过度"与"一个缺失"。结构优化具有动态性的特点,要求经济增长从增加产量、扩大规模为主,到存量调整、做优增量为主。引领经济新常态,打造中国经济升级版,需要爬坡过坎,从粗放到集约,从低端到高端,结构调整的任务更加艰巨。正如习近平指出的,要精心谋划用好我国经济的巨大韧性、潜力和回旋余地,依靠促改革调结构,坚持不懈推动经济发展提质增效升级,努力做到调速不减势、量增质更优。① 我们知道,结构动态优化是没有止境的,因为市场在变化,科技在发展,需求形势在变化。经济结构平衡、动态优化将成为经济的新常态,新常态的基础是增长速度、结构调整、动力转化的统一。目前中国经济结构中的产业结构、市场结构、区域结构、城乡结构、资本结构、分配结构等将发生新的转向与变化,进而实现中国经济结构多维度的、动态的调整、再平衡。从产业结构上,实现从制造大国走向制造强国,走向服务业强国;从区域结构上,从各自为战转向区域协同发展;从金融结构上,打破金融控制,让利实体经济的发展;从质量结构上,从"吹泡沫"到"挤水分",实现有效益、有质量的增长;从需求的角度调整经济结构,需要对需求结构的优化调整,从计划经济时期的供给约束型经济转变为社会主义市场经济条件下的需求约束型经济,要走主要依靠内需的发展道路,要解决好最终消费需求不足问题,增加城乡居民的最终消费需求,来保持经济长期稳定发展。从供给角度优化调整经济结构,必须充分认识生产要素低成本优势趋于减弱、资源环境硬约束增强、产能过剩矛盾加剧等经济发展客观条件的新变化,选准产业创新整合的突破口。此外,调整经济结构还要求提高经济增长的质量,还要把环保提高到新的阶段,要低碳,人民生活水平要随着经济增长而不断提高。目前中国经济的主要问题就是结构调整,只有经济结构调整、优化,经济增长才能质量提高,二者相辅

---

① 参见《习近平在中央经济工作会议上发表重要讲话》,人民网,2014 年 12 月 11 日。

相成。

在经济结构调整与动态优化过程中,要深化政府体制改革,政府转型是经济转型的前提,转变政府职能,改革完善投资、需求、产业、分配体制机制,理顺投资、需求、分配结构,保持宏观经济政策的连续性稳定性,充分发挥市场配置资源的决定性作用。实践证明,产业结构、需求结构是市场选择的结果,主体是企业。在市场经济条件下,政府创造公平市场竞争环境比赋予某些行业优惠政策重要,要改变政府习惯的产业管制、扶植的政策,因为一些产业扶植的政策往往会导致企业寻政策之租的来源,而不是把主要精力放在市场有效竞争上、放在产业价值链提升上、放在品牌拓展上。政府要充分发挥其在产权或权益保障、市场秩序完善、创新环境建设、公共服务与保障方面的作用。对政府职能做减法,实施负面清单管理模式,对政府而言,就是简政放权,该管的要管好,不该管的要放权,明晰政府权力清单、责任清单,对企业做加法,培育微观经济发展的持久动力,要激市场主体的"活力",把该放的权放到位,让市场主体真正放开手脚;就是要"补短板",把该做的事做好,增加公共产品有效供给;就是要"强实体",把该给的政策给足,夯实发展的微观基础。

4. 重视实体经济是经济新常态的内在要求

习近平总书记多次强调,工业化对于国家强大至关重要,国家强大要靠实体经济,不能泡沫化。国务院关于《中国制造2025》的通知强调:"制造业是国民经济的主体,是立国之本、兴国之器、强国之基。十八世纪中叶开启工业文明以来,世界强国的兴衰史和中华民族的奋斗史一再证明,没有强大的制造业,就没有国家和民族的强盛。打造具有国际竞争力的制造业,是我国提升综合国力、保障国家安全、建设世界强国的必由之路。"[①]实践证明,实体经济水平越高,经济实力就越强,抵抗风险的能力也越强,这是现代经济发展的硬道理。中国经济正在

---

① 《国务院关于印发〈中国制造2025〉的通知》,人民网,2015年5月19日。

向形态更高级、分工更复杂、结构更合理的阶段演化,做好实体经济是我国经济转型的重要举措。目前,中国经济发展中不平衡、不协调、不可持续等结构性矛盾和问题突出,主要症结在"实体经济不实,虚拟经济太虚",难点在于突破实体经济发展的困境,关键在于实体经济的升级转型。实体经济即制造业是国家的基础竞争力,必须毫不动摇积极发展现代制造业,美国服务业占国民经济70%以上,但近60%的是依靠制造业带动的生产性服务业,说明制造业对服务业的发展具有重要的支撑带动作用,例如先进的通信设备带动了年增加值约1.4万亿元的信息服务业,发达的汽车制造业将带动几倍于汽车售价的汽车后服务业。

强化实体经济,从消费方面,只有加快制造业升级,从制造大国走向制造强国,实现智能制造,向个性化定制、柔性化生产、网络化销售等先进制造方式、商业模式转型,满足日益个性化、多样化的消费需求,支撑消费结构升级。制造业是实施创新驱动发展战略的主要领域,制造业是研发投入的主要阵地,是创新最活跃、成果最丰富的领域,从根本上决定了国家整体创新水平。如出口方面,工业制成品已占全部出口的95%左右,调整优化产业结构和产品结构是提升"中国制造"竞争力的必由之路;从投资方面,中国目前的经济资本存量与人均资本存量与发达经济体差别很大,如总量是美国的30%、人均存量分别是美国的8%、韩国的17%,人均水电、铁路与教育、卫生投资占GDP比重都低于世界平均水平。投资有较大空间,国民储蓄率高,仍然高于40%以上,高储蓄率决定了高投资率,投资增长对GDP增长的贡献,消费增长对GDP增长的贡献,货物贸易与服务净增长对GDP增长的贡献。近年来工业物流、通信等基础设施和新技术、新产品、新业态、新模式的投资机会大量涌现,智能制造、智慧物流、高端装备、工业机器人、新能源汽车等正在成为投资新热点;就业方面,新兴服务业成长发展、传统产业结构优化升级,正在创造高质量就业岗位,带动整个就业结构改善。此外,我国在载人航天、探月工程、高速铁路、高性能计算机、新一代移动通信等领域取得重大突破,物联网、智能机器人等大量创新性技术广泛应用于各行各业,创新正在成为经济社会发展的主要驱动力。新一轮科技革命与产业变革风起云涌,工业技术与信息技术即"两个 IT"深度融合成为产业发展新趋势。只有加速推进信息化和工业化融合创新,真正把工业发展动力转到创新驱动的轨道上来,我国工业才能从全球价值链低端环节向高端环节跃升,实现由规模扩张向提质增效的根本性转变。

中国共产党第十八次全国代表大会于 2012 年 11 月 8 日至 14 日在北京举行(新华社发,庞兴雷摄)

(二) 如何把"看不见的手"与"看得见的手"都用好

政府和市场的关系是我国经济体制改革的核心问题。在市场作用和政府作用的问题上,要讲辩证法、两点论,"看不见的手"和"看得见的手"都要用好,努力形成市场作用和政府作用有机统一、相互补充、相互协调、相互促进的格局。使市场在资源配置中起决定性作用和更好发挥政府作用,二者是有机统一的,不是相互否定的,不能把二者割裂开来、对立起来,既不能用市场在资源配置中的决定性作用取代甚至否定政府作用,也不能用更好发挥政府作用取代甚至否定使市场在资源配置中起决定性作用。①

党的十八届三中全会明确提出"使市场在资源配置中起决定性作用和更好发挥政府作用"的科学论断,其核心是处理好"两只手"的关系,发挥市场配置资源的决定性作用。市场与政府这个问题能否解决好,不仅直接关系经济体制改革的方向,也关系整个全面深化改革的政策取向和成败。"惟其艰难,才更显勇毅;惟其笃行,才弥足珍贵。"政府和市场不是谁大谁小、"有你无我"的对立关系,而应"各就各位",成为优势互补的"黄金搭档"。政府要依靠法治界定和保护产权、保证合同履行和实施市场监管,维护公平有序竞争,规范市场主体行为,激发市场主体的积极性和创造性,引导市场主体合理配置资源,从而促进经济持续健康发展,让市场在资源配置中起决定性作用,重要基础是建设廉洁高效政府。政府与市场的关系就资源配置而言,市场要起决定性作用。资源配置从严格的经济学角度看主要是个微观问题,这句话意味着,在微观上要使市场起决定性作用。市场与政府应该做什么事情?需要把握以下几点认识。

1.政府是宏观管理者、企业是自主经营者

微观上是资源配置、厂商行为、产品、资源要素如何定价,产业分布,也包括如何确立产业结构,这些问题主要是市场竞争行为,而不是政府政策预先安排。比如企业的行为,就是企业的自主权,政府应少干预,政府制定规则,企业只要守法、依法纳税,合法经营,然后按市场追求利益最大化原则行事就好了。对企业行为的自主性这一点在认识上好像并没有什么分歧。产业结构问题是微观问题,不是宏观问题。结构问题更多是企业竞争之后形成的一种集合效应。目前为什么存在很

---

① 参见《习近平谈治国理政》,外文出版社 2014 年版,第 116—118 页。
　　注:本文为习近平总书记在中共中央政治局第十五次集体学习,使市场在资源配置中起决定性作用和更好发挥政府作用时的讲话。

严重的产能过剩？是市场盲目竞争所造成，还是政府计划、政府产业管制所造成？长期以来，发展改革委员会的"十五""十一五""十二五"期间列出了几大主导产业与几大新兴战略产业，全国就跟着走，地方政府以很便宜的地价、以政府信用作担保，银行按着这个搞贷款，各个开发区按着这个制定准入门槛，它不重复就怪了。产业发展的事情将来是不是政府可以少干点、如果指定计划也是指导性、不要扶植什么政策，而把它交给市场？政府应干点宏观的事情，而不要干微观的事情。即政府多干点让"规则"更趋完善，营造公平开放透明的市场环境的事，统一的市场准入、统一的市场监管，实行负面清单管理，使各类市场主体依法平等进入清单以外的领域，特别是消除对非公有制经济的各种隐性壁垒等。

2. 政府调控社会总供给、市场调节社会需求

因为消费、投资需求如何支出，这些更多应是市场行为、微观行为，是企业、消费者决定选择的事情，政府实际管不了，尤其是地方政府根本管不了。可能在总量控制中，宏观的供给管理和需求管理上，各级政府的管理重点不是需求，而是供给，是管住供给的质量，供给的安全标准。中国还没有到供给创造需求的时代，资本主义自由化时代只要生产出来，人们就有消费，但中国现在如果生产不出来好东西，怎么能带来消费需求？所以，在目前的体制深化转型期，对于宏观调控中供给和需求的管理，政府的重点是供给管理，应管住供给的质量和安全标准，而不是管住需求。政府要给市场主体创造更大发展空间。在这方面，目前政府权力清单与负面清单的改革就是实质性的改革，通过政府做减法，即简政放权，减出来的空间给了市场，给企业发展空间做加法，即赋予企业更多的创业空间；政府自身增加责任，要求有更精细化的管理和更高的工作效率。如对外商投资项目核准制、审批制改为备案制；工商登记注册资本实缴改认缴制；企业"先证后照"改"先照后证"；年检改年报，实施企业信息公示、经营异常名录；企业注册"一口受理""三证合一"、外资广告企业审批改备案；监管信息共享机制、综合执法体

系等推广。

政府要"创新和完善宏观调控方式。按照总量调节和定向施策并举、短期和中长期结合、国内和国际统筹、改革和发展协调的要求,完善宏观调控,采取相机调控、精准调控措施,适时预调微调,更加注重扩大就业、稳定物价、调整结构、提高效益、防控风险、保护环境"①。政府的职能是保持宏观经济稳定,加强和优化公共服务,保障公平竞争,加强市场监管,维护市场秩序,推动可持续发展,促进共同富裕,弥补市场失灵。这就明确了政府应该管什么、不应该管什么,为政府更好发挥作用划定了边界,为转变政府职能指明了方向。形象地说,就是要求政府当好国民经济的"掌舵人"、市场规则的制定者、市场运行的"裁判员"、基本公共服务的提供者、公平正义的维护者。即在供给管理方面,政府不管具体的项目和生产,而是管标准和秩序,尽可能不要提供私人产品。政府投资提供公共产品。中国不是公共品太多,而是严重匮乏。如环境治理、市场失灵、道路拥堵等城市病,这些多半都是公共品供给不足所造成。所以,政府投资应更多集中于真正意义上的公共品的提供,而不要集中于私人产品的提供。市场能生产的私人产品,就让市场去生产,政府不要去干。中国现在公共品的匮乏程度和中国的国家经济地位、中国现代化的要求相差非常大,可以借助市场,弥补政府开放建设资金不足,多渠道补民生短板,即现在讲的 PPP 模式,可以借助市场化,提高公共设施建设的效率与质量,降低社会资本进入基础设施与公共设施的门槛,积极推动审批制度改革,借助市场化,还可以提高公共管理事业的专业化、科学化水平。

3.政府、市场各就其位,发挥各自功能

中国经济持续旺盛高速增长甚至均衡增长,很重要的原因是政府在投资中扮演了重要的角色,这是一个优势,不能简单予以否定。需要

---

① 《中共中央关于制定国民经济和社会发展第十三个五年规划的建议》,新华网,2015 年11 月 3 日。

"深化行政管理体制改革,进一步转变政府职能,持续推进简政放权、放管结合、优化服务,提高政府效能,激发市场活力和社会创造力"①。中国的问题,不是政府的投资比西方高,而是政府的投资应当干什么。政府投资应更多用于公共品与公共基础设施,但由此不能否定中国各级政府在投资中起到了重要作用,这是中国反经济危机的一个优势。强调中国的经济增长,应该强调"三驾马车"的均衡。对于投资、消费和进出口,不能一段时期简单地强调其中某一个方面。这些年,过去强调投资,现在强调消费,这可能有不同时期的特殊考虑,应当强调三者的均衡。所以,在投资与消费这两方面,实际上政府能干的事情是,政府的重点还是在投资上,明确政府在投资上干什么,怎么干。消费领域里的事情更多应由市场去做。

在市场经济条件下,政府要耐得住寂寞,有形之手"少出手",政府之手不与市场争权、不要替代市场之手。实施政府体制改革,取消、下放行政审批事项,审批开放,减少审批——审批是什么? 是权力,是控制,是利益。政府的作用更多应体现于分配和再分配上。生产领域的事情是资源配置的微观行为,应更多交给市场。政府在国民收入的分配特别是再分配上,可能要扮演重要角色。国民收入分配中有宏观、中观、微观三个层面的问题。宏观上,国民收入在政府、企业和居民三者中分配,政府是财政收入,企业是资本盈余,居民是居民收入。这么多年这三个数字中增速最快的实际上是政府的财政收入,居民收入占GDP 的比重不断下降,根据国家统计局的统计最近十年平均每一年下降一个百分点,这就看出过去为什么说消费需求长期疲软,是因为在分钱的时候,大头给了政府和企业。基尼系数为 0.4。收入差距这么大,必然降低消费倾向,这是个大问题。中观是结构上的问题,中国收入差距这么大,表现在地区、产业、城乡的收入差距大,这需要运用国家财政转移支付政策、税收政策、货币政策进行调节。收入差距既包含宏观层

---

① 《中共中央关于制定国民经济和社会发展第十三个五年规划的建议》,新华网,2015 年11 月3 日。

面,也包含中观、微观层面。这些问题靠市场解决不了,必须靠政府解决,政府更多的关注重点应在分配领域,而生产领域的问题应更多交给市场解决。

4. 企业负责市场内在竞争机制,政府负责市场之外的竞争机制

市场内在竞争机制有两个:一个是主体秩序,另一个是交易秩序。前者是指企业产权制度,后者是指价格决定制度。前者回答的是谁在竞争的问题,后者回答的是怎样竞争的问题。市场内在竞争机制更多的是企业的事,是竞争者之间达成的事。市场之外的竞争机制,也有两方面:一个是道德秩序,另一个是法律秩序,这两方面靠市场本身很难形成有效的机制,在很大程度上要依靠国家和政府。孟德斯鸠有句名言,一个民族不在于其有无法律规定,而在于其有无法治精神。经济转轨时期,往往最匮乏的就是法治精神。我们有很多立法,这些法可能质量不是很好,但不要紧,慢慢改。最可怕的是立法者、执法者带头不遵守法律。这靠市场显然难以解决,必须依靠政府自身的改革。道德秩序方面,现代市场经济是诚信经济、信用经济,借贷、买卖、货币、契约全是信用关系,这取决于行为人对社会负责任的能力。但在转型期,以诚信为核心的道德大厦发生动摇,就如布坎南所说道德无政府状态。这种状态的匡正,首先要靠政府,靠政府加强法制让任何欺诈和不敬业行为付出足够的代价,而不是靠盲目分散的市场,因为市场是失灵的,起不了这个作用。为此,我们应大力倡导和切实贯彻市场主体"法无禁止皆可为"、政府"法无授权不可为""法定职责必须为"的法治经济理念,依法放开"无形之手",把资源配置的主导权交予市场,让市场主体的创造活力得以充分迸发,让创造财富的源泉充分涌流;依法管住"有形之手",规范政府行为,减少过多干预导致的市场扭曲,压缩滥用权力损害公共利益的空间。

处理好政府和市场这"两只手"的关系,关键是明晰"无形之手"与"有形之手"的功能、作用与局限,该政府的归政府,该市场的归市场,

如果"有形之手"之间过于偏爱短期内经济总量扩张竞赛,统一的市场和公平的竞争环境则难以内生形成;如果"有形之手"切断资源性产品价格形成机制,那么价格系统的基础信号、源头信息必然失真,产业结构失衡失序在所难免;如果"有形之手"对技术和人才市场的建设及功能做得不够,那么"创新"要么供给不够,要么成本太高,对创新驱动产生瓶颈制约。因此,完善现代市场体系需要"有形之手":先"破"后"立","破"不公平、不开放、不透明的市场规则,"立"负面清单、社会信用体系;有"放"有"管","放"不该管、管不好的资源性产品价格形成机制,"管"市场失序、市场失灵;既"灵"又"活","灵"在知道技术市场的运行规律和具体机制,又好又快地推动技术市场发育,"活"在千方百计集聚和用好各类优秀人才。在市场经济体制完善的进程中,向"强"市场方向演化需要"强"政府的支撑,但政府之"强"应该更多地体现在"破""立"的转化时间上,体现在"放""管"的坚决态度上,体现在"灵""活"的实际效果上。如果"有形之手"精准发力,意味着"无形之手"充分施展有了现实支点,也有了施展方向,更意味着"有形之手"在职能转变中正实现华丽转身。行进在社会主义市场经济这条大路上,有了持续释放的市场活力,有了科学有效的政府治理,中国经济的升级转型必将"化茧成蝶",才能实现瑰丽动人的中国梦想。①

(三) 经济新常态,如何打好结构调整的攻坚战

推进经济结构调整,实现经济结构的动态优化,是实现经济持续平稳增长的基础,是步入经济新常态的基本要求,而结构调整的内容极其复杂,而又十分关键。"加快推进经济结构战略性调整是大势所趋,刻不容缓。国际竞争历来就是时间和速度的竞争,谁动作快,谁就能抢占

---

① 参见刘伟:《对政府与市场关系问题的六点看法》,《华夏时报》2014 年 6 月 5 日。
　　注:本文为华夏时报记者商灏根据北大常务副校长刘伟教授在第二届民建"城市发展论坛"上所作演讲整理的材料。

先机,掌控制高点和主动权;谁动作慢,谁就会丢失机会,被别人甩在后边。"①正如习近平指出,"中国经济已经进入新的发展阶段,正在进行深刻的方式转变和结构调整。这就要不断爬坡过坎、攻坚克难。这必然伴随调整的阵痛、成长的烦恼,但这些都是值得付出的代价。彩虹往往出现在风雨之后。"②因此,经济结构调整什么、如何调整、谁来调整都需要好好推敲。

1. 经济结构调整不会一帆风顺,会有阵痛

世界经济发展的实践证明,一个国家或区域 GDP 总量虽然重要,但更重要的是经济结构的优化,是其全要素生产率的水平,是其经济增长的质量。中国经济过去虽然经历了总量扩张的繁荣,但却积累了明显的结构失衡问题,已步入结构调整加速期,从结构失衡到优化再平衡。从产业结构上看,以加工制造业为主的工业产能过剩,而服务业产能却不足,表现在看病难、上学难、融资难问题困扰民生福利改善与企业运行;从质量结构上看,政绩考核机制引发了各地方的招商引资竞赛,投资和出口超常增长,而消费占比却相对下滑;从地区结构上看,东部沿海地区快速崛起,而西部一些地区发展相对滞后,大城市尤其是特大城市的城市病愈发严重,而中小城市及小城镇内生性相对薄弱。经济结构优化往往比经济总量更重要。在经济发展问题上,要把握好速度、总量、结构的关系,处理好数量、质量、效益的关系,须臾不可违背辩证法。习近平指出:"块头大不等于强,体重大不等于壮,有时是虚胖。"③如果片面、简单化地把增加生产总值当发展,甚至"以 GDP 论英雄",只要"块头"和"体重",不注重质量和效益,不顾及环境资源代价,违背经济规律和自然规律,不仅是"虚胖",而且会加剧已有矛盾,积患成祸,带来诸多风险。例如 1840 年中英鸦片战争时,中国 GDP 总量居

① 《习近平在广东主持召开经济工作座谈会》,《人民日报》2012 年 12 月 11 日。
② 《深化改革开放 共创美好亚太——习近平主席在亚太经合组织工商领导人峰会上的演讲》,新华网,2013 年 10 月 8 日。
③ 《习近平总书记系列重要讲话读本》,学习出版社、人民出版社 2014 年版,第 65 页。

前,超出英国,但经济结构不行,中国 GDP 总量的产品主要是农产品和手工业品,其棉布是手工纺织的棉布,外贸出口是茶叶、瓷器、丝绸、桐油等。在 1840 年时,英国工业革命从 1770 年算起已有 70 年,工业化进展到了一定程度,英国 GDP 结构符合科技进步要求,钢铁产量比较高,技术设备制造发展,棉布全是用机器纺织的,其出口的一部分是机器制造的棉布,另一部分是蒸汽机机器设备,交通工具是轮船和火车。目前虽然中国经济总量已经第二,但经济结构还存在许多问题,与一些发达国家产业结构比,中国高新技术产品占 GDP 的比重低、处于全球产业价值链低端,第二次、第三次产业比例不合理,还有收入分配、城乡、区域发展结构都有进一步优化调整的空间,所以,当前中国改革重点难点是结构调整问题。大家知道,任何一次经济危机背后实质上是经济结构调整的过程,也是动态平衡、转型升级的过程,同样,任何国家的经济转型发展也会带来"阵痛"或困境。中国经济的转型发展也不会一帆风顺,调结构、转方式,实现创新驱动、转型发展绝非易事,不可能一蹴而就,需要经历较长的过程才能实现,经济转型发展的"痛苦"或"曲折"不可避免,非常必要。

目前,中国经济结构是基于经济开放、技术进步、全要素生产率提高要求,是基于一些经济结构失衡的背景下进行的调整,显然,结构调整与优化依靠要素资源的投入,尤其是资本积累的工业化在长期内是不可持续的,只有依靠技术进步,制度、模式创新,通过提高制度、技术效率和资源配置效率实现的发展才是可持续的、高效的。可持续发展道路不仅要追求科技含量高、资源消耗低、环境污染少、人力资源优势得到充分发挥,更要追求要素配置效率的优化。这种优化的前提条件是市场机制的充分发挥,尤其是市场制度的深化,而不是简单地从劳动与资本要素驱动转向创新要素驱动,这要求政府转型为其提供前提,为实现科技创新驱动、智能驱动转变,实施大众创新、万众创业提供制度安排。实践证明,若要素驱动模式若忽视了要素市场的培育,那必将导致要素价格的扭曲。没有哪个现代国家的工业化是在封闭条件下完成的,资源要素是在统一、开放的市场进行配置,这意味着新型工业化是以经济开放为背景;开放是获取新知识、进行制度创新,促进技术进步的有力手段,但此种获取方式取决于一国甚至一个行业内企业间的各种差异,尤其是技能劳动需求与供给、技术吸收能力和要素报酬差距。解决结构调整的体制困境,要明确哪些调整是通过市场价格、市场机制来完成的,哪些要通过政府体制改革,发挥政府职能完成。如在市场经济条件下,产能过剩问题可由市场来解决,而推进节能减排,建设美丽中国,则是政府必须努力的方向。产能严重过剩、企业竞争力、产业结构失衡的问题,主要原因在于体制机制改革不到位,解决这些复杂问题,取决于效率取向的市场制度创新,通过真正的市场化改革走出体制的困境。而收入分配结构的失衡一定要依靠政府调节而不能仅仅靠市场,市场在这些方面往往失灵的,政府要充分运用好财政、货币及税收政策,基础是做好第一次分配,辅助是第二次分配,完善是其他政策安排。在合理调整政府、企业与民众收入比例问题方面,如阶层之间收入基尼系数高,城镇内部贫富差距拉大,社会阶层就会固化等,要更好地发挥政府的作用。

2. 结构调整的关键是解决结构的失衡机制

中国经济运行中的结构失衡主要表现在三个方面。其一,是消费、投资与出口结构的失衡。当一国的经济增长过度依赖于某一种动力时,经济结构就会严重失衡,如中国的经济增长长期过度依赖出口与政府投资,居民消费就难以成为拉动经济增长的主动力,这种格局导致了产业结构的失衡。结构失衡累积的矛盾,随着经济规模进入中等收入水平后带来的规模报酬开始递减而越来越难以解决,并为经济结构调整造成了增长机制和利益分配的路径依赖,即"结构协调的增长"离不开原来增长机制的支持。因此,经济结构调整的难点在于找到脱胎于"结构失衡的增长"中某个增长机制,并使其在"结构协调的增长"中成为可能,是否可能的判断依据就是效率导向、持续发展的动力。通过结构失衡机制的矫正,充分发挥消费对增长的基础性作用,发挥投资对增长的重要动力功能,发挥出口对增长的重要支撑作用。其二,是实体经济与虚拟经济失衡。目前经济结构的失衡问题,不仅是产业结构失衡,是空间结构失衡,更是实体经济和虚拟经济之间发展的严重失衡,即"实体经济不实,虚拟经济太虚"。实体经济不实的主要表现:一是许多企业不愿做实业,愿意进入泡沫领域获取短期高利润。二是产业创新能力差,许多所谓的战略性新兴产业,实际上是戴着高新技术产业的"帽子",做的却是传统产业的活。三是生产率低、附加值低,因为无法抵消不断上涨的生产要素成本的压力,很多实体企业处于亏损的状态。而虚拟经济太虚的主要表现在于:一是真实利率高。不断上升的利率与人工成本,已使真实利率水平脱离了实体经济可以承受的极限,实体企业融资难、融资贵为普遍问题。二是汇率高。人民币汇率的持续大幅度攀升,导致出口企业的亏损倒闭。三是资产价格高。长期以来,以房地产为主体的资产价格不断地拉高 M2 水平、利率水平,抑制了民众消费和扩大内需战略的实施。四是债务率高。企业和地方政府负债体现在债务规模大、水平高,表现在债务结构上,负债的资产构成很多是回报率倒挂的公共基础设施项目,负债的抵押物主要是价格虚高的土地资产。其三,是工业化与城市化协调发展问题。从经济学的视角审视工业化、城市化,前者主要提供供给,后者主要影响需求,二者要协调发展。快速推进的工业化和城市化带动了中国经济的高速增长,而快速工业化与城市化的推进是经济结构调整中无法避开的问题,解决难题的关键在于走高效工业化道路或新型工业化道路。同样,城市化既是经济赶超时期的驱动力,又是导致结构失衡的重要原因。城市化不仅是脱胎于"结构失衡的增长"中的增长机制,而且是能成为"结构协调的增长"中的新路径,但前提是走高效城市化道路。

实践不断证明,结构调整的快慢,决定了经济动态平衡的速度,凡是进行结构性调整,速度很快,就复苏很快,如 2008 年金融危机后,通过雷曼兄弟公司的倒闭等削减债务,通过加州为代表的创新企业的重新涌现,以及以得州为代表的旧能源产业的新生页岩气的开采成本大幅下降,促进制造业回流进行结构调整,经济得以比较快地复苏。欧盟结构调整拖拖拉拉,债务难以消除,产业结构调整得慢,其经济复苏得也慢。而当下的中国经济结构调整已步入关键期、困难期,产业结构调整的主体是企业,同样要发挥好市场决定性作用与更好发挥政府的作用,产业结构是市场供给与需求平衡选择的结果,要改变以往政府习惯的产业管制政策,改革政府"点球式"产业扶植制度安排,因为一些不公平的产业扶植政策往往成为企业寻找政府政策之租的来源。在实践中,为什么一些产业往往"有心栽花花不开",如光伏产业,从一个新兴的产业很快进入一个产能过剩的产业,而另外一些行业却"无心插柳柳成荫",如阿里巴巴、腾讯、百度、京东等互联网企业发展很快。

3. 产业结构重点是存量调整、增量做优

当前传统产业增长动力减弱,新兴产业的动力尚没有跟上,暂时出现了"青黄不接"的尴尬,这很大程度上与产业结构调整相对滞后有关。从产业结构看,传统产业产能大幅超出需求,产品价格水平持续走低,企业经营困难加大,投资意愿和能力不足,化解产能过剩、企业兼并重组势在必行。与此同时,新一代信息技术加速与传统产业融合,新技术、新产品、新业态、新模式不断涌现,制造业的智能化、数字化、服务化特征日趋明显。产业结构调整的路径是促进传统产业升级转型、加快培育发展新兴产业。新一轮的世界产业革命,对中国产业变革,是一个技术上赶超发展、结构上加快升级的重大机遇。从规模上看,中国制造业成功超越日本成为世界第二,但从结构上来看,中国的先进制造业尤其是服务型制造业的比重明显偏低。制造业在大而不强的困境下,"制造强国"的梦想仿佛还在山那边。如何促进产业结构调整,主要选择是:一是促进制造业升级,消化产能过剩,鼓励企业兼并重组。结合"一带一路"行动规划,加大产业开放力度,实施产业输出。实施"中国制造2025"规划,明确十个重点行业,其中多数是战略经济产业、先进制造业,要加快制定每个行业的"2025专项计划",其他产业如钢铁、石化、有色金属、建材、纺织、轻工、食品等,这些关系到国计民生的基础行业也不能轻视,因为这些传统产业亟待用先进技术来改造提升。培育智能制造,开展数字化研发设计,《中国制造2025》提出到2025年要提高到84%,要进入推动仿真模拟、三维描述、高清运算、大数据等信息

工具来提升我们研发设计的效率和水准;把电子信息技术切入到产品里去,提高产品的质量、功能和附加值,特别是关键零部件、元器件、关键材料的质量和自给率,真正把代工组装变为自主制造;实施制造设备的数控化,推广高档数控机床,智能工业机器人,3D打印,生产制造;等等。二是推进制造业服务化发展。在信息化、网络化、智能化日益深化的背景下,以及经济全球化的加剧,各国制造业产业分工逐步细化,跨区域的产业融合不断升级,制造与服务融合型企业迅速增加。全球制造业发展基本趋势是从生产型制造向服务型制造转变。制造业服务化代表了全球制造业与新工业革命发展趋势。制造业服务化是突破产业链低端锁定、获取竞争优势的关键。在宏观层面表现为服务型经济的形成,在中观层面表现为从制造业城市向服务业城市转变,在微观层面表现为企业从生产型企业向服务型企业转变。德勤公司《基于全球服务业和零部件管理调研》表明,在其调查的80家制造企业中,服务收入占总销售收入的平均值超过25%;19%的制造业公司的服务收入超过总收入的50%。其中发达国家制造业服务化的水平明显高于正处在工业化进程中的国家。美国制造与服务融合型的企业占制造企业总数的58%;芬兰的这一比值为51%,荷兰为40%以及比利时为37%;中国制造业的服务化进程相对落后,具备服务型制造能力的企业仅占所有企业的2.2%。其一是依托制造业拓展生产性服务业:通用电气把服务渗透到了自己的日常作业管理之中,依托制造业积极发展商务金融、消费者金融、信息技术等利润丰厚、发展前景广阔的现代服务业。比如,通用电气公司既生产医疗器械,也提供医疗器械的融资租赁等相关金融服务,拉长了产业链条,增强了市场竞争力。通用电气已发展成为全球最大的多元化服务性公司,同时也是高质量、高科技工业和消费产品的提供者。其二是从销售产品,发展成为提供服务和成套解决方案的提供商:国际商业机器公司(IBM)是此领域的典型代表。IBM能够为客户提供集成了硬件、软件、融资和服务的成套解决方案,使IBM从硬件到软件和服务有机结合起来,强化了IBM满足客户需求的能力。其三是从制造企业转型为服务提供商:香港利丰集团没有一家自己的工厂,不拥有任何生产设备,但合作对象却超过 40 个国家约 7500 家供应商。拿到客户订单,利丰开展产业链管理,将每个环节外包给最好的生产商。比如一件衣服,可能里子在中国台湾生产,拉链在泰国生产,组装在中国大陆。这样,1 万员工的利丰身后实际工作者有 150 多万。目前,利丰的业务网络遍布全球,与超过 300 个跨国公司合作。这种无疆界生产、虚拟生产的模式不仅保证了产品质量,还将成本控制在最低水平。当今世界,凡是优秀的制造业企业都是服务型制造企业,基于制造的服务是企业收入增长的新来源,而服务产品创新是一个复杂而艰难的过程。三是开展"互联网+"行动规划。中国正处在工业化的关键阶段,互联网可以和任何产业相叠加,"互联网+"行动措施:要用新一代信息技术和平台去改造提升、优化相关业;要用互联网的理念思维去策划、设计产业的发展,企业是"互联网+"的行动主体,应该主动去拥抱互联网,增强内生动力,焕发内在活力,实现自我变革。"互联网+",应该是网络经济和实体经济的结合,应该是互联网企业和实体经济企业的结合。产业服务链的数字化和网络化、社会化,运用工业互联网发展现代智能物流、电子商务,大幅度降低制造成本,开展全周期的服务,使我们的消费者没有后顾之忧,这样可以进一步拉动消费,发展远程监控,在线维护,这样有助于长周期安全平稳地运行,制造业供应链和销售网的社会化、网络化,会适应生产模式的新变化,来推动生产型服务业快速发展。

4. 理顺分配收入机制、完善分配结构

国民收入的初次分配就是在国民收入"蛋糕"既定的前提下,如何处理好国家与个人的分配关系,实质是如何处理好积累和消费的关系。充分发挥政府的调节作用,积极主动地参与居民收入分配结构的调整。制约我国扩大城乡居民消费需求的主要因素:一是城乡居民可支配收入水平提高落后于经济增长,居民所得占国民收入的比重偏低。二是社会保障体系建设滞后。由政府提供的基本公共服务供给不足,导致居民预防性储蓄动机和意愿很强,边际消费倾向不高。三是收入分配

差距明显。高收入群体边际消费倾向递减,低收入群体没有能力增加消费,由此造成消费总量增长相对迟滞。要真正实现扩大城乡居民消费需求目标,除了实施系列行之有效的刺激消费政策,需要在治标的基础上,下大力气奠定治本之策,构建、完善推动消费需求持续增长的制度保障基础:适度提高居民收入在国民收入分配中的比重,合理调整国民收入分配关系,增加居民收入份额,降低政府收入比重,使人民群众有更多收入用于扩大消费;加快社会保障体系建设,推进基本公共服务均等化。加快完善社会保障体系,扩大社会保障覆盖面,逐步提高社会保障水平,并结合财税体制改革和转变政府职能,较大幅度增加财政对公共服务和公共产品的支出,解除群众扩大消费的后顾之忧;逐步缩小社会成员之间的收入差距。通过税收、转移支付等手段调整不同阶层、区域、城乡间的收入分配结构,增加占人口大多数的中低收入者收入,加大对困难群体的帮扶力度,逐步扩大中等收入阶层的数量。此外,工业化创造供给,城镇化创造需求。因此,要特别注重通过适度加快城镇化进程,推动消费需求的增长。加快推进户籍、金融、土地、社保等制度的改革,让农民工在所工作、生活的城市特别是在中小城市市民化,通过农民工这一为国家现代化作出巨大贡献的群体在城市安居乐业,使他们在创造巨大产能的同时,带动有效需求的持续增长。此外,政府可以通过财政的转移支付,将财力重点向经济欠发达地区或贫困地区倾斜,以改变区域发展的不平衡,增强经济欠发达地区或贫困地区的发展能力。既要重视国民收入的初次分配,又要重视国民收入的再次分配。国民收入初次的分配要保持国家、企业与社会消费、居民收入分配结构的优化。国民收入的再次分配通过政府财政对国民收入的重新分配,以调节优化国民收入分配的结构,消除不合理的分配结构。调整居民收入分配结构,缓解社会分配不公,目标是既要保低,又要限高;保障低收入者的收入,维护社会弱者的利益,提高高收入者的税收负担,但调整的重点是增加低收入者的收入,以缓解社会分配不公和贫富差距的扩大。在重视居民收入分配的公平同时,也要重视发展的机会均等。

（四）把创新驱动发展战略实施好

新常态是创新驱动型的经济,增长速度"下台阶",智造、创造、要素生产率、增长质量"上台阶"。加快从要素驱动、投资规模驱动发展为主,向以创新驱动发展为主的转变。党的十八届五中全会强调,实现"十三五"时期发展目标,破解发展难题,厚植发展优势,必须牢固树立并切实贯彻创新、协调、绿色、开放、共享的发展理念,鲜明地把创新摆在发展理念的首位。创新发展将成为"十三五"时期经济结构实现战略性调整的关键驱动因素,是实现"五位一体"总体布局下全面发展的根本支撑和关键动力。"要紧扣创新驱动发展目标,以推动科技创新为核心,以破除体制机制障碍为主攻方向,开展系统性、整体性、协同性改革的先行先试,统筹推进科技、管理、品牌、组织、商业模式创新,加快形成我国经济社会发展的新引擎,为建设创新型国家提供强有力支撑。"①

1. 经济新常态是创新驱动型的经济

原本依靠"要素驱动"和"投资驱动"的外延式、粗放型发展模式难以为继,由过度依赖要素增加转向靠深化改革,促进市场扩展、市场深化、制度创新来形成制度"红利",促进经济内生增长,必须把创新能力及其制度安排放在新常态经济的核心位置。经济新常态,从其表象上,是经济增长速度的换挡,其本质则是经济增长动力的转换,进而倒逼产业结构调整。从发展动力看,生产成本持续上升,资源环境约束不断强化,要素的规模驱动力减弱,必须更多依靠人力资本质量和技术进步,着力提升创新能力,通过供给创新激活消费需求,形成新的经济增长点。

创新驱动产生竞争新优势,带来发展新动力。为此需要培育发展

---

① 《习近平主持召开中央全面深化改革领导小组第十二次会议强调　把握改革大局自觉服从服务改革大局　共同把全面深化改革这篇大文章做好》,人民网,2015 年 5 月 6 日。

新动力,加快实现发展动力转换。优化劳动力、资本、土地、技术、管理等要素配置,一要激发创新创业活力,推动大众创业、万众创新,释放新需求。亚当·斯密认为人类社会经济增长的动力有赖于劳动分工和专业化所带来的劳动生产率的提高以及市场的深化和扩展。由于劳动分工提高了生产率,从而推动经济增长。对提高生产效率作用最大的分工和资本配置会在市场力量的作用下自然形成和有效实现,而政府的任务应该是维护稳定的法律制度和市场秩序,为经济增长提供制度保证。"GNP 之父"——库兹涅茨认为经济增长主要依赖于人口、资源等要素投入的增加,经济结构从农业生产占主导地位向制造业和服务业占主导地位转变。国家竞争力概念的提出者麦克尔·波特,在其"钻石理论"中分析一个国家某种产业为什么会在国际上有较强的竞争力,国家与区域竞争力的差异在于国家与区域拥有的现代通信、信息受过高等教育的人力、研究等高级生产要素不同。市场化改革应更多转向与创新活动相关的高级生产要素,包括人才、技术、金融、教育、品牌等应进行市场拓展与深化。产业要获得持久的竞争力,必须实现建立在初级生产要素之上的产业向高级生产要素提升,加快高级生产要素的市场化,在这个问题上有所突破,将会推动创新驱动和发展方式转变的实质性进展。熊彼特的"创造性破坏"经济动态下的技术进步、经济增长。结构的创造和破坏主要不是通过价格竞争而是依靠创新的竞争实现的。大规模的创新都淘汰旧的技术和生产体系,并建立起新的生产体系。

经济新常态,预示发展方式从规模速度型转向质量效率型,发展动力从要素驱动转向创新驱动,这构成了经济发展的大逻辑。在此背景下,创新驱动成为促进产业升级的不竭动力。企业既是市场主体、又是创新主体,政府制度安排支持创新型、充满活力的中小企业,促进传统产业改造升级,尽快形成新常态下新的经济增长点和产业驱动力。大力培育和发展战略性新兴产业,围绕战略性新兴产业需求部署创新链,突破技术瓶颈,掌握核心关键技术,加快新技术新产品新工艺研发应用,加强技术集成和商业模式创新;运用高新技术加快改造提升传统产业,在重点产业领域建设技术创新平台,加快科技成果转化应用,提升传统产业创新发展能力;着力强化企业技术创新主体地位,构建以企业为主体、市场为导向、产学研相结合的技术创新体系,建立企业主导产业技术研发创新体制机制,促进技术、人才等创新要素向企业研发机构流动,培育和壮大创新型企业。实施创新驱动,以全球视野谋划和推动创新,提高原始创新、集成创新和引进消化吸收再创新能力,更加注重协同创新,积极完善和落实促进科技成果转化,促进科技和金融结合,加强知识产权创造、运用、保护、管理,加强对科技创新活动和科技成果的法律保护,为科技创新提供有力保障;建立健全科研活动行为准则和规范,加强科研诚信和科学伦理教育,营造宽松包容、奋发向上的氛围,厚植创新的土壤;加快建设国家创新体系,着力构建以企业为主体、市场为导向、产学研相结合的国家创新体系,走创新驱动的内生增长之路,努力形成"人人创新""万众创新"的新局面。

实施创新需要创造新供给,推动新技术、新产业、新业态蓬勃发展,必须把发展基点放在创新上,形成促进创新的体制架构,塑造更多依靠创新驱动、更多发挥先发优势的引领型发展。需要培育以技术、标准、品牌、质量、服务为核心的对外经济新优势。提高劳动密集型产品科技含量和附加值,营造资本和技术密集型产业新优势,提高我国产业在全球价值链中的地位。创新驱动实质是人才驱动,要充分发挥科技第一生产力、人才第一资源的作用,破除体制机制障碍,着力破除一切阻碍创新驱动发展的壁垒,建立完善有利于创新的最优化的政策环境和制度。实现习近平总书记所讲"实施创新驱动发展战略,最根本的是要增强自主创新能力,最紧迫的是要破除体制机制障碍,最大限度解放和激发科技作为第一生产力所蕴藏的巨大潜能"①。深化体制机制改革,从政府管理、财税、金融、人才、教育、股权激励等多个方面开展突破、为创新驱动发展提供制度创新。如放开新兴行业准入管制,开展创新人

---

① 《习近平谈治国理政》,外文出版社 2014 年版,第 121 页。

注:本文为习近平主席 2014 年 6 月 10 日在中国科学院第十七次院士大会、中国工程院第十二次院士大会上的重要讲话。

才与教育制度,实施天使投资税制,推进商业银行与金融服务创新,对国有企事业创新实施股权激励等,进一步推动大众创业、万众创新,形成新的巨大动力,打造中国经济的新引擎,发展开放的创新创业生态系统,形成以知识创造、流通和应用为基础的创新型经济。

2. 体制机制创新是关键

党的十八届五中全会提出:"坚持创新发展,必须把创新摆在国家发展全局的核心位置,不断推进理论创新、制度创新、科技创新、文化创新等各方面创新,让创新贯穿党和国家一切工作,让创新在全社会蔚然成风。"①现行政府管理体制不适应创新驱动的要求,其主要表现:一是政府设计和运用创新政策的能力有待提高。如促进创新的"点球式"政策多,而普惠型政策少;政府供给型政策多,企业需求侧政策少;直接资助政策多,社会引导政策少,政府之间的政策协同性不足。二是政府GDP 考核、经济活动用旧思维对创新活动作取舍,创新价值和人员价值难以通过要素价格体现关注科技领域改革,国家没有从经济社会发展领域同步发力。三是对科技成果转移转化的市场化机制不到位。如对无形资产的认识和管理有待改进,对市场化的科技成果发现、转化、评估和收益分配机制尚未健全完善。四是宽容包容开放的创新创业氛围不足。缺少支持创新的社会氛围,全社会尊重创造、包容创新、宽容失败的氛围不够浓厚,缺乏激励创新的舆论环境,有关创新创业服务体系不健全。如专业化服务机构和人才缺乏,高校、科研院所与企业之间开放协同不足,创新要素流动不足。五是社会创新服务体系亟待优化。如政府公共资源分散,缺乏顶层设计和总体统筹,以企业为主体的科研投入和退出机制不完善,社会资本对于中小企业和早期初创企业支持严重不足等,上述因素影响了创新机制作用的发挥,也影响了企业与人员的创新活力。

---

① 《中共中央关于制定国民经济和社会发展第十三个五年规划的建议》,新华网,2015 年11 月 3 日。

诺斯把制度性因素作为经济增长的源泉,从而把经济增长与制度变迁联系起来,认为经济增长应该重点研究新增长背后的、能驱动经济增长的、由制度派生出来的激励结构,而这种激励结构可以降低交易费用进而推动经济增长的产权体系,包括国家制度创新、政府治理方式创新、产权激励机制、企业组织创新。如何推进市场制度的完善与深化,建设完善契约、诚信、平等的市场文化;如何加强知识产权保护与创新的激励,促使农村资产资本化、利率市场化等;如何让先进的技术能够从实验室到生产线;如何让融资、科研、制造、消费在内的整个市场体系按照现代经济的方式运转? 还有资本与技术之间的障碍、技术和产业之间的障碍、产业与市场的障碍、国内与国外资源的障碍,唯有通过制度变革,才有可能打破。创新发展的实践表明,企业作为自主创新主体,创新活动既要符合科技活动的规律,也要契合市场经济发展的内在需求。加强知识产权保障,保障创新者权益;鼓励更多人去创新创业,打造一个宽松的创新创业环境,通过制度创新,为企业技术、运行模式创新提供保障。可持续创新需要借助企业可持续创新来实现,将技术、组织、商业模式创新相结合,用制度、组织的创新成果去保障技术创新活动的开展。现实中,很多阻碍经济可持续发展的不是科技,而是制度或政策壁垒。因此,增强自主创新能力,最紧迫的是破除体制机制障碍,最大限度解放、激发科技作为第一生产力所蕴藏的巨大潜能。与低成本优势相比,技术创新具有不易模仿、附加值高等突出特点,由此建立的创新优势持续时间长、竞争力强。实现科技创新、制度创新、开放创新的有机统一和协同发展,向科技创新要速度、要后劲、要效益,把推动发展的立足点转到质量和效益上来,进而提高各个企业的核心竞争力。

3. 创新驱动的路径与模式

纵观全球新兴产业及其新模式、新业态的发展,在新的生产力逐渐兴起的浪潮中,技术驱动、市场驱动、制度驱动是其根本性推动力量。一是技术驱动。企业以前所未有的全新产品和服务,创造出新的需求和市场空间，即以供给创造需求。如 3D 打印技术问世后，2007 年 Shapeways 创建了"3D 云打印模式"。用户上传产品设计（或购买该网站上的 3D 设计图）并选择原材料付费后，由 Shapeways 打印出成品，用户也可以在线展示和销售产品，网站按利润的 3.5% 收取手续费。二是市场驱动。企业以全新的商业模式，实现更低成本、更便捷服务、更快速反应，满足市场需求、适应市场竞争。如 2014 年阿里巴巴与新浪微博的联姻。以 5.86 亿美元购入新浪微博 18% 的股份，正孕育"社交网络+电子商务+第三方支付"的新模式。三是制度驱动。是以制度调整或创设改变市场主体利益关系，为新兴产业的某些新模式、新业态提供巨大发展空间。如国际碳排放交易机制催生出 1400 亿欧元的全球性碳交易市场，推动碳交易、碳金融、碳审计、碳中介相关的新模式、新业态快速发展。为成功实现创新驱动模式，需要：其一是推动劳动力要素和资本要素的升级。深化改革高等教育体制，大学要把精英教育与创新、创业教育相结合，把"顶天"与"立地"相结合，加强职业技能教育体系，培养一大批适应产业升级和新兴产业发展的高水平技术工人。完善多层次资本市场，强化资本市场引导资本流动、支持创新、分散风险的能力；推动劳动力要素和资本要素的优化配置。加强知识产权保护力度，切实保护创新者的合法权益，提升知识产权附加价值。推进政府管理体制改革，健全有利于创新的公共服务体系。其二是按产业升级目标推进创新驱动战略的实施，以产业链引导创新链，以创新链支撑产业链。消除产业链与创新链优化配置和融合互动的体制机制障碍，实现创新资源整合共享，建立产业和创新要素合理分布与优化配置、上下游和各环节有机联动的机制。通过大力推进体制机制创新，营造良好产业生态，搭建创新服务平台，促进资金、人才、科研、信息、网络、数据等知识要素、创新要素集聚和共享。其三是协同推进、集中突破产业领域发展的若干重大关键技术和共性技术。围绕重点产业领域，通过财政、税收、金融等手段引导整合现有科研院所、企业形成关键技术和共性技术的研究开发体系，改革其管理体制和绩效考核机制，充分发挥其在关键技术和共性技术研发中的作用。

4. 良好的生态创新环境是基础

创新需要合适的环境,促进创新型企业家的出现,非常重要的因素是生态环境。自由、产权保障、法治、文化对创新非常重要。创新要有自由的心,要有法律的保障。如果知识产权保护很弱,法治很不健全,仍然会有套利的企业家,但是在这种环境下出现创新的企业家几乎不可能。为创新要自由,当你不会为了你的想法去冒险的时候,创新是不可能的。真正的创新需要的是专利的有力保护!没有有力的专利保护,创新的原动力就会枯竭!仔细考察各类创新,与时机相关,总是若干探索、尝试、错误、折回的综合体,充满了各种阴差阳错。大众创新可以,但创新成功往往是小众的事情或概率,这既取决于个人(团体)的创新能力,也取决于创新生态环境,有什么资源可以利用,有什么人员可以交流,创新者迈出的每一步,是否能寻找到相关的资源与机会,能否给你足够的反馈。如果把创新者视为青蛙,创新环境视为池塘,成功视为池塘彼岸,那么各种外部因素就相当于水面上的荷叶。想要抵达彼岸,你必须借助一片片的荷叶,但你永远无法知道跳上某片荷叶会遇到什么,也不知道它能通向哪几片其他荷叶。唯一能确认的是,荷叶越密集,荷叶之间的距离越短,抵达彼岸的几率就越大。在创新能力一定的情况下,能借助的外部因素越多,创新成功的可能性越大。

创新生态环境的建设要求政府创新的治理新体系,实现政府监管、商业环境、创新政策的创新,主要关注创新驱动发展的税收 Tax、贸易 Trade、技术 Technology、人才 Talent 的 4T 环境。因为科技创新不是管出来的,是放出来的,是执着求索出来的,是市场竞争出来的。政府一是"放",凡是市场机制能够实现或有社会组织能够替代的服务功能,主动转型、为之腾出空间,并给予必要支持。二是"退",对于市场导向明确的创新活动,减少对具体项目的选择和企业创新的干预。三是"进",进一步加强统筹协调和顶层设计,抓战略、抓重大、抓前沿、抓基础。政府加强创新的政策设计。改变点球式、供给侧、攀比型创新政策的安排,因为其边际效益明显递减,迫切需要在更高层面开展系统设计、协同推进。政府创新政策要更多地注重普惠,多予不如少取。如实施三大普惠型政策,即研发费用加计扣除、高新技术企业认定、技术先进型服务企业认定;政府的创新制度安排要有明确的稳定预期,让行政相对人有章可循。如欧盟每4—5年调整一次汽车排放标准,在全欧洲推行,并提前5年预告社会大众,倒逼汽车产业技术升级等。政府对待科技创新,既是当务之急,更要久久为功。政府及社会应当处理好显绩与潜绩的有机平衡,从注重当前发展转向可持续发展,围绕创新驱动发展进行要素配置,更加注重技术、人才、信息等要素的利用,将科技创新作为区域、行业、企业发展评价的关键衡量标准。实施创新驱动,要尊重科技创新和科技成果产业化规律,培育开放、统一、公平、竞争的市场环境,建立健全科技创新和产业化发展的服务体系和支持创新的功能型平台,建设各具特色的创新园区与平台,营造鼓励创新、宽容失败的创新文化和社会氛围,并通过制度创新,为企业技术、运行模式创新提供保障,鼓励更多的人去创新创业,打造一个宽松的创新创业环境。

通过市场化机制、专业化服务和资本化途径构建的低成本、便利化、全要素、开放式的创业服务组织,建立政府及社会从天使投资到财税政策,从知识产权保护到转变政府科技管理职能。在科技服务业上,科技中介服务、科技金融日趋关键,在经济结构上,民营中小企业成为创新主体。按照创新生态系统建设的需要,发展科技服务业,突出市场化、专业化、社会化。发展"众创空间",引导民营企业、社会资本参与孵化器建设运营,完善科技创业苗圃、孵化器和加速器构成的创业孵化链。制定天使投资制度安排,设立创业投资基金、税收支持,提供廉价的创新公共服务设施,降低企业内部的配套成本;降低创新创业企业运行成本,完善科技创新相关的税收抵免优惠政策。积极帮助科技创业者降低用工成本。如对符合规定的科技创业孵化企业,可提供社会保险费补助政策、政府廉价集体宿舍政策。对雇佣本地大学生就业或引进人才的,还可提供收入补助政策。建立技术创新的市场导向机制,技术研发方向、路线选择、资源、要素按市场导向优化配置。

思考题

1. 什么是经济发展新常态?
2. 如何理解供给侧结构性改革?

参考文献

1.《习近平谈治国理政》,北京:外文出版社,2014 年。

2. 中共中央宣传部:《习近平总书记系列重要讲话重要读本(2016 年版)》,北京:学习出版社、人民出版社,2016 年。

3.《中共中央关于制定国民经济和社会发展第十三个五年规划的建议》,新华社,2015 年 11 月 3 日。

4. 刘伟:《对政府与市场关系问题的六点看法》,《华夏时报》2014 年 6 月 5 日。

5.《"互联网+"重新定义信息化——关于"互联网+"的研究报告(上、下)》,《光明日报》2015 年 10 月 16 日。

二、全面深化改革

"改革开放是一项长期的、艰巨的、繁重的事业,必须一代又一代人接力干下去。必须坚持社会主义市场经济的改革方向,坚持对外开放的基本国策,以更大的政治勇气和智慧,不失时机深化重要领域改革,朝着党的十八大指引的改革开放方向奋勇前进。"——习近平在主持十八届中央政治局第二次集体学习时的讲话(2012 年 12 月 31 日)①

---

① 《改革开放只有进行时没有完成时》(2012 年 12 月 31 日),见《习近平谈治国理政》,外文出版社 2014 年版,第 67 页。

党的十八大以来,习近平总书记围绕全面深化改革、扩大开放作出一系列重要论述,其立意高远、思想深刻、内涵丰富、切中肯綮,实现了我党关于改革开放理论的新的拓展和突破,为全面深化改革、扩大开放提供了根本的遵循和指导。我们深入学习研究习近平总书记关于改革开放的重要论述,具有十分重要的政治、理论和实践指导意义。

(一) 为什么说改革开放是决定当代中国命运的关键一招

改革开放是决定当代中国命运的关键一招,也是决定实现"两个一百年"奋斗目标、实现中华民族伟大复兴的关键一招,实践发展永无止境,解放思想永无止境,改革开放也永无止境,停顿和倒退没有出路,改革开放只有进行时、没有完成时。①

改革开放对于中国共产党、中国人民、中华民族,乃至国际共产主义运动的作用怎么估计都不过分。习近平总书记用"决定当代中国命运的关键一招,也是决定实现'两个一百年'奋斗目标、实现中华民族伟大复兴的关键一招"来形容改革开放的作用是恰如其分的。

改革开放是我们党在新的时代条件下带领人民进行的新的伟大革命。之所以将改革开放上升到"革命"的高度,可以从以下 3 个维度来理解。一个是社会主义制度的自我完善和发展维度。事物是运动、变化和发展的,这是马克思主义的基本观点,社会主义制度同样如此。恩格斯早在 1890 年致奥·伯尼克的信中就谈到这个问题,他说:"所谓'社会主义社会'不是一种一成不变的东西,而应当和任何其他社会制度一样,把它看成是经常变化和改革的社会。"国际共产主义运动中,特别是苏联东欧的社会主义发展模式的僵化和封闭,最终导致这些国家社会主义制度被颠覆和破坏,使国际共产主义运动出现严重挫折和

---

① 参见《关于〈中共中央关于全面深化改革若干重大问题的决定〉的说明》(2013 年 11 月 9 日),见《习近平谈治国理政》,外文出版社 2014 年版,第 71 页。

低潮,这反过来印证了恩格斯观点的正确。新中国成立以后由于中国实行"一边倒"政策,中国共产党学习和照搬苏联模式建设社会主义,也曾出现超越生产力发展阶段的"一大二公""一平二调",片面追求生产关系上的"纯而又纯",甚至发生"文化大革命"这样的全局性错误,使我国的国民经济处于崩溃的边缘,党、国家和中华民族遭到严重浩劫。惨痛的历史事实教育了中国共产党和中国人民,我党对苏联模式的认识也由学习照搬、机械模仿发展到改革不适合经济发展阶段和社会实际的体制机制,探索中国特色社会主义的正确轨道上来,从而开启了立足国情实现社会主义制度自我完善发展的改革开放伟大历史进程,从而赋予社会主义制度以新的生机和活力。30多年的改革开放实践已经充分证明,中国的改革开放改变了中国共产党、中国人民和中华民族的面貌,改变了社会主义乃至国际共产主义运动的历史命运。一个是解放和发展社会生产力的维度。马克思在《〈政治经济学批判〉序言》中指出:"人们在自己生活的社会生产中发生一定的、必然的、不以他们的意志为转移的关系,这些生产关系的总和构成社会的经济结构,即有法律的和政治的上层建筑竖立其上并有一定的社会意识形式与之相适应的现实基础。"①生产力与生产关系、经济基础与上层建筑这是人类社会的基本矛盾,但在不同的社会历史条件下,这两对矛盾的性质是不同的,在社会主义以前的社会,这两对矛盾是对抗性质,在社会主义社会是非对抗性的,由于矛盾性质不同,因而解决的方法也就不同,前者是一个阶级推翻另一个阶级的革命,后者是统治阶级自觉推动的改革,主要目的是解决生产关系和上层建筑中不适应生产力和经济基础的那些方面,解放和发展社会生产力。我党领导和推动的改革开放事业属于后者。一个是全面深刻变革的维度。改革不是对旧的体制机制的细枝末节的修补,而是对体制机制全面而深刻的变革。经济基础决定上层建筑。中国的改革发端于经济领域,以经济体制改革为重点,但是上层建筑对经济基础具有反作用,因此改革必须由经济体制逐步

---

① 《马克思恩格斯文集》第 2 卷,人民出版社 2009 年版,第 591 页。

延伸到其他领域,努力推进经济体制、政治体制、文化体制、社会体制、生态文明体制和党的建设制度的全面深化改革,使这场革命更为全面和深刻。当然,经济体制改革对其他方面的改革具有重要影响和传导作用,重大经济体制改革的进度决定着其他方面体制改革的进度,具有牵一发而动全身的作用。正如习近平总书记所强调的那样,"在全面深化改革中,我们要坚持以经济体制改革为主轴,努力在重要领域和关键环节改革上取得新突破,以此牵引和带动其他领域改革"。① 从改革内容的全面深刻以及改革难度上说,全面深化改革都是一场革命。

改革开放是我们党和人民大踏步赶上时代前进步伐的重要法宝。新时期最鲜明的特色就是改革开放。党的十一届三中全会以来,我国的改革开放经历了从农村到城市、从经济领域到其他各个领域、从渐进式的改革到突破难点的改革历程;对外开放经历了由点到面、由浅入深,从经济特区和沿海开放城市为重点逐步向沿江沿边,从东部到中西部内陆地区推进的过程。伴随汹涌澎湃、势不可挡的改革开放洪流,我国经济社会发展实现"井喷式"发展,创造出"中国奇迹"、产生"中国震撼",取得举世瞩目的伟大成就。一是生产力快速发展。自 1978 年实行改革开放到 2014 年,我国国内生产总值由 3.64 千亿元人民币增长到 63.65 万亿元人民币,年均增长率接近 10%,是世界平均水平的 3 倍多。二是综合国力大为增强。至 2010 年,中国的 GDP 总量已上升到世界第二位。中国已经成为世界上第一大出口国,世界最大的外汇储备国。经过 30 多年的改革开放,中国综合国力大幅度增强以及国际政治中的地位和影响力显著提高,已经是一个不争的事实。三是人民生活水平迅速提高。改革开放 30 多年来,我国解决了 13 亿人的温饱问题,并逐步向小康迈进,人均收入发生显著变化,自 1978 年到 2014 年,中国城镇居民人均可支配收入由 343.4 元提高到 2.95 万元,农村居民家庭人均纯收入由 133.6 元提高到 9892 元。总之,30 多年来,中国人

---

① 《切实把思想统一到党的十八届三中全会精神上来》(2013 年 11 月 12 日),见《习近平谈治国理政》,外文出版社 2014 年版,第 94 页。

民的面貌、社会主义中国的面貌、中国共产党的面貌都发生深刻的变化,我国在国际社会赢得举足轻重的地位。之所以取得如此辉煌的成就,最根本原因还是在于改革开放。正如习近平总书记指出的,"35 年来,我们党靠什么来振奋民心、统一思想、凝聚力量?靠什么来激发全体人民的创造精神和创造活力?靠什么来实现我国经济社会快速发展、在与资本主义竞争中赢得比较优势?靠的就是改革开放。"①

改革开放是决定实现"两个一百年"奋斗目标、实现中华民族伟大复兴的关键一招。习近平总书记指出,"没有改革开放,就没有中国的今天,也就没有中国的明天"。② 党的十八大确定,在中国共产党成立一百年时全面建成小康社会,在新中国成立一百年时建成富强民主文明和谐的社会主义现代化国家。面对如此艰巨光荣的历史任务,我们必须通过全面深化改革,着力解决经济社会发展中存在的各种矛盾和问题,不断推进中国特色社会主义制度的自我完善和发展。应当清醒地认识到,我们面临的国内外环境发生和即将发生极为广泛和深刻的变化,我国经济社会发展面临一系列突出的矛盾和问题,实现"两个一百年"目标充满各种挑战,前进道路上还存在不少困难和问题。比如,面对世界经济低速增长、仍然处于深度调整期,国际竞争更加激烈,特别是在国内,经济增长已从原来的高速进入到中高速阶段,社会主义市场经济体制还不够完善,发展中不平衡、不协调、不可持续问题依然突出,科技创新能力不强,产业结构不合理,发展方式粗放,深化改革开发和转变经济发展方式任务艰巨;城乡区域发展差距和居民收入分配差距依然较大,社会矛盾明显增多,教育、就业、社会保障、医疗、住房等关系群众切身利益的问题较多,部分群众生活困难;文化发展同经济社会发展和人民日益增长的精神文化需求还不完全适应,文化在推动全民族文明素质提高中的作用亟待加强,一些领域存在道德失范、诚信缺失

---

① 《关于〈中共中央关于全面深化改革若干重大问题的决定〉的说明》(2013 年 11 月 9 日),见《习近平谈治国理政》,外文出版社 2014 年版,第 86 页。

② 《改革开放只有进行时没有完成时》(2012 年 12 月 31 日),见《习近平谈治国理政》,外文出版社 2014 年版,第 69 页。

现象,社会主义核心价值观教育需要进一步增强,文化软实力建设任务艰巨;水污染、空气污染、固体废物污染等比较突出,严重影响着人民生产和生活,生态文明建设任务繁重;形式主义、官僚主义、享乐主义和奢靡之风问题突出,一些领域消极腐败现象易发多发,反腐败斗争形势依然复杂严峻;等等。所有这些问题的破解和各方面风险与挑战的化解,除了深化改革开放,别无他途。

问题倒逼改革,改革在解决问题中得以深化。站在历史与未来的交汇点上,习近平总书记强调,"改革开放是决定当代中国命运的关键一招,也是决定实现'两个一百年'奋斗目标、实现中华民族伟大复兴的关键一招,实践发展永无止境,解放思想永无止境,改革开放也永无止境,停顿和倒退没有出路,改革开放只有进行时、没有完成时。"[①]

(二) 改革的目标任务

从形成更加成熟更加定型的制度看,我国社会主义实践的前半程已经走过了,前半程我们的主要历史任务是建立社会主义基本制度,并在这个基础上进行改革,现在已经有了很好的基础。后半程,我们的主要历史任务是完善和发展中国特色社会主义制度,为党和国家事业发展、为人民幸福安康、为社会和谐稳定、为国家长治久安提供一整套更完备、更稳定、更管用的制度体系。[②]

全面深化改革就是要统筹推进各领域改革,首要的是确立一个总的目标,还要有各个领域具体的目标。习近平总书记指出,过去,我们也提出过改革目标,但大多是从具体领域提的。比如,我们讲过,政治体制改革总的目标是巩固社会主义制度,发展社会主义社会的生产力,

---

① 《关于〈中共中央关于全面深化改革若干重大问题的决定〉的说明》(2013 年 11 月 9 日),见《习近平谈治国理政》,外文出版社 2014 年版,第 71 页。
② 参见《在省部级主要领导干部学习贯彻十八届三中全会精神全面深化改革专题研讨班上的讲话》(2014 年 2 月 17 日),见《习近平关于全面深化改革论述摘编》,中央文献出版社 2014 年版,第 27 页。

发扬社会主义民主,调动广大人民的积极性。党的十四大提出,我国经济体制改革的目标是建立社会主义市场经济体制。党的十八届三中全会提出全面深化改革的总目标,并在总目标统领下明确了经济体制、政治体制、文化体制、社会体制、生态文明体制和党的建设制度深化改革的分目标。

就总目标而言,习近平总书记指出,全面深化改革的总目标,就是完善和发展中国特色社会主义制度、推进国家治理体系和治理能力现代化。全面深化改革的总目标既包括改革的根本方向——完善和发展中国特色社会主义制度,又包括改革的根本路径——推进国家治理体系和治理能力现代化,是两个方面辩证的统一。30 多年中国特色社会主义发展和改革开放实践充分说明,坚持完善和发展中国特色社会主义制度是推进国家治理体系和治理能力现代化的前提和保证;而有效应对和妥善解决中国特色社会主义实践中出现的各种矛盾问题,不断夺取中国特色社会主义新胜利,需要不断提高国家治理体系和治理能力的现代化水平。

全面深化改革总目标的确立,既是改革进程本身向前拓展提出的客观要求,体现了我们党对改革认识的深化和系统化,同时也体现了我们党对社会主义建设规律认识的深化,体现了新一届党中央治国理政的新方略。无论从国际共产主义运动的历史来看,符合国情的社会主义制度的完善和发展,特别是如何有效治理社会主义这样一个新的社会,不仅马克思主义经典作家没有给出系统答案,而且从巴黎公社到苏联东欧社会主义实践都没能解决好这个问题。虽然中国共产党领导中国人民对上述问题进行了艰苦探索,尤其伴随改革开放的伟大历史进程,中国特色社会主义制度、国家治理体系和治理能力现代化取得重大成果、积累丰富经验,但是我们必须看到,相比我国经济社会发展和人民群众的要求,相比当今世界日趋激烈的国际竞争,相比实现国家长治久安,我们的制度还没有达到更加成熟更加定型的要求,我们在国家治理体系和治理能力方面还有许多亟待改进的地方,制度执行力、治理能力日益成为"短板""短腿"。因此,全面深化改革的总目标顺应改革大势而提出,揭示了改革的方向,成为全面深化改革的总引领,也是我们在推进全面深化改革中必须把握好的首要要求。我们必须努力完善和发展中国特色社会主义制度,为党和国家事业发展、为人民幸福安康、为社会和谐稳定、为国家长治久安提供一整套更完备、更稳定、更管用的制度体系。正如习近平总书记指出的,"这项工程极为宏大,零敲碎打调整不行,碎片化修补也不行,必须是全面的系统的改革和改进,是各领域改革和改进的联动和集成,在国家治理体系和治理能力现代化上形成总体效应、取得总体效果。"①

就各领域深化改革的分目标而言,习近平总书记从经济、政治、文化、社会、生态文明、国防和军队以及对外开放等方面对全面深化改革各领域主要任务和重大举措都进行了系统的论述。比如深化经济体制改革,这是全面深化改革的重点,其基本遵循是坚持社会主义市场经济改革方向,核心问题是处理好政府和市场的关系,使市场在资源配置中起决定性作用和更好发挥政府作用。比如深化政治体制改革,必须坚持正确政治方向,坚持中国特色社会主义政治发展道路,关键是要坚持党的领导、人民当家作主、依法治国有机统一,以保证人民当家作主为根本,以增强党和国家活力、调动人民积极性为目标,扩大社会主义民主,发展社会主义政治文明。比如深化文化体制改革,必须坚持走中国特色社会主义文化发展道路,弘扬社会主义先进文化,推动社会主义文化大发展大繁荣,增强全民族文化创造活力,让一切文化创造源泉充分涌流。比如深化社会体制改革,必须把促进社会公平正义、增进人民福祉,作为全面深化改革的出发点和落脚点,坚持发展为了人民、发展依靠人民、发展成果由人民共享,作出更有效的制度安排,把群众关心的教育、就业、收入分配、社会保障、医药卫生、住房、食品安全、安全生产等作为社会领域改革的重点。比如深化生态文明体制改革,坚持绿色发展,必须坚持节约资源和保护环境的基本国策,正确处理经济发展同

---

① 《在省部级主要领导干部学习贯彻十八届三中全会精神全面深化改革专题研讨班上的讲话》(2014 年 2 月 17 日),见《习近平关于全面深化改革论述摘编》,中央文献出版社2014 年版,第 27 页。

生态环境保护的关系,完善经济社会发展考评体系,健全国家自然资源资产管理体制,实行能源和水资源消耗、建设用地等总量和强度双控行动,完善对重点生态功能区的生态补偿机制等。比如深化国防和军队改革,必须坚持"建设一支听党指挥、能打胜仗、作风优良的人民军队"这一党在新形势下的强军目标,加快重要领域和关键环节改革步伐,进一步解放和发展战斗力,进一步解放和增强军队活力,为实现强军目标提供体制机制和政策制度保障。比如构建开放型经济新体制,将实行更加积极主动的开放战略,完善互利共赢、多元平衡、安全高效的开放型经济体系,促进沿海内陆沿边开放优势互补,形成引领国际经济合作和竞争的开放区域,培育带动区域发展的开放高地。

中国(上海)自由贸易试验区,是中国政府设立在上海的区域性自由贸易园区,位于上海浦东新区境内(新华社发,裴鑫摄)

总之,改革开放是一场深刻而全面的社会变革,我们必须深入学习研究习近平总书记关于改革开放顶层设计和总体规划的系列论述,牢牢把握方向目标,明确任务要求,既突出核心与重点环节,又注意整体推进与协同配合,深入研究各领域改革关联性和各项改革举措耦合性,深入论证改革举措可行性,把握好全面深化改革的重大关系,以形成深化改革、扩大开放的强大合力,确保实现改革开放目标任务。

（三）根本性问题与颠覆性错误

中国是一个大国,决不能在根本性问题上出现颠覆性错误,一旦出现就无法挽回、无法弥补。我们的立场是胆子要大、步子要稳,既要大胆探索、勇于开拓,也要稳妥审慎、三思而后行。我们要坚持改革开放正确方向,敢于啃硬骨头,敢于涉险滩,敢于向积存多年的顽瘴痼疾开刀,切实做到改革不停顿、开放不止步。[①]

习近平总书记早在党的十八届三中全会召开前一个月,在召开的亚太经合组织 2013 年工商领导人峰会上,作出"中国是一个大国,决不能在根本性问题上出现颠覆性错误,一旦出现就无法挽回、无法弥补"的论述,话所指、意所向,是十分清楚的。法国历史学家托克维尔曾精辟地指出,"小国的目标是国民自由、富足、幸福地生活,而大国则注定要创造伟大和永恒,同时承担责任与痛苦"。中国作为拥有 13 亿人口且在世界四大文明古国中文明唯一没有中断的大国,有义务和责任继续创造"伟大和永恒",而这些都决定了我们承担不起颠覆性错误的代价,其实世界也承担不起这种代价。

何为根本性问题? 改革开放作为一场深刻的革命,其方向目标、指导思想、出发点落脚点等都是根本问题。何为颠覆性错误? 所犯的原则性、根本性、全局性错误就是颠覆性的错误。我国的改革开放是社会主义制度的自我完善和发展,决不能在根本性问题上出现颠覆性错误。这就要求,全面深化改革必须高举中国特色社会主义伟大旗帜,坚持社会主义市场经济改革方向,以促进社会公平正义、增进人民福祉为出发点和落脚点,进一步解放思想、解放和发展社会生产力、解放和增强社会活力,坚决破除各方面体制机制弊端,不断推动中国特色社会主义制

---

① 参见《深化改革开放,共创美好亚太》(2013 年 10 月 7 日),见《习近平谈治国理政》,外文出版社 2014 年版,第 348 页。

度的自我完善和发展,开创中国特色社会主义事业更加广阔的前景。

方向决定道路,道路决定命运。既然中国特色社会主义是社会主义,那么不论如何改革、怎么开放,都必须坚持社会主义的方向,把党的基本路线作为生命线,始终把以经济建设为中心同坚持四项基本原则、坚持改革开放相结合,做到"一个中心、两个基本点"的有机统一。党的十八届三中全会《决定》明确指出,"改革开放的成功实践为全面深化改革提供了重要经验,必须长期坚持。最重要的是,坚持党的领导,贯彻党的基本路线,不走封闭僵化的老路,不走改旗易帜的邪路,坚定走中国特色社会主义道路,始终确保改革正确方向"。

我国30多年改革开放之所以取得巨大成功,就在于它是社会主义的改革开放,目的是巩固和发展社会主义事业。30多年来,我们党毫不动摇地坚持党的基本路线,在推进中国特色社会主义伟大事业中实现"一个中心、两个基本点"的辩证统一和有机结合,有效地经受住国际国内各种风险和挑战考验,为中国特色社会主义事业乃至国际共产主义运动注入勃勃生机。相反,世界上一些社会主义国家的大党、老党,它们也推进自身及所在国家的"改革",但它们的"新思维"背离了社会主义的原则和方向,其"改革"实践必然将社会主义事业引入歧途,遭受挫折甚至失败,其惨痛教训发人深省,必须引以为戒。当前,社会上一些偏于极端的思想、思潮,需要引起注意和足够的警惕,比如有的人以西方某些国家的政治观和价值观为圭臬,把改革开放定义为往西方"普世价值"、西方政治制度的方向改,否则就说是"不改革"。一些敌对势力和别有用心的人在那里摇旗呐喊、制造舆论、混淆视听,以各种各样的复杂心理,"预言"和期盼着中国在一些"根本性问题"上的变化甚至被"颠覆"。面对复杂形势和各种考验,我们必须保持政治定力,明确改革目标和方向,清楚改什么、不改什么。比如,我们全面深化改革的总目标,就是完善和发展中国特色社会主义制度、推进国家治理体系和治理能力现代化。必须完整理解和把握这一总目标,在这两句话中,前一句规定了全面深化改革的根本方向,后一句规定了在根本方向指引下完善和发展中国特色社会主义制度的鲜明指向。我们国家治理体系需要改进和完善,但怎么改、怎么完善,是由我们国家的历史传承、文化传统、经济社会发展水平决定的,是由中国人民的意志决定的,不能盲目崇拜、照抄照搬别人的制度模式,否则"就会画虎不成反类犬,不仅不能解决任何实际问题,而且还会因水土不服造成严重后果"①。在改革方向问题上,在改什么、不改什么这些实质性问题上,我们必须保持清醒头脑,既要"敢于啃硬骨头,敢于涉险滩,敢于向积存多年的顽瘴痼疾开刀,切实做到改革不停顿、开放不止步",又要"胆子要大、步子要稳,既要大胆探索、勇于开拓,也要稳妥审慎、三思而后行"。那些不能改的,包括中国特色社会主义基本路线、基本纲领、基本经验、基本要求等,不但现在不能改,今后仍然不能改,始终坚持改革开放的正确方向,坚持和完善党的领导,坚持和完善中国特色社会主义制度,切实做到在纷繁复杂的事物表象中把准改革脉搏,在众说纷纭中开好改革药方,不动摇、不懈怠、不折腾。

在坚持改革开放的社会主义方向不动摇的同时,还必须始终警惕和防止否定改革开放、否定中国特色社会主义的错误认识和错误思潮。邓小平早在南方谈话时就提出要"防止右,更要防止左"。"左"倾错误曾给党的事业带来多次严重损失,甚至几乎葬送中国革命。"左"的思潮在我党历史上从来没有销声匿迹过。伴随改革开放的历史进程,各种非议和否定改革开放的声音也一直存在。极端者有意曲解和放大改革开放以来中国在发展过程中出现的矛盾、困难和问题,指责中国进行的改革是变公有制为私有制的改革,是变社会主义为资本主义的改革,否定改革开放和中国特色社会主义道路,主张要彻底改弦更张,"再来一次全面拨乱反正",让中国重走封闭僵化的老路。邓小平同志指出:"不坚持社会主义,不改革开放,不发展经济,不改善人民生活,只能是死路一条。"当前,中国改革已进入攻坚期和深水区,正如习近平总书记指出的,"中国改革经过三十多年,已进入深水区,可以说,容易的、

① 《在省部级主要领导干部学习贯彻十八届三中全会精神全面深化改革专题研讨班上的讲话》(2014年2月17日),见《习近平关于全面深化改革论述摘编》,中央文献出版社2014年版,第22页。

皆大欢喜的改革已经完成了,好吃的肉都吃掉了,剩下的都是难啃的硬骨头。"①这个时候必须一鼓作气,"停顿和倒退没有出路"。瞻前顾后,畏葸不前,信心动摇,甚至放弃改革,中国改革开放 30 多年取得的进展将可能前功尽弃。改革开放符合党心民心,顺应时代潮流,只有改革开放才能发展中国、发展社会主义、发展马克思主义。

总之,只要不犯颠覆性错误,中国就能保持改革开放和民族复兴的大好势头,中国梦必将美梦成真。

（四）改革开放需要什么样的方法论

必须从纷繁复杂的事物表象中把准改革脉搏,把握全面深化改革的内在规律,特别是要把握全面深化改革的重大关系,处理好解放思想和实事求是的关系、整体推进和重点突破的关系、顶层设计和摸着石头过河的关系、胆子要大和步子要稳的关系。②

方法问题就如同过河的桥或船。改革开放是前无古人的崭新事业,必须坚持正确的方法论。习近平总书记从深入探索和牢牢把握改革开放的内在规律出发,深刻揭示、全面深化改革的一些重大关系,特别是在改革开放的方法上强调既要摸着石头过河,又要加强顶层设计;既要整体推进,又要重点突破;既要胆子大,又要步子稳,实现了对改革开放方法论的新拓展。

既要解放思想,又要实事求是。思想是行动的先导。改革开放 30 多年贯穿始终的一条主线就是解放思想。实践发展永无止境,解放思想也就永无止境。中国 30 多年波澜壮阔的改革开放事业发展到今天,同样需要新的思想引领,仍然需要以解放思想作为先导。没有大的思想解放,就不会有大的改革举措和大的改革成就。所谓解放思想,是指

① 《改革再难也要向前推进》(2014 年 2 月 7 日),见《习近平谈治国理政》,外文出版社 2014 年版,第 101 页。

② 参见《在湖北考察改革发展工作时的讲话》(2013 年 7 月 21 日至 23 日),见《习近平关于全面深化改革论述摘编》,中央文献出版社 2014 年版,第 37 页。

摆脱落后于实践的思想认识,目的在于更好地做到实事求是,而不是脱离实际的胡思乱想、天马行空和异想天开。这就要求我们,在推进改革发展上,必须立足中国国情和条件,一切从实际出发,立足人民群众的利益和呼声,既大胆探索又脚踏实地,不断推进理论创新和实践创新,有效化解前进道路上的各种风险挑战,把改革开放不断推向前进,始终走在时代前列。

既要整体推进,又要重点突破。改革开放是一场深刻而全面的社会变革,是一个系统工程,每一项改革都会对其他改革产生重要影响,每一项改革又都需要其他改革协同配合,因此"必须坚持全面改革,在各项改革协同配合中推进"①。如果不把握全局、不整体推进,很多单项改革都难以完成。因此,我们必须在把握全局的前提下整体推进改革,深入研究各领域改革关联性和各项改革举措耦合性,"使各项改革举措在政策取向上相互配合、在实施过程中相互促进、在改革成效上相得益彰"。② 但是,改革的整体推进,并不意味着平均用力、没有重点。必须坚持重点与两点的统一、整体推进与重点突破的统一。在改革发展进程中必须认清主要矛盾和矛盾的主要方面,分清轻重缓急,以更大的政治勇气和智慧,力求在改革的重点领域和重点环节有所突破,从而促进改革开放的全面推进和深入发展。

既要考虑全局,又要照顾到局部。全局由一个个局部组成,局部是全局中的局部,没有全局局部就不可能存在,没有局部也无所谓全局,既不能以局部代替全局,也不能只考虑全局而无视局部。在改革举措上,我们必须牢固树立高度自觉的大局意识,自觉从大局看问题,每一项改革都要从大局出发来统筹谋划,同时还要考虑局部的具体情况,因时因地制宜;在改革涉及的利益关系上,既要考虑人民群众的全局、整体、长远利益,还要考虑人民群众的局部、个体、眼前利益,正确处理好

---

① 《在十八届中央政治局第二次集体学习时的讲话》(2012 年 12 月 31 日),见《习近平关于全面深化改革论述摘编》,中央文献出版社 2014 年版,第 35 页。

② 《在中共十八届三中全会第二次全体会议上的讲话》(2013 年 11 月 12 日),见《习近平关于全面深化改革论述摘编》,中央文献出版社 2014 年版,第 44—45 页。

整体与局部的关系。

既要摸着石头过河,又要加强顶层设计。我国的改革开放是没有任何先例的创新性伟大事业,没有现成的答案和经验,只能"摸着石头过河"。习近平总书记指出,"摸着石头过河,是富有中国特色、符合中国国情的改革方法。摸着石头过河就是摸规律。"①中国特色社会主义道路就是在"摸着石头过河"中逐步探索出来的。这种渐进式改革,避免了因情况不明、举措不当而引起社会动荡,为稳步推进改革、顺利实现目标提供了保证。但当,随着改革开放的不断深入,深化改革的复杂性和艰巨性日益增大,在这种情况下,就需要我们在继续坚持摸着石头过河,继续鼓励大胆试验、大胆突破的同时,加强对改革的宏观思考和顶层设计,更加注重改革的系统性、整体性、协同性,使全面深化改革取得实质性进展。习近平总书记提出的"一带一路"战略,就是进行科学顶层设计的妙笔之作。

既要胆子大,又要步子稳。当前我国的改革已进入深水区和攻坚期,改革遇到的思想观念障碍、利益固化的藩篱、体制运行的惯性等多方面的阻碍掣肘,改革的艰巨性、复杂性、风险性凸显。"惟其艰难,才更显勇毅;惟其笃行,才弥足珍贵。"习近平总书记要求我们以"明知山有虎,偏向虎山行"的胆略和勇气,敢于担当,敢于啃硬骨头,敢于涉险滩,不断把改革推向前进。同时,习近平总书记谆谆告诫全党,"改革是循序渐进的工作,既要敢于突破,又要一步一个脚印、稳扎稳打向前走"。② 面对深化改革的艰巨性和复杂性,我们必须保持积极稳健的步伐,一切从实际出发,认真探索改革规律,做到审慎稳妥、稳扎稳打,"蹄疾而步稳"。

既要以改革促发展、用发展保稳定,又要靠稳定推进改革发展。改

---

① 《在十八届中央政治局第二次集体学习时的讲话》(2012 年 12 月 31 日),见《习近平关于全面深化改革论述摘编》,中央文献出版社 2014 年版,第 34 页。

② 《在省部级主要领导干部学习贯彻十八届三中全会精神全面深化改革专题研讨班上的讲话》(2014 年 2 月 17 日),见《习近平关于全面深化改革论述摘编》,中央文献出版社 2014 年版,第 151 页。

革发展稳定是我国社会主义现代化建设的重要支点。正确处理改革发展稳定的关系,实现三者的有机统一,是关系我国社会主义现代化建设全局的重要指导方针。发展是硬道理,是改革发展稳定的根本目的,是解决一切经济社会问题的关键;稳定是硬任务,为改革发展提供前提保障和基础条件;改革是硬功夫,是保持发展和稳定的强大动力。三者相互依托、相互支撑、相互为用、形成闭环。正确处理三者关系,就要坚持把改革的力度、发展的速度和社会可承受的程度有机统一起来,使改革发展稳定相互协调、相互促进,确保人民群众安居乐业,确保社会政治稳定和国家长治久安。

(五) 改革必须坚持和尊重人民主体地位

改革开放是亿万人民自己的事业,必须坚持尊重人民首创精神,坚持在党的领导下推进。改革开放是人民的要求和党的主张的统一,人民群众是历史的创造者和改革开放事业的实践主体。所以,必须坚持人民主体地位和党的领导的统一,紧紧依靠人民推进改革开放。①

人民群众是改革的主体。坚持和尊重人民主体地位,发挥群众首创精神,紧紧依靠人民推动改革,这是全面深化改革必须遵循的基本原则。

习近平总书记指出,"改革开放之所以得到广大人民群众衷心拥护和积极参与,最根本的原因在于我们一开始就使改革开放事业深深扎根于人民群众之中。"②回顾改革开放 30 多年的历程,我们不难看到,从大包干的探索到联产承包责任制的全面推开,从乡镇企业的异军突起到民营经济的半壁江山,从扩大企业自主权到国有企业改革,可以说,改革开放在认识和实践上的每一次突破和创新,改革开放中每一个

---

① 参见《在十八届中央政治局第二次集体学习时的讲话》(2012 年 12 月 31 日),见《习近平关于全面深化改革论述摘编》,中央文献出版社 2014 年版,第 138 页。
② 《切实把思想统一到党的十八届三中全会精神上来》(2013 年 11 月 12 日),见《习近平谈治国理政》,外文出版社 2014 年版,第 97 页。

新生事物的产生和发展,改革开放多领域多方面经验的创造和积累,无不来自人民群众的伟大创造和聪明智慧。人民群众对改革的积极支持和主动参与,是改革成功的动力之源。坚持以人为本,尊重人民主体地位,发挥群众首创精神,紧紧依靠人民推动改革,这是我党领导的 30 多年改革开放事业持续推进并取得成功的宝贵经验。

当前,国内外环境都在发生极为广泛而深刻的变化,我国面临一系列突出矛盾和挑战,前进道路上还有不少困难和问题。解决这些困难和问题,关键在于深化改革,而"中国改革经过三十多年,已进入深水区,可以说,容易的、皆大欢喜的改革已经完成了,好吃的肉都吃掉了,剩下的都是难啃的硬骨头"①。面对改革中的艰难险阻,只有紧紧依靠人民,得到人民群众的支持、拥护和参与,才能爬坡过坎、战胜困难,取得胜利。

习近平总书记一再强调,人民对美好生活的向往就是我们的奋斗目标,"要把实现好、维护好、发展好最广大人民根本利益作为出发点和落脚点,坚持以民为本、以人为本"②。在全面深化改革上坚持以人为本、以民为本,就是要把群众利益作为改革的出发点和落脚点,就要把人民满意作为衡量改革成败的根本标准。推进任何一项重大改革,都要站在人民立场上把握和处理好涉及改革的重大问题,都要从人民利益出发谋划改革思路、制定改革举措,时刻把群众安危冷暖放在心上,及时准确了解群众所思、所盼、所忧、所急,着力解决好人民群众最关心最直接最现实的利益问题,从群众最期盼的领域改起,从制约经济社会发展最突出的问题改起,坚持共享发展理念,让全社会感受到改革发展带来的实实在在的成果,让人民群众得到实实在在的利益,从而有更多获得感。同时要正确处理最广大人民根本利益、现阶段群众共同利益、不同群体特殊利益的关系,使"生活在我们伟大祖国和伟大时代的中国人民,共同享有人生出彩的机会,共同享有梦想成真的机会,共

① 《改革再难也要向前推进》(2014 年 2 月 7 日),《习近平谈治国理政》,外文出版社 2014 年版,第 101 页。

② 《把宣传思想工作做得更好》,见《习近平谈治国理政》,外文出版社 2014 年版,第 154 页。

同享有同祖国和时代一起成长与进步的机会"①。

人民群众是物质财富和精神财富的创造者,是变革社会的主体和决定性力量,必须坚持人民主体地位。毛泽东同志早在 1944 年《文化工作中的统一战线》一文中指出:"要联系群众,就要按照群众的需要和自愿。一切为群众的工作都是要从群众的需要出发,而不是从任何良好的个人愿望出发。……这里有两条原则:一条是群众的实际需要,而不是我们脑子里头幻想出来的需要;一条是群众的自愿,由群众自己下决心,而不是由我们代替群众下决心。"②我们订计划、做决策、办事情,是靠闭门造车、领导拍脑袋,还是靠深入群众、发动群众、集思广益,完全会是两种结果。群众主张提议的,一方面有了群众支持的力量;另一方面即使有不同的意见,也可以靠群众去开展说服工作。反之,如果是政府主观决定的事情,一方面,没有群众主动支持的基础;另一方面,反对的群众很难听进政府的解释,即使找来专家作评估解释,也很难说服群众,使群众产生自然的逆反心理。因此,党员干部必须牢固树立群众观点,站稳群众立场,不仅将联系群众、听取群众意见作为基本的工作方法和工作作风,而且作为党和政府工作的基本内容和形式。改革开放是群众共同的事业,改革的根本力量在于群众,办法来自基层,党员干部必须切实做到问政于民、问需于民、问计于民,切不可自说自话、关起门来搞改革,更不能异想天开、凭主观愿望拍脑袋。"大鹏之动,非一羽之轻也;骐骥之速,非一足之力也"。只有动员群众、依靠群众才能取得改革的胜利,正如习近平总书记指出的,"充分调动群众推进改革的积极性、主动性、创造性,把最广大人民智慧和力量凝聚到改革上来,同人民一道把改革推向前进。"③

---

① 《在第十二届全国人民代表大会第一次会议上的讲话》(2013 年 3 月 17 日),见《习近平谈治国理政》,外文出版社 2014 年版,第 40 页。

② 《文化工作中的统一战线》(一九四四年十月三十日),见《毛泽东选集》第三卷,人民出版社 1991 年版,第 1010—1011 页。

③ 《切实把思想统一到党的十八届三中全会精神上来》(2013 年 11 月 12 日),见《习近平谈治国理政》,外文出版社 2014 年版,第 98 页。

思 考 题

1. 为什么说改革开放是决定当代中国命运的关键一招?
2. 如何认识全面深化改革的目标任务?

参考文献

1.《习近平谈治国理政》,北京:外文出版社,2014 年。

2.《习近平关于全面深化改革论述摘编》,北京:中央文献出版社,2014 年。

三、全面依法治国

　　"全面贯彻实施宪法,是建设社会主义法治国家的首要任务和基础性工作。宪法是国家的根本法,是治国安邦的总章程,具有最高的法律地位、法律权威、法律效力,具有根本性、全局性、稳定性、长期性。……任何组织或者个人,都不得有超越宪法和法律的特权。一切违反宪法和法律的行为,都必须予以追究。"——习近平:《在首都各界纪念现行宪法公布施行 30 周年大会上的讲话》(2012 年 12 月 4 日)

党的十八大以来,习近平总书记连续发表了一系列关于依法治国的重要论述,党的十八届四中全会更是第一次以法治为主题做出了重要决定,对全面推进依法治国做出了重大部署,从而发动起了一场自新中国成立以来规模最为宏大、影响最为深远的法治运动。习近平总书记关于法治的重要论述十分全面深刻,涵盖了法治建设的方方面面,也正面回答了当前社会关于法治的许多困惑问题,纠正了许多认识上的误区,对于正确顺利推进法治中国建设起到了指路明灯的作用。学习习近平总书记的这些重要论述,对于加深理解党的依法治国新方略具有很强的指导性意义。

(一) 法治是治国理政的基本方式

习近平总书记将依法治国提高到治国理政的基本方略和基本方式的战略高度,是完全符合人类社会发展规律的科学论断。两千多年前,古希腊哲学家柏拉图在其名著《政治家》中,把各种政治制度分为"依法治理"和"不依法治理"两类,每一类又可以分为一个人的统治(君主制)、少数人的统治(贵族制)和多数人的统治(民主制),从而排列组合出了六种政治制度。在这六种政治制度中,柏拉图认为"依法治理的君主制"是最好的,"不依法治理的君主制"则是最坏的——"君主政体当它被良性规则或良法约束时,就是六种政体中最好的,当它不受法律约束时,就是最冷酷无情和最令人难以接受的。"①且不论柏拉图对于君主制、贵族制和民主制的看法是否全然正确,其对法治的推崇由此可见一斑。看来在柏拉图那里,权力的集中度是可以商量的,法治则是不能商量的。一句话,"法治才是硬道理"。到了今天这个时代,法治自然更是一个现代国家的底色,是国家治理体系和治理能力现代化不可缺失和不可撼动的基石。

---

① 【古希腊】柏拉图:《政治家》,云南人民出版社 2004 年版,第 17—19 页。

1.深化改革离不开法治

全面推进依法治国乃是"四个全面"的重要组成部分。习近平总书记在 2015 年中央党校省部级主要领导干部学习贯彻党的十八届四中全会精神全面推进依法治国专题研讨班开班仪式上指出,全面建成小康社会是我们的战略目标,全面深化改革、全面依法治国、全面从严治党是我们的三大战略举措。"四个全面"相辅相成、相互促进、相得益彰,要想准确把握全面依法治国的精神实质,就必须将其置于"四个全面"的战略布局背景之下,尤其是要深刻理解"全面依法治国"与"全面深化改革"之间的关系。党的十八届三中全会提出了"全面深化改革"的战略部署,四中全会又紧接着提出了"全面依法治国"的战略部署,充分证明改革与法治的关系乃是一个硬币的两面,又如鸟之双翼,车之两轮,是我们实现全面建成小康社会战略目标的两个基本路径。然而在目前的实践中,有些同志在如何认识改革与法治的关系问题上还存在着一些错误的观念,认为改革本身就是要突破法律的条条框框,因此两者存在着根本矛盾。这种观念是错误的,改革与法治乃是辩证统一的关系。习近平总书记在 2014 年 2 月 28 日中央全面深化改革领导小组第二次会议上强调,凡属重大改革都要于法有据,在整个改革过程中,都要高度重视运用法治思维和法治方式,发挥法治的引领和推动作用,加强对相关立法工作的配套衔接,确保在法治轨道上推进改革。良好的法治本身具备了很大的制度弹性和创新空间。在改革的关键时期,我们完全可以通过立法授权,赋予改革主体在底线约束的前提下充分发挥改革主动性的创新空间。即便遇到了重大的制度障碍,只要经过科学论证和民主程序,我们同样可以通过及时修订法律来为改革松绑,实现立法与改革决策相衔接,做到重大改革于法有据、立法主动适应改革和经济社会发展需要。对于实践证明行之有效的,要及时上升为法律。实践条件还不成熟的、需要先行先试的,要按照法定程序作出授权。对不适应改革要求的法律法规,要及时修改和废止。全面深化改革离不开法治的保障作用。

2. 经济发展离不开法治

党的十八届四中全会决定指出,社会主义市场经济本质上是法治经济。使市场在资源配置中起决定性作用和更好发挥政府作用,必须以保护产权、维护契约、统一市场、平等交换、公平竞争、有效监管为基本导向,完善社会主义市场经济法律制度。没有法治,市场交易就没有规则可循,市场竞争就会陷入恶性循环。毒奶粉和地沟油的出现,本质上就是唯利是图的市场竞争必然带来的逻辑结果。中国社会现在如此,西方社会也曾如此。马克思在《资本论》中揭露道:"糖有 6 种掺假方法,橄榄油有 9 种,奶油有 10 种,盐有 12 种,牛奶有 19 种,面包有 20种,烧酒有 23 种,面粉有 24 种,巧克力有 28 种,葡萄酒有 30 种,咖啡有 32 种。""每天吃的面包中含有一定的人汗,并且混杂着脓血、蜘蛛网、死蟑螂和发霉的德国酵母,更不用提明矾、砂粒以及其他可口的矿物质了。""他们在整整 10 年内,每天用 10 小时从那些必须靠人放到凳子上才能干活的幼童的血中抽出丝来。"[①]历史早已证明,一旦进入市场经济时代,如果没有同时建立起法治的底线防守和约束,市场竞争往往就是通往地狱的大门。要想解决市场竞争可能带来的恶果,只能通过强化法治,让市场经济在法治的约束和引导下健康发展。

3. 社会治理离不开法治

习近平总书记在 2013 年 2 月 23 日中共中央政治局第四次集体学习时指出,要深入开展法治宣传教育,在全社会弘扬社会主义法治精神,引导全体人民遵守法律、有问题依靠法律来解决,形成守法光荣的良好氛围。要坚持法制教育与法治实践相结合,广泛开展依法治理活动,提高社会管理法治化水平。中国曾经是一个乡土社会,如今正处在快速城市化的进程之中。数千年的农业生产方式和农村生活方式造就了一个"熟人社会",如今的工业生产方式和城市生活方式则造就了一

---

① 马克思:《资本论》第 1 卷,人民出版社 2004 年版,第 289 页。

个"生人社会"。"熟人社会"的组织方式必然是权力与人情，"生人社会"的组织方式则必然是法治与契约。换句话说，一个熟人社会可以用"王法之治"来管理，一个生人社会却只能用"约法之治"来治理。在一个具有亲缘关系的"熟人社会"里，由于人们彼此知根知底，低头不见抬头见，因此依托王法家规、民风民俗便足以约束一个人的行为。然而，一旦这种社会结构被打破，社会流动性的爆发式增长导致人们彼此

2015 年 3 月 2 日，众多媒体记者在最高法第一巡回庭审理的第一宗案件采访(新华社发，毛思倩摄)

不再相识，那么"游戏只玩一次"的道德风险便会迅速上升。在传统约束迅速松弛的情况下，法治的底线防守和约束就成为这个社会至关重要的稳定器。既然今天中国城市化的进程已经不可逆转，那么中国法治的进程自然也就不可逆转。关于社会治理的法治化，党的十八届四中全会决定已经做出了充分的阐述，提出要强化规则意识，倡导契约精神，要深化基层组织和部门、行业依法治理，支持各类社会主体自我约束、自我管理。发挥市民公约、乡规民约、行业规章、团体章程等社会规范在社会治理中的积极作用，发挥人民团体和社会组织在法治社会建

设中的积极作用,支持行业协会商会类社会组织发挥行业自律和专业服务功能。社会治理现代化离不开法治。

4. 民主发展离不开法治

党的十八届四中全会决定指出,制度化、规范化、程序化是社会主义民主政治的根本保障。民主与法治是一对孪生兄弟,却又有着各自独立的品格。法国的勒庞曾经诠释过民主与法治的关系问题:"没有民主的支持,宪政就是'恶法'体系的领头羊,宪政的建立是民主革命的结果;然而,没有宪政的约束,民主亦是脆弱的,常常成为多数一时的冲动,甚至沦落为暴政的工具。"①作为"约法之治",法治乃是民主博弈的结果,然而法治一旦形成,又反过来确立了民主博弈的规则和底线。历史经验表明,在民主与法治"蛋生鸡、鸡生蛋"的关系中,法治的确应该先行一步。拿破仑的威权高压最终给法国带来了不朽的1804年《法国民法典》,人民行动党的长期执政也并不妨碍新加坡成为一个真正的法治国家,可见法治权威的初次建立的确有可能通过政治核心的自觉行动来推动。而法治的底线一旦确立,民主博弈的乱局危险就会大大降低。在缺乏法治的国家,民主的滥觞如同缺乏堤坝约束的洪水,往往会带来可怕的乱局。党的十六大以来,我们党在总结了正反两方面的历史经验教训之后,强调要坚持党的领导、人民当家作主、依法治国的有机统一,就是基于对民主与法治内在关系的深刻认知而做出的正确判断。

5. 民族和谐离不开法治

在2014年第二次中央新疆工作座谈会上,习近平总书记提出了"依法治疆、团结稳疆、长期建疆"的治疆战略;在中央第六次西藏工作座谈会上,习近平总书记又提出了"依法治藏、富民兴藏、长期建藏"的治藏战略。新疆和西藏处于我国反分裂反暴恐的第一线,如何治理好

---

① 【法】古斯塔夫·勒庞:《革命心理学》,广东人民出版社2012年版,第20页。

新疆和西藏,维护国家统一与民族和谐,一直是全党全国认真思考的重大问题,而习近平总书记的讲话旗帜鲜明地把法治摆到了最重要最优先的位置,这是对法治在维护民族和谐问题上发挥基础性战略性作用的深刻认识。世界上任何国家都会有自己不可触碰的底线原则,将这些底线原则用法律的形式固定下来,就构成了这个国家的法治底线。对于中国这样一个"天下国家"来说,维护国家统一、反对国家分裂乃是国家和民族的最高利益,任何人不得以任何形式触碰和践踏这条底线,否则必定自动触发法律的严厉制裁。一个法治国家在自己的底线问题上是没有商量余地的,必须以最坚决的态度来捍卫法治的尊严,以不可挑战的确定性来遏制任何心存侥幸的言行。1964 年独立建国之前,新加坡曾经发生过两次严重的马华种族冲突,死伤数百人。独立建国之后,新加坡采用了多种手段来遏制种族宗教因素对国家团结的侵害,其中就包括严厉的法治手段。1990 年,新加坡颁布《维持宗教和谐法案》,划定宗教活动的行为界限,赋予内政部长下达限制令的权力。如果内政部长认定任何宗教团体机构中成员或神甫、僧侣等具有或试图具有以下行为——"导致不同宗教团体之间的敌视、仇恨、恶意情绪;借宣传、信仰任何宗教之名进行推动政治事业或政党事业的活动;借宣传、信仰任何宗教激发对新加坡总统或政府的不满,发现有人企图利用宗教危害社会安全、种族、宗教和谐的言论",部长可以发出限制令,限制此人的言论和行动。违犯限制令者,地方法院可以依法处罚。在法治的高压态势下,新加坡的种族宗教因素基本上被约束在法治轨道之内,20 多年来几乎无人敢于挑战该法案,基本实现了种族宗教的和谐。以史为鉴,以人为鉴,中国的反分裂斗争同样离不开法治的基础性作用。

6. 反腐倡廉离不开法治

2013 年 1 月 22 日,在十八届中央纪律检查委员会第二次全体会议上,习近平总书记指出,要加强反腐败国家立法,加强反腐倡廉党内法规制度建设,深化腐败问题多发领域和环节的改革,确保国家机关按照法定权限和程序行使权力。要加强对权力运行的制约和监督,把权力关进制度的笼子里,形成不敢腐的惩戒机制、不能腐的防范机制、不易腐的保障机制。党的十八届五中全会再次强调,要坚持全面从严治党、依规治党,深入推进党风廉政建设和反腐败斗争,巩固反腐败斗争成果,健全改进作风长效机制,着力构建不敢腐、不能腐、不想腐的体制机制。从历史上看,由于独特的地缘政治结构使然,中国社会自古以来就具有十分深厚的行政集权传统。为了有效地控制行政集权的滥用,中国社会自然而然地发展出了与行政集权相对应的御史监察制度。在两千多年时间里,御史监察制度一直都是中国体制的支柱之一,其基本职能也十分稳定,那就是作为一个专司监督的机构直接隶属于最高统治者,独立于行政体系之外并强力监督之。除了御史台的最高长官之外,监察御史的品级往往很低,也没有什么行政权能,却拥有十分自由和强大的监察权和弹劾权,其锋镝所向,即便当朝宰相也要惧其三分。我国台湾地区的监察院、新加坡的反贪污调查局(CPIB)、我国香港地区的廉政公署(ICAC)以及我国内地的纪委体制,从某种意义上讲都是这种御史监察传统的当代继承。然而在法治时代,这种历史继承必须接受严格的法治化改造。从某种意义上说,CPIB 和 ICAC 已经成功地完成了这种改造,从而缔造了亚洲第一和亚洲第二的廉洁社会。无论在执行任务的时候有多么广泛的权力,CPIB 和 ICAC 都严格按照法律规定的程序和内容予以执行,不能越雷池一步,尤其还要受到检控权和审判权的有力制约。这显然与古代人治传统下允许"风闻言事"的御史监察有着本质上的区别,更不是锦衣卫之流的特务机构所能比拟的。中国当前的反腐斗争成绩卓著,有目共睹,如果还有哪方面需要继续提高的话,那就是希望能够进一步提高反腐败的法治化水平。脱离法治轨道的反腐斗争在一个现代社会里是经不起推敲的,也是注定走不远的。

(二) 党的领导和依法治国的有机统一

2015 年 2 月,在省部级主要领导干部学习贯彻十八届四中全会精神全面推进依法治国专题研讨班上，习近平总书记再次深刻阐述了党的领导和依法治国之间的关系这个法治建设的核心问题，指出中国共产党是中国特色社会主义事业的领导核心，处在总揽全局、协调各方的地位。社会主义法治必须坚持党的领导，党的领导必须依靠社会主义法治。

依法治国是否还需要坚持党的领导，这是中国法治建设的关键问题，也是社会共识能否形成的关键问题。要想正确理解这个问题，我们需要借鉴一下系统科学的理论。古希腊哲学家柏拉图在《理想国》中说："当一个国家最最像一个人的时候，它是管理得最好的国家。比如像我们中间某一个人的手指受伤了，整个身心作为一个人的有机体，在统一指挥下，对一部分所感受的痛苦，浑身都感觉到了，这就是我们说这个在手指部分有痛苦了。这个道理同样可应用到一个人的其他部分，说一个人感到快乐或感到痛苦。"①柏拉图用最简单的语言描述了一个系统科学的道理。系统科学认为，每一个生命系统就是一个命运共同体，各系统要素之间既是有层次有差别的，又是不可分割的；系统科学还认为，每个社会系统的发展目标，就是进化成一个类生命的高级系统。在一个社会"命运共同体"内部，社会的各个组成部分之间既是有层次有差别的，又是不可分割的，既是分工合作的，又是命运与共的。

倘若这个判断成立的话，那么就不难理解：就像一个人的大脑会指挥身体去工作，但是如果身体受了伤，也会通过神经系统来告诉大脑，让大脑重视并帮助解决问题一样，一个社会同样也有着自己的"大脑""身体"以及连接其间的"神经系统"，而法治就是这样的一种"神经系统"。从这个意义来说，一个社会缺乏法治，就如同一个人缺乏神经系统一样，不知道伤害什么时候发生，发生在哪里，也不知道伤害会有多严重，其后果显然是不堪设想的。同时，系统科学还认为，一个高级生命系统既是一个有机的整体，各个子系统又应该拥有一定的"自组织"

---

① 【古希腊】柏拉图:《理想国》,商务印书馆 2002 年版,第 197 页。

能力。这就好比一个人睡觉的时候,是不用担心自己的心跳和呼吸会停止一样,因为心肺子系统拥有"自组织"的能力,会按照自己的节奏自我运作。大脑虽然是全身最为高级的控制系统,但是大脑不可能时时刻刻指挥心肺运作。所谓法治,从某种意义上就表现为社会各个子系统的自组织能力。

我们不妨以党的领导与司法之间的关系为例进一步阐述。无须讳言,当前社会上有些人一直提倡在中国应该实现"司法独立",并以此作为是否实现法治的根本标志。其实在我们看来,与其提倡"司法独立",不如提倡"独立司法"。这并不是一个文字游戏,"司法独立"中的"司法"是一个名词,表达的是一种主体独立的概念;而"独立司法"中的"司法"则是一个动词,表达的是一种功能独立的概念,二者有着本质的区别。从系统科学的角度来说,"党的领导"好比一个国家和社会的"大脑系统",凝聚的是这个国家和社会的灵魂和意志。"独立司法"则好比一个国家和社会的"肝肾系统",专司这个社会矛盾纠纷的"排毒"功能。一个人的肝肾系统很显然是不可能脱离这个人的身体而独立存在的,因此彻底的"司法独立"本质上是一个伪命题。即便是西方社会的所谓"司法独立",究其本义,其实也不过是在表达一个功能独立的概念。然而,肝肾的排毒功能的确又是专属的,即便是作为全身控制系统的大脑,也不可能具备排毒的功能,因此也就根本不可能替代肝肾排毒,否则大脑必然会因此而中毒。由此可见,一个真正的法治社会必须有效排除权力对正常的司法活动尤其是对司法个案的干预。习近平总书记在 2014 年 1 月 7 日中央政法工作会议上强调,要正确处理坚持党的领导和确保司法机关依法独立公正行使职权的关系。各级党组织和领导干部要支持政法系统各单位依照宪法法律独立负责、协调一致开展工作。党的十八届四中全会的决定也旗帜鲜明地要求,各级党政机关和领导干部要支持法院、检察院依法独立公正行使职权。要建立领导干部干预司法活动、插手具体案件处理的记录、通报和责任追究制度。任何党政机关和领导干部都不得让司法机关做违反法定职责、有碍司法公正的事情,任何司法机关都不得执行党政机关和领导干部违法干预司法活动的要求。应该说,这两段表述已经十分清楚地表达了党的领导对司法系统功能独立的最大尊重。

与此同时,司法的功能独立并不意味着否定党的领导。还是借用一下人体生命系统的比喻。倘若一个人有一天得了脂肪肝,那么他的大脑必须控制自己注意饮食,坚持锻炼,必要的时候还要适当吃点药。倘若这个人判断自己的肝肾得了肿瘤呢?那么大脑很可能就要做出一个十分重大的决定,在合适的时候将自己送上手术台开刀。党的十八届三中全会和十八届四中全会先后对司法改革作出了周密的战略部署,其涉及面之广,对旧体制触动之深,在近几十年的历史中可谓空前。从某种意义上说,这次司法改革的重要性和难度已经无异于对司法系统进行一次手术治疗。这种外科手术式的改革举措很显然不可能由司法系统自我发动,而必须依靠政治核心的坚强政治意志,以及对历史和人民负责的高度政治自觉。没有党的坚强领导,包括司法改革在内的各项改革都可能沦为水中月、镜中花。当然,无论是饮食控制还是开刀吃药,大脑对肝肾的所谓干预的最终目的只是为了让后者恢复独立运作的自组织功能,一旦后者恢复健康,则不再干预也不可能干预其独立运作。这就是系统科学中控制系统与子系统之间的科学关系,也可以借用来帮助我们理解党的领导与依法治国之间的有机统一。

(三) 依法治国与以德治国相得益彰

党的十八届四中全会指出,坚持依法治国和以德治国相结合。国家和社会治理需要法律和道德共同发挥作用。必须坚持一手抓法治、一手抓德治,大力弘扬社会主义核心价值观,弘扬中华传统美德,培育社会公德、职业道德、家庭美德、个人品德,既重视发挥法律的规范作用,又重视发挥道德的教化作用,以法治体现道德理念、强化法律对道德建设的促进作用,以道德滋养法治精神、强化道德对法治文化的支撑作用,实现法律和道德相辅相成、法治和德治相得益彰。

　　依法治国是否应该与以德治国相结合,在中国的知识界是有一定争论的。有些人认为,今天中国提出依法治国是一种进步,但是提出以德治国又为人治留下了空间。这个问题需要我们全面和辩证地看待。从权力制约的角度来讲,法治的确是权力的笼子。2013 年 1 月 22 日,习近平总书记在中国共产党第十八届中央纪律检查委员会第二次全体会议上指出,"要加强对权力运行的制约和监督,把权力关进制度的笼子里。"习近平总书记的这句话给人们留下了深刻的印象,并迅速地成为人们谈及法治与权力制约时的口头禅。其实不管是在中国还是在西方,"把权力关进制度的笼子"已经成为人们的一种普遍共识。19 世纪的英国历史学家阿克顿勋爵在其名著《自由与权力》中有一句名言:"权力导致腐败,绝对的权力绝对导致腐败。"(Power tends to corrupt, and absolute power corrupts absolutely)认识到权力的危险性并能够运用民主法治的原则予以制约,这的确是人类社会发展史上值得赞美的一次飞跃。在这个问题上,中国还有很多需要向其他国家学习的地方,还有很长的路要走。

　　然而只把权力关进笼子就够了吗? 仔细想想,人们为了保护自己,常常会把什么东西关进笼子呢? 大概会有两种——一种是动物园里的野兽,另一种是监狱里的罪犯。之所以要把他(它)们关进笼子,就是因为他(它)们有能力伤害我们。然而就算把野兽和罪犯关进笼子,我们敢亲近他(它)们吗? 我们能够指望他(它)们为人民服务吗? 我们当然不指望野兽和罪犯为人民服务,可是我们希望权力为人民服务。原来说到底,权力终究不应该是野兽和罪犯,不应该是我们的敌人。如果权力只是居心叵测的敌人,那么就算把它关进制度的笼子,我们依然只成功了一半,却输掉了另一半。因为"把权力关进制度的笼子"只是法治的一半内涵,法治的另一半内涵是——把掌握权力的好人关进制度的笼子。

　　何谓"权力"? 孟子曰:"夫道二,常之谓经,变之谓权。怀其常道而挟其变权,乃得为贤。"《公羊传》曰:"权者何? 权者反于经,然后有善者也。"常与变,经与权,让我们想起了法治与权力之间的关系。权者,变也。权力的本质其实就在于必要的自由裁量空间,无论一个社会如何用制度来限制和规范权力,都无法彻底消灭这种自由裁量空间,这就是权力的真相之一。美剧《纸牌屋》描绘的不一定是事实,然而其折射出来的政治生态告诉我们:哪怕自诩民主法治如美国者,其精英阶层依然掌握着很大的权力空间。可见,一个好社会即便制度健全,也应选贤与能,因为权变的空间永远存在。法治不仅要将权力关进制度的笼子,还要保证这些必要的权变空间掌握在好人的手里。制度的笼子可以让权力想作大恶而不得,好人掌握权力则可以让权力不仅不作小恶,而且愿意为人民服务。

这个问题触及西方和中国不同的政治理念。西方的政治理念乃是怀疑主义,前提假设是政治家都是坏人。阿克顿的那句名言后面其实还跟着一句更激烈的话——"伟人几乎总是坏人"(Great men are almost always bad men)。而中国的政治理念则是德治与仁政,前提假设是政治家应该是君子,就像孔子所说的那样:"为政以德,譬如北辰,居其所而众星共之。"这两种政治理念在亚欧大陆的两端花开两朵,各表一枝,各有其历史渊源,也各有其合理性,分别帮助西方和中国建构起自己的政治大厦并屹立数千年之久。尽管今天的中国正在努力学习西方的政治理念,学习如何编织制度的笼子以制约权力的滥用,然而从长远看,中国人切不可对自己的政治传统毫无信心,导致从一个极端走到另一个极端。无论民主法治的倒逼机制如何完善,也永远取代不了执政者道德自觉的价值。而这正是习近平总书记在倡导法治的同时,依然一再强调"要始终坚持人民利益高于一切,紧紧依靠人民,全心全意为人民服务"的根本原因所在。2013 年 11 月习近平总书记在考察山东时指出,国无德不兴,人无德不立。必须加强全社会的思想道德建设,激发人们形成善良的道德意愿、道德情感,培育正确的道德判断和道德责任,提高道德实践能力尤其是自觉践行能力,引导人们向往和追求讲道德、尊道德、守道德的生活,形成向上的力量、向善的力量。只要中华民族一代接一代追求美好崇高的道德境界,我们的民族就永远充满希望。从某种意义上讲,法治与德治同样也是治国理政的鸟之双翼、车之双轮。制度的核心是怀疑,道德的核心是信任,一个好社会,应该是用怀疑的外壳装载着信任的内核。从这个意义上讲,"法"的确应该与"礼"相辅相成,"依法治国"的确应该与"以德治国"相得益彰。在法治建设领域,中西文明同样应该做到莱布尼茨所说的那样,"正宜两好合一,取长补短,用一盏灯点燃另一盏灯"。①

(四) 治国理政中的法治思维与底线思维

党的十八大以来,习近平同志多次强调,要坚持底线思维,不回避矛盾,不掩盖问题,凡事从坏处准备,努力争取最好的结果,这样才能有备无患、遇事不慌,牢牢把握主动权。李克强、张高丽等其他新一届中央领导也分别在不同的场合强调发展要坚持底线思维。随后中央各部委和地方各省市也都从自身的工作角度出发,纷纷强调底线思维的重要性。谈到底线思维,不由令人联想起党的十八大以来中央强调的另一种思维方法——法治思维。党的十八大报告指出,要提高领导干部运用法治思维和法治方式深化改革、化解矛盾、推动发展、维护稳定的能力。那么,什么是底线思维? 什么是法治思维? 底线思维与法治思维之间究竟是什么关系?

从治国理政的角度看,法治思维与底线思维应该是两种既有交叉又有不同的思维方法。法治思维是领导干部治国理政的主体思维,涵盖了当今社会改革、发展、稳定三大领域;而底线思维是领导干部治国理政的重要思维方法之一,其大部分内涵可以为法治思维所含摄,当然也有其独特的内涵和外延,比如特定时期的经济增长率底线和失业率底线,比如党组织对党员干部提出的高于法律要求的某些道德底线和纪律底线等。然而就总体而言,底线思维的大部分内涵的确可以为法治思维所含摄。我们不妨从法治的视野诠释一下底线思维的内涵,以论证两种思维之间的联系,揭示底线思维的法治属性。

---

① 【德】莱布尼茨:《中国近事》,大象出版社 2005 年版,第 2 页。

1. 底线刚性思维

法治的底线是确定性的、刚性的,是一个社会保护其成员生命财产安全的最后防线。一旦法律制定,底线就随之确立,任何人不得以任何理由予以突破。我国宪法规定,一切国家机关和武装力量、各政党和各社会团体、各企业事业组织都必须遵守宪法和法律。一切违反宪法和法律的行为,必须予以追究。任何组织或者个人都不得有超越宪法和法律的特权。而对于执法者而言,这条底线的确定性和刚性不仅意味着被动地守法,更意味着主动地执法。

这就是法治的底线刚性思维。事实证明,这条底线的刚性越强,对犯罪的阻遏力度和威慑程度就越强,社会管理的成本就越低。这条底线的刚性越弱,犯罪的侥幸心理就越严重,社会管理的成本就越高。从遏制暴行到防止腐败,从社会管理到廉政建设,底线刚性思维都是这个社会不可突破、不可触碰、不可或缺的"高压线"。任何权变的空间都必须被牢牢地限制在这条"高压线"之内,否则必将受到法律的严惩。

2. 底线公平思维

在 2013 年年底的中央经济工作会议上,习近平总书记强调,要继续按照守住底线、突出重点、完善制度、引导舆论的思路,统筹教育、就业、收入分配、社会保障、医药卫生、住房、食品安全、生产安全等,切实做好改善民生各项工作。党的十八届五中全会进一步提出了共享发展的理念,要按照人人参与、人人尽力、人人享有的要求,坚守底线、突出重点、完善制度、引导预期,注重机会公平,保障基本民生,实现全体人民共同迈入全面小康社会。习近平总书记的讲话和中央的精神为我们如何看待民生的底线公平问题指出了明确的方向。

众所周知,近些年来全国各地不断发生一些针对无辜群众的公共安全事件。无论是校园惨案还是公交车纵火案,那些残害无辜的罪犯理应受到最严厉的惩罚和最愤怒的谴责,然而一个法治社会的反思绝不应该停留于此。在一个动物世界里,食肉动物与食草动物之间的相互残杀是无关于道德和法律的。因为在那里,它们的最高法则就是生存。生活需要讲规则,生存是不择手段的。人类首先是一种动物,同样具备动物的本能,同样有可能因为生存而相互残杀。然而人类社会之所以不再是动物世界,就是因为人类社会已经建立起了一条底线,底线之上称之为生活,底线之下称之为生存;底线之上是人类社会,底线之下是动物世界。就像电影《一九四二》所描述的那样,1942 年河南大旱之后,人们的生活底线被彻底洞穿。在这种情况下,无论是囤着粮食的东家,还是家无余粮的长工,最终都无法在混乱的旋涡中保护住自己的生命财产安全,因为底线的失守顷刻间就让人类社会倒退成了动物世界。在今天这样一个差别化已经成为不争现实的社会里,当所有人都在底线之上生活的时候,这个差别化的社会依然可以维持稳定,此时每个人的幸福度很大程度上是由自己决定的。然而一旦有人跌穿生活的底线进入生存状态的时候,这个社会的幸福度很可能就是由最不幸福的那个人决定的。

在一个差别化的社会里,由于法律保护个人的私有财产权和继承权,所谓的起点公平和结果公平事实上是一个很难证明的命题。差别化的社会最值得追求的公平是底线公平,也就是对所有的社会成员做出一个不可撤销的坚定承诺,保证每个人过上最基本的有尊严的生活。唯有如此,这个社会的成员才不会在陷入困境时丧失生活的信心,进而铤而走险危害社会。正如马斯洛的需求层次理论所揭示的,生存与安全乃是人类最基本的需求,这种最基本的需求实际上就是每个人的底线。在这条不可后撤的底线上,每个人都是绝对公平的。在一个差别化的社会里,每个人的身份有差别,财富有多寡,然而在对生命的尊重和保护上,每个人都是一样的。一个平民也许可以接受一个富人开着豪车而自己挤着地铁,但绝不会接受他开着豪车随意撞人而不受到公平的惩罚。这就是一个差别化社会的底线公平思维。一旦底线公平被击穿,这个社会将很快陷入动荡,直至最后被彻底颠覆。

法治必须为社会守护这条公平的底线。而这条底线也并非恒定不变,它会随着时代条件的变化而不断做出调整。俗话说"水涨船高",倘若一个社会最终摆脱了生存与温饱的困扰,那么这条社会底线应该设定在哪里呢? 习近平总书记在 2013 年年底的中央经济工作会议上的讲话已经为我们指明了努力的方向,一个好政府应该尽可能动用公共资源为社会守护这条公平的底线。当然,需要指出的是,守护底线公平不等于养懒人,底线公平与机会公平是相辅相成的。底线公平的价值在于维护稳定,机会公平的价值在于激励发展。一个不稳定的社会最终是无法发展的,一个不发展的社会最终也是无法稳定的。因此一个好社会的公平观是"倒 T 字"形的——底部一横的底线公平,纵向一竖的机会公平。有底线,有机会,人生就没有真正的遗憾,社会就没有真正的失败。

3. 底线倒逼思维

2013 年 9 月 17 日,习近平同志在党外人士座谈会上指出,改革是由问题倒逼而产生,又在不断解决问题中而深化。2013 年 11 月 12 日,党的十八届三中全会通过了《中共中央关于全面深化改革若干重大问题的决定》,正式吹响了全面深化改革的号角。从某种意义上说,与 1978 年的改革开放一样,这场全面而深刻的改革的确是由问题倒逼出来的。1978 年的中国,"文革"浩劫刚刚过去,国民经济已经接近于崩溃的边缘,社会各领域同时面临着各种严重的问题。此时的国家命运与党的命运,都已经站在了最后的生死底线之上,只要再后撤一步,必将陷入万劫不复的历史深渊。于是,不甘就此沉沦的中国人民在以邓小平同志为核心的党中央领导下,绝地反击,将问题的倒逼转化为改革的自觉,成功地建立起社会主义市场经济体系,经过 30 多年艰苦卓绝的努力,将中国的经济总量推上了世界第二的高峰。生死存亡的底线困境没有让中国人和中国共产党沉沦,而是成功地倒逼出了改革的自觉。1978 年改革开放的思维是如此,如今全面深化改革的思维同样也是如此,这种思维就是底线倒逼思维。

底线倒逼思维广泛存在于各种社会生活之中。企业要想经营好,离不开市场思维的倒逼,市场就是企业的底线;军队要想有战斗力,离不开战场思维的倒逼,战场就是军队的底线。同理可证,政府要想执好政,同样离不开法治思维的倒逼,法治就是政府的底线。法治源自人民群众的意志,违背人民群众意志的政府就如同违背市场规律的企业和违背战场规律的军队一样,终将被无情地淘汰进历史的垃圾堆。因此,要想不被市场淘汰,企业就必须自觉地遵循市场规律,努力生产出受市场欢迎的商品;要想不被战场淘汰,军队就必须自觉地按照战场的标准开展演练,以生成真正的战斗力;同理可证,要想不被人民的意志淘汰,政府就必须自觉地遵循法治的要求,运用法治思维深化改革、化解矛盾、推动发展、维护稳定。

一个自觉的政府必须对法治的底线倒逼常怀敬畏之心。人民意志的底线倒逼其实有着多种表现形式,法治的底线倒逼只是其中一种,这种倒逼本质上乃是一种建设性倒逼或制度性倒逼。倘若一个政府拒不接受或拒不建立法治的底线倒逼,那么人民意志最终也会通过暴力革命予以实现,到头来同样可以实现对政府的倒逼,而此时的倒逼本质上就是一种破坏性倒逼。中国古代"其兴也勃焉,其亡也忽焉""水能载舟,亦能覆舟"的王朝周期律,就是这样的一种破坏性倒逼。而一旦王朝周期律登场,这个社会就一定要付出玉石俱焚的高昂代价。秦末农民起义,"项羽引兵西屠咸阳,杀秦降王子婴,烧秦宫室,火三月不灭;收其货宝妇女而东"(《史记·项羽本纪》)。唐末农民起义,黄巢两度攻破长安,"纵兵屠杀,流血成川,谓之洗城"(《资治通鉴》卷第二百五十四)。公元 2 年,西汉全国人口 5959 万,经过数十年的血腥内战,到了公元 57 年的东汉,人口仅余 2100 万,真可谓是赤地千里,十室九空。这就是王朝周期律破坏性倒逼的恐怖力量。唯有深刻认识到破坏性倒逼的可怕性,才能最终倒逼出制度性倒逼的自觉性。从这个意义上说,法治的底线倒逼思维乃是破解王朝周期律的真正法宝。

由此可见,底线倒逼思维乃是一种动态思维。鉴于突破底线的可怕后果,人们必须尽可能地远离底线,而不是停留在底线边缘,甚至故意踩着底线行走。常言道,常在河边走,怎能不湿鞋。踩着底线行走的人随时都有可能跌穿底线,从而给自己带来不测。因此,对于一个自觉的政府或官员来讲,底线乃是倒逼自己努力向上、努力向前的起跑线、动力源,而对于一个不自觉的政府或官员来讲,底线很可能就是最终葬送自己命运的死亡线。明确底线,倒逼自觉,这就是法治的底线倒逼思维,也是习近平总书记所讲的"凡事从坏处准备,努力争取最好的结果"的真正要义所在。

尊重底线的刚性,守护底线的公平,服从底线的倒逼,这就是法治视野下的底线思维。当代领导干部唯有牢固树立起法治的底线思维,才能够真正做到有备无患、遇事不慌,牢牢把握主动权,才能够真正提高自己深化改革、化解矛盾、推动发展、维护稳定的能力,为全面建设小康社会贡献自己的力量。

思 考 题

1. 为什么说中国共产党的领导是中国特色社会主义法治之魂?
2. 为什么说法治是治国理政的基本方式?

参考文献

1.《习近平谈治国理政》,北京:外文出版社,2014 年。
2.《〈中共中央关于全面推进依法治国若干重大问题的决定〉辅导读本》,北京:人民出版社,2014 年。

四、推进协商民主

　　"社会主义协商民主,是中国社会主义民主政治的特有形式和独特优势,是中国共产党的群众路线在政治领域的重要体现。中共十八大提出,在发展我国社会主义民主政治的进程中,要完善协商民主制度和工作机制,推进协商民主广泛多层制度化发展。中共十八届三中全会强调,在党的领导下,以经济社会发展重大问题和涉及群众切身利益的实际问题为内容,在全社会开展广泛协商,坚持协商于决策之前和决策实施之中。这些重要论述和部署,为中国社会主义协商民主发展指明了方向。"——习近平:《在庆祝中国人民政治协商会议成立 65 周年大会上的讲话》(《人民日报》2014 年 9 月 22 日)

"协商",是一个人们十分熟悉的词语;"民主",对大家来说,更是不会陌生。然而,当"协商"与"民主"合并起来,形成了"协商民主"这个"新概念"时,或许就会使人感到有些"新鲜"、不容易把握了。近期来"协商民主"得以"高密度""高频率"地亮相,多种版本的"解读"也络绎不绝、层出不穷。伴随着30多年来改革开放发展进程,长期以来一些认为"一脚长"(经济建设发展快)、"一脚短"(政治建设发展慢)的观点;认为民主党派作为"花瓶党",政党协商就是"装装样子""不说白不说、说了也白说"的观点,以及认为统一战线、参政议政无非就是"招招生、举举手、拍拍手、挥挥手"的观点等,在一定的场合,还是"涛声依旧",那些视而不见、听而不闻当下客观实际,总是"重复那昨天的故事"的现象,仍然有着一定的市场,等等,这些都"倒逼"人们及时全面、准确把握社会主义协商民主的科学内涵、精神实质、实践举措,坚定中国特色社会主义民主政治建设的自信,无论是从理论上看,还是从实践上看,其意义是多么重要和紧迫。

(一) 协商与民主

什么是"社会主义协商民主"? 习近平开明宗义指出:"社会主义协商民主,是中国社会主义民主政治的特有形式和独特优势,是中国共产党的群众路线在政治领域的重要体现。"大千世界,无奇不有。人类共同生存的"地球村"中,打着"民主"旗号的,比比皆是;标榜"协商民主"的,也举不胜举。习近平以十分严谨、缜密的逻辑判断明确指出的"社会主义协商民主",是一个完整的科学范畴。"社会主义"四个字不能"省略",因而不能笼统地简称为"协商民主"。"社会主义协商民主",深刻揭示和表明了协商民主的社会主义根本属性和本质。

强调科学范畴的特性和实质,是习近平一贯的逻辑思维方式方法。深入学习习近平系列重要讲话精神,我们不仅要认真学习这些讲话所阐述的重要思想和基本内容,而且还要深刻领悟习近平在阐述这些重要思想和基本内容过程中所孕育的科学思维方法。把握好习近平科学的思维方法,对于完整、准确领会习近平系列重要讲话的精神实质,有着重要的意义。党的十八大以来,习近平始终要求全党要"坚持和发展中国特色社会主义",并且"快人快语""开门见山":"中国特色社会主义是社会主义而不是其他什么主义,科学社会主义基本原则不能丢,丢了就不是社会主义"。① 社会主义协商民主,是同社会主义基本制度紧密结合在一起的。社会主义协商民主,"社会主义"几个字是不能没有的,这并非多余,并非"画蛇添足",而恰恰相反,这是"画龙点睛"。所谓"点睛",就是点明我们的协商民主的性质。

2014 年 9 月 21 日,庆祝中国人民政治协商会议成立 65 周年大会在北京召开(新华社发,刘卫兵摄)

1. 社会主义协商民主:中国社会主义民主政治的特有形式和独特优势

"人民民主是社会主义的生命。""人民当家作主是社会主义民主

---

① 参见:《习近平在新进中央委员会的委员、候补委员学习贯彻党的十八大精神研讨班开班式上发表重要讲话》,《人民日报》2013 年 1 月 6 日。

政治的本质和核心。"概括地说,人民民主、人民当家作主,就是坚持人民主体地位,坚持国家的一切权力属于人民。90多年中国共产党发展的历史、60多年中华人民共和国发展的历史、30多年改革开放和社会主义现代化建设发展的历史一再表明,"中国共产党领导人民实行人民民主,就是保证和支持人民当家作主"。"保证和支持人民当家作主",不是一句"口号",更不是一句"空话",而是落实在国家政治生活和社会生活之中,保证人民依法有效行使管理国家事务、管理经济和文化事业、管理社会事务的权力。

"鞋子合不合脚,自己穿了才知道。"习近平这一著名的"鞋子论",言简意赅,通俗而意蕴深刻。正所谓:"履不必同,期于适足;治不必同,期于利民。"一个国家的发展道路究竟合不合适,只有这个国家的人民才最有发言权。"世界这么大",各国和各国人民应该共同享受尊严。也正是在这样一个大前提下,习近平提出,我们一贯主张,"要坚持国家不分大小、强弱、贫富一律平等,尊重各国人民自主选择发展道路的权利,反对干涉别国内政,维护国际公平正义"。[①]他还明确指出,"一个国家实行什么样的主义,关键要看这个主义能否解决这个国家面临的历史性课题"。选择什么样的发展道路如此,选择什么样的主义如此,选择什么样的民主方式——同样如此。习近平同志的"鞋子论",好似"绵里藏针",朴实中浸润着的底气,蕴含着理性,既让人听着亲切,又让人感受赞同,在这形象的比喻中,向世界传递了我们始终坚持和发展中国特色社会主义的坚定自信。

习近平坦诚地指出,"中国特色社会主义政治制度之所以行得通、有生命力、有效率,就是因为它是从中国的社会土壤中生长起来的。中国特色社会主义政治制度过去和现在一直生长在中国的社会土壤之中,未来要继续苗壮成长,也必须深深扎根于中国的社会土壤。"[②]同样,"保证和支持人民当家作主"是基本要求和内容,需要有相应的形

---

① 习近平:《在莫斯科国际关系学院发表重要演讲》,《人民日报》2013年3月24日。

② 习近平:《在庆祝全国人民代表大会成立60周年大会上的讲话》,《人民日报》2014年9月6日。

式和方式来实行。实践表明,当今世界,实现民主的形式是丰富多样的,不能拘泥于刻板的模式,"更不能说只有一种放之四海而皆准的评判标准"。基于此,对别国的发展道路选择、政治制度"说三道四""横加指责",或者硬要把自己的民主形式套在其他国家的头上是极不理智的,也是根本不现实的。

人民当家作主,是与人民所享有的权利相匹配的。选举、投票,是人们在日常生活中"感受"较为"明显"的方式——不知不觉中,往往会把"直选""公投"当作是民主进程衡量"标准"。选举和投票,的确是实行民主的重要方式和手段,但不是问题的全部。我们判断人民是否享有民主权利,不仅"要看人民是否在选举时有投票的权利,也要看人民在日常政治生活中是否有持续参与的权利";不仅"要看人民有没有进行民主选举的权利,也要看人民有没有进行民主决策、民主管理、民主监督的权利"。这两者相互联系,相互促进,前者容易"显现",但后者尤为"深刻"。"社会主义民主不仅需要完整的制度程序,而且需要完整的参与实践。"据此,习近平以三个"具体地、现实地",作了进一步的阐述,这就是人民当家作主,必须:具体地、现实地体现到中国共产党执政和国家治理上来;具体地、现实地体现到中国共产党和国家机关各个方面、各个层级的工作上来;具体地、现实地体现到人民对自身利益的实现和发展上来。

总之,从各国的具体国情出发,"保证和支持人民当家作主",既可以通过依法选举的方式,也可以通过让人民的代表来参与国家生活和社会生活的管理的方式,通过选举以外的制度和方式让人民参与国家生活和社会生活的管理也是十分重要的。在现实生活中,我们不能机械地、片面地把"选举"当作唯一的民主方式,更不能当作是"最佳"的民主方式。习近平深刻而尖锐地指出,"人民只有投票的权利而没有广泛参与的权利,人民只有在投票时被唤醒、投票后就进入休眠期,这样的民主是形式主义的"。

我国人民民主实践充分表明,在我们这个人口众多、幅员辽阔的社会主义国家里,关系国计民生的重大问题,在中国共产党领导下进行广泛协商,体现了民主和集中的统一;人民通过选举、投票行使权利和人民内部各方面在重大决策之前进行充分协商,尽可能就共同性问题取得一致意见,是中国社会主义民主的两种重要形式。在中国,这两种民主形式不是相互替代、相互否定的,而是相互补充、相得益彰的,共同构成了中国社会主义民主政治的制度特点和优势。

习近平多次强调,中国特色社会主义最本质的特征就是坚持中国共产党的领导。在我们这样一个世界人口第一的发展中大国,取得任何事业的进步,没有中国共产党领导的"核心力量",都是"一事无成"的,历史和现实已经并将不断充分证实这一颠扑不破的科学论断。历史和现实也已经并将不断充分地证实协商民主深深嵌入了中国社会主义民主政治全过程。我国的社会主义协商民主,既坚持了中国共产党的领导,又发挥了各方面的积极作用;既坚持了人民主体地位,又贯彻了民主集中制的领导制度和组织原则;既坚持了人民民主的原则,又贯彻了团结和谐的要求。所以说,中国社会主义协商民主丰富了民主的形式、拓展了民主的渠道、加深了民主的内涵。

2. 社会主义协商民主是中国共产党的群众路线在政治领域的重要体现

"老百姓是地,老百姓是天,老百姓是共产党永远的挂念。老百姓是山,老百姓是海,老百姓是共产党生命的源泉。"中国共产党"两个先锋队"的性质,决定了党的宗旨是全心全意为人民服务。这一宗旨,是坚持马克思主义唯物史观的根本要求。人民群众是历史的创造者,是推动历史进步的动力。中国共产党领导全国各族人民建立的中华人民共和国,当家作主的是广大人民群众。《中华人民共和国宪法》规定,国家的一切权力属于人民,一切国家机关和国家工作人员必须依靠人民的支持,经常保持同人民的密切联系,倾听人民的意见和建议,接受人民的监督,努力为人民服务。因此,无论何时何地,治国理政、管理社会,必须紧紧依靠人民。

以马克思主义唯物史观为遵循,中国共产党在自己的工作中实行群众路线。群众路线是中国共产党人把马克思主义基本原理同中国具体实际相结合的重要理论创新与实践成果,是我们党把马克思列宁主义关于人民群众是历史创造者的原理,系统地运用在党的全部活动中,形成了群众路线这一党的根本工作路线。这一根本的工作路线,"是实现党的思想路线、政治路线、组织路线的根本工作路线"。① 历史经验表明,群众路线和实事求是、独立自主一道,是毛泽东思想活的灵魂。

党的群众路线,不能随意地"简化"为"从群众中来,到群众中去"。《中国共产党章程》的规范表述是,"党在自己的工作中实行群众路线,一切为了群众,一切依靠群众,从群众中来,到群众中去,把党的正确主张变为群众的自觉行动。"②这是由"价值意蕴"(一切为了群众,一切依靠群众)、"途径方式"(从群众中来,到群众中去)、"目标导向"(把党的正确主张变为群众的自觉行动)三部分组成的有机整体。习近平在党的群众路线教育实践活动工作会议上再次强调,"群众路线是我们党的生命线和根本工作路线","历史和现实都告诉我们,密切联系群众,是党的性质和宗旨的体现,是中国共产党区别于其他政党的显著标志,也是党发展壮大的重要原因;能否保持党同人民群众的血肉联系,决定着党的事业的成败"③。

习近平指出,"全心全意为人民服务,始终代表最广大人民根本利益,是我们能够实行和发展协商民主的重要前提和基础。"中国共产党自诞生那天起,就明确表示,党除了工人阶级和最广大人民群众的利益,没有自己特殊的利益。党及其领导的国家是代表最广大人民根本利益的,其一切理论和路线方针政策,其一切工作部署和工作安排,都应该来自人民,都应该为人民利益而制定和实施。在这个大政治前提下,我们应该也能够广泛听取人民内部各方面的意见和建议。

① 《十一届三中全会以来党的历次全国代表大会中央全会重要文献选编》(下),中央文献出版社 1997 年版,第 47 页。
② 《中国共产党第十四次全国代表大会文件汇编》,人民出版社 1992 年版,第 94 页。
③ 习近平:《在党的群众路线教育实践活动工作会议上的讲话》,《人民日报》2013 年 8 月 5 日。

　　实践生动地表明，在中国共产党统一领导下，通过多种形式的协商，广泛听取意见和建议，广泛接受批评和监督，深刻体现了中国社会主义协商民主的独特优势所在，也有益于以下五个"可以"和五个"有效"：可以广泛达成决策和工作的最大共识，有效克服党派和利益集团为自己的利益相互竞争甚至相互倾轧的弊端；可以广泛畅通各种利益要求和诉求进入决策程序的渠道，有效克服不同政治力量为了维护和争取自己的利益固执己见、排斥异己的弊端；可以广泛形成发现和改正失误和错误的机制，有效克服决策中情况不明、自以为是的弊端；可以广泛形成人民群众参与各层次管理和治理的机制，有效克服人民群众在国家政治生活和社会治理中无法表达、难以参与的弊端；可以广泛凝聚全社会推进改革发展的智慧和力量，有效克服各项政策和工作共识不高、无以落实的弊端。

　　社会主义协商民主是中国共产党的群众路线在政治领域的重要体现，深刻表明国家各项工作都要贯彻党的群众路线，密切同人民群众的联系，倾听人民呼声，回应人民期待，不断解决好人民最关心最直接最现实的利益问题，凝聚起最广大人民的智慧和力量。

　　我们已经跨入我国国民经济和社会发展第十三个五年规划（"十三五"）的重要历史发展时期。"十三五"时期，是全面建成小康社会的"决胜"阶段，我们党确定的"两个一百年"奋斗目标的第一个百年奋斗目标，将在"十三五"时期胜利实现。如期实现全面建成小康社会奋斗目标，推动经济社会持续健康发展，必须遵循符合我国国情的一系列重要的、基本的原则。其中，首先就是要"坚持人民主体地位"。《中共中央关于制定国民经济和社会发展第十三个五年规划的建议》（以下简称"建议"）指出，"人民是推动发展的根本力量，实现好、维护好、发展好最广大人民根本利益是发展的根本目的。必须坚持以人民为中心的发展思想，把增进人民福祉、促进人的全面发展作为发展的出发点和落脚点"。据此，中央明确提出，要"发展人民民主，维护社会公平正义，保障人民平等参与、平等发展权利，充分调动人民积极性、主动性、创造性"。当前，从各层次、各领域扩大公民有序政治参与，发展更加广泛、更加充分、更加健全的人民民主,应进一步扩大人民民主,健全民主制度,丰富民主形式,拓宽民主渠道。

全面建成小康社会、实现"两个一百年"奋斗目标,事关亿万人民群众根本利益和中华民族伟大复兴。因此,"建议"强调指出,要"动员人民群众团结奋斗","充分发扬民主,贯彻党的群众路线,提高宣传和组织群众能力,加强经济社会发展重大问题和涉及群众切身利益问题的协商,依法保障人民各项权益,激发各族人民建设祖国的主人翁意识"。在实际工作中,要创新群众工作体制机制和方式方法,"正确处理人民内部矛盾,最大限度凝聚全社会推进改革发展、维护社会和谐稳定的共识和力量"。①

社会主义协商民主,是"中国社会主义民主政治的特有形式和独特优势,是党的群众路线在政治领域的重要体现"。这一重要论断,经受了历史的检验,经受了实践的检验。历史和实践也同时雄辩地表明:"社会主义协商民主在我国有根、有源、有生命力,是中国共产党人和中国人民的伟大创造"。②

(二)不实在,非民主

1.社会主义协商民主,应该是实实在在的、而不是做样子的

习近平明确指出,"民主不是装饰品,不是用来做摆设的,而是要用来解决人民要解决的问题的。"③言行一致、真抓实干,是中国共产党人的一贯品行;不搞"形式主义"、不做"表面文章",是党的思想路线的内在要求。社会主义民主政治建设,不是写在纸上,喊在嘴上,挂在墙

① 《中共中央关于制定国民经济和社会发展第十三个五年规划的建议》,《人民日报》2015年11月4日。
② 习近平:《社会主义协商民主在我国有根有源有生命力》,《人民日报》2014年10月28日。
③ 习近平:《在庆祝中国人民政治协商会议成立65周年大会上的讲话》,《人民日报》2014年9月22日。

上的,而是要"实实在在"付诸社会生活之中的。结合社会主义协商民主的发展过程,"社会主义民主不仅需要完整的制度程序,而且需要完整的参与实践"。这样由亿万人民群众参与的实践,而且是"完整"的参与实践,是有着基本的要求,充分体现在三个"具体"和"现实"方面的,即:具体地、现实地体现到中国共产党执政和国家治理上来;具体地、现实地体现到中国共产党和国家机关各个方面、各个层级的工作上来;具体地、现实地体现到人民对自身利益的实现和发展上来。

更进一步说,现实而又严峻的国内外形势,客观地要求社会主义协商民主必须是"实实在在"的,不能够做样子的,也是不允许做样子的。从国内来讲,改革开放进程中利益格局深刻调整呈现出新形势、社会新旧矛盾相互交织呈现出新变化、市场经济条件下思想观念多元多样呈现出新情况;从国际来讲,世界范围内不同政治发展道路竞争博弈呈现出新挑战,因而,不断加强社会主义协商民主"实实在在"的建设,意义重大而深远,这深刻表现在五个"有利于":有利于扩大公民有序政治参与、更好实现人民当家作主的权利,有利于促进科学民主决策、推进国家治理体系和治理能力现代化,有利于化解矛盾冲突、促进社会和谐稳定,有利于保持党同人民群众的血肉联系、巩固和扩大党的执政基础,有利于发挥我国政治制度优越性,增强中国特色社会主义道路自信、理论自信、制度自信。

"民主不是装饰品",一语中的、一锤定音:这既是对社会主义协商民主发展的要求,也是对中国特色社会主义民主政治建设的客观评价。那些把我国诸多参政党民主党派调侃为"花瓶党",把具有中国特色的"政治协商"浓缩为"招招手、举举手、拍拍手、挥挥手",浑然全是"形式主义",是不符合实际的。坦率而又坦诚地说,社会主义协商民主发展进程中无疑有着有待改进、完善的地方,但更要充分肯定所取得的进展及准确把握其实质性的贡献。"民主不是装饰品,不是用来做摆设的,而是要用来解决人民要解决的问题的。"这就是科学的结论。

政党协商是中国特色社会主义民主政治的独特优势,在党和国家工作大局中具有不可或缺的重要地位和作用。新中国成立前夕,中国人民政治协商会议第一届全体会议召开。会议代表全国各族人民意志,代行全国人民代表大会职权,通过了具有临时宪法性质的《中国人民政治协商会议共同纲领》和《中国人民政治协商会议组织法》、《中华人民共和国中央人民政府组织法》,作出关于中华人民共和国国都、国旗、国歌、纪年4个重要决议,选举中国人民政治协商会议全国委员会和中华人民共和国中央人民政府委员会,宣告中华人民共和国的成立。这一系列充分民主协商的"标志性"成果,展现了人民政协为新中国的成立作出的重大的、"实实在在"的贡献。

政党协商也是国家治理体系的重要方面。新中国成立以后,无论是资本主义工商业社会主义改造等内政问题,还是抗美援朝等外部事务,中国共产党都与各民主党派进行广泛、深入的协商,直到达成共识以后,再付诸行动,受到社会各方面的拥护和支持。改革开放初期,为调动广大工商界投身经济建设的积极性,邓小平同志邀请中国民主建国会(民建)中央、全国工商联5位领导同志座谈,"五老火锅宴"成为一段佳话。而92岁高龄的中国农工民主党(农工党)季方主席和民建中央胡厥文主席、全国工商联胡子昂主席联名提出了《关于振兴和发展中药事业的建议书》,得到了中共中央高度肯定,"三老上书"成为多党合作历史上的又一段佳话。

进入新世纪,振兴东北老工业基地、建立海峡西岸经济区、建立中原经济区等,都是由民主党派中央参与调研提出,并成为推动我国区域发展的重大战略。党的十八大以来,民主党派中央就促进京津冀协同发展、应对雾霾污染等问题提出了很多务实有效的意见和建议。通过政党协商,搭建了制度化的表达意见、沟通协商的平台,广泛凝聚了社会各方面的智慧和力量,促进了国家治理决策的科学化、民主化。

中国特色社会主义的伟大实践,为进一步激励和发挥各参政党的特点和优势,推进多党合作事业和社会主义协商民主建设,凝心聚力,共同助力全面建成小康社会发展,提供了宽广的舞台。社会主义协商民主的成果和营养,为党和国家高度重视,切切实实地转化为方针政策,付诸实践。调查研究、参政议政、政治协商的丰硕成果,得到了党和政府及有关部门的吸收和采纳。

认真回顾和总结历史和现实经验,我们可以清晰地认识到,社会主义协商民主的多种方式和多种渠道,为恢复和发展国民经济、巩固新生人民政权、推动各项社会改革、促进社会主义革命和建设,在全面建成小康社会、不断推进社会主义现代化建设事业进程中,作出了"实实在在"的历史性贡献。在新的历史发展时期和发展阶段,以习近平同志为核心的党中央,进一步准确把握人民政协性质定位,充分发挥人民政协作为协商民主的重要渠道作用,围绕"团结"和"民主"这两大主题,推进政治协商、民主监督、参政议政制度建设。人民政协和社会主义协商民主工作,在继承中发展、在发展中创新,紧紧围绕中心、服务大局,聚焦全面深化改革凝聚共识、汇集力量、建言献策,作出了新的积极贡献。这是任何不戴"有色眼镜"的人们"有目共睹"的、不容置疑的。

遵循辩证唯物主义和历史唯物主义的观点,我们既要看到社会主义协商民主在"实实在在"方面,有着长足的推进,但也要看到,协商民主建设是一个不断发展的过程。新形势、新任务,有着新问题、新挑战,因此,在新的历史发展时期和新的历史发展阶段,要"支持鼓励协商民主建设探索创新",尊重群众首创精神,注重实践经验提炼总结,并适时上升为制度规范。努力做到三个"加强":加强领导和组织协调,鼓励探索创新,通过各种途径、各种渠道、各种方式进行广泛协商,建立健全提案、会议、座谈、论证、听证、公示、评估、咨询、网络、民意调查等多种协商方式;加强中国特色新型智库建设,建立健全决策咨询制度;加强协商民主理论研究,不断丰富和发展社会主义协商民主理论体系。

2.构建程序合理、环节完整的协商民主体系

习近平提出社会主义协商民主应该是"全方位"的、"全国上上下下都要做的",深刻揭示了社会主义协商民主是一个由诸多要素有机组成的"系统工程",强调了"构建程序合理、环节完整的社会主义协商民主体系"的重要性和必要性。

习近平总书记还就"构建程序合理、环节完整的社会主义协商民

主体系"提出了明确的要求,其中包括:拓宽国家政权机关、政协组织、党派团体、基层组织、社会组织的协商渠道;深入开展立法协商、行政协商、民主协商、参政协商、社会协商;发挥统一战线在协商民主中的重要作用,发挥人民政协作为协商民主重要渠道的作用,完善人民政协制度体系,规范协商内容、协商程序,拓展协商民主形式,更加活跃有序地组织专题协商、对口协商、界别协商、提案办理协商,增加协商密度,提高协商成效。①

之所以强调人民政协协商民主建设及具体的要求,在于人民政协协商民主是社会主义协商民主的重要组成部分。在《中共中央关于加强社会主义协商民主建设的意见》颁布以后不久,2015 年 6 月 25 日,新华社全文刊登了中共中央办公厅印发的《关于加强人民政协协商民主建设的实施意见》。人民政协协商民主是在中国共产党领导下,参加人民政协的各党派团体、各族各界人士履行政治协商、民主监督、参政议政职能,围绕改革发展稳定重大问题和涉及群众切身利益的实际问题,在决策之前和决策实施之中广泛协商、凝聚共识的重要民主形式。人民政协以宪法、政协章程和相关政策为依据,以中国共产党领导的多党合作和政治协商制度为保障,集协商、监督、参与、合作于一体,成为各党派团体和各族各界人士发扬民主、参与国是、团结合作的重要平台,是适合中国国情、具有鲜明中国特色的制度安排。长期以来,人民政协作为协商民主重要渠道和专门协商机构的作用,对于广纳群言、广谋良策、广聚共识,促进党和政府决策科学化、民主化,更好实现人民当家作主,化解矛盾、促进社会和谐稳定,进而不断推进国家治理体系和治理能力现代化,作出了许多重要的贡献。

细细"品味"社会主义协商民主体系的基本要素,不难发现,这是一个在深化政治体制改革中逐步构建"3+3+1"的逻辑框架。这第一个"3",指的是"政党协商、政府协商、政协协商";这第二个"3",指的是

---

① 习近平:《关于〈中共中央关于全面深化改革若干重大问题的决定〉的说明》,《人民日报》2013 年 11 月 16 日。

"人大协商、人民团体协商、基层协商";这最后一个"1",指的是"社会组织协商"。值得认真学习和把握的是,在这"3+3+1"体系内容方面,相应的"限定词"是不尽相同的。第一个"3",其要求是"重点加强";这第二个"3",其要求是"积极开展";而这最后一个"1",则是"逐步探索"。这不仅是语词上有所差异,而且内含着分层、分类指导的辩证法思维。在实践中,建构、完善这"3+3+1"的逻辑体系,为的是发挥各协商渠道自身优势,做好衔接配合,不断健全和完善社会主义协商民主制度。需要强调的是,各类协商要根据自身特点和实际需要,合理确定协商内容和方式,使人民群众可以通过多种多样的民主通道,享受知情权、参与权、表达权、监督权,共同参与民主协商。

就目前人们所达到的实践水平和认识水平,架构起社会主义协商民主体系,既要注重这"3+3+1"的基本方式和渠道,同时也要注重要坚持从实际出发,按照科学合理、规范有序、简便易行、民主集中的要求,制订协商计划、明确协商议题和内容、确定协商人员、开展协商活动、注重协商成果运用反馈,确保协商活动有序务实高效。

需要指出的是,突出"全方位""全国上上下下"的要求,归根到底,就是要牢牢把握人民群众是社会主义协商民主这一重中之重的观点。大力发展基层协商民主,重点在基层群众中开展协商。凡是涉及群众切身利益的决策都要充分听取群众意见,通过各种方式、在各个层级、各个方面同群众进行协商。要完善基层组织联系群众制度,加强议事协商,做好上情下达、下情上传工作,保证人民依法管理好自己的事务。要推进权力运行公开化、规范化,完善党务公开、政务公开、司法公开和各领域办事公开制度,让人民监督权力,让权力在阳光下运行。

2015年10月29日中国共产党第十八届中央委员会第五次全体会议通过的《中共中央关于制定国民经济和社会发展第十三个五年规划的建议》指出,"巩固和发展最广泛的爱国统一战线,全面落实党的知识分子、民族、宗教、侨务等政策,充分发挥民主党派、工商联和无党派人士作用,深入开展民族团结进步宣传教育,引导宗教与社会主义社会相适应,促进政党关系、民族关系、宗教关系、阶层关系、海内外同胞关系和谐,巩固全国各族人民大团结,加强海内外中华儿女大团结"。①
这对于我们在"十三五"期间,全面建成小康社会这一决胜阶段,发挥
统一战线在协商民主中的重要作用,实现"两个一百年"和中华民族伟
大复兴,有着重要的指导意义。

3. 真协商就要协商于决策之前和决策之中

习近平强调,"协商就要真协商,真协商就要协商于决策之前和决
策之中,根据各方面的意见和建议来决定和调整我们的决策和工作,
从制度上保障协商成果落地,使我们的决策和工作更好顺乎民意、合
乎实际。"②实行人民民主,保证人民当家作主,要求我们在治国理政时
在人民内部各方面进行广泛商量。开展广泛的商量,是中国共产党人
的优良传统。大到"共商国是",小到"鸡毛蒜皮",商量不可或缺。正
因为如此,毛泽东指出,"国家各方面的关系都要协商。"他还如此坦诚
相告:"我们政府的性格,你们也都摸熟了,是跟人民商量办事的"。据
此,特地为其起了名字,"可以叫它是个商量政府"。毛泽东风趣而又
深刻的话语,展现了人民政府为人民的真谛。既然是个"商量政府",
那么如何商量,就成为一个"问题"。于是乎,周恩来就十分明确提出,
"议事精神不在于最后的表决,主要是在于事前的协商和反复的讨
论。"岁月流逝、斗转星移。时空变化,在所难免,但"跟人民商量办
事","主要是在于事前的协商和反复的讨论","真协商就要协商于决
策之前和决策之中",中国共产党人注重决策前商议的理念,真可谓是
世代相传。

习近平指出,"在人民内部各方面广泛商量的过程,就是发扬民
主、集思广益的过程,就是统一思想、凝聚共识的过程,就是科学决策、
民主决策的过程,就是实现人民当家作主的过程。这样做起来,国家治

---

① 《中共中央关于制定国民经济和社会发展第十三个五年规划的建议》,《人民日报》2015
年11月4日。

② 习近平:《在庆祝中国人民政治协商会议成立65周年大会上的讲话》,《人民日报》2014
年9月22日。

理和社会治理才能具有深厚基础,也才能凝聚起强大力量。"长期以来,中国共产党人始终坚持通过各种途径、各种渠道、各种方式就改革发展稳定重大问题特别是事关人民群众切身利益的问题进行广泛协商,既尊重多数人的意愿,又照顾少数人的合理要求,广纳群言、广集民智,增进共识、增强合力。

社会主义协商民主的实践,生动地勾勒出"有事要商量"——"有事好商量"的逻辑轨迹。商量,不仅有其重要性和必要性,而且有其可能性和实效性。这就表明了,在中国社会主义制度下,"有事好商量",众人的事情由众人商量,找到全社会意愿和要求的"最大公约数",是人民民主的真谛。"有事好商量",表明了在中国特色社会主义建设事业中,有事可以商量,有事能够商量,通过商量,最大限度地把事情办好。把"人民政府"真正办成"商量政府",商量的关键,在于三个"多商量":即:有事多商量,遇事多商量,做事多商量,总之,"商量得越多越深入越好"。

值得注意的是,在实际工作中,不同的商量内容,要采取不同的商量范围,这也就是说,涉及全国各族人民利益的事情,要在全体人民和全社会中广泛商量;涉及一个地方人民群众利益的事情,要在这个地方的人民群众中广泛商量;涉及一部分群众利益、特定群众利益的事情,要在这部分群众中广泛商量;涉及基层群众利益的事情,要在基层群众中广泛商量。

历史和现实一再告诉人们,"在人民内部各方面广泛商量的过程,就是发扬民主、集思广益的过程,就是统一思想、凝聚共识的过程,就是科学决策、民主决策的过程,就是实现人民当家作主的过程。这样做起来,国家治理和社会治理才能具有深厚基础,也才能凝聚起强大力量。"①

"真协商就要协商于决策之前和决策之中",揭示了协商有着两种

---

① 习近平:《在庆祝中国人民政治协商会议成立 65 周年大会上的讲话》,《人民日报》2014年 9 月 22 日。

可能性：一种是"真协商"，另外一种就是"假协商"。既然"真协商就要协商于决策之前和决策之中"，那么，"假协商"的表现至少有一点，就是协商于决策之后。强调协商、商量要在决策前和决策中，说深刻，很深刻；说简单，也很简单。每个人都明白，决策以后再搞协商和商量，只能是"马后炮""事后诸葛亮"，既是深恶痛绝的"形式主义"，也是缺乏尊重、"忽悠百姓"、令人反感的"愚民政策"。

实践证明，围绕大政方针与涉及人民群众利益的相关问题，在决策之前和决策实施之中开展广泛协商，努力形成共识，避免在大的问题上出现颠覆性错误，是政党协商的重要经验。党和国家在确立重大方针政策前与各民主党派进行协商，认真听取各民主党派的意见，各民主党派围绕大政方针与涉及人民群众利益相关问题，从自己独特的角度提出意见和建议，也展现了参政党的自身优势和作用。更进一步说，决策前、决策中开展广泛协商的过程，既是我们党广泛听取民主党派意见和建议的过程，也是民主党派了解和接受我们党的政治主张，不断增强中国特色社会主义道路自信、理论自信、制度自信的过程。

协商于决策之前和决策之中的"真协商"，需要在制度建设上得以保障。近年来，中央连续就协商民主颁布了一系列文件，推动社会主义协商民主更加制度化、规范化、程序化。就加强政党协商来说，目前已明确，中共中央总书记每年固定 4 次召开协商座谈会，分别就经济社会发展的建议、半年度经济工作、中央全会文件、中央经济工作会议文件等内容，与民主党派中央和无党派人士代表协商，为推动社会主义协商民主广泛多层制度化发展丰富了内涵、拓宽了渠道。

（三）协商民主是个"舶来品"吗

有道是"言必称希腊"。一提起"协商民主"，有些人总是会自觉不自觉地马上联想起古希腊，或者都以为罗尔斯、哈贝马斯等西方学者是协商民主的"创始人"。应当充分看到，在人类社会发展的进程中，世界各国对民主的内容和形式有着名目繁多、多种多样的探索，我国的协商民主也需要对其他国家的协商民主有所了解,但不能简单、粗糙地把"协商民主"的"发明专利权",拱手让给西方,以为我国社会主义协商民主"来源"于西方,"移植"于我国。于是乎,"协商民主"成了"舶来品"——事实果真如此吗?

社会主义协商民主是中国共产党和中国人民的伟大创造,是中国社会主义民主政治的特有形式和独特优势,是中国共产党的群众路线在政治领域的重要体现。社会主义协商民主不同于西方协商民主的理论和内涵,其产生的理论源泉、制度基础、政治实践以及文化背景均有着极大的不同。社会主义协商民主深深地植根于中国历史文化,产生于近代以后中国人民革命的伟大斗争,发展于中国特色社会主义的光辉实践,是实现国家富强、民族振兴、人民幸福的重要保障。

习近平总书记曾以三个"独"、五个"源"、四个"基础"的高度概括,深刻揭示了社会主义协商民主的中国特色、中国风格、中国气派。社会主义协商民主"是中国社会主义民主政治中独特的、独有的、独到的民主形式,它源自中华民族长期形成的天下为公、兼容并蓄、求同存异等优秀政治文化,源自近代以后中国政治发展的现实进程,源自中国共产党领导人民进行革命、建设、改革的长期实践,源自新中国成立后各党派、各团体、各民族、各阶层、各界人士在政治制度上共同实现的伟大创造,源自改革开放以来中国在政治体制上的不断创新"。进而,习近平总书记既高屋建瓴、又言简意赅地总结道,社会主义协商民主,"具有深厚的文化基础、理论基础、实践基础、制度基础"。这也深刻昭示着我国社会主义协商民主,绝不是照搬照抄西方民主形式的"舶来品"。

1. 深厚的文化基础

我国是一个有着数千年的文明积淀的泱泱大国,中华传统文化博大精深,其中不仅包含了关于政治协商的思想学说和制度实践,而且在根源上显示出与协商民主相契合的文化精神和价值关切,从而成为中国当代协商民主建设的源头活水。概括起来说,其中包括了珍贵的

"天下为公""兼容并蓄""求同存异"等民本思想、价值观念、和谐精神的思想财富,与此相关联的"民惟邦本、治国为民","导民使言、兼听纳谏";"和而不同""重义轻利",以及"和合""谏言"等范畴,都为造就我国源远流长的政治协商传统,起到了重要的作用。

2. 科学的理论基础

社会主义协商民主是马克思主义基本原理同中国具体实际相结合的伟大创造和最新成果,是中国特色社会主义理论体系的重要内容,具有独到牢固的理论基础。这其中主要包括:

一是马克思主义有关政党理论、国家理论,以及民主政治理论。马克思主义提出的关于无产阶级政党必须坚持领导权,就应该团结其他工人政党,应该与其他民主政党结成同盟的观点;关于国家的起源和本质、无产阶级夺取政权以及应该如何运用无产阶级政权等观点;关于资产阶级革命实现了在私有制基础上的政治民主,但它是少数人的、虚假的民主等观点,都为社会主义协商民主建设提供重要的理论指导。

二是我们党有关统一战线理论。作为"三大法宝"之一,统一战线一直贯穿于中国的革命、建设和改革开放实践,团结一切可以团结的力量、最大限度调动一切积极因素,既是其核心精神,也是我们党治国理政的一条宝贵经验。社会主义协商民主既坚持人民民主的原则,又贯彻团结和谐的要求,是对统一战线理论的灵活运用和创造性发展。

三是我们党有关群众路线的理论。我们党始终坚持群众路线,代表最广大人民群众的根本利益,紧紧依靠人民治国理政、管理社会,广泛听取人民内部各方面的意见和建议,接受人民的监督。站在新的历史起点,我党强调社会主义协商民主是党的群众路线在政治领域的重要体现,协商于民、协商为民,展现出社会主义协商民主的价值追求。

3. 坚实的实践基础

社会主义协商民主根植于中国广袤的土壤,是中国共产党领导人民在长期的革命、建设和改革开放的伟大实践中,不断探索中国特色社会主义政治发展道路的必然结果。新民主主义革命时期,中国共产党在"三三制"民主政权建设中有效地进行了协商民主实践,开启了中国协商民主的萌芽和雏形。1948年4月30日,"五一"劳动节前夕,中国共产党为动员全国各阶层人民实现建立新中国的光荣使命,发布了具有重要历史意义的纪念"五一"劳动节口号,号召各民主党派、无党派人士和社会贤达迅速召开政治协商会议,并得到了社会各界的踊跃响应,为协商建国吹响了胜利的前奏曲。1949年9月,中华人民共和国第一届政治协商会议召开,协商建立中华人民共和国,正式确立中国共产党领导的多党合作和政治协商制度,标志着协商民主这种新型民主形式开始在全国范围内实施。

值得提出并关注的是,这一时期的全国政协,发挥着"特殊"的作用,具有"双重"的属性。一方面,它是人民民主统一战线的组织形式;另一方面,它又是中央国家政权的组织形式,在当时属于最高权力机关——全国人民代表大会的替代形式。这是当时历史条件下政治协商会议的特殊性质和历史作用。历史的时针到了1954年9月,第一届全国人民代表大会第一次会议召开,人民代表大会制度成为国家的根本政治制度。全国政协不再具有以前曾经具有的替代全国人民代表大会的性质和作用。这时,全国政协面临着两种"前途":一种是由于不再发挥替代人民代表大会的作用,而退出历史舞台;一种是虽然不再发挥替代人民代表大会的作用,但是仍然作为人民民主统一战线的组织形式保留下来。智慧的中国人民和中国共产党人,选择了"后者",予以"保留"。历史证明,这是一个正确的选择。正是这一个具有深远意义的选择,开辟了具有中国特色的人民民主两种实践形式的道路。

改革开放以来,社会主义协商民主在继承中发展、在发展中完善。从党的十三大提出"建立社会协商对话制度"构想,到2007年《中国的政党制度》白皮书首次提出"选举民主"和"协商民主"概念、再到党的十八大和十八届三中全会作出健全社会主义协商民主制度,推进社会主义协商民主广泛多层制度化发展的战略部署,我国已逐步形成了符合中国国情的协商渠道,协商民主从党际协商向社会协商不断拓展,从

政治领域向社会生活领域不断拓展,从国家层面向地方和基层不断
拓展。

4. 系统的制度基础

我国社会主义协商民主基本形成了以宪法为根本保障、以基本政
治制度为重要支撑、以党的方针政策为实践依据的较为完备的制度
体系。

首先,国家宪法这一根本大法,为社会主义协商民主的发展和完善
提供了法律保障,从法律的角度,强调了坚持和发展人民政协、统一战
线、政治协商制度等的重要作用和意义;

其次,基本的政治制度和一系列重要文献的颁发,是巩固和发展社
会主义协商民主的重要支撑,形成了国家层面的政治协商、国家与社会
之间的社会协商,以及社会层面的公民协商这一具有中国特色的协商
民主体系。简要地作一梳理:1949 年的协商建国,标志着中国共产党
领导的多党合作和政治协商制度正式确立;1989 年年底,中共中央颁
布《关于坚持和完善中国共产党领导的多党合作和政治协商制度的意
见》,把中国共产党领导的多党合作和政治协商制度作为我国的基本
政治制度;1997 年,党的十五大将其纳入社会主义初级阶段的三大基
本纲领之一;2005 年,中共中央下发《关于进一步加强中国共产党领导
的多党合作和政治协商制度建设的意见》,对多党合作和政治协商制
度作了进一步的重申和强化。2012 年,党的十八大作出了一个十分重
要的决定,通过党代会把协商民主作为人民民主的一种重要形式确立
起来,健全社会主义协商民主制度。党的十八大以后,党中央又相继颁
发了《中共中央关于加强社会主义协商民主建设的意见》《关于加强
人民政协协商民主建设的实施意见》,对在新形势下推进社会主义协
商民主建设,有着重要的理论意义和实践意义。

最后,党的一系列方针政策是社会主义协商民主建设的基本依据。
当前,健全社会主义协商民主制度、推进社会主义协商民主广泛多层制
度化发展,在指导思想、基本原则、工作举措、协商渠道、协商程序、工作

保障等方面,都有了明确的要求,是推进社会主义协商民主的行动指南和重要遵循,在实践中得以认真的贯彻和落实。

(四) 在当代中国,既然能够实行"多党合作", 为什么不能实行"多党制"

乍一看,"多党合作"和"多党制"这两个概念十分"相似",都嵌入了"多党"的意思,但实际上两者有天壤之别,存在着本质的区别。"世界这么大",各国有着各自不同的国情。选择什么样的政治制度如同选择什么样的发展道路一样,是各国人民的自主选择。当代中国实行"多党合作",而不是行"多党制",同样是中国人民的自主选择。这是中国特色社会主义的政党制度,也是当代中国的一项基本政治制度,是马克思主义政党理论、统一战线理论、社会主义民主政治理论同中国具体实践相结合的伟大创造。另一方面,深入分析西方"多党制"的实质,有益于我们明确这一政治制度不适合我国国情,进而坚定走中国特色社会主义政治发展道路。诚然,我们也不应对实行"多党制"的国家予以过多的评价、更不能加以一味指责。问题在于,"多党合作",不是"多党制";"一党执政",不是"一党专政";中国共产党与民主党派之间,更不是"执政党"与"在野党""反对党"之间的关系。事关这些重大理论问题,是来不得半点的"马虎"和"含糊"的。

我国不能实行"多党制",是人民的选择,也是历史的选择。正如习近平指出的那样,"在中国建立什么样的政治制度,是近代以后中国人民面临的一个历史性课题。为解决这一历史性课题,中国人民进行了艰辛探索。"[1]"往事并不如烟"。在中国近现代史上,不少人曾经把资本主义"多党制"当作是包治百病的"救国良方",辛亥革命以后,又纷纷仿效西方这一政治制度,霎时间政党林立,一度达到300多个,但

---

[1] 习近平:《在庆祝中国人民政治协商会议成立65周年大会上的讲话》,《人民日报》2014年9月22日。

最后都以"草草收场"而告终，都未能改变中华民族落后挨打的态势。抗日战争胜利以后，又有人主张走"第三条道路"，仍然要扯起"多党制"的这面旗号，但实行专制独裁统治的国民党粉碎了这些人的幻想。历史一再表明，"多党制"在中国"走不通"，这是以鲜血和生命所换得的沉痛经验。

习近平以高超的辩证法思维作出以下鲜明的判断，值得我们认真学习和把握："设计和发展国家政治制度，必须注重历史和现实、理论和实践、形式和内容有机统一。要坚持从国情出发、从实际出发，既要把握长期形成的历史传承，又要把握走过的发展道路、积累的政治经验、形成的政治原则，还要把握现实要求、着眼解决现实问题，不能割断历史，不能想象突然就搬来一座政治制度上的'飞来峰'。"他还进一步指出，"政治制度是用来调节政治关系、建立政治秩序、推动国家发展、维护国家稳定的，不可能脱离特定社会政治条件来抽象评判，不可能千篇一律、归于一尊"；他特别强调："在政治制度上，看到别的国家有而我们没有就简单认为有欠缺，要搬过来；或者，看到我们有而别的国家没有就简单认为是多余的，要去除掉。这两种观点都是简单化的、片面的，因而都是不正确的。"①

"橘生淮南则为橘，生于淮北则为枳"。照抄照搬他国的政治制度行不通，会水土不服，会画虎不成反类犬，甚至会把国家前途命运葬送掉。不顾自己的实际国情，照搬照抄他国的模式，昨天行不通、今天行不通、明天还是行不通；先前行不通、当下行不通、今后和将来，仍然行不通。总之，"只有扎根本国土壤、汲取充沛养分的制度，才最可靠、也最管用"，"中国特色社会主义政治制度过去和现在一直生长在中国的社会土壤之中，未来要继续茁壮成长，也必须深深扎根于中国的社会土壤"②。这些经典论述，理当铭记在心。

---

① 习近平：《在庆祝中国人民政治协商会议成立 65 周年大会上的讲话》，《人民日报》2014年 9 月 22 日。
② 习近平：《在庆祝中国人民政治协商会议成立 65 周年大会上的讲话》，《人民日报》2014年 9 月 22 日。

需要指出的是,"多党合作"只是"简称",规范的表述是"中国共产党领导的多党合作和政治协商制度",虽然字数比较多,但必须完整、准确理解,尤其是"中国共产党领导"不能省略。习近平明确指出,"中国共产党的领导是包括各民主党派、各团体、各民族、各阶层、各界人士在内的全体中国人民的共同选择,是中国特色社会主义最本质的特征,也是人民政协事业发展进步的根本保证。"①概言之,中国共产党的领导,是首要的前提和根本的保证,多党合作是核心内容。共产党领导、多党派合作,共产党执政、多党派参政,这是我们中国特色社会主义政党制度的显著特征。

1. 实行中国共产党领导的多党合作和政治协商制度,体现了社会主义民主政治的本质要求

在政党的相互关系方面,共产党处于领导地位。这种领导地位是中国人民和各民主党派在长期革命、建设和改革实践中的正确选择和国情使然。在当代中国,没有任何一个政党能够取代共产党从而成为13亿人民的领导核心。各民主党派也都清醒地认识到接受中国共产党领导的重要性、必要性和现实意义,有着接受共产党领导、真诚合作、共同奋斗的愿望。

在政党与国家政权的关系上,共产党是执政党,各民主党派是参政党。共产党的执政地位是历史形成的,是宪法赋予并明确规定的。民主党派的参政党地位是根据其在历史上和当代中国政治生活中的有益作用确立的。民主党派作为各自所联系的一部分社会主义劳动者、社会主义建设者和拥护社会主义的爱国者的政治联盟,在共产党领导下参加国家政权、参与社会事务管理,是人民民主的重要体现。这与那些"一党制""两党制"及"多党制"均有所不同。在我国,民主党派作为参政党,其参政地位受到法律保护,各民主党派在分享国家政权、共同

---

① 习近平:《在庆祝中国人民政治协商会议成立 65 周年大会上的讲话》,《人民日报》2014年 9 月 22 日。

向人民负责的基础上同共产党实行广泛与密切的合作。各民主党派和无党派人士在各级权力机关中均占有一定比例,各级人大、政府、法院、检察院中都有民主党派成员、无党派人士担任领导职务。

从政党和社会的关系看,各民主党派同共产党团结合作,共同担负起社会管理职能。在当代中国,由执政的共产党承担领导社会管理的职能是理所当然的。但随着市场经济的深入发展,社会结构分化重组,出现了许多新兴社会阶层和群体。民主党派与许多新兴社会阶层有着历史的、天然的密切联系,这样就形成了共产党代表最广大人民群众,民主党派和无党派人士代表各自所联系的一部分社会阶层和群体,共同致力于社会主义建设事业的局面。多党合作和政治协商制度有利于发挥民主党派广泛联系不同社会阶层和群体的政治优势,协同执政党做好领导社会管理的工作。

2. 实行中国共产党领导的多党合作和政治协商制度,有利于国家政治生活民主化

这一基本政治制度是实现人民当家作主的重要形式,丰富了民主的形式,使各民主党派、无党派人士广泛参加国家和社会管理,促进决策的民主化和科学化,为发扬社会主义民主、实现国家政治生活民主化提供了重要保障。中国共产党领导的多党合作和政治协商制度是民主协商的重要实践。各民主党派以参政党身份参加对国家大政方针的政治协商和对国家事务的民主监督,在各个领域与共产党合作共事,推进了国家政治生活民主化。

3. 实行中国共产党领导的多党合作和政治协商制度,有着重要的维护社会稳定的功能

历史和现实都表明,一个世界上最大的发展中国家进行现代化建设,需要共产党这个强有力的领导核心;同时,社会转型、利益多元化等客观形势的变化,要求有更加有效的民主参与。多党合作有助于形成多元利益表达渠道,动员广泛的社会政治资源,解决各种利益矛盾,化解利益冲突,促进社会稳定,把民主党派、无党派人士所联系的那部分群众的积极性、创造性充分调动起来,充分发挥其聪明才智,妥善处理人民内部矛盾和协调各种利益关系。

4. 实行中国共产党领导的多党合作和政治协商制度,有利于加强和改善共产党的领导

通过政党之间的互相监督,尤其是民主党派和无党派人士对共产党的监督,能够使执政党随时听到不同的意见和批评,更好地接受人民群众的愿望和诉求,克服和纠正官僚主义、以权谋私等不正之风,及时改正错误。民主党派的监督职能是有效防止执政党腐败的重要机制。加强和改善共产党的领导,必须改善执政方式,建立健全适合国情的人民民主监督机制,使党和国家机关更好地接受人民群众的监督。当然,中国共产党与民主党派的相互监督,是在四项基本原则基础上,通过提出批评、意见、建议,通过调研和磋商等方式进行的政治监督,是多党合作的一种重要形式,目的是更好地致力于共同事业,实现共同目标,而不是为了把对方搞垮。这种相互监督是积极的、善意的、良性的,同西方政党之间相互倾轧、尔虞我诈那一套,有着根本的不同。正如习近平所言,"我们要坚持和完善中国共产党领导的多党合作和政治协商制度,加强社会各种力量的合作协调,切实防止出现党争纷沓、相互倾轧的现象",总之,"我们要坚持发挥党总揽全局、协调各方的领导核心作用,提高党科学执政、民主执政、依法执政水平,保证党领导人民有效治理国家,切实防止出现群龙无首、一盘散沙的现象"。①

■ 思考题

1. 什么是"社会主义协商民主"?

2. 为什么在中国不能实行"多党制"?

_____

① 习近平:《在庆祝全国人民代表大会成立 60 周年大会上的讲话》,《人民日报》2014 年 9 月 6 日。

参考文献

1. 习近平:《在庆祝中国人民政治协商会议成立 65 周年大会上的讲话》,《人民日报》2014 年 9 月 22 日。

2. 习近平:《在庆祝全国人民代表大会成立 60 周年大会上的讲话》,《人民日报》2014 年 9 月 6 日。

3.《中共中央关于制定国民经济和社会发展第十三个五年规划的建议》,新华社,2015 年 11 月 3 日。

五、塑造中国精神

我们党始终把思想建设放在党的建设第一位,强调"革命理想高于天",就是精神变物质、物质变精神的辩证法。我们必须毫不放松理想信念教育、思想道德建设、意识形态工作,大力培育和弘扬社会主义核心价值观,用富有时代气息的中国精神凝聚中国力量。——习近平在主持中央政治局第二十次集体学习时强调(2015 年 1 月 23 日)

中国特色社会主义是经济社会全面发展的社会主义新形态,社会主义文化建设是全面发展的一个重要方面。党的十八大以来,习近平非常重视先进文化及精神文明的建设,他从实现中华民族伟大复兴中国梦的角度提出,我们不仅要有物质财富的极大丰富,还要有精神财富的极大丰富。我们要继续锲而不舍、一以贯之抓好社会主义精神文明建设,要加强对中华优秀传统文化的挖掘和阐发,努力实现中华传统美德的创造性转化和创新性发展,为全国各族人民不断前进提供坚强的思想保证、强大的精神力量、丰润的道德滋养。只有人民有信仰,民族才有希望,国家就有力量。

(一) 为什么说意识形态工作是党的一项极端重要的工作

习近平在 2013 年全国宣传思想工作会议的讲话(以下简称"8·19 讲话")中指出,"经济建设是党的中心工作,意识形态工作是党的一项极端重要的工作。"在习近平的这一论断中,经济建设与意识形态工作并列提出,意识形态工作不是重要而已,而是"极端重要",揭示了社会主义文化建设的核心问题。

1.意识形态工作是党的一项极端重要的工作

历史和现实告诉我们,能否做好意识形态工作,事关党的前途命运,事关国家长治久安,事关民族凝聚力和向心力。国家既要有硬实力,也要有软实力,既要切实做好中心工作、为意识形态工作提供坚实物质基础,又要切实做好意识形态工作、为中心工作提供有力保障;既不能因为中心工作而忽视意识形态工作,也不能使意识形态工作游离于中心工作。忽视意识形态工作则后患无穷,这方面有着深刻教训。1989 年发生的北京政治风波,邓小平同志就明确认为这是党内思想政治工作、意识形态工作失误的后果。而在国际上,邓小平同志在 1992 年南方谈话中说:"苏联这么强的国家,几个月一下子就垮了。如果中国不接受这个教训,在苗头出现时不注意,就如戈尔巴乔夫那样的'新思维'出来以后没注意那样,就会出事。"①

我们要坚持唯物辩证法,要深刻认识经济基础对上层建筑的决定作用,也要深刻认识上层建筑对经济基础的反作用——忽视意识形态工作就是不承认这一反作用。事实证明,国家发展好了,意识形态和宣传思想工作就好做;反过来说,意识形态和宣传思想工作做好了,国家才能发展得更好。意识形态工作属于精神文明建设的范畴,只有物质文明建设和精神文明建设都搞好,中国特色社会主义事业才能顺利向前推进。

2. 意识形态工作面临所未有的挑战和困难

对于意识形态工作的实际状态,习近平在"8·19讲话"中高屋建瓴地指出,我们正在进行具有许多新的历史特点的伟大斗争,面临的挑战和困难前所未有,必须坚持巩固壮大主流思想舆论,弘扬主旋律,传播正能量,激发全社会团结奋进的强大力量。

为什么说我们"面临的挑战和困难前所未有"呢?这一论断基于当前我国意识形态领域存在十分复杂的情况:由于改革进入深水区,各种社会矛盾在利益诉求的驱动下有所激化,人们的价值取向呈现出"独立性、选择性、多变性、差异性"的局面;与此同时,西方敌对势力对我国实施西化、分化举措从来没有停止过,思想文化领域是长期渗透的重点领域;在此背景下,加上网络化时代的技术特征,各种不同利益诉求、不同价值观和文化追求,甚至个人的情绪宣泄,都在网络上得到快速传播和蔓延。那些对中国共产党、社会主义基本制度、中国特色社会主义建设成就心怀不满的人,都会通过网络进行诽谤、造谣、污名化等破坏活动,以历史虚无主义、新自由主义等为代表的错误思潮也异常顽固,不时泛滥;而在意识形态的领导权方面,存在着不同程度的"软弱涣散"状态。

---

① 吴松营:《邓小平南方讲话真情实录》,人民出版社 2012 年版,第 66—67 页。

3. 巩固马克思主义在意识形态领域的指导地位

种种问题都指向意识形态领导权状态,首要的解决之途亦在于此。习近平强调,意识形态和宣传思想工作就是"要巩固马克思主义在意识形态领域的指导地位,巩固全党全国人民团结奋斗的共同思想基础。党员、干部要坚定马克思主义、共产主义信仰,脚踏实地为实现党在现阶段的基本纲领而不懈努力,扎扎实实做好每一项工作,取得'接力赛'中我们这一棒的优异成绩"。

在马克思主义指引下解决中国的社会发展道路问题、实现中华民族的伟大复兴,这就是一代又一代中国共产党人的"接力赛",马克思主义就是我们的"接力棒"。习近平尖锐批评了一种现象:"在我们党员、干部队伍中,信仰缺失是一个需要引起高度重视的问题。在一些人那里,有的以批评和嘲讽马克思主义为'时尚'、为噱头。"[①]

因此,习近平特别关注领导干部这一"关键少数",强调领导干部特别是高级干部要把系统掌握马克思主义基本理论作为"看家本领",老老实实、原原本本地学习。各级党校、干部学院、社会科学院、高校、理论学习中心组等都要把马克思主义作为必修课,成为马克思主义学习、研究、宣传的重要阵地,让各级干部学会运用马克思主义立场、观点、方法观察和解决问题,坚定理想信念。

4. 坚持团结稳定鼓劲、正面宣传为主的重要方针

首先,党的领导在事关大是大非和政治原则问题上,必须增强主动性、掌握主动权、打好主动仗。所谓"主动",就是要保持政治敏锐性,洞察形势,帮助干部群众划清是非界限、澄清模糊认识。特别是对于西方敌对势力散布的政治价值观,对于那些身在体制内,吃共产党的饭却砸共产党的锅的人,必须断然表示拒绝。各级领导决不能为了赢得所

---

① 中共中央纪律检查委员会、中共中央文献研究室:《习近平关于党风廉政建设和反腐败斗争论述摘编》,中央文献出版社、中国方正出版社 2015 年版,第 17 页。

谓"开明绅士"的名誉,"爱惜羽毛",放弃政治原则。宣传思想部门必须守土有责、守土负责、守土尽责。

其次,既要总结经验,又要善于创新,抓好理念创新、手段创新、基层工作创新。当前社会上思想活跃、观念碰撞,互联网等新技术新媒介日新月异,只有审时度势、因势利导,创新内容和载体,改进方式和方法,才能使意识形态工作和精神文明建设始终充满生机活力。关键是要提高质量和水平,把握好时、度、效,增强吸引力和感染力,让群众爱听爱看、产生共鸣,充分发挥正面宣传鼓舞人、激励人的作用。

有理由坚信,只要全党动手做好意识形态这一极端重要的工作,我们就能实现习近平在2015年新春的展望:"人民有信仰,民族有希望,国家有力量。"

(二) 如何在世界文化激荡中站稳脚跟

在民族国家时代,文化必然具有民族性。在由西方现代性开启的全球化时代,中华文化与西方文化及世界文化的关系是不可回避的问题,正确处理这个问题是中国文化建设的重要方面。在中西方文化关系中,中华文化的基本定位是什么呢? 习近平指出,培育和弘扬社会主义核心价值观必须立足中华优秀传统文化。习近平还站在历史的制高点上,审时度势,开创性地提出"博大精深的中华优秀传统文化是我们在世界文化激荡中站稳脚跟的根基"这一命题。回望中西方文化关系史,可以说习近平的论断扭转了近代以来中华文化的颓势,意义非凡。

1. 中华文化为中华民族提供丰厚滋养

中华民族有五千年的文明史,创造了源远流长的古老文化。为什么别的古老文明衰落了,而中华文明却从未发生根本的断裂呢? 习近平在一系列讲话中回答了这个问题,他说:"在几千年的历史流变中,中华民族从来不是一帆风顺的,遇到了无数艰难困苦,但我们都挺过来、走过来了,其中一个很重要的原因就是世世代代的中华儿女培育和发展了独具特色、博大精深的中华文化,为中华民族克服困难、生生不息提供了强大精神支撑。"①首先来说,中华文化为中华民族提供了创新精神。我们的先人们早就提出:"周虽旧邦,其命维新。""天行健,君子以自强不息。""苟日新,日日新,又日新。"可以说,创新精神是中华民族最鲜明的禀赋。在5000多年的文明发展进程中,中华民族创造了高度发达的文明,我们的先人们发明了造纸术、火药、印刷术、指南针,在天文、算学、医学、农学等多个领域创造了累累硕果,为世界贡献了无数科技创新成果,对世界文明进步影响深远、贡献巨大,也使我国长期居于世界强国之列。

其次表现在中华文化的变通性上。在5000多年的文明发展进程中,中华民族创造了博大精深的灿烂文化,中华文化在坚守自身时,很早就意识到了"文明因交流而多彩,文明因互鉴而丰富"的道理,在长期演化过程中,中华文明从与其他文明的交流中获得了丰富营养,也为人类文明进步作出了重要贡献。丝绸之路的开辟,遣隋遣唐使大批来华,法显、玄奘西行取经,郑和七下远洋,等等,都是中外文明交流互鉴的生动事例。对人类社会创造的各种文明,无论是古代的中华文明、希腊文明、罗马文明、埃及文明、两河文明、印度文明等,还是现在的亚洲文明、非洲文明、欧洲文明、美洲文明、大洋洲文明等,我们都应该采取学习借鉴的态度,都应该积极吸纳其中的有益成分。通过文化自信以及文明的交流和互鉴,中国人民的理想和奋斗,中国人民的价值观和精神世界,既始终深深植根于中国优秀传统文化沃土之中,同时又随着历史和时代前进而不断与日俱新、与时俱进。

2. 中华文化的新崛起

由于中国拥有悠久的古老文明,在许多方面领先于西方,因而在中

---

① 习近平:《在文艺工作座谈会上的讲话》(2014年),《人民日报》2015年10月15日。

西方文化关系中,18世纪还一度形成了"中学西渐"的局面,中国"开始被推举为模范文明"。但是,到了19世纪,西方在工业革命的带动下全面开启了全球化进程。1840年,中英鸦片战争爆发,中国在自己的土地上战败,被迫向西方打开国门。在强大的西方工业文明面前,关注并学习西方成为近代中国有识之士的思想选择。从19世纪末到20世纪初所发生的这一幕,无论中国人的主观情感反应如何,客观上显示的就是中国传统文化的颓势。从百年巨变的角度来看待中国传统文化的颓势,辩证分析的结论是:其积极意义是导致中国文明发生现代转型,而其消极意义便是打击了中国人的文化自信心。

自鸦片战争以来,经过170多年的国家探寻,今天的中国已经重新崛起,成为世界第二大经济体,其对世界经济的贡献超过了1/3。中国已经发展起来了,中华民族被外族任意欺凌的时代已经一去不复返了。现在,中国的国际地位不断提高、国际影响力不断扩大,这是中国人民用自己的百年奋斗赢得的尊敬。

从文化意义上说,中国的崛起意味着中华文化的颓势已经终结,中华文化已经自立于世界文化之林,"言必称西方"的时代已经过去,中国人应该具有新的文化自觉。

3. 中国特色社会主义道路是中国历史传承和文化传统决定的

习近平在深入思考中国发展道路的历史路径时,运用马克思主义的辩证法对近百年中国思想文化史进行理性反思:在肯定西方先进文化对中国现代化的积极意义时,透视出表象之下的另一面——中国优秀传统文化尽管一度处于守势,但从来就没有完全断裂过,而是在不断纠正西方文化之偏颇,开辟中国自己的发展道路。

习近平从文化与国家发展之间的关系角度指出:中华优秀传统文化是我们最深厚的文化软实力,也是中国特色社会主义植根的文化沃土。每个国家和民族的历史传统、文化积淀、基本国情不同,其发展道路必然有着自己的特色。数千年来,中华民族走着一条不同于其他国家和民族的文明发展道路。我们开辟了中国特色社会主义道路不是偶然的,是我国历史传承和文化传统决定的。

如何理解中国特色社会主义道路"是我国历史传承和文化传统决定的"呢?表面上看,20世纪初的新文化运动导致了对中国传统文化统治地位的放弃,也收获了对西方文化的开放式吸收,但是,在中国道路的展开过程中,中国优秀传统文化的潜在影响以及对形形色色的西化诉求的拒绝,却成了实际上的主旋律。

习近平在回顾中国近代史时指出,为了挽救民族危亡、实现民族振兴,中国人民和无数仁人志士孜孜不倦寻找着适合国情的政治制度模式。辛亥革命之前,太平天国运动、洋务运动、戊戌变法、义和团运动、清末新政等都未能取得成功;辛亥革命之后,中国尝试过君主立宪制、帝制复辟、议会制、多党制、总统制等各种形式,各种政治势力及其代表人物纷纷登场,都没能找到正确答案,只有中国共产党领导的革命才从根本上改变了近代以后中国内忧外患、任人宰割的悲惨命运。而中国共产党领导的革命恰恰是从中国国情出发的,是将马克思主义与中国优秀传统文化相结合的。习近平实际上揭示出20世纪中国革命具有一种高度的文化自觉意识,并在这种自觉意识的引领下正确探寻中国的道路,中国道路的文化意义就在于反思西化。

今天,中国已经发展起来,但民族复兴的中国梦还未完全实现,全面深化改革的任务还未完成,保持中国发展道路的中国特色依然是我们的历史自觉意识。习近平说得好,中国有960多万平方公里土地、56个民族,我们能照谁的模式办?谁又能指手画脚告诉我们该怎么办?照抄照搬他国的政治制度行不通,会水土不服,会画虎不成反类犬,甚至会把国家前途命运葬送掉。只有扎根本国土壤、汲取充沛养分的制度,才最可靠、也最管用。需知,"本国土壤"之重要内涵就是优秀的传统文化。

面对历史,面对中国的发展道路,有什么理由怀疑中华文化是我们在世界文化激荡中站稳脚跟的根基呢?没有。

（三）为什么说构建核心价值观是国家治理
体系和治理能力的重要方面

2013 年党的十八届三中全会提出了"国家治理体系和治理能力现代化"这一概念,引起高度关注,引发社会热议,其中有一个倾向是以现代西方政治理念作为参照来解读,有意或无意地忽略中国历史文化背景,而习近平 2014 年 2 月 24 日的讲话则凸显了中国历史文化背景,纠正了某些偏颇。

1. 中国传统政治哲学对"两个关系"的验证

为什么说核心价值观建设是国家治理体系和治理能力的重要方面呢? 习近平同志提出了"两个关系",一是关系社会和谐稳定,一是关系国家长治久安,应该说,"两个关系"早已得到中国传统政治哲学、首先是秦汉之际的政治哲学的验证。

中国历史上不断混战的战国时期是以秦灭六国为终结的,鉴于秦以暴力而取天下的路径,汉朝最初的统治者也迷信"马上而得之"的治理方式,不屑于运用《诗》、《书》这些儒家经典去构建价值观。直到汉武帝时,为了国家治理的长期性,著名儒生董仲舒以周秦为例,说周之失掉天下是由于"大为亡道",而秦同样如此。因此,"今师异道,人异论,百家殊方,指意不同,是以上亡以持一统,法制数变,下不知所守。臣愚以为诸不在六艺之科、孔子之术者,皆绝其道,勿使并进。邪辟之说灭息,然后统纪可一而法度可明,民知所从矣。"董仲舒的意思是,如果社会没有统一的"道",即价值观,大众就会不知道应该坚守什么。解决这个问题,就必须统一对"道"的阐释与提倡,使"邪辟之说灭息",民众便知道如何行事了。这就是历史上有名的"罢黜百家,独尊儒术"。①

---

① 《汉书·董仲舒传》。

由于董仲舒的献策与汉武帝的采纳,克服了社会治理问题上的无为而治的乌托邦倾向,也克服了单纯依靠政治统治、忽视人的思想观念培养的硬性方式,从而奠定了价值观建设对社会稳定、国家治理的正面意义,确认了社会价值观的核心诉求。

关于儒家价值观对中国社会治理乃至中国文明延续的积极意义,历史一直在予以证明。德国前总理施密特在近期与中国学者的对话中指出,三千年前已经存在的古文明不止中国一个,还有埃及、伊朗、希腊、罗马。但那些古文明都已经消逝了,可是中国依然存在,而且又突然复兴了。他注意到,在中国的文明史过程中,儒学差不多覆盖了一半。

在世界现代性潮流的冲击之下,"独尊儒术"的文化格局于 19 世纪后期逐渐式微,民族复兴与追求社会主义目标的革命成为 20 世纪中国的主旋律。引人注目的一个事实是,尽管儒家思想本身在革命过程中是处在遭受批评的地位上,但是,革命在改变旧制度、建立新制度的同时,中国共产党人继承了中国文化中一贯重视价值观建设的传统,制度革命与人的改造、道德的升华一同发展。美国著名学者莫里斯·迈斯纳说,"为了研究中国共产党的意识形态,弄清楚价值观与目标之间的相互关系,真正理解后者如何使前者变得'有意义',乃是特别重要的事。"他认为毛泽东的马克思主义中最大也是最有意义的特点就是,"普及正确的社会价值观并在普及过程中使之内在化,创造共产主义社会的物质前提,共产主义才会实现"①。

应该说,习近平同志的论断既继承了中国文化的优良传统,也继承了中国共产党自身历史上的优良传统,符合社会治理的客观规律。

2.核心价值观建设要适应国家治理体系和治理能力现代化

社会历史是发展的,一般地肯定核心价值观建设是国家治理体系

---

① 莫里斯·迈斯纳:《马克思主义、毛泽东主义与乌托邦主义》,中国人民大学出版社 2005 年版,第 104 页。

和治理能力的重要方面还不够,党的十八届三中全会提出了"国家治理体系和治理能力现代化",这就产生了核心价值观建设适应"国家治理体系和治理能力现代化"的问题。

在另一场合,习近平指出,"推进国家治理体系和治理能力现代化,要大力培育和弘扬社会主义核心价值体系和核心价值观,加快构建充分反映中国特色、民族特性、时代特征的价值体系。要加强对中华优秀传统文化的挖掘和阐发,努力实现中华传统美德的创造性转化、创新性发展,把跨越时空、超越国度、富有永恒魅力、具有当代价值的文化精神弘扬起来,把继承优秀传统文化又弘扬时代精神、立足本国又面向世界的当代中国文化创新成果传播出去。"①这就是说,社会主义核心价值观必须以自身的现代化,去适应国家治理体系和治理能力的现代化。

关于国家治理体系和治理能力的现代化之必然性,习近平指出,国家治理体系和治理能力是一个国家的制度和制度执行能力的集中体现,两者相辅相成。我们的国家治理体系和治理能力总体上是好的,是有独特优势的,是适应我国国情和发展要求的。同时,我们在国家治理体系和治理能力方面还有许多亟待改进的地方,在提高国家治理能力上需要下更大气力。可以理解为,现代化就是针对那些"许多亟待改进的地方"而言的,改进了才能说实现了国家治理体系和治理能力的现代化。

比如"民主"这个价值范畴,在共产党人的思想体系中,民主的原则与无产阶级、人民大众的价值取向是完全吻合的。以人口的绝大多数为自己的道义出发点,这本身就体现了民主的要求。因而,党的十八届三中全会突出强调了坚持人民主体地位和发展社会主义民主政治,国家治理要以保证人民当家做主为根本。必须从社会根本制度的设计到基础社会机制的运行上,有助于健全民主制度、丰富民主形式。由此,与国家治理体系和治理能力的现代化中的民主诉求相适应的是,社

---

① 《习近平在省部级主要领导干部学习贯彻十八届三中全会精神全面深化改革专题研讨班开班式上发表重要讲话》,《人民日报》2014 年 2 月 18 日。

会主义核心价值观的 24 个字中,民主也被列为基本范畴,使得国家制度的现代化得到现代化价值观在理念上的支持。

的确,民主自由这样的概念在来源上与西方文化有着更密切的联系,源于希腊字"demos"的民主意为人民,在西方文化中,民主权利的实现与个体的自由选择是密切相关的。24 个字的社会主义核心价值观确认民主自由,说明社会主义核心价值观的现代化构建是符合文化发展规律的。习近平在承认文化的"跨越时空、超越国度、富有永恒魅力、具有当代价值"的特性的基础上,提出了"继承优秀传统文化又弘扬时代精神、立足本国又面向世界"的要求,这意味着,价值观建设既然要弘扬时代精神,面向世界,那就必须把世界文明广泛承认的民主、自由这些范畴吸收进来。只是说,中国不会由于这一吸收而听命于国外势力的支配,中国会坚持自己对于民主、自由这些范畴的中国特色社会主义的理解。

(四) 为什么要对"去中国化"现象说"不"

习近平 2014 年 9 月 9 日在北京师范大学考察时,谈到课本中的古诗词问题,用了"'去中国化'是很悲哀的"这一重要判断。在一个月后的文艺工作座谈会上,进一步明确指出,"增强文化自觉和文化自信,是坚定道路自信、理论自信、制度自信的题中应有之义。如果'以洋为尊'、'以洋为美'、'唯洋是从',把作品在国外获奖作为最高追求,跟在别人后面亦步亦趋、东施效颦,热衷于'去思想化'、'去价值化'、'去历史化'、'去中国化'、'去主流化'那一套,绝对是没有前途的!"[1]这表明他敏锐地感觉到,在当下所谓"全球化"的浪潮中,存在着一种文化危险——唯西方文化是瞻,以"去中国化"为荣,长此以往,西化、分化的图谋将轻而易举地实现,中华民族复兴的中国梦也许将毁于此。

---

① 习近平:《在文艺工作座谈会上的讲话》(2014 年),《人民日报》2015 年 10 月 15 日。

1. 直面西方文化冲击中国传统文化的现象

不必讳言,自改革开放以来,西方文化产品大量进入中国,对中国传统文化的冲击是前所未有的。对中国文化版图的变化,美国《纽约时报》2002 年 2 月 25 日载文称:

"在过去几年里,中国的大城市以惊人的速度冒出了美国商店和餐厅,包括星巴克、普尔斯马特、必胜客、麦当劳以及 Esprit 服装店等。新建的住宅小区用上了'橘郡'和'曼哈顿花园'之类的美式名字。人们梦寐以求的豪华汽车是高档的别克车。

"欧洲人也许习惯于把麦当劳的每一个'巨无霸'汉堡包都看成是美国文化帝国主义的标志,然而中国人大多欢迎这种入侵——事实上他们已经使它成为自己的一部分。"

时间又过去了十多年,此一趋势并未减缓,在中国的诸多建筑设施中,诸如"中国的百老汇""中国的好莱坞""中国的泰晤士""东方巴黎"……屡见不鲜,似乎不扯上西方,这个地方就一钱不值。

此外,重英语而轻汉语已成痼疾。由于社会机制的存在,从幼儿园开始到中青年职业人士,无不以皓首穷经之势刻苦攻读英文,中文素养却越来越差,以至于形成庞大的英语培训产业。甚至,在我们这个以汉语为母语的国家,国内召开的学术会议,只要冠以"国际"一词,就得一律使用英语。在此背景下,课本中去掉中国古诗词,的确是"去中国化"泛滥之必然后果。

2. 本土文化被摧毁是一个民族的悲剧

如何看待全球化时代"去中国化"现象的存在呢?对全球化最早作出概括和描述的其实是马克思、恩格斯,他们在《共产党宣言》中指出:资产阶级,由于开拓了世界市场,使一切国家的生产和消费都成为世界性的了。资产阶级挖掉了工业脚下的民族基础,古老的民族工业被消灭了。它们被新的工业排挤掉了,新的工业的建立已经成为一切文明民族的生命攸关的问题。这些工业所加工的不是本地的原料,而是来自极其遥远的地区的原料；它们的产品不仅供本国消费，而且同时供世界各地消费。过去那种地方的和民族的自给自足和闭关自守状态，被各民族的各方面的互相往来和各方面的互相依赖所代替了。

"物质的生产是如此，精神的生产也是如此。各民族的精神产品成了公共财产。民族的片面性和局限性日益成为不可能，于是由许多种民族的和地方的文学形成了一种世界的文学。""资产阶级，由于一切生产工具的迅速改进，由于交通的极其便利，把一切民族甚至最野蛮的民族都卷到文明中来了。它的商品的低廉价格，是它用来摧毁一切万里长城、征服野蛮人最顽强的仇外心理的重炮。它迫使一切民族——如果它们不想灭亡的话——采用资产阶级的生产方式；它迫使它们在自己那里推行所谓的文明，即变成资产者。一句话，它按照自己的面貌为自己创造出一个世界。"①

这就是说，民族文化的被摧毁，并不是这个民族的幸事，甚至也不是中性的事件，而是民族的悲剧，是被西方资产阶级强加于上的，结果是使自己这个民族更加适合于接受西方的奴役和剥削。近代史上一度出现过"全盘西化"思潮，实质上也是"去中国化"，极端化者如胡适，他说："我们必须承认我们自己百事不如人，不但物质机械上不如人，不但政治制度不如人，并且道德不如人，知识不如人，文学不如人，音乐不如人，艺术不如人，身体不如人。"②所以必须"死心塌地地"学习西方文明。

3. 只有阻止"去中国化"，中国才能崛起。

可以说，如果不是中国共产党领导的革命实际上阻止了"去中国化"的推行，中国的重新崛起是不可能的。今天的中国，比历史上任何时期都更接近实现中华民族伟大复兴的目标，比历史上任何时期都更有信心、更有能力实现这个目标，也更应该阻止"去中国化"。

---

① 《马克思恩格斯选集》第 2 卷，人民出版社 1995 年版，第 276 页。
② 胡适：《介绍我自己的思想》，见《胡适全集》第 4 卷，安徽教育出版社 2003 年版，第 667 页。

对于中华民族的复兴,世界已经不能无动于衷了。2009 年,英国学者马丁·雅克(Martin Jacques)的新著《当中国统治世界》在英美引起极大影响。雅克认为,在 21 世纪上半叶,支离破碎的全球秩序将会代替西方统治,使得多种货币(美元、欧元以及人民币)和经济/军事影响范围(就像美国对欧洲、亚洲西南部和南亚的影响,以及中国对东亚和非洲的影响)都会受到各自文化传统的统治(欧美文化、儒家思想等)。但是他预测,在 21 世纪下半叶,具体的数字将证明一切,中国将统治世界,世界将被东方化。"在整个世界,人们会忘记过去欧美统治的辉煌成就。他们会学说普通话,而不是英语,他们会纪念郑和,而不是哥伦布;他们会学习儒家思想而不是柏拉图理论,并且他们会对中国的文艺复兴人物沈括惊叹不已,而不是对达·芬奇感到赞叹。"①对"去中国化"的批判,本质上是对"全盘西化"的批判,是对"中国特色"的自觉与自信,是对西方话语霸权的摆脱。

思考题

1. 为什么说意识形态工作是党的一项极端重要的工作?

2. 为什么说构建核心价值观是国家治理体系和治理能力的重要方面?

参考文献

1. 习近平:《在文艺工作座谈会上的讲话》(2014 年),《人民日报》2015 年 10 月 15 日。

2. 中共中央纪律检查委员会、中共中央文献研究室:《习近平关于党风廉政建设和反腐败斗争论述摘编》,北京:中央文献出版社、中国方正出版社,2015 年。

---

① 伊恩·莫里斯:《西方将主宰多久》,中信出版社 2014 年版,第 392 页。

六、改善社会民生

　　我们的人民热爱生活，期盼有更好的教育、更稳定的工作、更满意的收入、更可靠的社会保障、更高水平的医疗卫生服务、更舒适的居住条件、更优美的环境，期盼孩子们能成长得更好、工作得更好、生活得更好。人民对美好生活的向往，就是我们的奋斗目标。——习近平在十八届中央政治局常委同中外记者见面时的强调（《人民日报》2012 年 11 月 16 日）

习近平总书记特别关注民生改善与社会建设问题,多次强调民生的重要性。改善民生涉及诸多方面,就业是根本民生问题,要努力增加就业岗位;收入是热点民生问题,要努力实现劳动报酬增长和劳动生产率提高的同步;教育是长远民生问题,要努力办好人民满意的教育;社会保障是普惠托底的民生问题,要建立更加公平、可持续的社会保障制度;消除贫困是紧迫民生问题,要格外关注困难群众;等等。要求全党必须保持清醒头脑,强化底线思维,有效防范、管理、处理各种安全风险,及时有力地处置、化解社会安全所面临的挑战。要把握社会发展大势,回应社会呼声和群众关切,创新社会治理体制,提高社会治理水平。

(一) 我们需要什么样的民生观

党的十八大以来,习近平总书记多次阐明其"民生观",提出民生工作的着力点就是将广大人民群众凝聚到追求幸福生活的目标上来。2013 年 4 月 8 日,习近平在海南考察时强调,抓民生要抓住人民最关心最直接最现实的利益问题,抓住最需要关心的人群,一件事情接着一件事情办、一年接着一年干,锲而不舍向前走。民生就是老百姓的生计,是人民群众最关心最直接的切身利益,是人民幸福之基、社会和谐之本。[1]

民生连着民心,民心关系着国运。治国理政的最大难题就是民生问题,解决民生问题是执政党最大的政治,能否改善民生也是最重要的政绩。各级领导干部必须牢固树立民生导向的政绩观,持之以恒地把民生工作抓好,保障和改善民生,这既是我们党全心全意为人民服务宗旨的根本要求,也是立党为公、执政为民执政理念的具体体现。"让老百姓过上好日子是我们一切工作的出发点和落脚点"。要把做好民生工作、让人民群众满意作为最大的政绩,以人民群众的忧乐为忧乐,踏踏实实为群众办好事、办实事、解难事,更多地让群众发言,让百姓评

---

[1] 参见《加快国际旅游岛建设 谱写美丽中国海南篇》,《人民日报》2013 年 4 月 11 日。

价,让人民群众在改革发展中有更多更实的"获得感"。

1."民生"就是"国计",事关国泰民安的根基

国泰民安是中国人自古以来的梦想,"治理之道,莫要于安民;安民之道,在于察其疾苦"。只有把国民的生计与生活问题解决好了,才能实现长治久安。民生问题从来没有像今天这样得到国家的空前重视,它不仅涉及人民群众的根本利益,而且也影响到国家改革发展的大局,民生解决得愈好,经济社会发展就会愈顺利,因而需要"让发展的成果惠及全体人民"。中央"十三五"规划的建议中,更加强调共享理念,"必须坚持发展为了人民、发展依靠人民、发展成果由人民共享,作出更有效的制度安排,使全体人民在共建共享发展中有更多获得感"。①

目前,人民生活水平普遍提高,可谓衣食无忧,但市场化的快速推进也在不断放大各类民生问题。市场调节的自发性、盲目性和滞后性,使人们在体味经济快速增长快乐的同时,也面对许多新的风险和各种不确定性因素,这些因素不断内化为新的民生问题。比如,人们对于就业的不满意,对教育公正、医疗、社会保障、分配不均等,都有了新的更高需求。要看到,民生毕竟是一个动态持续发展的过程,其外延和内涵都会随着社会发展和进步而不断扩展和升级。而民生诉求的多样性、复杂性又反过来增加了政府有效供给的难度。因此,关注民生问题始终是党和政府肩负的重要职责,是社会和谐的基础和保障。民生改善"没有最好,只有更好"。2013 年 5 月 14 日,习近平总书记在天津考察时提出,保障和改善民生是一项长期工作,没有终点站,只有连续不断的新起点。

要持之以恒把民生工作抓好,善于把改善民生工作转化为经济发展新"引擎"。有的地方政府在解决民生问题的过程中,把"民生"视同"包袱",认为抓民生只是投入,只有花钱,不能正确理解民生与发展的

---

① 《中共中央关于制定国民经济和社会发展第十三个五年规划的建议》,《文汇报》2015 年 11 月 4 日。

关系,把两者对立起来。其实,如果换一种视角、换一种思维,就会看到问题的另一面,这是唯物辩证法的基本原理,民生与发展具有良性互动的一面。在经济新常态下,民生项目和工程是又一个新的增长点,既能增加投资,又能拉动消费,是具有乘数效应的新动力。同时,民生问题解决好了,有利于凝聚民心,激发社会创业创造创新的活力。为此,各级地方政府一方面要不断增加公共产品和服务供给,加大政府对教育、医疗卫生、保障房等的投入;另一方面还要努力推进大众创业、万众创新,孵化和培育经济社会发展新动力。

2. 民生连着百姓的幸福,是人类文明进步之源

追求快乐和幸福是人类社会的永恒主题,也是政府出台公共政策所应追求的终极目标。哲学家休谟说过:"一切人类努力的伟大目标在于获得幸福"。每个人的追求可能千差万别,但人类奋斗不息的终极目的,简单说就是追求幸福快乐,党和政府推进社会发展的目的也应该是人民的幸福。实现经济增长是为了人民的幸福,达到政治"善治"也是为了人民的幸福,促进文化发展同样是为了人民的幸福,纵览人类历史,不难发现民生幸福不仅是和谐社会的重要内容,而且是人类文明之源,实现社会和谐之本。

GDP 被西方经济学界称为"伟大的发明",成为评价世界各国社会发展的重要标准,但它不能反映国民民生状况的全面真实信息,更不能提供公众生活福利的全部状况,当 GDP 达到一定水平后,决定人们生活幸福状态的不再是物质财富增长,而是其他非经济因素。幸福指数(Gross National Happiness,GNH)近年来得到重视,成为衡量国稳、民福的重要参考指标。幸福指数不仅有助于监控经济社会运行态势,而且能了解民众的生活满意度,是社会运行状和民众生活状态的"晴雨表"。

对于幸福指数问题,目前还存在争论,因为幸福是人们对生活满意程度的一种主观感受,确实难以找到客观的衡量标准,但"幸福的人都是相似的",其相似之处在于,它是一种良性的快感,是人们追求的终极目标。将"幸福指数"首次付诸实践的是不丹国王吉格梅·辛格·

旺楚克(Jigme Singye Wangchuck),他认为,政府施政应该以实现幸福为目标,注重物质和精神之间的平衡发展。基于此,1970 年,不丹政府把经济增长、政府善治、文化发展和环境保护视为国家发展的四大支柱。时至今日,"国民幸福指数"这一概念逐渐得到国际认同。比如,2008 年,法国总统萨科齐组建了一个专家组,成员包括以诺贝尔经济学奖获得者约瑟夫·斯蒂格里茨和阿马蒂亚·森等在内的 20 多名世界知名专家,进行了一项名为"幸福与测度经济进步"(Happiness and Measuring Economic Progress)的研究。该项研究认为应当对国民经济核算方式进行改革,将国民主观幸福感纳入衡量经济表现的指标,以主观幸福程度、生活质量及收入分配等指标来衡量经济发展。

2015 年 12 月 16 日,江西省东乡县王桥镇塘下村困难户冯新兴(前右)在江西绿沐农业开发有限公司基地收获花果芋,该公司采取"公司+合作社+基地+农户"的方式种植 1500 余亩本地特色产品花果芋,带动附近近 800 户农户脱贫致富(新华社发,宋振平摄)

目前,我国已有许多地方政府提出以"幸福"为目标的城市发展战略,社会的发展应该与让人民享受幸福生活的方向相一致,这体现了治国理政理念的进步。当然,各地政府也不能以建设"幸福城市"为幌子,跟风追新,不从根本上解决问题。幸福城市建设要真正让老百姓幸福,必须紧紧围绕"民生"二字,使城市不仅宜居、宜业,而且还能在民生服务方面实现全方位覆盖,在百姓安居乐业的同时,实现老有所养、幼有所教、贫有所依、难有所助,让百姓真正获得"幸福生活"。

(二) 保障和改善民生的"底线"在哪里

2013 年 12 月 13 日,习近平在中央经济工作会议上强调必须做好保障和改善民生工作,要继续按照守住底线、突出重点、完善制度、引导舆论的思路,统筹教育、就业、收入分配、社会保障、医药卫生、住房、食品安全、安全生产等,切实做好改善民生各项工作。[①] 他还在许多场合提出民生工作与守住底线问题,要按照"守住底线、突出重点、完善制度、引导舆论"的思路做好民生工作。必须明确社会保障政策的重点,从而为全面深化民生领域改革指明方向。在"十三五"规划全面建成小康社会的收官阶段,更要"坚守底线、突出重点、完善制度、引导预期,注重机会公平,保障基本民生,实现全体人民共同迈入全面小康社会"[②]。

关注和重视民生,不断保障和改善民生,就是要抓住人民群众最关心最直接最现实的利益问题,抓住最需要关心的人群,一件事情接着一件事情办,一年接着一年干,锲而不舍向前走。党员干部必须要及时准确地了解群众所思、所盼、所忧、所急,把群众工作做实、做深、做细、做透。那么,怎样才能做好民生工作呢?重要的是守住底线,即"社会政策要托底",这意味着好的社会政策必须做到普惠、持久、有效。"普惠"就是让发展成果惠及每一个人,每个人禀赋不同,能力有异,业绩

---

① 参见《中央经济工作会议在北京举行》,《人民日报》2013 年 12 月 13 日。
② 《中共中央关于制定国民经济和社会发展第十三个五年规划的建议》,《文汇报》2015 年 11 月 4 日。

有优劣,机遇有差异,但社会应该提供基本生活保障。"持久"就是社会福利的供给水平要与实际发展水平相适应,要尽力而为、量力而行,不能使社会福利过度膨胀,避免债台高筑、失信于民。"有效"就是社会保障和社会福利的提供要有利于形成鼓励"通过勤劳致富改善生活"的机制,不是搞平均主义,更不能罚勤赏懒,要通过建立公平竞争的机制保持社会的活力。

1. 守住底线体现出党和政府必须承担起应负的民生责任

所谓"底线"是要表明政府承担着不可推卸的责任,必须努力做到。我们知道,足球场上守门员的重要性,"一个好的门将赛过半支球队",守门员的工作就是守住底线,如果底线被破,就意味着比赛的失败。守住底线强调的是时刻要有戒备心和责任,要有危机意识,防范可能出现的危机。在民生问题上,守住底线意味着维护最起码的社会公平,要让老百姓吃住无忧,安居乐业,要通过政府的一系列社会政策向居民提供最基本的需求。比如,在满足低收入群体温饱需求的低保制度方面,在"三险一助"的医疗保障体系方面,在义务教育制度方面,等等,都需要依靠国家的制度保障和财政支持来解决,这些基本需求是属于普惠性的民生权益。

2. 守住底线需要得到各方力量共同参与,为民生建设出力

事实上,发挥市场配置资源的决定性作用与坚守底线公平并不矛盾,关键在于能否从市场机制资源配置最薄弱的环节着手,"从坏处准备",有效解决市场失灵问题。从建立贫穷边远地区教师财政补贴机制,到中央经济工作会议多次强调大型企业应当履行社会责任并提高劳动要素参与财富分配的份额,再到城乡大病医保借助商业保险经办机制提高制度运行效率……这些教育、收入分配和社会保障领域的底线公平,既离不开国家强有力的干预,又离不开企业、社会和个人的多方参与。在扶贫攻坚工程方面,也要"健全东西部协作和党政机关、部队、人民团体、国有企业定点扶贫机制,激励各类企业、社会组织、个人

自愿采取包干方式参与扶贫"①。对企业而言,建立员工福利制度是增强员工凝聚力的有效人力资本投资,是对底线思维的有效补充和回应。对个人而言,也应当在全社会底线公正的守护下树立正确的价值观,勤劳致富,而非靠投机违法妄想一夜暴富。

3. 守住底线就是让低收入群体感到生活"有底"

"守住底线"就是要保证普通民众,特别是低收入群体的生活水平稳中有升。为了加大对中低收入群体的扶助力度。近年来,我国采取了一系列举措,比如,连续上调最低工资、基本养老金和低保补助标准,增加中低收入人群收入,上调个人所得税起征点,等等。当然,城乡最低生活保障标准,一定要根据当地经济发展水平和财力状况适时作出调整,以保障困难群众基本生活需要。以养老保险待遇水平为例,近年来企业退休人员享受养老金"十连调",在增长10%的同时也存在制度可持续性的风险。德国的经验表明,养老金水平要与居民消费价格指数(CPI)挂钩以保持购买力,同时也应当与社会发展水平(如当年 GDP增长率等)建立一定关联,以期让全体国民共享经济发展成果。底线思维既不是冒进主义,也不是国家责任的退缩,而是要基于制度理性的适度推进。

4. 要突出重点,着力解决民生的紧迫问题

"突出重点"就是要抓住一些民生最紧迫的问题,比如,要注意稳定和扩大就业,做好以高校毕业生为重点的青年就业工作,"加强就业援助,帮助就业困难者就业"②。要完善就业服务体系,提高就业服务能力;要善待和支持小微企业发展,强化大企业社会责任;要继续加强保障性住房建设和管理,加快棚户区改造;等等。"突出重点",表明在

---

① 《中共中央关于制定国民经济和社会发展第十三个五年规划的建议》,《文汇报》2015 年11 月 4 日。
② 《中共中央关于制定国民经济和社会发展第十三个五年规划的建议》,《文汇报》2015 年11 月 4 日。

目前我国资源财力有限的情况下,要把有限的资源用来解决群众反映强烈的、关乎百姓福祉的突出问题。习近平总书记提出,对困难群众要格外关注、格外关爱、格外关心,这"三个格外"提醒着各级干部要关注重点群体。2012 年 12 月底,习近平总书记上任伊始,就冒着零下十几摄氏度的严寒,赶赴河北阜平县,看望慰问困难群众,考察扶贫开发工作。他强调,消除贫困、改善民生、实现共同富裕,是社会主义的本质要求。①

5. 要完善制度,让制度"红利"惠及更多百姓

底线思维要求不断完善制度设计,具体到民生领域,就是要不断夯实国家的制度建设责任和财政责任,承担转移支付、提供公共服务、培育产业力量三大责任。以养老保障制度为例,2012 年,城镇居民社会养老保险试点全面铺开,新型农村社会养老保险向全覆盖的目标迈进。但由于养老保险基础水平较低,异地转换以及接续不便等问题仍然困扰部分群众。如何完善制度,让制度"红利"惠及更多民众是需要努力的方向。在老年服务和残疾人服务等方面,既要从坚守底线公平的角度补贴需方,又要从长远考虑,"争取最好的结果",扶持和补贴老年人服务和残疾人护理等产业。在制度设计过程中,既要在总量上扩大政府投入,又要从结构上明确各级财政(中央与地方)对各项民生工程的分责机制;既要不断完善低保制度、社会保险等收入保障制度,又要进一步做好老少边穷地区义务教育机会公平等一系列公共服务体系建设。

(三) 怎样不断促进公平正义、增进人民福祉

2013 年 7 月 23 日,习近平在武汉主持召开部分省市负责人座谈

---

① 参见《把群众安危冷暖时刻放在心上把党和政府温暖送到千家万户》,《人民日报》2012
年 12 月 31 日。

会时提出,进一步实现社会公平正义,通过制度安排更好保障人民群众各方面权益。要在全体人民共同奋斗、经济社会不断发展的基础上,通过制度安排,依法保障人民权益,让全体人民依法平等享有权利和履行义务。① 中央在"十三五"规划的建议中,特别强调人民主权地位问题,"发展人民民主,维护社会公平正义,保障人民平等参与、平等发展权利,充分调动人民积极性、主动性、创造性"②。

人类社会的发展进步,从一定的角度来看,主要表现在两个方面的关系变化上:一是人与自然的关系,即经济发展问题;二是人与人的关系,即社会的公平正义问题。人与自然的关系,主要是为了解决人类的生存问题,核心是如何使生存条件变得越来越好,也就是说让人们生活得幸福。生存条件是人类发展乃至从事一切社会活动的基础,这是马克思主义经济基础决定上层建筑的基本原理。要不断改善人们的生存条件,就必须解放和发展社会生产力。随着生产力的发展,财富越来越多,出现了财富占有的多寡问题,也就是社会的公平正义问题。财富积累愈多,公平问题就愈突出。古今中外,历史上大的社会动荡乃至改朝换代,大部分是因为社会不公、贫富差距过大引发矛盾,矛盾尖锐到极点就是社会革命。

1. 促进公平正义是对日益强烈社会呼声的积极回应

随着我国经济社会发展水平和人民生活水平的不断提高,人民群众的公平意识、民主意识、权利意识不断增强,对社会不公问题反映越来越强烈。比如:有的人靠钻空子、搞歪门邪道一夜暴富,有的人靠"拼爹"获得"火箭式提拔";由于政策制度不完善的原因,不同身份的居民在收入、医疗、教育、养老等方面的待遇差别较大,受到不公正对待;中国奢侈品消费居世界第二,但还有不少人生活在贫困线以下;等等。过去,不公平的事件和现象传播慢、影响范围窄;而今,互联网、手

---

① 参见《习近平在武汉召开部分省市负责人座谈会》,《人民日报》2013 年 7 月 25 日。

② 《中共中央关于制定国民经济和社会发展第十三个五年规划的建议》,《文汇报》2015 年 11 月 4 日。

机等新媒体的快速发展,人人充当"记者",一旦发生不公平事件,便很快传开,再加上有的人看待不公平现象时,容易带有非理性和极端化情绪,故意渲染炒作,夸大了不公平的程度。"事不公则心不平,心不平则气不顺"。公平正义问题成为社会诸多矛盾的交结点,大众关注度很高。

公平正义问题不抓紧解决,不仅会影响人民群众对改革开放的信心,而且会影响社会和谐稳定。因此,中央在"十三五"规划的建议中,提出,"建立更加公平更可持续的社会保障制度。实施全民参保计划,基本实现法定人员全覆盖。坚持精算平衡,完善筹资机制,分清政府、企业、个人等的责任。"①如果不能带给老百姓实实在在的利益,不能创造更加公平的社会环境,今天的发展将不可持续,我们所进行的改革开放又有何意义。公平正义问题是我们党正在面临的一个重大问题,关系到党能不能长期执政。我们究竟能不能解决好这个问题,还面临着考验。习近平总书记对此十分重视,高瞻远瞩地洞察到这个事关党的兴衰存亡的问题,告诫全党:"这个问题不抓紧解决,不仅会影响人民群众对改革开放的信心,而且会影响社会和谐稳定。"②党的十八大报告强调:"逐步建立以权利公平、机会公平、规则公平为主要内容的社会公平保障体系,努力营造公平的社会环境,保证人民平等参与、平等发展权利。"③在追求公平正义的道路上,中国必须举起改革的大旗。

2. 追求公平正义是马克思主义的基本要求,也是改革的体现

对于公平正义这个古老而又常新的话题,人类从未停止思考和孜孜不倦的追求。从柏拉图到亚里士多德,再到早期空想社会主义者,思

---

① 《中共中央关于制定国民经济和社会发展第十三个五年规划的建议》,《文汇报》2015年11月4日。

② 习近平:《切实把思想统一到党的十八届三中全会精神上来》,《人民日报》2014年1月1日。

③ 胡锦涛:《坚定不移沿着中国特色社会主义道路前进 为全面建成小康社会而奋斗》,人民出版社2012年版,第14—15页。

想家们曾描绘过一种没有剥削压迫、社会实行公平正义的图画。但由于历史局限,他们无法找到实现理想社会的途径。马克思、恩格斯在分析资本主义基本矛盾的基础上,运用唯物史观和剩余价值学说,创建了科学社会主义理论,使社会主义真正成为一种社会运动。资本主义生产方式虽然创造了巨大社会财富,但其制度天然制造贫富分化,必须加以改变。马克思关于未来理想社会的设想,无论是按劳分配的共产主义低级阶段,还是按需分配的共产主义高级阶段,基本原则都是公平正义和人的解放。

改革是社会主义制度的自我完善和发展,在改革发展成就基础上必须体现社会公平正义、增进人民福祉的要求。近年来随着社会领域改革的推进,民生建设取得显著的成就。但也要看到,在现有发展水平上,社会上还存在不少有违公平正义的现象。譬如不同行业、不同地域间收入差距过大;一些地方土地征用和房屋拆迁中暴力执法引起干群关系紧张;环境污染、食品安全、高房价、看病难、看病贵等问题突出,这都反映出社会公正问题。在社会发展水平和人民生活水平不断提高的情况下,居民的公平意识、民主意识、权利意识会不断增强,对社会不公的反映也会越来越强烈。邓小平晚年特别关心公平公正问题,强调"十二亿人口怎样实现富裕,富裕起来以后财富怎样分配,这都是大问题,题目已经出来了,解决这个问题比解决发展起来的问题还困难"。如果在发展起来之后不能创造更加公平的社会环境,甚至导致更多不公平,改革就失去意义,可以说,促进公平正义是人类躲不开、绕不过的一个重大问题。

3. 要在实践中不断探索实现公平正义的路子

在改革开放之初,我们党就意识到公平与效率的关系问题。"做大蛋糕"与"分好蛋糕",孰轻孰重? 答案是不分伯仲,缺一不可。改革开放初期在发展的压力下,人们偏向于效率,注重做大蛋糕;而在富裕了之后,对公正的呼声越来越强烈,也有必然性。怎样办? 党的十八届三中全会《决定》中指出,"全面深化改革必须以促进社会公平正义、增进人民福祉为出发点和落脚点。"如果不能给老百姓带来实实在在的利益,如果不能创造更加公平的社会环境,甚至导致更多不公平,改革就失去意义,也不可能持续。要通过深化改革,完善制度,强化监管,综合施策,努力形成合理有序的收入分配格局,使发展成果更多更公平惠及全体人民。

如何正确处理公平与效率的关系,是每一个国家在发展中都会遇到的一个难题。这个问题处理好了,既有利于经济发展,也有利于社会和谐稳定。处理不好,经济很难发展,即使一段时间发展了也难以持续,甚至可能出现大的社会动荡。从总体上看,多年来我国在这个问题上处理得是比较好的。尤其是在改革开放之初,我国的经济社会发展既提高了效率,也兼顾了公平,因而极大地调动了广大人民群众的积极性和创造性,使生产力得到了空前的解放。今天,我们逐步摆脱了贫穷落后的状况,经济总量跃居世界第二位,人均收入进入中等国家行列。但由于我国人口多,城乡、区域差距大,各地发展很不平衡。

4. 通过全面深化改革为公平正义的实现保驾护航

实现社会公平正义是由多种因素决定的,最主要的还是经济社会发展水平。在不同发展水平上,在不同历史时期,不同思想认识、不同阶层的人对社会公平正义的认识和诉求也会不同。我国现阶段存在的有违公平正义的现象,许多是发展中的问题,是能够通过不断发展,通过制度安排、法律规范、政策支持加以解决的。我们讲促进社会公平正义,就要从最广大人民根本利益出发,从社会发展水平、从社会大局、从全体人民的角度看待和处理这个问题。必须牢牢抓住经济建设这个中心,推动经济持续健康发展,进一步把"蛋糕"做大,为保障社会公平正义奠定更加坚实的物质基础。同时要通过建立公平合理的收入分配制度分好"蛋糕",努力提高居民收入在国民收入中的比重,提高劳动报酬在初次分配中的比重,实现居民收入增长和经济发展同步,劳动报酬增长和劳动生产率提高同步,加快形成合理有序的国民收入分配格局,切实缩小收入分配差距。

从我国国情出发,实现社会公平正义,从根本上要靠制度来保障。要通过创新制度安排,努力克服人为因素造成的有违公平正义的现象,保证人民平等参与、平等发展权利。习近平总书记指出:"要把促进社会公平正义、增进人民福祉作为一面镜子,审视我们各方面体制机制和政策规定,哪里有不符合促进社会公平正义的问题,哪里就需要改革;哪个领域哪个环节问题突出,哪个领域哪个环节就是改革的重点。"① 对由于制度安排不健全造成的有违公平正义的问题要抓紧解决,使我们的制度安排更好体现社会主义公平正义原则,更加有利于实现好、维护好、发展好最广大人民根本利益。要在全体人民共同奋斗、经济社会发展的基础上,加紧建设对保障社会公平正义具有重大作用的制度,逐步建立以权利公平、机会公平、规则公平为主要内容的社会公平保障体系,努力营造公平的社会环境,保证人民平等参与、平等发展权利。制度建设的核心是要合理解决权力配置问题,完善有利于公平正义的法治基础,防止因权力滥用造成的社会不公。要通过改革转变政府职能,消除垄断现象,破除各种特殊利益集团,给每个人都创造能够靠自己的努力和才能实现梦想的平等机会。要通过改革给占人口一半以上的农村居民以迁徙自由,消除由于户籍制度不合理而造成的社会分层的不公正。

（四）公民与社会组织如何参与社会治理

2014 年 3 月 5 日,习近平在参加十二届全国人大二次会议上海代表团审议会时强调,加强和创新社会治理,关键在体制创新,核心是人。解决社会矛盾和问题必须坚持以人为本,牢固树立社会治理一切为了人民群众的理念,做到为民、亲民、爱民、利民。② 要深入基层调研,满足人民群众日益增长的需求,适应群众民主意识、法治意识不断提高的

---

① 习近平:《切实把思想统一到党的十八届三中全会精神上来》,《人民日报》2014 年 1 月 1 日。
② 参见习近平:《推进上海自贸区建设　加强和创新特大城市社会治理》,《人民日报》2014 年 3 月 6 日。

现实,吸引每一个公民参与到社会治理过程中,以便更有效地解决各类社会矛盾和社会问题。中央在"十三五"规划建议中,明确提出"推进社会治理精细化,构建全民共建共享的社会治理格局。健全利益表达、利益协调、利益保护机制,引导群众依法行使权利、表达诉求、解决纠纷。增强社区服务功能,实现政府治理和社会调节、居民自治良性互动。"①

当今社会事务,可谓千头万绪。实践证明,政府包揽一切,既做不好,也行不通。怎么办?最好的办法就是吸引广大公民和社会组织参与社会治理,通过社会协同、公众参与的方式,实现社会资源的有效整合利用。从世界范围来看,现代社会治理,就是一种在规范的公共治理结构下的公民参与以及公民与政府之间进行良性互动的协同治理。目前,我国社会组织发展迅速,在维护社会稳定、提供公共服务和促进科教文卫事业发展等方面发挥着作用,成为社会治理的重要参与者。当然,由于社会组织的发展还处于起步阶段,在数量、规模以及能力方面都还存在着一定差距,难以充分发挥他们在社会治理中的协同作用。因此,各级政府在社会治理过程中,要有意识地调动社会组织以及广大公民参与的积极性,促进社会自治与公民自我服务能力的提升。

1. 社会组织要适应当今社会发展的趋势,转变观念,敢于作为

社会组织对于现代社会来说,是独立于政府和市场之外的另一支重要力量,对于纠正政府权力过于集中、市场力量过于垄断的倾向,具有不可替代的重要作用。我国社会组织近年来虽有所发展,但与西方发达国家相比仍显不足。每万人拥有社会组织的数量只有 3.2 个,仅为美国的 1/16,日本的 1/31,法国的 1/34。尤其是社会急需的行业类、科技类、公益慈善类、城乡社区服务类社会组织需要加速发展。各地政府正在采取措施,积极主动地培育和推进社会组织成长。作为公民和

---

① 《中共中央关于制定国民经济和社会发展第十三个五年规划的建议》,《文汇报》2015 年 11 月 4 日。

社会组织自身,更应该积极主动地承接政府转移的社会管理职能。除了更多、更好地承接政府委托购买的社会服务项目之外,社会组织还要发挥主观能动性,承担起社会治理主体的责任,主动承担政府转移的社会管理职能,进而加快政府职能的转移和让渡,以实现现代协同治理模式。比如,老年协会逐步承担起社区为老年人服务的职能,残疾人协会逐步承担起为残疾人服务的职能,青少年组织更多地发挥先锋队的作用,引领志愿者新风尚。

2. 加强社会组织自身建设,规范内部治理,不断提升能力

社会组织要成为公共服务的承担者,就必须不断完善内部治理,加强机构自身能力建设,不断提升自身发展的竞争力。许多地方已经开始注重战略谋划,立足长远目标,加强社会组织的规范管理,以促进其健康发展。比如,上海市自2002年以来,相继制定了《上海市行业协会管理暂行办法》、《关于进一步推进本市民间组织参与社区建设和管理的意见》、《关于进一步加强本市社会组织建设的指导意见》、《关于鼓励本市公益性社会组织参与社区民生服务的指导意见》等。一方面,积极培育和鼓励社会组织参与社会治理;另一方面,制定完善相关的法律、法规和政策,支持和引导社会组织合法、有序参与社会治理。要加强和改进政府监管,推进建立社会组织信息公开和评估制度,健全、整合退出机制,保障社会组织规范地展开活动。各类社会组织必须按照法人地位明确、内部治理结构完善、管理运行规范的要求,制定内部治理的规章,实行民主选举、民主决策、民主管理、民主监督,促进社会组织人才队伍的专业化和职业化,提升自身的公信力和服务能力。

3. 提供专业化的服务,优化社会资源配置,实现社会协同治理

社会组织参与社会治理的基本形式,就是提供更加专业的社会服务,这直接关系到社会组织的生存发展。提供公益性、非营利性服务,是现代社会特别是社会转型期对社会组织的基本要求。社会组织应围

绕发挥服务功能,切实代表和维护好特定群体和会员的合法权益和共同利益。同时,可利用自身机制、资源、人才等方面优势,发挥出政府、市场机制难以提供的公共服务职能,在政府和市场不能或不愿做的领域起到补充作用。比如,在城市社区沉淀了很多未开发的资源,有许多没利用的硬件设施、居民闲置的小额资金等,对于这些资源的整合和配置,政府往往无暇顾及,而单个居民的力量又有限,社会组织则可施展能力。以专业化的服务满足社区居民之需,除了满足社区居民生活服务和文娱方面的需求之外,随着生活水平的提高,居民越来越提出更精细化要求,如社区居民对于教育(早教)、卫生(专业陪护)和法律(老年人房产纠纷)等专业性服务的需求增长迅速,而社会组织具有覆盖面广、机制灵活等优势,能够做到更细致、更贴心的服务。社会组织可通过接受委托、参与招标等方式,承接一些社会管理和公共服务职能。实践证明,社会组织在满足特殊群体、弱势群体需求,解决社会问题等方面具有独特优势。充分发挥各类社会组织优势,有利于形成政府、市场、社会组织的有效协同,有效配置社会资源,加强社会协调,化解社会矛盾,通过专业化社会服务全方位地满足社会需求。

思考题

1. 党和政府为什么要高度重视民生问题?
2. 如何看待改革过程中的公平正义问题?

参考文献

1. 中共中央文献研究室编:《习近平总书记重要讲话文章选编》,北京:党建读物出版社、中央文献出版社,2016年。

2.《中共中央关于制定国民经济和社会发展第十三个五年规划的建议》,新华社,2015年11月3日。

3. 罗会德:《国外执政党解决民生问题的经验及启示》,《中共天津市委党校学报》2012年第1期。

七、建设生态文明

建设生态文明是关系人民福祉、关乎民族未来的大计,是实现中华民族伟大复兴中国梦的重要内容。"我们既要绿水青山,也要金山银山。宁要绿水青山,不要金山银山,而且绿水青山就是金山银山。"——《习近平总书记系列重要讲话读本》,学习出版社、人民出版社 2014 年版,第 120 页

（一）生态兴则文明兴

2013 年 5 月，习近平在主持中共中央政治局第六次集体学习时指出，"生态兴则文明兴，生态衰则文明衰"。这一论断深刻揭示了生态环境与人类文明兴衰的关系，彰显了中国共产党人对人类文明发展规律、自然规律和经济社会发展规律的深刻认识，揭示了人类文明发展的客观规律和生态建设的极端重要性，丰富发展了马克思主义生态观。

中华文明传承五千多年，积淀了丰富的生态智慧。中国儒家所提出的"仁者以天地万物为一体"、道家所提及的"天人合一""道法自然""天地与我并生，而万物与我为一"等思想，"劝君莫打三春鸟，儿在巢中望母归"的经典诗句，"一粥一饭，当思来之不易；半丝半缕，恒念物力维艰"的治家格言，无不展现着古代哲人认识人与自然关系的智慧，至今仍给人深刻启迪。生态环境是人类文明赖以存在和发展的自然前提和物质基础。没有生态环境，也就没有人类文明的起源和延续，生态环境影响与制约着人类文明的历史进程和发展水平。从历史的视野来看，一些古代文明的衰落与生态环境破坏紧密相关，譬如：古巴比伦文明、古印度哈巴拉文明、中美洲玛雅文明等古代文明都因林茂、水丰的生态环境而兴，又因生态平衡破坏而衰。在《自然辩证法》中，恩格斯就曾指出，"美索不达米亚、希腊、小亚细亚以及其他各地的居民，为了得到耕地，毁灭了森林，但是他们做梦也想不到，这些地方今天竟因此而成为不毛之地"。"我们不要过分陶醉于我们人类对自然界的胜利。对于每一次这样的胜利，自然界都对我们进行报复"。

自然生态是人类的栖息之所，是人类社会产生、存在和发展的基础和前提。古往今来，人们一直生活在大自然的厚泽之下，自然生态为人类活动提供了丰富的生产和生活资料，如同一位慈祥的母亲哺育人类的成长发展，此谓"天地之大德"。远古时期，人们对大自然充满敬畏，匍匐在苍穹之下寻找最基本的生活资源。大自然也关爱生命，关爱人类，它使人类成为生命演化链条上的最终成果，成为大地上最为璀璨的一粒明珠。进入工业文明以来,人与自然的关系被异化,人们信奉"人是万物主宰",人类贪婪地、肆无忌惮地向大自然开战,以从未有过的热情改造自然、利用自然。在生产力空前发展的同时,也以前所未有的速度和程度改变了生态环境系统,并因生态环境的破坏而对人类自身的生活和存在产生了巨大影响。许多国家都曾经历"先污染后治理"的过程,水被污染了,土壤被污染了,至今都没有完全恢复。英国是最早开始走上工业化道路的国家,伦敦在很长一段时期是著名的"雾都"。19世纪末,英国伦敦的光化学烟雾,在短期内致使数千人死亡。20世纪30年代,比利时爆发了世人瞩目的马斯河谷烟雾事件。20世纪40年代,美国洛杉矶由于上百万辆汽车排出的废气造成的光化学烟雾,导致很多人生病、死亡。

在我国,经过三十多年的快速发展,所累积的生态环境问题进入高发频发阶段。一些地方、一些领域并没有处理好经济发展同生态环境保护的关系,在"财富—欲望"的过度追求中按捺不住向苍山、湖沼、草原要粮的热情,无节制地开发资源,毁林开荒、滥垦草原、围湖造田。滥垦草原带来的土地沙漠化使土地的生产力下降,越来越多的沙尘暴遮天蔽日,像幽灵一样飘浮在城市的上空。在全国74个按新的空气质量标准监测的城市中,大气达标比例仅为4.1%,全国频繁出现大范围长时间的雾霾污染天。围湖造田使湖泊蓄水面积不断缩小,削弱了湖泊天然的蓄洪和调洪能力,恶化了湖泊周围的生态。全国约2/3的大中城市用水紧张,江河水系、地下水污染相当严重。全国耕地逼近18亿亩红线,1.5亿亩耕地受污染、四成多耕地退化,有的地区重金属、土壤污染比较严重。毁林开荒使森林覆盖率严重下降,森林"地球之肺"的功能正在日益丧失,加剧气候变暖的进程。大规模水土流失引发越来越多洪水和泥石流等自然灾害,吞噬着人们赖以生存的家园……一个又一个的生态悲剧不断上演。据有关部门统计,各地因环境污染造成的损害,包括空气污染引发的疾病、森林退化等造成的全部损失可能达到GDP的5%—6%。生态环境的破坏正在导致哮喘、气管炎、高血压、癌症等各种疾病的加剧发生,严重威胁人类健康,导致人类退化。人们竭尽全力地发展所谓的工业文明,却也诱发了人与自然的疏远。

人类文明与生态环境是相互依存、相互联系的整体。与一个充满生命活力的自然生态和睦相处、共生共荣是人类的生命和精神所需,是文明延续传承的基石。2014 年 12 月,习近平在中央政治局常委会会议上再次谈及,必须从中华民族历史发展的高度来看待这个问题,为子孙后代留下美丽家园,让历史的春秋之笔为当代中国人留下正能量的记录。

金昌市将山水林田湖是一个生命共同体的理念融入城市建设之中,积极探索独具特色的"景中城""城中景"个性化城市建设;图为金昌市紫金花城景区(新华社发,范培坤摄)

(二) 绿水青山就是金山银山

2013 年 9 月,习近平在哈萨克斯坦纳扎尔巴耶夫大学回答学生问题时指出,我们绝不能以牺牲生态环境为代价换取经济的一时发展,我们既要绿水青山,也要金山银山。宁要绿水青山,不要金山银山,而且绿水青山就是金山银山。

党的十八大以来,无论是政治局集体学习,还是同人大代表讨论交流,无论是在深入基层乡村的调研中,还是在远渡重洋的国外访问时,习近平总书记反复强调这"两座山",生动形象地阐明了经济发展与生态保护的辩证关系,坚定诠释与传递着这一执政理念。习近平曾对"两山论"进行过深入分析:在实践中对绿水青山和金山银山这"两座山"之间关系的认识经过了三个阶段:第一个阶段是用绿水青山去换金山银山,不考虑或者很少考虑环境的承载能力,一味索取资源。第二个阶段是既要金山银山,但是也要保住绿水青山,这时候经济发展和资源匮乏、环境恶化之间的矛盾开始凸显出来,人们意识到环境是我们生存发展的根本,只有留得青山在,才能有柴烧。第三个阶段是认识到绿水青山可以源源不断地带来金山银山,绿水青山本身就是金山银山,我们种的常青树就是摇钱树,生态优势变成经济优势,形成了浑然一体、和谐统一的关系,这一阶段是一种更高的境界。习近平总书记关于"保护生态环境就是保护生产力,改善生态环境就是发展生产力"的战略思想深刻阐述了生态环境与生产力的内在关系。在保护生态环境中发展生产力,在发展生产力中改善生态环境,实现生产力发展与生态环境改善的同步与协调。

习近平总书记对绿水青山与金山银山关系的清晰认知并非一天两天,而是源于数十年来的"久久为功"。1999 年,习近平到长汀调研,之后十年,长汀的水土流失一直被列入福建省为民办实事项目。长汀是客家人重要的聚居地,历史上山清水秀,林茂田肥,人们安居乐业。由于近代以来森林遭到严重破坏,长汀成为当时全国最为严重的水土流失区之一。1985 年,长汀水土流失面积达 146.2 万亩,占全县面积的31.5%,不少地方出现"山光、水浊、田瘦、人穷"的景象。绿水青山没了,何谈金山银山?在福建工作期间,习近平五下长汀,走山村,访农户,摸实情,谋对策,大力支持长汀水土流失治理。经过连续十几年的努力,长汀治理水土流失面积 162.8 万亩,减少水土流失面积 98.8 万亩,森林覆盖率由 1986 年的 59.8% 提高到现在的 79.4%,实现了"荒山—绿洲—生态家园"的历史性转变。长汀的生态治理样本,折射出习近平清晰的生态理念。2005 年 8 月,时任浙江省委书记习近平同志来到浙江省安吉县调研时,首次提出"绿水青山就是金山银山"的重要论述,提出如果能够把这些生态环境优势转化为生态农业、生态工业、生态旅游等生态经济的优势,那么绿水青山也就变成了金山银山。2006 年 3 月 23 日,习近平同志在"之江新语"专栏上刊发了《从"两座山"看生态环境》一文,再次系统论述了"两座山"之间辩证统一的关系。

时光荏苒,走过十年,"绿水青山就是金山银山",已在浙江大地呈现出神形兼备、丰盈充实的全域化格局。各地巧借山水、盘活资源,"美丽经济"多姿多彩,生态红利持续释放。

习近平总书记考察过的安吉县余村,借力当时天荒坪风景名胜区编制总体规划契机,制定了生态旅游、生态居住、生态工业"三区规划",有效地将村民生活、生产与发展的空间作了合理布局。

村民潘春林原是矿山的一名拖拉机手。"记得从 2005 年开始,村里陆续带着我们到外面取经,鼓励大家发展农家乐等休闲旅游经济"。带着对美好生活的憧憬,潘春林拿出全部家当,办起了"春林山庄"。10 年间,"春林山庄"已发展成为当地最大的农家乐,还先后获得了市服务业百家优强企业、安吉县美丽农家乐示范点等称号。

潘春林十年来的变化,是余村转型发展的一个缩影。从"卖石头"到"卖风景",从简单粗放的生产方式中走了出来,虽说同样是靠山吃山,但余村人收获的却是人与自然和谐共处的那份愉悦,真切体会到了绿水青山中蕴含的含金量。

村民盛小梅家的业晟竹木工艺品位于村里的生态工业区内。这里共有 32 家企业,其中 25 家是竹制品企业。这些企业背靠村里的 6000 亩毛竹山,就地取材,充分享受着生态红利。村民胡加兴利用越来越清澈的河流,办起了荷花山漂流,夏季游人如织;村民俞金宝看到村里越来越多的游客,便结束在外闯荡的日子,回家办起了生态种植采摘园……2014 年,余村村民人均可支配收入 27677 元,是 2004 年年底的近5倍。

余村的绿水青山迎来了投资商的目光。现在,由外来投资商投资的荷花山景区一年有近10万人次的游客;由上海客商投资的金栖堂度假酒店正在建设之中……截至2014年年底,余村已拥有旅游景区3个,农家乐14家、床位410张。

人改变了环境,环境又反过来改变了人。余村人的改变,在64岁的村民洪月仙眼里看得尤为真切:"邻里间没有矛盾,不用调解;游客一扔烟蒂,很快会有村民捡走放进垃圾桶……"古银杏树,流水潺潺,余村这幅美图,正是"两座山"科学论断的一个生动写照。

2015年3月中央政治局会议提出一个让人耳目一新的概念:"绿色化"。"绿色化"概念的提出是对党的十八大提出的"新四化"的拓展与延伸,是中国经济社会发展的必然,也是中央领导同志高度重视生态环境的必然。生态文明建设不仅有了理论上的"抓手",也有了实践的路径。何为"绿色化"? 在经济领域,它是一种生产方式,"科技含量高、资源消耗低、环境污染少的产业结构和生产方式"。"绿色化"也是一种生活方式,"生活方式和消费模式向勤俭节约、绿色低碳、文明健康的方向转变,力戒奢侈浪费和不合理消费"。同时,"绿色化"还是一种价值取向,"把生态文明纳入社会主义核心价值体系,形成人人、事事、时时崇尚生态文明的社会新风"。让生产方式变"绿",生活方式变"绿",价值取向变"绿",实现"绿水青山"与"金山银山"相得益彰。

如今,"绿水青山就是金山银山"的发展理念,已成共识。2015年5月,中共中央、国务院正式公布《关于加快推进生态文明建设的意见》。在"两山"重要思想的引领下,中国正阔步迈进生态文明建设的美丽新时代。

(三) 生态红线是怎么回事

2013年5月24日,习近平总书记在中共中央政治局第六次集体学习时再次强调,要划定并严守生态红线,牢固树立生态红线的观念。

在生态环境保护问题上,就是要不能越雷池一步,否则就应受到惩罚。党的十八届三中全会更是把划定生态保护红线作为改革生态环境保护管理体制、推进生态文明制度建设最重要、最优先的任务。

近年来,随着工业化和城镇化快速发展,我国资源环境形势日益严峻。尽管我国生态环境保护与建设力度逐年加大,但总体而言,资源约束压力持续增大,环境污染仍在加重,生态系统退化依然严重,生态问题更加复杂,资源环境与生态恶化趋势尚未得到逆转。已建各类保护区空间上存在交叉重叠,布局不够合理,生态保护效率不高,生态环境缺乏整体性保护,且严格性不足,尚未形成保障国家与区域生态安全和经济社会协调发展的空间格局。

在此背景下,为强化生态保护,2011 年,《国务院关于加强环境保护重点工作的意见》(国发〔2011〕35 号)明确提出,在重要生态功能区、陆地和海洋生态环境敏感区、脆弱区等区域划定生态红线。这是我国首次以国务院文件形式出现"生态红线"概念并提出划定任务。国家提出划定生态保护红线的战略决策,旨在构建和强化国家生态安全格局,遏制生态环境退化趋势,力促人口资源环境相均衡、经济社会和生态效益相统一。划定生态红线实行永久保护,体现了我国科学规范生态保护空间管制并以强制性手段构建国家生态安全格局的政策导向和决心。

那么,什么是生态红线呢?生态红线有哪些重要内涵?生态保护红线是指对维护国家和区域生态安全及经济社会可持续发展,保障人民群众健康具有关键作用,在提升生态功能、改善环境质量、促进资源高效利用等方面必须严格保护的最小空间范围与最高或最低数量限值,具体包括生态功能保障基线、环境质量安全底线和自然资源利用上线,可简称为生态功能红线、环境质量红线和资源利用红线。其中,生态功能红线是指对维护自然生态系统服务,保障国家和区域生态安全具有关键作用,在重要生态功能区、生态敏感区、脆弱区等区域划定的最小生态保护空间;环境质量红线是指为维护人居环境与人体健康的基本需要,必须严格执行的最低环境管理限值;资源利用红线是指为促进资源能源节约,保障能源、水、土地等资源安全利用和高效利用的最高或最低要求。

这里需要对生态、资源、环境这三个概念的含义及其相互关系做一些阐述。从生态学的角度讲,生态是自然生态系统的简称,指的是在一定的空间和时间范围内,各种生物之间以及生物与其环境之间,通过能量流动和物质循环而相互作用的统一整体。生态(系统)的主体是生物,包括植物、动物和微生物。生态(系统)中的生物周围的事物(即生物所依存的条件),在生态学中称为环境。人们通常所说的资源,指的是在生物所依存的环境中被生物消耗的东西,包括食物、光、营养物(对植物)和重要的空间等。也就是说,生物和环境都只是生态(系统)的构成要素,资源则只是环境的组成部分,它们都不能包含生态(系统)的整体,当然也不能代指生态(系统),所以当我们只讲"资源保护"或"环境保护"时并不能包含整个生态(系统)保护。生态(系统)则不然,因为它是由生物、环境、资源等要素有机构成的复合体,既包含了环境,也包含了资源,当然也包含了生物,所以当我们讲"生态保护"时也就自然包含了"资源保护"和"环境保护""生物保护"的内容。这也就是党的十八届三中全会《决定》之所以用"划定生态保护红线"而不用"划定资源保护红线"和"划定环境保护红线"的原因之所在。

目前,我国在计划生育、节约资源(保护耕地、水资源和能源)两大基本国策中已相继设立红线,而且红线的约束性极强。同样,生态红线是生态文明和可持续发展的顶层红线管理规划。我国应该建立一个基于"人口—资源—环境"三大基本国策的红线管理体系,而生态红线只是其中一束。生态红线其实质就是要树立一种"底线"思维。

我国在短短几十年里,走过了发达国家几百年才完成的工业化、城镇化过程;与之相伴,发达国家一两百年间逐步出现的环境问题在我国集中显现,呈现明显的结构型、压缩型、复合型特点。环境问题的形成非一日之功,治理起来也不可急于求成。扭转依然严峻的环境形势注定是一场持久战,需要付出长期艰苦努力。这就要求我们适应这一新常态,划定并严守生态红线,切实树立底线思维。从制度上保障生态红线,让透支的资源环境逐步休养生息,扩大森林、湖泊、湿地等绿色生态空间,增强水源涵养能力和环境容量。在操作过程中,生态红线划定难,划定以后真正严格实施则更难。真正让生态环境休养生息,就要让红线成为"高压线",保证生态红线划得定、守得住,使生态红线像人口红线、耕地红线、水资源红线一样,作为硬约束、硬指标来执行。

牢固树立生态红线理念,要加强生态文明宣传教育,尤其要将生态文明建设、严守生态红线的相关内容纳入干部教育培训工作之中,促使各级领导干部树立生态红线意识,将生态保护理念切实引入决策全过程,将环境影响评价扎实贯穿监督各环节,在绿色发展、清洁生产和低碳生活方面起到引领和示范作用。同时,增强全民节约意识、环保意识、生态意识,在全社会形成知晓红线存在、参与红线划定、监督红线执行、保障红线功能的良好氛围。

此外,科学调整生态政绩考核体系。完善经济社会发展考核评价体系,把资源消耗、环境损害、生态效益等体现生态文明建设状况的指标纳入经济社会发展评价体系,使之成为推进生态文明建设的重要导向和约束。不同的功能区实行不同的绩效评价体系和政策导向。对于生态红线区域范围内的政绩考核体系,应侧重衡量提供绿色 GDP、综合提升环境承载力和改善生态环境的测评等方面绩效。同时,在干部使用问题上,应让"生态政绩"显性化,不仅使出生产力的地方出干部,也让出生态力的地方出干部。

(四) 为什么说"加强生态环境保护,这里面有很大的政治"

2013 年 4 月,习近平总书记在十八届中央政治局常委会会议上的讲话中谈道:"如果仍是粗放发展,即使实现了国内生产总值翻一番的目标,那污染又会是一种什么情况?届时资源环境恐怕完全承载不了。经济上去了,老百姓的幸福感大打折扣,甚至强烈的不满情绪上来了,那是什么形势?所以,我们不能把加强生态文明建设、加强生态环境保护、提倡绿色低碳生活方式等仅仅作为经济问题。这里面有很大的政治。"

我们在积极推动经济发展的同时，也要认识到环境是一种重要资源，同时又是一种公共产品。城市中的空气、水和土壤都可以被看作是公共产品，都具有政治性，对环境和资源的开发利用是攸关公平公正的问题。近年来，大城市地区高密度的人口和高强度的经济活动使得城市环境污染问题加剧，不仅造成巨大的经济损失，也直接危及人体健康，成为社会危机的主要因素之一。2015年5月5日，党中央、国务院审议通过的《关于加快推进生态文明建设的意见》，正式向全社会公开发布。《意见》着重指出，近年来由于环境污染造成的群体性事件、项目选址导致的环境"邻避"问题屡现网络、报纸，群众关注度高、社会反响强烈。近年来，由于环境污染问题引发的群体性事件呈多发态势。仅从2007年算起，引起较大舆论关注的，就有：2007年6月福建厦门PX项目引发"集体散步"事件；2008年上海市民"散步"反建磁悬浮事件；2009年11月广东番禺兴建垃圾焚烧厂引发群众抗议事件；2011年8月辽宁大连PX项目引发群众抗议事件；2012年4月天津PC项目污染引发群众"集体散步"事件；2012年7月初的什邡事件和7月底的启东事件；2014年5月杭州余杭兴建垃圾焚烧厂引发群众抗议事件；2015年4月四川威远冷凝气泄漏事件引发的群众抗议煤焦化厂事件；等等。

分析这些事件可以发现，因环境污染引发的群体性事件多建立在集体公共利益诉求的基础上，相较于其他群体性事件，其人数众多（根据中国社科院2014年《法治报告》，环境污染问题是引发万人规模以上群体性事件的主要原因），声势浩大，当地政府的应对和控制能力较为薄弱。而且最终解决往往都是以当地政府迅速宣布停建污染项目，事件才得以平息，容易造成"一地闹事，邻里围观，全国评理"的局面。此类事件有几个亟待思考的共同问题：相关项目的污染到底有多严重？地方政府是否存在重经济轻环保的倾向？这些项目当初的环境影响评估是否完善？政府的决策是否公开透明？与其事后维稳，为何不事先让公众充分参与？公众的群体行为是否全都理性、合法？为何群体性事件总是夹杂着"打砸抢"行为？政府对突发事态应如何应对？"一闹就停"是否会进一步丧失政府公信力？

目前，我国已进入一个环境问题敏感时期。作为一个发展中大国，经济发展快，环境污染严重，同时群众的环境意识有了很大提高，依法维护自身环境权益的愿望日益强烈，各方矛盾不断累积。城市化进程的快速推进和多方矛盾的急剧积累，不断倒逼政府提高解决问题的效率。同时，政府在处理这些问题时，往往在制度上、认识上或应对实践上，存在着准备不足，无法适应形势需要的问题。有些地方政府长期以来重经济、轻环保，为体现政绩招商引资往往降低环保门槛，使得很多直接影响群众健康的污染问题埋下了隐患。一旦此类问题突破了人民群众的心理底线，就容易引发群体性事件。另外，后期处置工作不得当，对群众依法维护自身环境权益的强烈愿望认识不足，与群众的有效沟通不够，也是使得矛盾激化、事态进一步扩大的主要原因。

环境污染群体性事件的发生，可以视作是快速城市化背景下，公众积累的大量社会情绪的释放。这种释放背后所折射出的，既有我国当前相关环境问题治理的体制机制问题；政府在民众心目中的公信力问题；政府与民众之间沟通不顺的问题；地方政府在 GDP 与生存环境之间、效率与民意之间的优先抉择问题；也有多方参与科学决策、社会风险评估的长效机制问题。这些问题如果从根源上得不到解决，民众的诉求得不到合理的回应，将诱发大规模的群体性事件，并最终对我们稳定的社会生活和政治生态造成恶劣的影响。

保护和改善生态环境关系到一个国家综合国力的提高。实践证明，脱离环境保护搞经济发展是"竭泽而渔"，离开经济发展抓环境保护是"缘木求鱼"。经济发展决定人们的生活水平，生态环境决定人们的生存条件。只强调保护和发展生产力而不保护环境，或者离开经济发展而只抓环境保护，都是不可取的。

生于忧患，死于安乐。我们要时刻保持对环境怀有一颗敬畏之心，把环境保护放在社会发展的重要位置；水可载舟，亦可覆舟。我们要时刻牢记生态环境与政治稳定、经济发展的关系，把环境保护视作社会发展的首要任务;鲧禹治水,堵不如疏。我们要时刻认识到保护生态环境的公民责任,把环境保护融入到我们日常的政治生活中。只有加强生态环境保护,社会政治才能更加稳定,同时稳定的社会政治也有利于营造更为和谐美好的生态环境!

思考题

　1.为什么必须建设社会主义生态文明?

　2.为什么要把划定生态保护红线作为推进生态文明制度建设最重要、最优先的任务?

参考文献

　1.《中共中央国务院关于加快推进生态文明建设的意见》,北京:人民出版社,2015年。

　2.《为了中华民族永续发展——习近平总书记关心生态文明建设纪实》,北京,新华网,2015年3月9日。

八、全面从严治党

　　"党要管党，才能管好党；从严治党，才能治好党。对我们这样一个拥有八千五百多万党员、在一个十三亿人口大国长期执政的党，管党治党一刻不能松懈。如果管党不力、治党不严，人民群众反映强烈的党内突出问题得不到解决，那我们党迟早会失去执政资格，不可避免被历史淘汰。这决不是危言耸听。"——习近平：《在全国组织工作会议上的讲话》(2013年6月28日)

面对复杂多变的国际形势和艰巨繁重的国内改革发展任务,实现党的十八大确定的各项目标任务,进行具有许多新的历史特点的伟大斗争,关键在党,关键在人。打铁还须自身硬。习近平同志围绕从严治党提出了一系列新思想新观点新要求,强调"从严治党必须具体地而不是抽象地、认真地而不是敷衍地落实到位"。这些重要论述,为在新的历史起点全面推进党的建设新的伟大工程指明了方向。

（一）为什么要突出强调从严治党

全面从严治党,是党中央根据新形势新任务的要求,为进一步加强和改善党的领导、推进党的建设新的伟大工程而作出的重大战略部署,是新的时代条件下管党治党的总要求。推进全面从严治党,对进行具有许多新的历史特点的伟大斗争,实现中华民族伟大复兴的中国梦,具有十分重要的意义。

1. 从严治党是我们党的优良传统和重要经验

中国共产党从成立之日起,就注重加强党的建设,强调严守党的纪律,坚持从严治党。在党的二大确立的党章中就专门有党的纪律的部分,规定了九个方面的情况,比如,无故连续两次不到会、三个月欠交党费、连续四个星期不为本党服务都要开除。党的二大对党员提出了七个方面的要求,指出,我们党应当是无产阶级中最有革命精神的、把群众组织起来的为无产阶级之利益而奋斗政党。土地革命战争时期,我们党于 1929 年 12 月召开了古田会议,首次提出了从思想上建党问题。这次会议也对党员也提出非常具体的标准,比如政治观念没有错误、忠实、有牺牲精神、没有发洋财的观念、不吃鸦片不赌博等。抗日战争时期,在 1938 年的中共六届六中全会上,毛泽东还提出共产党员在各方面都应该成为模范,包括英勇作战的模范、执行命令的模范、遵守纪律的模范、政治工作的模范、内部团结统一的模范、多做工作少取报酬的模范、实事求是的模范、远见卓识的模范以及学习的模范等。1939 年

10月,毛泽东在《〈共产党人〉发刊词》一文中,总结了中国革命的经验教训,把党的建设作为"三大法宝"提了出来。1941年到1944年,我们党开展了延安整风运动,创造了通过整风集中解决党内突出问题的有效途径。新中国成立前夕,毛泽东在中共七届二中全会上提出了"两个务必"的要求,即务必继续保持谦虚、谨慎、不骄、不躁的作风,务必继续保持艰苦奋斗的作风。新中国成立后,我们党成为执政党,党所面临的形势、任务、地位和作用都发生了根本性的变化。在新中国成立之初的"三反"运动中,我们处决了腐败分子刘青山、张子善,表明我们党从严治党、除恶务尽的决心,在当时起到了敲山震虎、扶正祛邪的良好效果。"文革"结束后,我们党总结"文化大革命"的教训,更加明确地提出了从严治党问题。改革开放之初,有人提出不仅要给企业"松绑",也要给纪律"松绑"。陈云同志批示:"党性原则和党的纪律不存在'松绑'的问题。没有好的党风,改革是搞不好的。共产党不论在地下党时期或执政时期,任何时候都必须坚持党的纪律。"1987年党的十三大正式提出把从严治党作为新时期加强党的建设的基本方针。1992年党的十四大首次把坚持从严治党载入党章的总纲。九十多年来,我们党之所以能够从小到大、由弱到强,成为世界上最大的社会主义国家执政党,成功地领导中国人民在革命、建设和改革道路上取得一个又一个伟大胜利,关键就在于我们坚持党要管党、从严治党,不断增强党的创造力、凝聚力、战斗力,始终保持和发展党的先进性和纯洁性,从而为事业胜利提供根本保证。

2. 全面从严治党,是适应新形势、新挑战的客观要求

在全面建成小康社会的决定性阶段,我们党肩负着光荣而伟大的历史使命,也面临诸多挑战和风险。这种挑战和风险,既有来自国际的,也有来自国内的,但最根本的还是来自党内的。从国际看,当今世界正处于大变革大调整时期,世界形势正发生复杂而深刻的变化。一方面,和平与发展仍然是时代的主题。世界多极化、经济全球化深入发展,社会信息化继续推进,科技创新不断取得新成果,各国相互依赖达

到前所未有的程度。另一方面,国际金融危机影响深远,发达国家经济增长乏力,保护主义抬头,霸权主义、强权政治和新干涉主义上升,恐怖主义猖獗,局部动荡频发。从我国与世界的关系看,通过多年快速发展,我国的综合国力和国际地位不断上升,影响力不断扩大。这一方面使我国推动世界和平与发展的能力得到增强,另一方面也使一些国家对我国抱持戒备心理,加大制约和遏制力度或采取敌对立场。从国内看,经过改革开放 30 多年的发展,人民群众的物质文化生活水平得到很大提高,城乡面貌发生巨大改变。但我国仍处于并将长期处于社会主义初级阶段的基本国情没有变,我国作为世界上最大发展中国家的特性没有变。我国发展面临的不平衡、不协调、不可持续问题突出,城乡区域发展差距和居民收入差距较大。特别是改革进入攻坚期和深水区,各种思想观念的障碍和利益固化的藩篱,严重制约着改革的进程。意识形态领域局部多元、多样、多变的趋势日益明显,主流意识形态与多样化社会思潮长期并存、相互激荡。所有这些,都对我们党提出了严峻挑战。从党的自身看,我们正在进行具有许多新的历史特点的伟大斗争,经受着时代考验。与国内外形势发展变化相比,与党所承担的历史任务相比,党的领导水平和执政水平、党组织建设状况和党员干部素质、能力、作风,都还有不小差距,党内存在一些亟待解决的突出问题。一些党员、干部理想信念动摇、宗旨意识淡薄,得过且过,庸懒散奢等不良风气在一些党员干部身上滋长蔓延;一些基层党组织战斗堡垒作用不强,有的甚至软弱涣散;一些党员先锋队意识淡化,组织纪律性不强,不能发挥先锋模范作用;一些党员干部作风问题比较突出,有的严重脱离群众,对群众疾苦漠然置之,甚至欺压群众、侵害群众利益;形式主义、官僚主义问题较为普遍地存在,奢侈浪费现象严重。一些领域消极腐败现象易发多发,不仅大案要案时有发生、令人触目惊心,而且发生在群众身边的腐败现象较多存在。这些问题为什么会存在?习近平总书记指出:这些年来,一些地方和部门之所以存在纪律松弛、组织涣散,正气上不来、邪气压不住,党内和社会上潜规则越来越盛行,政治生态和社会环境受到污染,根子就在从严治党没有做到位。有些地方和单位看起来党在管党治党,但没有管到位上,没有严到份上。这种状况如果任其发展下去,是非常危险的。习近平总书记指出:如果管党不力、治党不严,人民群众反映强烈的党内突出问题得不到解决,那我们党迟早会失去执政资格,不可避免被历史淘汰。这决不是危言耸听。什么"两个一百年"的目标,什么中华民族复兴的中国梦,都无从谈起。因此,要坚持治国必先治党、治党务必从严,不断提高自我净化、自我完善、自我革新、自我提高能力,靠"自身硬"凝聚起不可战胜的磅礴力量,创造无愧于历史的辉煌业绩。

3. 全面从严治党是吸取苏联共产党经验教训得出的必然结论

20 世纪 80 年代末 90 年代初,一些长期执政的社会主义国家政党纷纷垮台,原因是多方面的,而其中最根本的原因,是这些国家的执政党长期忽视自身的建设,纪律松弛,腐化变质,导致组织分崩离析。以苏联为例,为什么曾经在十四国武装侵略中凯歌行进、面对德国法西斯铁蹄不曾弯腰并创造过巨大经济奇迹的苏联共产党,却在没有外敌入侵和内部暴乱的情况下,"忽喇喇似大厦倾",顷刻之间解体覆亡了呢?原因当然是多方面的,但毫无疑问,管党不力、治党不严是其中最重要的原因之一。比如,在所谓的"民主化""公开性"的幌子下,从 1990 年苏共中央二月全会、经苏共二十八大到 1991 年 7 月中央全会,戈尔巴乔夫对党的指导思想作出根本性修改,放弃马克思主义的"垄断"地位,承认指导思想多元化。结果造成广大党员干部思想的极大混乱,共产党也因之失去了凝聚力、战斗力。"8·19 事件"后,苏共迅速瓦解,从一定意义上讲,正是苏共容忍反共反社会主义思潮的泛滥,使党失去马列主义指导思想的必然结果。比如,苏共在"党内生活民主化"的口号下,戈尔巴乔夫抛弃了民主集中制组织原则。苏共抛弃民主集中制组织原则带来的两个直接后果就是党的派别化和联邦化。由于没有有效的游戏规则和组织纪律约束,党内各种派别之间争斗不断,严重影响了党的战斗力和完整统一,使党处于四分五裂的状态之中。比如,不适当强调党政分开,使苏共失去对政权的领导。苏共十九次代表会议提出"一切权力归苏维埃",其结果是,苏维埃代表大会成为各派政治力量权力斗争的场所,造成全国性的"权力真空"。由于失去苏共党组织的支撑,苏联国家管理体系也很快就陷入全面混乱。总之,正如习近平总书记指出的:"苏联解体前,在所谓'公开性'、'民主化'的口号下,苏共放弃了民主集中制原则,允许党员公开发表与组织决议不同的意见,实行所谓各级党组织自治原则,一些苏共党员甚至领导层成员成了否定苏共历史、否定社会主义的急先锋,成了传播西方意识形态的大喇叭,苏共党内从思想混乱演变到组织混乱。最后,这样一个有着90多年历史、连续执政70多年的大党老党就哗啦啦轰然倒塌了。"从苏共执政失败中吸取教训,避免重蹈苏共遭遇的挫折,就必须坚持全面从严治党。列宁下面的一段话对于我们党来说分明具有别样的意义,他说:"无论过去和现在,我们的力量就在于我们对最惨重的失败也能给予十分冷静的估计……如果昨天的经验教训没有使我们看到旧方法的不正确,那么我们今天就决不能学会用新方法解决自己的任务。"

中国共产党第十八届中央委员会第六次全体会议于 2016 年 10 月 24 日至 27 日在北京举行(新华社发,庞兴雷摄)

（二）坚持从严治党，从严在何处

坚持全面从严治党，必须在"全"字上下足功夫，在"严"字上用力气，把从严治党的要求贯彻到党的建设的各方面和全过程，真正做到思想教育从严、干部管理从严，作风要求从严，组织建设从严、制度执行从严。

1. 思想教育从严，坚守共产党人的精神追求

求木之长者，必固其根本；欲流之远者，必浚其泉源。对党员、干部来说，思想上的滑坡是最严重的病变，"总开关"没拧紧，不能正确处理公私关系，缺乏正确的是非观、义利观、权力观、事业观，各种出轨越界、跑冒滴漏就在所难免了。"思想上松一寸，行动上就会散一尺。"因此，必须把思想建党放在首位，加强理想信念教育，铸牢从严治党的思想基础。

理想信念是一个国家、民族和政党团结奋斗的精神旗帜。党的十八大以来，习近平总书记高度重视理想信念问题，强调指出：坚定理想信念，坚守共产党人精神追求，始终是共产党人安身立命的根本。对马克思主义的信仰，对社会主义和共产主义的信念，是共产党人的政治灵魂，是共产党人经受住任何考验的精神支柱。形象地说，理想信念就是共产党人精神上的"钙"，没有理想信念，理想信念不坚定，精神上就会"缺钙"，就会得"软骨病"。当前，在我们党员、干部队伍中，信仰缺失、理想动摇是一个需要引起高度重视的问题。比如，有的对共产主义心存怀疑，认为那是虚无缥缈、难以企及的幻想；有的不信马列信鬼神，从封建迷信中寻找精神寄托，热衷于算命看相、烧香拜佛，遇事"问计于神"；有的是非观念淡薄、原则性不强、正义感退化，糊里糊涂当官，浑浑噩噩过日子；有的甚至向往西方社会制度和价值观念，对社会主义前途命运丧失信心；有的在涉及党的领导和中国特色社会主义道路等原则性问题的政治挑衅面前态度暧昧、消极躲避、不敢亮剑，甚至故意模

糊立场、耍滑头；等等。事实一再表明，理想信念动摇是最危险的动摇，理想信念滑坡是最危险的滑坡。一些党员、干部出这样那样的问题，说到底是信仰迷茫、精神迷失。

习近平同志强调，看一个干部是否合格，第一位的就是看理想信念是否坚定。如果理想信念不坚定，不相信马克思主义，不相信中国特色社会主义，这样的干部能耐再大也不是我们党需要的好干部。习近平强调，没有远大理想，不是合格的共产党员；离开现实工作而空谈远大理想，也不是合格的共产党员。也就是既要仰望星空又要脚踏实地。如果丢失了我们共产党人的远大目标，就会迷失方向，变成功利主义、实用主义。而有了坚定的理想信念，站位就高了，眼界就宽了，心胸就开阔了，就能坚持正确政治方向，永葆共产党人政治本色。但是，我们强调党员、干部坚定理想信念，不是说要天天高喊共产主义口号，去干"跑步进入共产主义"那种事。我们要脚踏实地为实现党在现阶段的基本纲领——建设中国特色社会主义而不懈奋斗，扎扎实实做好当前每一项工作。

要坚定理想信念，炼就"金刚不坏之身"，必须用科学理论武装头脑，系统掌握马克思主义科学理论，把的理想信念建立在对马克思主义真理性、社会主义共产主义必然性的真正认识和科学把握的基础之上。习近平总书记强调，面对着十分复杂的国内外环境，肩负着繁重的执政使命，如果缺乏理论思维的有力支撑，是难以战胜各种风险和困难的，也是难以不断前进的。党的各级领导干部要原原本本学习和研读经典著作，认真学习马克思主义哲学，特别是历史唯物主义。广大党员领导干部，都要认真学习马克思主义基本理论，特别是中国特色社会主义理论体系，不断增强工作的科学性、预见性、主动性，使各项决策体现时代性、把握规律性、富于创造性。党校、干部学院、社会科学院、高校、理论学习中心组等都要把马克思主义作为必修课，成为马克思主义学习、研究、宣传的重要阵地，教育引导党员、干部认真学习马克思主义理论，不断提升理论素养、精神境界，不断提高运用马克思主义解决实际问题的能力。特别是党校，要定好位，干部到党校来学习，必须把坚定理想信念、提高思想政治水平放在首位,老老实实、原原本本学习马克思列宁主义、毛泽东思想特别是邓小平理论、"三个代表"重要思想、科学发展观、习近平同志系列重要讲话。新干部、年轻干部尤其要抓好理论学习,通过坚持不懈学习,学会运用马克思主义立场、观点、方法观察和解决问题,坚定理想信念,提高辩证思维能力,做到虔诚而执着、至信而深厚。他强调指出,到党校适当扩大一些知识学习是可以的,但不能喧宾夺主、主次颠倒,党校一定要把理论学习的气氛搞得浓浓的。

2. 干部管理从严,管好干部这一"关键的少数"

习近平总书记强调,党要管党,首先是管好干部;从严治党,关键是从严治吏。要着力培养选拔党和人民需要的好干部,要把从严管理干部贯彻落实到干部队伍建设全过程,坚持从严教育、从严管理、从严监督,要让每一个干部都深刻懂得,当干部就必须付出更多辛劳、接受更严格的约束,没有这样的思想准备和觉悟,就不要进入干部队伍。

以什么样的标准选人用人,是干部工作的首要问题。新时期党和人民需要的好干部的标准是什么? 习近平总书记在全国组织工作会议上鲜明地概括为五个方面、二十个字,即信念坚定、为民服务、勤政务实、敢于担当、清正廉洁。把党和人民需要的好干部选出来,必须切实做到"四个坚持"。一是坚持党管干部,保证党对干部工作的领导,解决"为谁选人"的问题;坚持五湖四海、任人唯贤,落实立党为公的执政理念,解决"用什么理念选人"的问题;坚持德才兼备、以德为先,保证干部政治坚定、作风优良,解决"选什么样的人"的问题;坚持注重实绩、群众公认,靠实践检验干部,解决"依据什么选人"的问题。要做到这"四个坚持",必须把加强党的领导和充分发扬民主统一起来,强化党委(党组)的领导和把关作用,重视在发扬民主的各种方式中、在正确分析和对待推荐测评结果上、在决定任用的关键环节把好关,不简单以票数、分数定取舍,真正把好干部及时发现出来、合理使用起来。一要把忠诚、干净、担当作为选人用人的重要导向,鲜明确立起来,大力选拔信念坚定、心系人民、襟怀坦白的干部,坚决不用信念动摇、背离人民、欺骗组织的干部;二要大力选拔遵纪守法、为政清廉、品行端正的干部,坚决不用目无法纪、以权谋私、道德败坏的干部;三要大力选拔坚持原则、认真负责、敢抓敢管的干部,坚决不用投机钻营、敷衍塞责、争功诿过的干部。

好干部不会自然而然产生。成长为一个好干部,一靠自身努力,二靠组织培养。要切实抓好成千上万各级干部的教育培训,特别是重要岗位、关键岗位干部的教育培训,教育和引导广大党员干部坚定理想信念、加强道德养成、规范权力行使、培育优良作风,自觉履行党章赋予的各项职责,严格按照党的原则和规矩办事。要拓宽实践锻炼的途径,积极为干部锻炼成长找寻平台,引导干部深入基层、深入实际、深入群众,把基础搞扎实。加强干部跨条块、跨领域、跨区域和上下交流,使干部经历一些难事、急事、大事、复杂的事。有计划地安排优秀年轻干部到艰苦岗位、到基层磨炼。完善优秀年轻干部培养选拔的政策制度,进一步拓宽来源、优化结构、改进方式、提高质量。

现实当中,一些干部出现这样那样的问题,主要是干部自身放松了要求,也与干部管理工作跟不上、干部管理制度有漏洞密切相关。要加强对干部的日常管理和监督,进一步完善相关措施,强化组织监督、舆论监督、群众监督,使领导干部无论八小时之内还是八小时之外,都受到约束。习近平总书记强调,没有监督的权力必然导致腐败,这是一条铁律。组织上培养干部不容易,要管理好、监督好,让他们始终有如履薄冰、如临深渊的警觉。对干部身上出现的苗头性、倾向性问题,要及时"咬咬"耳朵、扯扯袖子,不能睁一只眼闭一只眼,更不能哄着、护着,防止小毛病深化成大问题。着力加强遵守纪律特别是政治纪律、执行民主集中制、改进工作作风、履行岗位职责、解决自身问题等方面的监督,加强上级党组织对下级一把手的监督,强化领导班子成员之间的相互监督。党的十八大后,我们制定领导干部在企业兼职(任职)的规定,2014 年共清理在企业兼职 6.3 万人次,其中省部级干部 229 人。制定配偶子女移居国外的领导干部管理办法,明确"裸官"不得在党和国家机关重要岗位任职,2014 年全国对 3200 余名副处级以上"裸官"进行了清理。健全领导干部个人有关事项报告制度,2014 年对全国 6 万多名领导干部个人有关事项报告进行抽查核实,其中一些人因发现问题被取消提拔资格,有的还受到处理。从 2015 年起,对领导干部报告个人有关事项报告随机抽查比例提高到 10%,对新提任的县处以上干部做到"凡提必查"。此外,还开始对领导干部配偶、子女及其配偶经商办企业行为进行规范,对干部政策执行情况进行专项整治等等,目的就是把从严管理干部的要求落实到制度规范上、落实到干部工作各个环节。

习近平总书记指出,从严管理的要求能不能落到实处,领导机关和领导干部带头非常重要。领导机关和领导干部做出样子,下面就会跟上来、照着做。各级干部特别是领导干部要按照"三严三实"要求,深学、细照、笃行焦裕禄精神,努力做焦裕禄式的好干部。各级党组织要旗帜鲜明肯定表彰锐意进取的干部,教育帮助"为官不为"的干部,支持和鼓励干部一心为公、兢兢业业、敢于担当。如果失职渎职给党和人民事业造成损失的,必须严肃处理。

3. 作风要求从严,使党的作风全面纯洁起来

以习近平同志为核心的新一届党中央,以作风建设为切入点和突破口拉开全面从严治党的大幕。党的十八大以来,从制定出台改进工作作风、密切联系群众的"八项规定",到深入开展以为民务实清廉为主要内容的党的群众路线教育实践活动,以及在县处级以上领导干部中开展"三严三实"专题教育……让人民群众看到了实实在在的成效和变化,得到人民群众广泛认同和衷心拥护。

习近平总书记指出:工作作风上的问题绝对不是小事,如果不坚决纠正不良风气,任其发展下去,就会像一座无形的墙把我们党和人民群众隔开,我们党就会失去根基、失去血脉、失去力量。"奢靡之始,危亡之渐。"不正之风离我们越远,群众就会离我们越近。我们党历来强调,党风问题关系党的生死存亡。古今中外,因为统治集团作风败坏导致人亡政息的例子多得很!我们一定要引为借鉴,以最严格的标准、最

严厉的举措治理作风问题。不可否认的是,在发展社会主义市场经济条件下,商品交换原则必然会渗透到党内生活中来,这是不以人的意志为转移的。社会上各种各样的诱惑缠绕着党员、干部,"温水煮青蛙"现象就会产生,一些人不知不觉就被人家请君入瓮了。这么多年,作风问题我们一直在抓,但很多问题不仅没有解决、反而愈演愈烈,一些不良作风像割韭菜一样,割了一茬长一茬。症结就在于对作风问题的顽固性和反复性估计不足,缺乏常抓的韧劲、严抓的耐心,缺乏管长远、固根本的制度。因此,作风建设不可能一蹴而就、毕其功于一役,更不能一阵风,刮一下就停,必须经常抓、长期抓,在改进作风上立新规、动真格、求实效、防反弹。

当前,党内作风上的问题集中表现在"四风"上。习近平总书记指出,形式主义、官僚主义、享乐主义和奢靡之风,是当前群众深恶痛绝、反映最强烈的问题,也是损害党群干群关系的重要根源。"四风"问题解决好了,党内其他一些问题解决起来也就有了更好条件。他强调,解决"四风"问题要对准焦距、找准穴位、抓住要害。反对形式主义,就要着重解决工作不实问题,着力改进学风、文风、会风和工作作风,真正把功夫下到察实情、出实招、办实事、求实效上;反对官僚主义,就要着重解决在人民群众利益上不维护、不作为问题,坚决整治消极应付、推诿扯皮、侵害群众利益问题;反对享乐主义,就要着重克服及时行乐思想和特权现象,牢记"两个务必",保持昂扬向上、奋发有为的精神状态;反对奢靡之风,就要着重狠刹挥霍享乐和骄奢淫逸的不良风气,做到艰苦朴素、精打细算,勤俭办一切事情。从 2013 年 6 月开始,教育实践活动自上而下分两批开展,2014 年 10 月基本结束。在这次教育实践活动中,中央政治局率先垂范,全党自上而下,按照"照镜子、正衣冠、洗洗澡、治治病"的总要求,以整风精神开展活动,对作风之弊、行为之垢进行大排查、大检修、大扫除,有力整治了形式主义、官僚主义、享乐主义和奢靡之风问题,脱离群众现象明显扭转,党风、政风和社会风气为之一新。

事实告诉我们,作风问题具有反复性和顽固性,抓一抓会好转,松一松就反弹,不可能一蹴而就、毕其功于一役,更不能一阵风,刮一下就停。反"四风"的实践也说明,抓和不抓大不一样,真抓和假抓大不一样,严抓和松抓也大不一样。当前,"四风"问题在面上有所收敛,但不良风气积习甚深,树倒根在,稍有松懈,刚刚压下去的问题就可能死灰复燃,防反弹、防回潮任务依然艰巨。"作风建设永远在路上,永远没有休止符"。要以踏石留印、抓铁有痕的劲头,锲而不舍、驰而不息地抓下去,如果前热后冷、前紧后松,就会功亏一篑。要完善并严格执行作风建设各项制度,强化执纪监督,把顶风违纪搞"四风"列为纪律审查的重点,建立健全管用的体制机制,自觉接受群众评议和社会监督。习近平总书记要求,各级领导干部都要既严以修身、严以用权、严以律己,又谋事要实、创业要实、做人要实。"三严三实"是广大党员干部特别是各级领导干部的为政之道、成事之要、做人准则,是对党员干部的新要求,是加强作风建设的再启程、再出发。"三严三实"专题教育作为党的群众路线教育实践活动的延展深化,作为加强党的思想政治建设和作风建设的重要举措,对于进一步祛除歪风邪气、树立清风正气,推动作风建设取得新成效必将发挥重要作用。

"不矜细行,终累大德。"各级干部要从我做起、从小事做起,带头坚守正道、弘扬正气,努力营造良好从政环境。要紧紧盯住作风领域出现的新变化新问题,及时跟进相应的对策措施,做到掌握情况不迟钝、解决问题不拖延、化解矛盾不积压,谁以身试法就要坚决纠正和查处。要从解决"四风"问题延伸开去,努力改进思想作风、工作作风、领导作风、干部生活作风,努力改进学风、文风、会风,加强治本工作,使党员、干部不仅不敢沾染歪风邪气,而且不能、不想沾染歪风邪气,使党的作风全面纯洁起来。

4.组织建设从严,始终保持党的组织坚强有力

列宁说:"无产阶级在夺取政权的斗争中,除了组织而外,没有别的武器。"习近平总书记强调:越是情况复杂、基础薄弱的地方,越要健全党的组织、做好党的工作,确保全覆盖,固本强基,防止"木桶效

应"。因此,必须把从严治党的要求贯彻和体现到党的组织建设之中。

党员是党的肌体的细胞。从严治党的要求必须落实到党员队伍的管理中去。2003年1月28日,习近平总书记主持召开中共中央政治局会议,对加强新形势下党员发展和管理工作进行了研究和部署,提出按照"控制总量、优化结构、提高质量、发挥作用"的总要求。要控制总量,加强发展党员工作宏观指导,制定和落实发展党员规划,保持党员队伍适度规模。要严把入口,始终把政治标准放在首位,决不能让那些动机不纯、一心想借入党捞好处的人进入党内,从源头上保证党员的质量。要改善结构,着力在工人中发展党员,继续做好在农民中发展党员工作,重视从青年工人、农民、知识分子中发展党员。要强化日常教育和管理,严格党内组织生活,使广大党员平常时候看得出来、关键时刻站得出来、危急关头豁得出来,充分发挥先锋模范作用。要疏通出口,及时处置不合格党员,对不符合党员标准的要坚决清退、对不起作用的党员要予以除名,对贪污腐败、违法违纪行为要依法处理。

党的基层组织是党的全部工作和战斗力的基础。贯彻党要从严治党方针,必须扎实做好抓基层、打基础的工作。要健全党的基层组织体系。在新形势下,党的组织建设和国家政权建设出现了上层健全、基层薄弱的新情况新问题。要做好扩大基层组织覆盖的工作,加大在农民合作社、城乡接合部、流动人口聚集地、产业园区等建立党组织的力度,构建城乡统筹的基层党建新格局。切实把整顿软弱涣散基层党组织作为当务之急,结合《中国共产党农村基层组织工作条例》修订,结合国有企业基层党组织建设、社会组织党建工作意见办法的制定,进一步规范基层党组织职责定位、工作要求和活动方式,使基层党组织真正强起来。要建立严密的基层党组织工作制度,推动服务群众、做群众工作制度化、常态化、长效化,把基层党组织的工作重心转到服务发展、服务民生、服务群众、服务党员上来,使基层党组织领导方式、工作方式、活动方式更加符合服务群众的需要。要把热情关心和严格要求结合起来,对基层干部给予更多理解信任和关心爱护,加强教育培训,宣传先进典型,使他们辛苦得愉快、干得光荣,更好地服务群众。各级都要重视基层、关心基层、支持基层,加大投入力度,加强带头人队伍建设,确保基层党组织有资源、有能力为群众服务。

党内政治生活是党组织教育管理党员和党员进行党性锻炼的主要平台。贯彻全面从严治党的要求,必须严肃党内政治生活。然而,由于受种种因素影响,党内生活制度在一些地方没有得到很好的落实,党内生活庸俗化、娱乐化、业务化、随意化倾向突出,分散主义、好人主义、个人主义盛行,甚至一些人不知党内政治生活为何物,是非判断十分模糊。这次群众路线教育实践活动,实际上就是一次健康严肃的党内生活,党员干部普遍受到了一次很好的党性锤炼和精神洗礼。要继续扩大成果,进一步完善和落实党内生活各项制度,使党内政治生活在全党严肃认真开展起来。如何严肃党内政治生活?习近平总书记强调要坚持和用好民主集中制、开展批评和自我批评、严格党内生活、加强党的团结统一这"四大法宝"。第一,要认真执行党的民主集中制。要发扬党内民主,营造民主讨论的良好氛围,鼓励讲真话、讲实话、讲心里话,允许不同意见碰撞和争论,同时善于进行正确集中,防止议而不决、决而不行。严格按程序办事、按规则办事、按集体意志办事,坚决反对和防止个人或少数人专断。第二,坚持用好批评和自我批评武器。党内政治生活质量在相当程度上取决于这个武器用得怎么样。对批评和自我批评这个武器,我们要大胆使用、经常使用、用够用好,使之成为一种习惯、一种自觉、一种责任,使这个武器越用越灵、越用越有效果。党内要开展积极健康的思想斗争,帮助广大党员、干部分清是非、辨别真假,坚持真理、修正错误,统一意志、增进团结。坚持把民主生活会作为解决领导班子自身问题的重要平台,领导带头、开门纳谏,开展积极健康的思想斗争,切实提高民主生活会质量。第三,要坚持严格党内组织生活,增强政治性、原则性、战斗性,使各种方式的党内生活都有实质性内容。第四,要坚持党性原则基础上的团结,坚决反对和纠正表面一团和气、实际上相互较劲设防的假团结。

5.制度执行从严,运用党内法规把从严治党落到实处

在担任总书记之前,习近平同志就明确地指出,解决从严治党问题,最根本的是严格遵循执政党建设规律进行制度建设,不断增强党内生活和党的建设制度的严密性和科学性,既要有实体性制度又要有程序性制度,既要明确规定应该怎么办又要明确规定违反规定怎么处理,减少制度执行的自由裁量空间,推进党的建设的科学化、制度化、规范化。党的十八大以来,结合群众路线教育、党风廉政建设和反腐败的实践,习近平总书记更是从党的生死存亡高度对制度管党治党问题发表了一系列的论述,强调要加强党内法规制度建设,完善党内法规制定体制机制,形成配套完备的党内法规制度体系,运用党内法规把党要管党、从严治党落到实处,促进党员、干部带头遵守法规制度。他指出:把中央要求、实际需要、新鲜经验结合起来,制定新的制度,完善已有的制度,废止不适用的制度。他认为:不管建立和完善什么制度,都要本着于法周延、于事简便的原则,注重实体性规范和保障性规范的结合和配套,要体现改革精神和法治思维,把中央要求、群众期盼、实际需要、新鲜经验结合起来,努力形成系统完备的制度体系,以刚性的制度规定和严格的制度执行,确保改进作风规范化、常态化、长效化,不能把制度变成"稻草人"。

习近平总书记强调,法规制度的生命力在于执行。贯彻执行法规制度关键在真抓,靠的是严管。要强化法规制度意识,在全党开展法规制度宣传教育,引导广大党员、干部牢固树立法治意识、制度意识、纪律意识,形成尊崇制度、遵守制度、捍卫制度的良好氛围,坚持法规制度面前人人平等、遵守法规制度没有特权、执行法规制度没有例外。要加大贯彻执行力度,让铁规发力、让禁令生威,确保各项法规制度落地生根。要加强监督检查,落实监督制度,用监督传递压力,用压力推动落实。对违规违纪、破坏法规制度踩"红线"、越"底线"、闯"雷区"的,要坚决严肃查处,不以权势大而破规,不以问题小而姑息,不以违者众而放任,不留"暗门"、不开"天窗",坚决防止"破窗效应"。党的十八大以来,党内法规制度的"笼子"编织得更加紧密、牢固。首次发布《中国共产

党党内法规制定条例》和《中国共产党党内法规和规范性文件备案规定》,迈出用制度约束权力的重要一步;集中清理1978年以来制定的党内法规和规范性文件,近四成党内法规和规范性文件被废止或宣布失效;出台了20余项廉政新规定,涵盖的内容大到干部选拔任用、公务接待、机关会议费,小到公共场所禁烟、寄送贺年卡、购买赠送烟花爆竹等,一边建章立制,一边狠抓落实,已经取得了明显的成效。

(三) 党员干部为什么要做守纪律讲规矩的表率

习近平总书记反复强调党的各级组织和全体党员特别是党的领导干部,必须遵守党的纪律,按党的规矩办事。在十八届中央纪委五次全会上,他着重阐述严明党的纪律和规矩等重大问题,再次着重地强调,要加强纪律建设,把守纪律讲规矩摆在更加重要的位置。党的十八大以来,我们把严明纪律作为从严治党的重要措施,通过加强纪律建设、严格执纪,纪律的刚性约束明显强化。当然,我们也要看到,这些成效是阶段性的,必须持之以恒、驰而不息地继续加强纪律建设,使纪律真正成为"带电的高压线",在党内真正形成守纪律讲规矩的生动局面。

中共中央政治局审议通过的《中国共产党廉洁自律准则》和《中国共产党纪律处分条例》等,是落实党的十八大和习近平总书记系列重要讲话精神、加强党内法规制度建设的重要成果,是加强党的建设、落实全面从严治党的治本之道。广大党员特别是党员领导干部,要自觉在廉洁自律上追求高标准,在严守党纪上远离违纪红线,以自身的表率作用,引领全党形成尊崇制度、遵守制度、捍卫制度的良好风尚。

1. 从严治党,要靠严明的纪律和规矩

任何政党都有纪律和规矩,没有纪律和规矩就不成其为政党。在世界上最早产生近代政党的英国,其政党都有严格的纪律和规矩。例如,英国工党早在1903年就明确提出党的议员要增进党的利益、不得反对本党决定的"誓约"。不仅如此,欧美国家的不少政党都设

有议会党团督导员,亦即所谓的"党鞭",其主要职责就是督促本党议员遵守党的规矩,对不遵守规矩的议员采取惩戒措施。历史的经验表明,没有规矩不成其为政党,更不成其为马克思主义政党。如果纪律松弛、规矩不张,任何政党都难逃衰败甚至垮台的厄运。苏联共产党最后失败的一个重要原因就是放弃民主集中制原则和党的严格纪律。

中国共产党是一个具有革命理想和铁的纪律的马克思主义政党,纪律严明是党的优良传统和政治优势。新的历史条件下,我们党要团结带领人民实现"两个一百年"的目标,同样要靠严明的纪律和规矩。应当说,党的纪律和规矩都不是新近才提出来的,但为什么党的十八大以来党中央和习近平总书记突出地强调党的纪律和规矩问题呢?就是因为一个时期以来,从严治党没有做到位、严到份,导致一些党员干部把党的纪律当作"稻草人""橡皮泥",根本不把党的纪律和规矩当成一回事,破坏党的纪律和规矩甚至到了肆无忌惮、胆大妄为的地步!这种状况如果得不到及时有效解决,那么我们党迟早会出大问题。因此,习近平总书记强调:"党要管党、从严治党,靠什么管,凭什么治?就要靠严明纪律。"我们党有8800多万党员,在一个13亿多人口的发展中大国执政,必须把守纪律讲规矩摆在更加重要的位置。

2. 第一位的是严守政治纪律和政治规矩

党的纪律和规矩有成文的,也有不成文的,党在长期实践中形成的优良传统和工作惯例,有的可能不成文,但也是党员干部必须遵守的规矩。在成文的规矩中,包括1部党章,2部准则,还有20多部条例,以及数量更多的规则、规定、办法、细则。其中党章是党的"根本大法"和全党同志必须遵守的总规矩。新修订的《中国共产党廉洁自律准则》和《中国共产党纪律处分条例》是对党章规定的具体化,都是全党必须遵守的纪律和规矩。在党的各类纪律和规矩中,党的政治纪律和政治规矩是最重要、最根本、最关键的纪律和规矩。党的组织纪律、工作纪律、群众纪律等是党的政治纪律在不同方面和环节的反映。不管违反哪方面的纪律,最终都会侵蚀党的执政基础,破坏政治纪律。而守住了党的政治纪律和政治规矩,思想上清醒政治上坚定,就容易守住其他各项纪律和规矩的防线。可见,遵守党的政治纪律和政治规矩是遵守党的全部纪律的重要基础。

遵守党的政治纪律和政治规矩,最核心的,就是坚持党的领导,坚持党的基本理论、基本路线、基本纲领、基本经验、基本要求,同党中央保持高度一致,自觉维护中央权威。党的政治纪律和政治规矩不是抽象的,而是具体的,同党中央保持一致也不是一个空洞的口号,而是一个重大政治原则。《中国共产党纪律处分条例》针对现阶段违纪问题的突出表现,强调政治纪律和政治规矩,对反对党的领导和党的基本理论、基本路线、基本纲领、基本经验、基本要求行为作出处分规定。要永远把严守政治纪律和政治规矩排在第一位,切实遵守《中国共产党纪律处分条例》关于政治纪律的规定,通过严肃政治纪律和政治规矩带动其他纪律严起来。

3. 守纪律讲规矩是对党员干部党性的考验

党的纪律和规矩就是对党组织和党员确立的行为标尺,国家的法律法规是面向全体公民的行为底线。党的性质和宗旨都决定了党的纪律和规矩严于国家的法律法规。"破国法"者必先"破党规"。只有切实把纪律和规矩挺在前面,落实抓早抓小,才能防止小错酿成大祸,才能防止"要么是好同志,要么是阶下囚"的问题,避免党员干部滑向违法犯罪的深渊。守纪律讲规矩是对党员、干部党性和忠诚度的重要考验。党员领导干部要发挥表率作用,带头践行廉洁自律规范,自觉维护纪律的严肃性和权威性;带头学习宣传阐释《中国共产党廉洁自律准则》、《中国共产党纪律处分条例》和党的各种规矩,提高守纪律讲规矩的思想自觉,始终把党规党纪刻印在心上,做学习宣传党的纪律和规矩的"明白人";坚持从我做起,向我看齐,坚决摒弃"特殊党员"思想,按规矩办事、按规矩用权,要求别人做到的自己首先做到,要求别人不做的自己首先不做,自觉接受党组织和党员的监督约束,做遵守党的纪律和规矩的"带头人";忠诚履职,落实从严治党责任,带头正风肃纪,对包括本单位内存在的问题,对违反纪律、破坏规矩的行为要进行严肃处理,不能装聋作哑、避重就轻,当"老好人",确保把纪律和各项党内法规执行到位,做党的纪律和规矩的"守护人"。

（四）如何理解"把抓好党建作为最大的政绩"

在 2014 年 10 月召开的党的群众路线教育实践活动总结大会上,习近平总书记强调:"各级各部门党委(党组)必须树立正确政绩观,坚持从巩固党的执政地位的大局看问题,把抓好党建作为最大的政绩。"他指出:"如果我们党弱了、散了、垮了,其他政绩又有什么意义呢?"习近平总书记关于"把抓好党建作为最大的政绩"的重要论述,精辟地阐明了新形势下党建工作的重要地位,具有极其重要的现实针对性和深远意义,在广大党员干部中引起热烈反响。然而,一些同志在思想上也还存在一些疑惑,比如"抓好党建是最大政绩"与我们一直在讲的"发展是第一要务"有没有矛盾? 是不是今后主要抓好党建就行了,抓不抓发展不重要了? 等等。答案当然是否定的。那么,抓好党建是最大政绩与发展是第一要务之间究竟是何种关系,如何正确认识和准确把握两者的关系?

1. 抓发展必须抓党建,抓党建是"坚持发展是第一要务"的必然要求

中华民族的独立和解放,是在党的领导下取得的;解决 13 亿多人民温饱问题和初步建成小康社会,也是在党的领导下实现的。没有共产党就没有新中国,就没有中国特色社会主义,就没有社会主义现代化,这是总结中国近代以来全部历史经验得出的基本结论。在新的历史条件下,党要带领人民进行具有许多新的历史特点的伟大斗争,应对和战胜前进道路上的各种风险和挑战,首要的和根本的就在于把党建设好,这是实现"两个一百年"奋斗目标的基本前提和根本保证。如果

我们党弱了、散了、垮了,中国特色社会主义事业就会被断送,什么国家发展繁荣、民族伟大复兴、人民幸福安康,全都无从谈起。正如邓小平同志指出的,在中国这样的大国,没有共产党的领导,必然四分五裂、一事无成。同样,如果风气坏了、队伍垮了、人心散了,即使取得一时的发展成就,但这种发展决不是我们要的发展。同时,各级领导干部应该认识到,片面的发展绩效并不会自然转化为政治认同。如果经济发展了,但是腐败却更严重了,这会人民群众剥夺感相对更为强烈。邓小平早在 20 世纪 80 年代就曾告诫全党,"风气如果坏下去,经济搞成功又有什么意义?会在另一方面变质,反过来影响整个经济变质,发展下去会形成贪污、盗窃、贿赂横行的世界。"从这个意义上说,抓发展必须抓党建,抓好党建无疑是最大的政绩。发展政治学的研究也表明:一个强大的政党对于后发现代化国家的稳定和发展至关重要。中国现代化的成功,"中国奇迹"的创造,都源于中国共产党的坚强领导。办好中国的事情,关键在党,这是我们总结中国近代以来历史经验得出的必然结论。因此,各级各部门党委(党组)必须树立抓党建是本职、不抓党建是失职、抓不好党建是不称职、党建出了问题是渎职的意识,把抓好党建作为最大的政绩,聚精会神抓好党的建设,为实现"两个一百年"的奋斗目标提供坚强的政治保证。

2. 抓党建就要抓发展,抓发展是"抓好党建是最大政绩"的题中之义

近代以后中国落后挨打的屈辱的历史告诉我们,一个民族只有自强,才能在世界民族之林自立。发展是硬道理,是解决中国所有问题的关键。我们用几十年的时间走完了发达国家几百年走过的历程,最终靠的是发展。实现"两个一百年"奋斗目标、实现中华民族伟大复兴的中国梦,归根到底也要靠发展。现阶段,中国仍是世界上最大的发展中国家,仍处于并将长期处于社会主义初级阶段,因此,以经济建设为中心仍然是兴国之要,发展仍然是我们党执政兴国的第一要务。只有推动经济持续健康发展,才能筑牢国家繁荣富强、人民幸福安康、社会和

谐稳定的物质基础。党的建设历来是同党的政治路线联系在一起的，是为党的历史任务和中心工作服务的。在现阶段，党的建设必须以实现"两个一百年"的奋斗目标为根本方向，紧紧围绕发展这个党执政兴国的第一要务来进行，努力把党建优势转化为国家发展的优势，把党建成果转化为国家发展的成果，使党的建设更加符合社会主义现代化事业发展的要求。党的建设也只有服务于党和国家工作大局，才能在中国特色社会主义伟大实践中找到自己的依托和归宿，为自己开辟宽阔舞台和活力源泉。因此，各级各部门党委（党组）必须始终坚持把发展作为执政兴国的第一要务，一心一意谋发展，推进国家经济、政治、文化、社会和生态文明建设全面、协调、可持续发展，为抓好党建、巩固党的执政地位奠定坚实的基础。

把党建和发展有机结合起来，真正做到聚精会神抓党建、一心一意谋发展。党建是发展的支撑和保证，发展是抓好党建的依托和归宿，两者是相辅相成、缺一不可、有机统一的关系。然而，长期以来，一些党委、党组和党员领导干部不能正确认识和把握两者关系，认为发展是硬任务，党建是虚功夫，不必那么上心用劲，重发展轻党建、"一手硬、一手软"的现象较为普遍。为什么长期以来"四风"问题越积越多、潜规则越来越盛行、政治生态越来越差？根子就在党建工作没有做到位，从严治党的要求没有真正落到实处。各级党委（党组）要准确把握党建和发展的关系，既克服"唯 GDP 论英雄"的偏向，也防止"就党建抓党建"的局限，坚持党建工作和中心工作一起谋划、一起部署、一起考核，把每条战线、每个领域、每个环节的党建工作抓具体、抓深入，真正做到"两手抓、两不误、两促进"。

各级党委（党组）必须把从严治党责任扛在肩上，切实把全面从严治党责任落实到位。习近平总书记在党的群众路线教育实践活动总结大会上的讲话中对落实管党治党责任问题作了全面论述，提出了明确的要求。首先，习近平总书记在讲话中明确提出了"三不"，即历史和现实特别是这次活动都告诉我们，不明确责任，不落实责任，不追究责任，从严治党是做不到的。因此，从严治党，必须提高对从严治党责任制重要性的认识,增强治党的意识和责任感。紧接着,习近平总书记发出了治党"三问"。他指出,经过这些年努力,各级建立了党建工作责任制,党委抓、书记抓、各有关部门抓、一级抓一级、层层抓落实的党建工作格局基本形成。"然而,是不是各级党委、各部门党委(党组)都做到了聚精会神抓党建?是不是各级党委书记、各部门党委(党组)书记都成为了从严治党的书记?是不是各级各部门党委(党组)成员都履行了分管领域从严治党责任?"他认为,一些地方和部门还难以给出令人满意的答案。总书记的治党"三问"振聋发聩、发人深省。习近平总书记一针见血地指出了落实从严治党责任方面存在的"三个误区":一是在一些领导干部眼中,抓党建同抓发展相比要虚一些,不容易出显绩。二是一年开几次会布置一下就可以了,不必那么上心用劲。三是一些人认为,在发展社会主义市场经济条件下,从严治党面临两难选择:过宽没有威慑力,会导致越来越多人闯"红线",最终法不责众;过严会束缚人手脚,影响工作活力,干不成事,甚至还会影响自己的选票。这些认识都是不对的。因此,各级各部门党委(党组)必须树立正确政绩观,坚持从巩固党的执政地位的大局看问题,把管党治党作为重大政治责任,切实做到"三个一起",即各级党委要把从严治党责任承担好、落实好,坚持党建工作和中心工作一起谋划、一起部署、一起考核,把每条战线、每个领域、每个环节的党建工作抓具体、抓深入,坚决防止"一手硬、一手软"。对各级各部门党组织负责人特别是党委(党组)书记的考核,首先要看抓党建的实效,使党委(党组)书记成为真正从严治党的书记;考核其他党员领导干部工作也要加大这方面的权重,促使他们认真履行分管领域从严治党责任,保证从严治党要求落到实处。

思考题

1. 中国共产党为什么要突出强调全面从严治党?

2. 中国共产党全面从严治党,"严"在何处?

参考文献

1. 中共中央宣传部:《习近平总书记系列重要讲话重要读本(2016年版)》,北京:学习出版社、人民出版社,2016年。

2. 中共中央文献研究室:《习近平关于全面从严治党论述摘编》,北京:中央文献出版社,2016年。

3. 中共中央纪律检查委员会、中共中央文献研究室:《习近平关于党风廉政建设和反腐败斗争论述摘编》,北京:中央文献出版社、中国方正出版社,2015年。

Preface

What is the state system of China? How has the Communist Party of China (CPC) managed to exercize long-term governance and to lead the Chinese people from one victory to another? What are the 'secrets' of the CPC's governance? What is China's development road? What significant strategies have been adopted in China? What is the next step in China's development? Why has China been able to achieve such rapid economic development? These are just some of the many questions frequently asked by the international community, especially foreign political parties and statesmen on their visits to China. For the purpose of providing answers to these questions and enabling readers to be informed about the real China and the CPC, we arranged for the *Understanding Modern China* Series (hereinafter referred to as the Series) to be written, to serve as elementary documents introducing the CPC, as well as China's development road, development theories and development experience.

The *Series* is inspired by the new philosophies, new ideas and new strategies for the country's governance put forward by General Secretary Xi Jinping since the 18th National Congress of the CPC, aimed at the following aspects: strenuously reflecting the development vision of 'the Chinese Dream' and the development prospects of the 'Two Centenary Goals'; strenuously reflecting the coordinated promotion of the overall situation of a five-pronged approach to building socialism with Chinese characteristics (to build up socialist economy, socialist democracy, socialist advanced culture, socialist harmonious society, and socialist ecological civilization), and the 'Four-Pronged Comprehensive Strategy' (comprehensively completing the building of a Moderately Prosperous Society, comprehensively deepening reform, comprehensively advancing the rule of law, comprehensively exercising strict party goverance); strenuously reflect the 'new normal' facilitating and leading China's economic development and the implementation of the 'five major development concepts' (to promote innovative, coordinated, green, open, and shared development); strenuously reflecting the three major economic development strategies of the 'Belt and Road', the coordinated development of Beijing, Tianjin and Hebei province, and the Yangtze river economic belt. On the basis of a great number of fresh cases and experiences, the Series tells China's story, transmits China's voice, analyzes China's problems, and offers China solutions.

The Series has been written on the basis of telling China's story and transmitting China's voice, oriented around the following four aspects: the first is to illustrate the new measures taken to deepen reform since the 18th National Congress of the CPC, the new ideas on economic development and the new philosophy on foreign affairs, on the basis of an all-round introduction to the achievements since the reform and opening up; the second is to analyze the reason for the achievements, the underlying operating law, and the process of evolution, while presenting the development achievements of China's economy and society; the third is to keep to problem orientation and demand orientation, rather than attempt to be all-embracing and systematic, so as to clear up targeted doubts and confusion on the basis of the demands of foreign readers; the fourth is to introduce China not only in terms of 'where it is coming from', but also in terms of 'where it is going', for the purpose of enabling readers to know about China's historical development process on the one hand, and on the other hand, exemplifying and clarifying how China assures the organic unification of its past, present and future, the organic combination of inheritance and innovation, and how China is planning its future development.

Under the guidance of the International Department of the CPC Central Committee, the writing of the Series has been organized by China Executive Leadership Academy Pudong (CELAP).

The International Department of the CPC Central Committee is the functional department of the CPC in charge of foreign affairs. So far, the CPC has established connections of various types with more than 600 political parties and organizations in over 160 countries and regions, which include left-wing and right-wing parties; both ruling parties and opposition parties. Foreign affairs work is of paramount importance to the CPC, and an indispensable component of national diplomacy as a whole, whose target is to promote state-to-state and people-to-people communication and understanding.

CELAP is a national leadership institution in China, and as a platformon which international cooperative training and exchange are carried out, CELAP has held fast to its characteristics of internationality and openness since March 2005 when it was founded. CELAP spares no effort in implementing international cooperative training, with target participants being foreign political parties and statesmen, high-ranking business executives and senior professionals. By the end of 2015, CELAP had offered training programs to more than 6,000 participants from over 130 countries, and thus has won wide recognition and received a favorable reception from the countries, regions and participants that are involved.

To cater for the needs of foreign participants, CELAP initiated the writing of the Series at the beginning of 2012, and after four years of modifications and improvements, the finalized manuscripts were completed at the end of 2015. The first batch of 10 books to be published in this Series are: *China's New Strategies for Governing the Country; The Communist Party of China: the Past, Present and Future of Party Building; China's Reform, Opening Up and Construction of Development Zones; An Insider's Guide to the Inner Workings and Structure of the Chinese Government and Public Services; New Analysis of Urbanization in China; China's Agriculture and Rural Development in the Post-Reform Era; The Evolution of China's Diplomacy in the Modern Era; The Selection and Appointment of Officials in China; Leadership Education and Training in China; and Shanghai – the 'Pacesetter' of China's Reform and Opening Up.*

The authors of the Series are mainly professionals in CELAP, and functionaries and specialists in the Development Research Center of the Shanghai Municipal People's Government, Shanghai Institute for International Studies and Hangzhou Research Center for Urban Studies.

The Series is published in Chinese and English, with the English translation done mainly by senior professors at Shanghai International Studies University, to whom thanks are due. Gratitude also goes to the People's Publishing House for its great support and positive suggestions in the process of writing and translating.

Writing such a series of textbooks for mature foreign students is a first in China. Constructive criticism is welcome, for the Series as a new endeavor can hardly be free from mistakes.

Editorial Committee of the *Understanding Modern China* Series
January 2016
(Translator: Wang Xin)

Alain Charles Asia (ACA) Publishing Ltd is delighted to be associated with the People's Publishing House to bring this series of 10 *Understanding Modern China* books to an English-speaking readership.

ACA, formerly known as ACP (Alain Charles Publishing) Ltd Beijing, was founded in October 1989 and was the first foreign-owned publishing company to be allowed to open an office in China.

In 2007, ACP Beijing was renamed ACA Publishing Ltd to better reflect its focus on China and the Asia-Pacific region. The company specialises in publishing books about China for international readers and has offices in Beijing and London.

ACA Publishing Ltd,
April 2016

Contents

Contents

Introduction

At the 18th National Congress of the Communist Party of China (CPC) in November 2012, the CPC elected and established a new Party Central Committee with Comrade Xi Jinping as its core and at the same time set new goals for China's development and new strategies for the governance of China, thereby ushering in a new era in the history of China.

At the 18th CPC National Congress, the CPC as a governing party put forward the 'Two Centenary Goals' for China's future development. As is widely known, around 2020 the CPC - founded in 1921 - will mark its centenary, and around 2050, the PRC established in 1949 will celebrate its centennial. The CPC led the whole nation in completing the New Democratic Revolution, establishing a New China, realizing national independence and liberating the whole of the Chinese people. The CPC has become the governing party and chosen to take the path of socialism. Since 1978 when China initiated its policy of reform and opening up, the country has embarked on the path of socialism with Chinese characteristics. More than 30 years' implementation of the policy has led to the country's prosperity and strength as well as to the people's wellbeing. A continuous high growth rate over 30 years has enabled China to develop into the world's second largest economy. How should China continue to develop in the future? Undoubtedly, China will continue to follow the path of socialism with Chinese characteristics. "As long as we remain true to our ideal, are firm in our conviction, never vacillate in or relax our efforts or act recklessly, and forge ahead with tenacity and resolve, we will surely complete the building of a moderately prosperous society in all respects when the CPC celebrates its centenary, and turns China into a modern socialist country that is prosperous, strong, democratic, culturally advanced and harmonious when the PRC marks its centennial. The whole

Party should have every confidence in our path, in our theories and in our system."[1]

I. Building a Moderately Prosperous Society in All Respects

'To Complete the Building of a Moderately Prosperous Society in All Respects' is the first 'Centenary Goal'. The concept of 'a moderately prosperous society', formerly known and translated as 'a well-off society', was introduced by Mr. Deng Xiaoping in his meeting with Japanese Prime Minister Masayoshi Ōhira on December 6, 1979. Deng, for the first time, expounded his views on "a well-off life" and his conception of "a well-off society" that was expected to be put in place by the end of the 20th century. This very concept was officially approved and adopted in the report to the 12th CPC National Congress in 1982, and set forth as the strategic goal to be accomplished by the end of the 20th century. In 1997, Comrade Jiang Zemin officially established 'Building a Well-off Society' as a new historic mission in the report to the 15th CPC National Congress. In 2002, the 16th CPC National Congress set the goal for *Completing Building a Well-off Society in an All-Round Way* by 2020. In 2007, the report to the 17th CPC National Congress noted clearly that every effort must be made to ensure the attainment of the goal for 'Building a Moderately Prosperous Society in all Respects' by 2020, and set new requirements for promoting economic, political, cultural, social and ecological progress. The report to the 18th CPC National Congress required endeavours to be made to ensure completing the Building of a Moderately Prosperous Society in all Respects by 2020.

In traditional Chinese culture, 'moderate prosperity' is a relative concept that denotes 'affluence and being a person of substance', but to develop 'a moderately prosperous society' has definite and specific quantitative indices. Let us take economic index as an example. The 16th CPC National Congress stated that efforts should be made to quadruple China's 2000 GDP by 2020. The 17th CPC National Congress continued to use that index but with more emphasis on balanced development to ensure sound and rapid economic growth. The 18th CPC National Congress put forward the 'Two Doubles' for its economic objectives: one is to double China's 2010 GDP and the other is to double the same year's per-capita income for both urban

---

[1] *Hu Jintao's Report to the Eighteenth National Congress of the CPC: Firmly March on the Path of Socialism with Chinese Characteristics and Strive to Complete the Building of a Moderately Prosperous Society in all Respects*

and rural residents. Besides economic indices, there are other development requirements for socialist democracy, ethics, culture, social undertakings and environmental protection.

The essence of 'Building a Moderately Prosperous Society in All Respects' by 2020 set out at the 18th CPC National Congress lies in 'All Respects'. 'All Respects' means that the goal of a moderately prosperous society is to benefit all the Chinese people without any exception or without leaving anyone behind, and regardless of regional differences, covering the whole population of over 1.3 billion. 'All Respects' also means that the goal, involving all areas of endeavour, is an overall plan for the promotion of economy, politics, society, culture and ecological progress. The moderately prosperous society requires 'upright officials, clean government and clear politics'. It attempts to 'secure the greatest achievements in response to all the wishes and needs of the people'. It will 'break down the dichotomized structure of urban and rural areas and help farmers live a pleasant life in their sweet homes'. It aims to 'strengthen our national material and spiritual power, and improve the physical and mental life of the Chinese people of all ethnic groups'. It will 'bring back to life our unpolluted homeland so that we can bear in our mind sweet reminiscences about our homes with green mountains and clear waters'. To complete the 'Building of a Moderately Prosperous Society in All Respects' is a strategic goal of paramount importance.

There are only five years to go before completing the building of a moderately prosperous society in all respects. This is our goal in the near future, but how will China continue to develop around 2050, 30 years from now? China will undoubtedly continue to follow the path of socialism with Chinese characteristics. By doing so, we must, 'under the leadership of the CPC, based on the essential realities of the state, around the core of economic advancement, sticking to Four Cardinal Principles, and to the policy of reform and opening up, liberate and develop our productive force, to foster a socialist market economy, socialist democracy, socialist advanced culture, a socialist harmonious society and socialist ecological progress so as to promote the well-rounded development of the individual, and gradually achieve the common prosperity of all the people to build a prosperous, strong, democratic, culturally advanced, and harmonious modern socialist country'.[1] 'To build a prosperous, strong, democratic, culturally advanced,

---

[1] *Hu Jintao's Report to the Eighteenth National Congress of the CPC: Firmly March on the Path of Socialism with Chinese Characteristics and Strive to Complete the Building of a Moderately Prosperous Society in All Respects*

and harmonious modern socialist country' includes the requirements to promote the well-rounded development of the individual and to achieve prosperity for all the people. This is exactly the second 'Centenary Goal' to be achieved around 2050: 'the Chinese Dream' of 'the Rejuvenation of the Chinese nation'.

II. The Chinese Dream

To fulfill the goals and tasks requires a core concept to cover all aspects, together with a spiritual banner to boost the morale of the people and to stimulate the positive forces of the whole society. General Secretary Xi Jinping established the concept of 'the Chinese Dream' in his improvised speech to the press when he and other Party and state leaders visited the exhibition entitled 'The Road to Rejuvenation' on November 29, 2012. He developed the connotations of 'the Chinese Dream' on several subsequent occasions. 'The Chinese Dream' connotes 'the greatness and prosperity of China, the rejuvenation of the Chinese nation, the happiness of the Chinese people'. To realize the rejuvenation of the Chinese nation has been the greatest dream of China in modern times. 'The Chinese Dream' is the dream of the people, of the nation, of every Chinese family and even every individual, enabling every Chinese citizen to share equal opportunities, enjoy the excellence of life and make their dreams come true. It is the response to the calls and expectations of the people. The people's aspiration for a better life is our goal to strive for. To realize 'the Chinese Dream', we must keep to our socialist path, carry forward our Chinese spirit and pool our own strength. Meanwhile, 'the Chinese Dream' has much in common with the dream of people in other countries all over the world. To complete the 'Building of a Moderately Prosperous Society in All Respects' is a momentous milestone in the process of realizing the rejuvenation of the Chinese nation. "China has entered a decisive historic stage to completing the Building of a Moderately Prosperous Society in All Respects. To accomplish this goal is a key step in realizing 'the Chinese Dream' of the Rejuvenation of the Chinese nation." The proposal of 'the Chinese Dream' is vivid and inspiring. It is the 'greatest common denominator' of the strength from all sectors of the society, and has become the theme of the times for which the CPC has been leading and striving together with the Chinese people of all ethnic groups. The Chinese Dream has become an important guiding principle and governing concept put forward by Comrade Xi Jinping since the 18th CPC National Congress.

III. The Five-pronged Approach to Building Socialism with Chinese Characteristics

The report to the 18th CPC National Congress set forth an overall plan for seeking economic, political, cultural, social, and ecological progress as a five-pronged approach to building socialism with Chinese characteristics. In other words, to develop socialism with Chinese characteristics, we should make concerted efforts to promote economic, political, cultural, social and ecological progress in all areas of endeavour. To be more specific, we are going to 'build up socialist economy, socialist democracy, socialist advanced culture, socialist harmonious society, and socialist ecological civilization'. The focus of economic advancement is laid on 'accelerating the improvement of the socialist market economy and the change of the growth model'. The political advancement stresses 'keeping to the socialist path of making political advance with Chinese characteristics and promoting reform of the political structure'. The cultural advancement highlights the mission of 'building a culturally strong socialist country and strengthening the core socialist value system'. Social advancement accentuates 'improving people's living standard and innovating social management'. Ecological progress emphasizes the following tasks as 'conserving resources, protecting the environment and striving for green, sustainable and low-carbon development so as to make China a beautiful country'. All these five respects are indispensable to building socialism with Chinese characteristics, which is an overall strategic plan. The Party's leadership lies at the core of the grand undertaking of completing socialism with Chinese characteristics and guarantees its foundation and development. Accordingly, the overall plan for seeking economic, political, cultural, social, and ecological progress should incorporate one more respect, that is, Party building.

IV. The Four-pronged Comprehensive Strategy

In November 2012, the report to the 18th National Congress of the CPC put forward the goal of 'completing the Building of a Moderately Prosperous Society in All Respects'. Since then, the CPC Central Committee with Comrade Xi Jinping at its core has successively initiated the 'Two Centenary Goals' and the goal of 'Realizing the Chinese Dream of the Rejuvenation of the Chinese Nation'. In November 2013, the Third Plenary Session of the 18th CPC Central Committee called forth 'intensifying reform in all respects', and fixed its general goal as 'improving and developing socialism with Chinese characteristics and promoting the modernization drive of the national governance system and capacity'. The Fourth Plenary Session of the 18th CPC Central Committee held in October 2014, brought forward the goal of 'comprehensively advancing the rule of law' and defined its overall target as 'building the legal system of socialism with Chinese characteristics and developing socialist country built on the rule of law'. Later, 'to exercise strict self-governance by the Party in every respect' was proposed by Xi Jinping during an tour of inspection in Jiangsu Province on December 13 and 14 of 2014, and thus together with other three strategies, it was integrated into the 'Four-pronged Comprehensive Strategy' which was illustrated and established as a holistic development arrangement. The 'Four-pronged Comprehensive Strategy', just as the term indicates, has four principal strands, pinning down strategies to help continue and develop the path, the theories and the system of socialism with Chinese characteristics.

The 'Four-pronged Comprehensive Strategy' was brought forth as a response to our ever-changing national development conditions and as an answer to the earnest expectations of the people to tackle pronounced conflicts and problems confronting us. In respect of governing the whole country, this strategy captures the key target for a stable reform and development, covers a general development plan of China, and specifies the work of the Party and the country under new circumstances regarding strategic development direction, key areas and major targets. Adhering to the question-oriented approach and a scientific outlook, laying the base on Chinese realities and drawing on Chinese experience, General Secretary Xi Jinping has proposed the Four-pronged Comprehensive Strategy for tackling Chinese problems, from a comprehensive perspective of a modern Chinese communist member with a strategic vision and firm confidence in China. These four strategies are interconnected in facilitating, promoting and complementing each other. They include one target and three measures. In other words, they contain a general plan as well as specific key points, with each strategy directed at a matter of paramount strategic significance. Among them, 'to complete the Building of a Moderately Prosperous Society in All Respects' is the general strategic target, while the other three are specific measures. Among them, 'intensifying reform in all respects' and 'governing the country thoroughly based on law' are parallel strategies, as in, 'both wings of a bird and two wheels of a cart'. A further strategy, 'exercising strict self-governance in every respect' is a political safeguard for forging a more solid core leadership for our cause. These four strategies are not simply paralleled but organically integrated and interrelated in their top-level design, sketching a promising blueprint of socialist China where one can find a moderately prosperous society aglow with revolutionary spirit, the people sharing a solid view of law-based governance, and a ruling party strictly and completely self-governed.

V. The Five Major Development Concepts

The Fifth Plenary Session of the 18th CPC Central Committee, held in Beijing from October 26 to 29, 2015, mainly deliberated on the economic and social development of China in the following five years (2016 – 2020), and approved the document *Central Committee of the CPC: Recommendations for the 13th Five-Year Plan for Economic and Social Development*. The period of the '13th Five-Year Plan' is the decisive stage in finishing building a moderately prosperous society in all respects, while the most noteworthy contribution highlighted by the Fifth Plenary Session of the 18th CPC Central Committee is the proposal to promote innovative, coordinated, green, open, and shared development. These 'Five Major Development Concepts set out methods, direction and focus of national development during the 13th Five-Year Plan period, or even longer. They fully embody our experience of development over the past three decades of reform and opening up, and reflect our Party's new understandings on our internal laws of development.'[1] They enrich and elaborate the Party's theories on development. They demonstrate a breakthrough in, and new development of, the Scientific Outlook on Development; they summarize and conclude new ideas, new thoughts and new strategies concerning governance of the country under the guidance of the Party Central Committee with Comrade Xi Jinping at its core.

Firstly, among the five concepts, innovation is prioritized to an unprecedented extent. In pursuing innovative development, 'Innovation should be placed at the heart of China's development and promoted in every field, from theory to institutions, in science, technology, and culture. Innovation should permeate all work of the party and the country and become an inherent part of the society.'[2] Since the 16th CPC National Congress, our party has been governing the state involving all parts of work in accordance with the principle of reform and innovation and in an effort

---

[1] Xi Jinping. *Explanatory Notes for the Central Committee of the CPC: Recommendations for the 13th Five-Year Plan for Economic and Social Development.*

[2] *Central Committee of the CPC: Recommendations for the 13th Five-Year Plan for Economic and Social Development* (Adopted at the Fifth Plenary Session of the 18th Central Committee of the CPC on October 29, 2015)

to improve our self-initiated innovation capability and develop our country into an innovative state. The 18th CPC National Congress put forward the innovation-driven development strategy, and required us to conduct reform in every area and at all levels in economic and social development, and to promote innovative development through reform. At the Fifth Plenary Session of the 18th CPC Central Committee, innovation was cited as 'the primary driving force for development', and was put in 'a central place in China's development strategy'. This is a significant development of concepts and approaches, functioning as a response to requirements of the times. Accordingly, this concept involves 'innovation in our theories, institutions, science and technology, and culture' - rather than scientific and technological innovation alone. The first and foremost aspect of innovation is theoretical innovation. The Four-pronged Comprehensive Strategy is a kind of theoretical innovation; so too are the 'Five Development Concepts'. Theory is the precursor, the soul and the master switch. With the guidance of new theories, the direction of development and the path to be followed are clear. Institutional innovation is next in terms of importance. Modernization of the national governance system and its capacity is the overall goal of a comprehensive reform agenda, as well as being the greatest institutional innovation that guarantees other kinds of innovation. The key matter of scientific and technological innovation is the most dynamic innovation. That is why we should promote public entrepreneurship and innovation, and drive the emergence of new technology, new formats and new industries. Cultural innovation in a broad sense refers not only to the innovation in various areas of arts, cultural undertakings and industries but also to that of socialist core values, spiritual, political and ethical culture. 'Innovation should permeate all work of the party and the country, and become an inherent part of society.' This is a remarkable breakthrough in the Scientific Outlook on Development.

Secondly, the Five Major Development Concepts lay greater stress on coordinated development. In pursuing coordinated development, "While keeping firmly in mind the overall strategy of socialism with Chinese characteristics, we should properly handle relationships between major areas of development, focusing on promoting balanced development between urban and rural areas as well as between different regions; promoting coordinated economic and social development; and promoting the synchronized development of a new type of industrialization, information technology, urbanization, and agricultural modernization. While increasing China's hard power, we should also work to enhance its soft power, striving constantly to make development more comprehensive."[1] Besides the notions of 'promoting balanced development between urban and rural areas as well as between different regions' and 'promoting the synchronized development of a new type of industrialization, information technology, urbanization, and agricultural modernization', two more notions are proposed. These are; 'coordinating material progress and cultural and ethical progress' and 'integrating the development of the economy and national defense'. In this context, coordinated development is extended to cover a wider and larger scale, and will substantially realize 'a comprehensive, balanced and sustainable development' rather than economic coordination alone. For the first time, cultural and ethical progress is included in coordinated development, demonstrating determination to promote both material progress and cultural and ethical progress without favouring either at the expense of the other. Their coordinated development is a prerequisite to upholding and developing socialism with Chinese characteristics and a fundamental task in building a moderately prosperous society in all respects.

Third, the Five Major Development Concepts accentuate a harmonious green development between the people and nature. In pursuing green development, "We should adhere to the fundamental state policy of conserving resources and protecting the environment so as to promote sustainable development, and pursue a civilized development path that ensures increased levels of production, better living standards, and a sound ecology. We should move faster to build a resource-conserving, environmentally friendly society and bring about a model for modernization in which mankind develops in harmony with nature. We should move forward with building a Beautiful China and make new contributions toward ensuring global ecological security."[2] We should make green development a mode of production, a way of life, even a fashion of the society. 'Green development' corresponds to 'sustainable development' in the Scientific Outlook on Development, but it enriches the latter concept. Besides 'promoting low-carbon and sustainable development, conserving resources wherever possible and putting them to efficient use, stepping up environmental governance efforts and building ecological security shields', "We should take a green approach to developing a prosperous China and ensuring the wellbeing of its people. We should provide more quality green products for the people, encourage green forms of development and green lifestyles, and ensure that all work is in concert

---

[1] Ibid
[2] Ibid

to help the people become prosperous, make our country strong, and build a Beautiful China." Compared with the past, this principle highlights the concept of harmony between human and nature, stresses the notion of functional zones, and adds the goal of building a Beautiful China.

Fourth, the Five Major Development Concepts highlight open development. In pursuing open development, "In adapting to China's ever-deepening integration into the global economy, we should pursue a mutually beneficial strategy of opening up. We should develop a new level of openness within our economy, participate actively in global economic governance and the global supply of public goods, seek to have a greater say in the institutions for global economic governance, and look to build communities of common interests with more international partners."[1] Over 30 years have elapsed since the implementation of reform and opening up. At the start of this century, we proposed the integration of two approaches of 'bringing in' and 'going global' as our opening-up strategy. Since the 18th CPC National Congress, the situation concerning opening up has changed tremendously. In the past, we made more efforts to introduce the outside world to China, follow the world political and economic order and integrate ourselves into their institutions, and use others' platforms to display ourselves and promote our work. However, today we are increasing our efforts to go to the outside world, build up our own platforms for international collaboration, and set up new political and economic institutions as in the practices of the 'Belt and Road' Initiative, the Asian Infrastructure Investment Bank, the Silk Road Fund and Free Trade Zone. In changing circumstances, we should adapt to China's ever-deepening integration into the global economy, put into perspective the international and domestic conditions, and develop an open economy at a higher level. We should upgrade our opening-up strategy to establish a new framework. In addition, we should construct a new layout of complete openness for synchronized development of both land and marine economies, together with opening up to both east and the west regions. We should also leverage international and domestic markets and resources. We should participate actively in global economic governance in an effort to have a greater say in its institutions, and look to build communities of common interests with more international partners. China has become the world's second largest economy. To demonstrate our trustworthiness as a big country, we are going to assume more international responsibilities and obligations. The concept of open development reflects

---

[1] Ibid

our new perspectives on, and understanding of, opening-up policy under current world circumstances, and it is a renewal of the Scientific Outlook on Development.

Fifth, the Five Major Development Concepts underscore shared development. In pursuing shared development, "we should ensure that development is for the people, that it is reliant on the people, and that its fruits are shared by the people. We should improve our institutions to ensure that the people have a greater sense of benefit as they contribute to and share in development, thus strengthening the impetus for development, enhancing unity among the people, and helping them move steadily toward common prosperity."[1] Over the past 30 years of reform and opening up, we have shifted from a focus on development rate, efficiency and effectiveness, to place more emphasis on the people's standard of living, and have paid more and more attention to fairness and justice. Since the 16th CPC National Congress, we have proposed, 'the principle of all the people building and sharing a harmonious socialist society', and have created 'a lively situation in which everyone is duty-bound to work for, and benefit from, social harmony.' The concept of shared development embodies the orientation of the party's work to the people and the principle of putting the people first, and requires us 'to ensure that living standards are improved through the involvement and dedication of all people and the shared enjoyment of benefits therein' and to take the fundamental interests of the people as our starting point and as the ultimate goal of our work, to enable the people's expectations to be met. The key features of shared development proposed at the Fifth Plenary Session of the 18th CPC Central Committee lie in their orientation to people's wellbeing and fairness. They are illustrated by the following aspects: bridging the income gap, ensuring that personal income grows in step with economic growth, and that remuneration for labour grows in step with rising productivity. In addition, to combat poverty, we should adopt targeted measures to alleviate and eliminate poverty in light of local conditions. To proactively respond to population aging, we should establish a multilevel elderly support system, providing more services and products for the elderly. To promote the building of a Healthy China, we should implement a food safety strategy. To promote balanced population development, we should implement the policy of allowing all couples to have two children. All of these points are shining examples, signalling innovative ideas and highlighting new development.

---

[1] Ibid

Development is the theme of the times and a common objective in all countries of the world. The 'Five Major Development Concepts' constitute a development theory that is completely in step with the times, and are evidence of a change in the mode and approach of thinking. It is a synthetic application of dialectical and systematic methodology with a consideration of the worst-case-scenarios.

The Party Central Committee with Comerade Xi Jinping at its core is leading the Chinese people in accomplishing the following missions: attaining the Two Centenary Goals; completing the Building of a Moderately Prosperous Society in All Respects; realizing the Chinese Dream of the Great Rejuvenation of the Chinese Nation; conducting the Five-pronged Approach to an overall plan for promoting all-round economic, political, cultural, social, and ecological progress towards socialism with Chinese characteristics; coordinating the progress of the Four-pronged Comprehensive Strategy; and putting into practice the 'Five Major Development Concepts'. All these key words epitomize the core contents of the new principles and strategies for the governance of China under the leadership of General Secretary Xi Jinping.

Feng Jun is the chief editor of the book. Each section and chapter of the book is written by different authors, and they are, respectively: Introduction is written by Feng Jun, Chapter One by He Lisheng, Chapter Two by Wang Youming, Chapter Three by Liu Zhexin, Chapter Four by Hu Hanjin, Chapter Five by Huang Lizhi, Chapter Six by Yu Hongsheng, Chapter Seven by Yan Nailing, and Chapter Eight is written by Liu Jingbei.

Chapter 1

China's New Normal

China is still in a significant period of strategic opportunity. We must boost our confidence, adapt to the 'new normal' condition based on the characteristics of China's economic growth in the current phase; and stay cool-minded. China should also attach great significance to preventing a range of risks for its economy and take timely countermeasures to reduce potential negative effects.

— Xi Jinping's Speech during an Inspection Tour in Henan Province in May 2014.[1]

I. The New Normal of Economic Growth: Upgrading China's Economy

Literally, 'new normal' contains two terms, in which the 'new' means a different economic growth model compared with the 'old' one, and the term 'normal' refers to a usual state. Making the distinction from an economy that is overly driven by input and investment and grows inefficiently at a high rate, the economy under the 'new normal' condition refers to a long-lasting growth model with a lower rate of growth, a more optimized structure, a progressive transition to innovation as its key driver, and a deeper reform of its system. Adapting to the 'new normal' of growth indicates that China envisages a new period of economic development moving towards structural upgrading and relying more on domestic market. "Under the 'new normal' condition", as pointed out by General Secretary Xi Jinping, "China's economic development has three major features: a lower growth rate, an

---

[1] When Inspecting in Henan Province, Xi Jinping Stressed that We Must Deepen the Reform, Capitalize on Advantages, Innovate Ideas, and Make Overall Plans and Take All Factors into Consideration to Ensure Stable and Sound Economic Development as well as a Harmonious and StableSociety. People's Daily, May 11, 2014(1).

optimized structure and a different motive force. Specifically, the economy will shift gear from the previous high speed to a medium-high speed growth; the focus of growth model will be shifted from scale and speed to quality and efficiency; the economic structure will be changed from the expansion of production volume and capacity, to the dual goal of adjusting stock and upgrading the quality of production, instead of continuing to rely on natural resources and low-cost labor, the leading engine of development will be innovation. Independent of man's will, all this must be carried out according to the current development phase of the China's economy."[1]

1. Shifting gear from the previous high speed to a medium-high speed growth is the basic characteristic of the 'new normal' economy.

China is changing gear from an annual growth rate of 10% to a lower rate of about 7%, which is a manifestation of the 'new normal'. Because of the increasing costs or prices of labor, resources, land and other factors, the peak growth rates of the past cannot be sustained or afforded. Contributing factors include the enormous stress caused by the limitations imposed by environmental factors, consumption of resources and market restrictions. Therefore, it is impossible for the model of economic development that is driven only by elements of input, expansion and investment-driven growth to go further. Although seeing a lower growth rate under the 'new normal' situation, China still "aims to double the 2010 GDP and per capita income of urban and rural residents by 2020 on the basis of making China's development much more balanced, inclusive and sustainable,"[2] and continues to be the most vigorous economy leading global growth.

China is striving to achieve the 'Two Centenary Goals' as a grand blueprint and to accomplish the building of a moderately prosperous society in all aspects by 2020. Economically, as long as China keeps its growth rate at 7% during the 10 years from 2010 to 2020, even if the GDP drops by 1% every 10 years thereafter, namely at 6% from 2020 to 2030, 5% from 2030 to 2040, and 4% from 2040 to 2050, it will be an economy with GDP growth rate equal to that of America in 2030, and its economy will exceed that of America by 1.34 times in 2050. As General Secretary Xi Jinping pointed out in the Boao Forum for Asia Annual Conference 2015, "When looking at

---

[1] Xi Jinping. Explanatory Notes for the *Central Committee of the CPC: Recommendations for the 13th Five-Year Plan for Economic and Social Development*. Xinhuanet. November 3, 2015.
[2] *Central Committee of the CPC: Recommendations for the 13th Five-Year Plan for Economic and Social Development*. Xinhuanet. November 3, 2015.

China's economy, one should not focus on growth rate only. As the economy continues to grow in size, around 7% growth would be quite impressive, and the momentum it generates would be larger than that of the double-digit growth in previous years."[1]

2. Economic growth under the 'new normal' situation is genuine and uninflated.

When assessing the economic growth rate in an objective manner, it is crucial to take into account economic size as well as the quality and efficiency of development. Since the introduction of the reform and opening-up policy, China has witnessed a high economic growth rate. However, during this period, some regions and fields have seen the problems of 'GDP only' and inappropriate pursuit of a high growth rate regardless of other factors, which is closely related to problems such as over exploitation of resources, severe environmental pollution, and unhealthy economic structure we are encountering. Therefore, General Secretary Xi Jinping has repeatedly emphasized that "we must fully realize the relationship between sustainable and healthy economic development and GDP growth", and that, "we must avoid simply measuring development by the GDP growth rate." Avoiding simply measuring development by the GDP growth rate is an essential requirement for China's economy under the 'new normal' situation.

Since China has become the second largest economy in the world after more than three decades of high-speed growth, it is no longer realistic to continue to grow at this pace and at double-digit-percentage rates on the higher base level of economic activity. In addition, limitations of resources and environmental pollution, rule out continuing to pursue those levels of growth rate. Besides, solving the deep-seated problems accumulated during the high-speed development requires us to shift the economy to an appropriate speed, sparing space for stable and sustainable economic development.

Since China's economic aggregate activity and the base figure of GDP have already increased greatly after over three decades of high-speed development, an increase in economy of 1% GDP growth is by no means a negligible figure. Statistics show that China's GDP reached Rmb63.6 trillion in 2014 (calculated at current price, with the same factor applied hereafter),

---

[1] A Keynote Speech at the Boao Forum for Asia Annual Conference 2015 Delivered by President Xi Jinping. Xinhuanet. March 29, 2015.

exceeding $10 trillion at the current exchange rate, representing 13.3% of the world economy. Its annual increase in GDP was equivalent to the aggregate economic output of a medium-size developed country; the per capita GDP totaled $7,594, which, according to the World Bank estimates, placed China at a mid level among the countries with medium-to-high income in the world. The per capita disposable income of urban and rural residents is respectively Rmb29,000 and Rmb11,000.

Compared with that of 2013, the economic output of 2014 increased $866.5 billion, which means that at present the increase that China achieves in one year exceeds its total economic output in 1996, by $5.7 billion. Measured against other economies, that increase is $27.5 billion more than the aggregate economic output in 2013 of Turkey, which is the 17th largest economy in the world. Contrasts are even greater if we compare the figures for 2014 with those of 2007. Although the GDP growth rate in 2014 fell to 7.4%, the lowest since the beginning of the 21st century, every percentage point of GDP growth brings about an increase of $117.1 billion, twice as much as that of 2007. If we take the adjustment of industrial structure into consideration, every percentage point of GDP growth of 2014 is estimated to create 1.8 million new jobs. And the target of growth rate in 2014 means an increase of over Rmb5 trillion, equivalent of the entire economic output in 1994.

Each year since 2013, the increase created by the tertiary industry (service sector) in China as a proportion of GDP has surpassed that of the secondary industry. However, the service sectors in some developed countries have already accounted for more than 80% of their GDPs. Thus, the proportion of this sector in China's economy will be increasing for a long time under the 'new normal' situation. During the period of a change in the pace of economic growth, China has to emerge from the phase of rapid growth and develop at a reasonable growth rate, ensuring that the economy operates within an appropriate range. It is both possible and necessary to maintain a medium-high growth rate and keep the economy developing towards a medium-high level.

What speed, therefore, is it appropriate for China to grow at? "To achieve the goal of doubling per capita income by 2020 from its 2010 level, China must maintain an average annual economic growth rate at 6.5% or above while seeing growth of both income and the economy during the 13th Five-Year Plan period. Medium-high economic growth will help improve the living standards and quality of life with people truly enjoying the fruits brought about during the building of a moderately prosperous society in all respects."[1]

An excessively low growth rate will bring about many problems associated with structure rebalancing, employment security, improvement of livelihood and social stability. If the growth drops too fast or even goes into a stall, government revenue will shrink. This would be followed by a decrease in public expenditure, a soaring unemployment rate and a sharp fall in income, which would go beyond acceptable limits of social endurance.

Therefore, avoiding simply measuring development by the GDP growth rate does not mean ignoring economic growth. Instead, great importance is attached to an efficient, high-quality and sustainable growth. When determining a certain growth rate, we must take into consideration the need to finish building a moderately prosperous society in all respects, the necessities of expanding economic output and upgrading structure, the principles of reality and economic development, the requirements of both stabilizing economic growth and rebalancing the economic structure, and the pursuit of full employment and stably increasing income.

In general, the 'new normal' growth involves a dynamic balance of industrial structure, real improvement of social welfare, coordinated development between regions, integration of quality and efficiency as well as energy conservation and environmental protection. In other words, the economic growth under the 'new normal' situation is genuine and uninflated.

Just as General Secretary Xi Jinping stressed in the Central Economic Work Conference in December 2013, "The growth rate we are pursuing is genuine and not inflated, and is the one that could improve people's wellbeing and help achieve full employment. At this kind of rate, the economy should develop both in higher quality and efficiency and with no after-effects, and at the same time the labor productivity will be raised, economic vitality increasingly injected, and economic structure effectively adjusted."[2] We strive for sustainable economic growth accompanied by a transformation of the growth model, optimization of economic structure, improvement in the ecological environment and growth of quality and efficiency.

---

[1] Xi Jinping. Explanatory Notes for the *Central Committee of the CPC: Recommendations for the 13th Five-Year Plan for Economic and Social Development*. Xinhuanet, November 3, 2015.
[2] *Central Committee of the CPC: Recommendations for the 13th Five-Year Plan for Economic and Social Development*. Xinhuanet. November 3, 2015.

3. Structural optimization is an inherent feature of the 'new normal'.

What we are supposed to see when the restructuring starts to be carried out is that "major economic indices will be balanced and coordinated; the space and layout of development will be optimized; efficiency of investment and performance of enterprises will be improved; industrialization and informatization will be further integrated to raise the level of development; the development of industries will be promoted toward the medium-high end; the development of advanced manufacturing industry will accelerate, new industries will keep growing, the services industry will account for a higher proportion of the national economy; economic growth will be increasingly driven by consumption; the population urbanization rate will be improved rapidly; and major progress in agricultural modernization will be made. Fulfilling these objectives will turn China into an innovative and talent-rich country."[1]

China has accomplished remarkable achievements in its economy since the policy of opening up and reform was implemented, and its model and path of economic development have been recognized globally. The rapid-economic-growth model did fit China as an emerging economy, and as a post-industrial country with comparative advantages as a developing country. During that period it supported China's uninterrupted growth at a high rate. However, this kind of growth model has led to some serious structural problems and conflicts, including inefficient economic growth, a deteriorating trade environment, and energy, resources and the environment under heavy pressure or even too weak to support the growth.

For example, China's development has been excessively reliant on high investment; in the global division of labor it has been excessively reliant on trade linked to processing and manufacturing. It has depended excessively on cost price to prevail in international competition. But at the same time, high-value-added elements such as R&D and design, marketing, brand management and supply chain management in both industrial and value chains, have been absent. That can be summarized as 'three excessives' and 'one deficiency'. Dynamic structural optimization requires a focus on economic growth to shift from merely increasing output and expanding the operating base, to stock adjustment and quality upgrading. To lead the 'new normal'

---

[1] An important speech at the Central Economic Work Conference delivered by Xi Jinping. Xinhuanet. December 11, 2014.

and complete the upgrading of its economy, China needs to address certain problem areas and drive its economy from extensive model to intensive one, It must move from a low-technology model to a high-end one and overcome further difficulties, among which structure rebalancing is highlighted as a rather tough one.

Just as Xi Jinping put it, "We must capitalize on the resilience and great potential of China's economy, which still has much leeway to grow, to persist in improving its quality and efficiency and upgrading through reform and restructuring. And what we are striving to achieve is lower-speed economic growth without losing momentum and a growing economy providing higher-quality production."[1] As we know, the economic structure is required to be dynamically optimized all the time due to the constant change of market, technology and demand. The balance of economic structure and dynamic optimization will become the 'new normal' of the economy, which is based on the integration of growth rate, restructuring and power transformation.

Concurrently, we will bring revisions and changes into China's economic structure in terms of industrial structure, market structure, regional structure, urban and rural structure, capital structure and distribution pattern. Then, we will achieve multidimensional and dynamic adjustment and rebalancing of the economic structure. In terms of the industrial structure, we should pursue a transformation from a large manufacturing country to a country with both powerful manufacturing and service industries; in terms of regional structure, we should pursue a pathway of regional coordinated development instead of a separate one. As for the financial structure, we will get rid of financial controls to facilitate development of the real economy; and with respect to quality and structure, China has experienced a time when quantity and scale mattered most. But now we strive for efficient growth of high quality. Economic restructuring based on demand requires optimization of the demand structure. To maintain long-term stable economic growth, we must realize the transformation from a supply-constrained economy during the period of the planned economy to a demand-driven economy characterized by the socialist market economy, that is, we must develop domestic demand to address the inadequacy of final consumption. At the same time we must increase demand for final consumption by urban and

---

[1] An important speech at the Central Economic Work Conference delivered by Xi Jinping. People.cn. December 11, 2014.

rural residents with the goal of maintaining long-term economic stability and development. When optimizing the economic structure from the perspective of demand, we must recognize that the advantage of low costs of production factors is lessening, the constraints of limited resources and environmental pollution are increasing, and the conflicts caused by overcapacity are growing. Only with a full understanding of these changes in the process of economic development can we choose the optimum path for industrial innovation and integration. Besides, economic restructuring requires improvement of the quality of economic growth, the promotion of environmental protection to a new level, a low-carbon approach, and the consistent enhancement of people's living standards with the growth of the economy. The main challenge China is facing is restructuring. Only through the restructuring and optimization of the economy, can the quality of economic growth be improved quantitatively and qualitatively in a mutually complementary fashion.

Since government transformation is a prerequisite for economic transformation, during the economic restructuring and dynamic optimization, we must deepen the reform of the government system. This specifically includes the transformation of government functions, reform and improvement of the institutions and mechanisms concerning investment, demand, industry, and distribution, and a clear understanding of the structures of investment, demand, and distribution. We should maintain the consistency and stability of macroeconomic policies and let the market play the decisive role in allocating resources. Practice has shown that it is the market that chooses the present industrial and demand structures in which businesses are the main body. In the market economy, compared with preferential policies granted to some industries by the government, a leveled playing field is more important. We must change the customary policies of regulation and support for some industries because some of these policies breed profiteering practices by businesses instead of encouraging a focus on effective competition in the market, or improving the industrial value chain and brand promotion. The government must fully perform its functions in protecting property right or rights and interests, improving market conditions, providing infrastructure upgrades and ensuring public services and security. We must limit governmental functions and focus efforts on addressing negative aspects. In other words, the government should concentrate on effectively managing all issues that fall within its purview, and appropriately delegating powers where that is apporpriate. We must ensure that governments at all levels identify their powers and responsibilities, and encourage businesses through deregulation. We must build a sustained force to drive microeconomic development, and give vitality to market entities through delegating powers; we must fill gaps, ensuring that all things have been done well, and increasing the supply of public goods; we must boost the real economy, issue effective, necessary policies and lay a solid microeconomic foundation for economic growth.

4. Valuing the real economy is an inherent demand of the 'new normal'.

General Secretary Xi Jinping has repeatedly stressed that industrialization is significant for building a strong nation that relies on the real economy and under no circumstances tolerates economic 'bubbles'. In *Made in China 2025*, the State Council emphasized that "the manufacturing industry is the main body of the national economy, the foundation of the state, an important way to rejuvenate our country, and the base of building a stronger China. Since the industrial civilization was welcomed in the middle of the 18th century, the rise and fall of great powers in the world and China's history of struggle have proved again and again that a country would never be strong and prosperous if a powerful manufacturing industry is not achieved. Thus building an internationally competitive manufacturing industry is the only path we can take to enhance China's comprehensive strength, defend national security, and propel it to become one of the strongest countries around the world."[1]

Practice has proved that with greater maturity in the real economy, the stronger the economy becomes and the greater the risk tolerance is. This is a hard truth of modern economic development. Since China's economy is evolving into more sophisticated forms, more complicated division of labor, and more rational structures, a key part of China's economic transformation is to enhance the real economy. At present, the nub of some structural problems and conflicts such as the lack of balance, coordination and sustainability in economic development lies in the statement, 'the real economy has not been purely 'real' and the virtual economy is overly inflated'. The difficulty lies in finding a new way out of the negative situation of the real economy in which we are trapped: it is crucial to upgrade and transform the real economy. The real economy, or manufacturing, is the pillar of national competitiveness, so we must unwaveringly take positive steps

---

[1] Notice of the State Council on Issuing *Made in China 2025*. people.cn. May 19, 2015.

to develop a modern manufacturing industry. The service sector accounts for more than 70% of the national economy of the US, but nearly 60% of it goes to services driven by manufacturing industry. This indicates that manufacturing industry plays an important role in supporting and leading the service sector. For example, advanced communication equipment helps drive information services, which creates an annual increase of about Rmb1.4 trillion an advanced automobile industry will boost the automobile customer service industry with the market potential being several times higher than that of a car.

In order to strengthen the real economy from the perspective of consumption, only by accelerating the upgrading of manufacturing industries can China transform from a large manufacturing country to a powerful one. We aim to realize intelligent manufacturing and move towards an advanced manufacturing and commercial model, including elements such as personalized customization, flexible production and network sales. This will be required to meet the needs of growing personal and diversified consumption and to support the upgrading of consumption structure. Manufacturing industry is the main field for implementation of the development strategy driven by innovation. It is the main battlefield for research and development, and the most active and fruitful field, which will fundamentally determine the overall innovation capacity of China. For example, in respect of exports, manufactured products account for 95% of all the exported goods. It is a necessity for us to adjust and optimize the structure of industry and products so as to improve the competiveness of 'Made in China' products. From the perspective of investment, there exists a big gap in terms of economic capital stock and per capita stock between China and developed economies. For example, the gross capital stock of China is equivalent to 30% of that of the US, and per capita stock is equivalent to 8% and 17% of that of the US and of the Republic of Korea respectively. The proportions of those figures relating to water and electricity, and to investment in railway, education and health per capita to GDP are all lower than world average.

There is more room for investment in China. The country's high national saving rate, which now stands at over 40%, has led to high investment rate, high contribution of investment growth, consumption growth and net growth of goods and services to GDP growth. In recent years, investment opportunities have emerged in great numbers in the fields of industrial logistics, communication and other infrastructures, as well as new technologies, new products, new forms of business and new models. At the same time, intelligent manufacturing, intelligent logistics, high-end equipment, industrial robots, new energy vehicles and other investment fields are becoming new 'hot spots'. In terms of employment, the development of an emerging service industry and the optimization and upgrading of industrial structure are creating high-quality jobs, improving the entire employment structure.

Additionally, significant breakthroughs have been made in manned space flight, the lunar exploration program, high-speed rail transport, high performance computers and new generation mobile communications. The 'Internet of Things', intelligent robots and other innovative technologies have been widely used in a variety of industries, and innovation is becoming the main driving force of economic and social development. A new round of scientific, technological and industrial revolution is surging. The deep integration of industrial technology and information technology has become the new trend in industrial development. Only by accelerating integration and innovation in ICT and industrialization, and shifting the driving force of industrial development to innovation-driven development, can we shift China's industries from the low-end to the high-end on the global value chain, enabling the fundamental change from expansion of scale to a new model featuring better quality and higher efficiency.

The 18th National Congress of the CPC was held in Beijing from November 8 to 14 in 2012. (Xinhua News Agency)

II. Rational Coordination of the 'Invisible Hand' and the 'Visible Hand'

The relationship between the government and the market represents a core issue in our economic structural reform. Concerning their roles, we should appeal to both dialectical and dichotomous approaches so as to reasonably coordinate and make full use of the market, the 'invisible hand', and the government, the 'visible hand'. They should complement and coordinate with each other to form an integral and reciprocal force. Letting the market play the decisive role in allocating resources and letting the government better perform its functions are not contradictory. It does not mean that the market can replace the government's functions, nor vice versa.[1]

The Third Plenary Session of the 18th CPC Central Committee clearly put forward a scientific judgment of "letting the market play the decisive role in allocating resources and the government better perform its functions", the core of which is balancing the relationship between the market, the 'invisible hand', and the government, the 'visible hand', and allowing the market to play the decisive role in allocating resources.

The relationship between the market and the government is directly related to not only the direction of the reform of the economic system but also the orientation and result of all-round and deeper-level reform. "Only when in trials and tribulations, can one's courage be revealed; and it is the sincere practice that makes it precious." The government and the market are not contradictory, nor is one superior to the other; instead, they should take up their respective positions and complement each other's advantages. The government should define and protect property rights, guarantee the performance of contract and conduct market oversight by relying on monocracy. The government should also maintain fair and orderly competition, regulate behaviors of market entities, inspire the creativity and energy of market entities, and guide them through rational resource allocation to promote sustained and sound economic development. The important foundation of letting the market play a decisive role in allocating resources is the construction of an efficient government. In terms of allocation

---

[1] The"Invisible Hand"and the"Visible Hand"(May 26, 2014). *The Governanceof China*, Eng.ed.Foreign Languages Press. Oct 2014. p. 128.

Note: This is the speech delivered by General Secretary Xi Jinping at the 15th group study session of the Political Bureau of the 18th CPC Central Committee. The theme of the speech is to let the market play the decisive role in allocating resources, while allow the government to better perform its functions.

of resources, the market plays a decisive role in the relationship between the market and the government. From a strict economic perspective, the allocation of resources is mainly a microscopic problem, which means the market should be allowed to play the decisive role on a micro level. So what are the market and the government supposed to do? We need to understand the following points.

1. The government is the macro-manager, and the enterprise is the autonomous operator.

From a microscopic perspective, such issues as allocation of resources, manufacturer behaviors, the pricing of products and resource elements, industrial distribution, and the determination of industrial structures are mainly defined as market competition behaviors rather than being subject to prearrangement by government policies. For example, the government should reduce intervention in enterprise behaviors, which is rightfully an autonomy matter for enterprises. The government enacts market rules, and what the enterprises should do is to abide by the law, pay tax by law, operate legally, and act on the principle of maximum benefit in the market. There seems no difference in the understanding of autonomy of enterprise behavior. Industrial structure is a micro issue rather than a macro one. Industrial structure is determined by the hub effect that is developed amid competition among enterprises.

Why is excess production capacity such a serious problem? Is it caused by blind market competition, government plans or government industry regulation? For a long time, during the period of 'the Tenth Five-Year Plan', 'the Eleventh Five-Year Plan' and 'the Twelfth Five-Year Plan', the National Development and Reform Commission listed several leading industries and emerging strategic industries, which immediately attracted great attention across the whole nation. Local governments used low land prices and government credit as a guarantee, on the basis of which, banks engaged in loan activity; and development areas were set up before markets were ready, thus, repetition was not surprising. If the appointed plans are instructive without fostering policy, will the government streamline administration of industrial development and leave it to the market? The government should act on macroscopic rather than on microscopic levels. That is, the government should make efforts to perfect 'rules', and create an environment that is fair, open and transparent, and to implement unified market access and uniform market oversight. And on the basis of a negative list, all kinds of market entities may do business in sectors excluded from the negative list, equally and legally. We must strive to remove all hidden barriers of the non-public sectors in particular.

2. The government controls social aggregate supply, and the market regulates social needs.

The distribution of consumption and investment demand is rather about microscopic behaviors of the market. It depends upon the discretion of enterprises and consumers and is well beyond the capacity of the government, especially the local government. In terms of aggregate control as well as macroscopic management of supply and demand, the emphasis of governments at all levels should be on the supply side rather than on the demand side, which means keeping quality and safety standard of supplies under control. China has not operated in an era when supplies create demands. At the stage of capitalist liberalization, products would be consumed as long as they were produced. However, the goal of consumption would come to nothing if we failed to produce qualified goods in China. Therefore, during the current period of deepening transformation in systems, for the macroscopic supply management and demand management, the emphasis of the government is on supply management. The government should lay more stress on controlling the quality and safety standard of supplies rather than demands. The government should create larger development space for market entities.

In this respect, there is susbstantial scope for reform of what is and is not in the area of government power. To cut government power, that is, to streamline administration and delegate more powers to lower-level governments, will give more space to market for the development of enterprises. More responsibilities should be undertaken by the government; leaner management and a higher efficiency are in demand. For example, we should change the ratification system and approval system on foreign investment projects into a record system; change the paid-in capital registration system of business registration into a subscribed capital registration system; turn certification before licensing of enterprises into licensing before certification. We should replace annual inspection with an annual report, and implement transparency of information on enterprises information and anomalies in their operation. We should offer one-stop service for business registration procedures, take gradual steps to integrate the business license, the certificate of organization codes, and the certificate of taxation registration into one certificate, and change wholly foreign-invested advertising enterprise examination and approval for the record; and supervise the information sharing mechanism and comprehensive law enforcement system.

The government should "develop new ways of conducting and improving macro regulation. In response to the requirements of developing gross adjustment and adopting targeted steps simultaneously, it should take into consideration both the domestic and international situations and coordinate reform and development; the government should improve macro regulation, adopt a precise and well-timed regulation, timely and moderate pro-cyclical fine-tuning, pay more attention to expand employment, keep prices stable, make structural adjustments, improve the performance, guard against risks and protect the environment."[1] The function of the government is to maintain the stability of the macro-economy, strengthen and improve public services, safeguard fair competition, strengthen the oversight of the market, maintain market order, promote sustainable development and common prosperity, and intervene in situations where the market fails. This clarifies the responsibility of the government, better defines the function of the government and points out the direction to transform government functions. That is to say, the government should be the 'navigator' of national economy, the drafter of market rules, the 'judge' of the market operation, the provider of basic public services and the watchdog of fair play and justice. In supply management, the government does not interfere in any specific project and its production, but administers standards and orders, and seeks to refrain from providing private goods.

The government invests in public goods. In fact, China is suffering from a lack of public goods rather than an excess, as is evidenced by the so-called 'city diseases', like environmental pollution, market failures and traffic congestion, which are mostly caused by inadequate supply of public goods. Thus, the government investment should focus more on the provision of public goods, instead of on private products. Where the market can produce private goods, the government should not interfere. At present, there is a huge gap between the limited provision of public products and China's economic status and requirement of modernization. We can make up for the shortage of government funding in its open construction with the help of the market. We can strengthen the weaknesses in people's livelihood through

---

[1] *Central Committee of the CPC: Recommendations for the 13th Five-Year Plan for Economic and Social Development.* Xinhuanet. November 3, 2015.

multi-channel, which is the PPP model. We will improve the efficiency and quality of the development of public facilities, lower the entry barriers to infrastructure and public utilities for private capital, and deepen the reform of the system concerning matters subject to government examination and approval through market-based mechanisms. We will also improve the professional and scientific level of public utilities.

3. The government and market should take up their positions and perform their respective functions.

China's economy continues to enjoy a high-speed, robust and even balanced development. A vital reason is that the government plays an important role in investment, which is an advantage that cannot be denied. We should "further transform government's functions through deepening the reform of the administrative management system, so as to streamline administration and delegate power to the lower levels with the combination of surveillance, and optimize our services. We should improve the efficiency and capability of the government, so as to catalyze the dynamism of the market and the creativity of our society."[1]

The problem with government investment in China is not that it is higher than that in Western countries but rather, where it should be directed. The government should invest more in public goods and public infrastructure. However, the critical role that governments of all levels have played in guiding investments cannot be denied, since it served as one of China's strengths in counteracting the economic crisis. We should emphasize the balance of 'the troika' of investment, consumption and foreign trade in China's economic growth. We should not simply stress any specific one of the above three aspects during a certain period. Because of special consideration in different periods, we emphasized investment in the past, while we pay more attention to consumption at present. We should emphasize balanced development of these three factors. Thus, in investment and consumption, the government should lay emphasis on investment and have a clear set of goals and pathways. In the field of consumption, the market should play a dominant role.

In the socialist market economy, the government should use the 'visible hand' less, and should not compete with the market for the power of manipulation or take its place. We should implement structural reform

---

[1] *Central Committee of the CPC: Recommendations for the 13th Five-Year Plan for Economic and Social Development*. Xinhuanet. November 3, 2015.

of the government, cancel the requirement for verification or approval for professional qualifications, open the approval system and reduce approval items. What is the approval system? It is about powers, control, and interests. The role of the government should be more reflected in the allocation and reallocation. The issues in production are micro behaviors in the allocation of resources and should be delegated more to the market. The government may play an important role in allocation, and especially the reallocation, of national income. We can discuss the issues in the allocation of national income from macro-view, medium-view and micro-view levels, respectively. At the macro level, the national income is allocated to governments as fiscal revenue, to enterprises as capital surplus and to residents as income.

In fact, government revenue has grown fastest among these three factors in recent years. The percentage of residents' income as a proportion of GDP has been decreasing continually. According to the China's National Bureau of Statistics, residents' income has been dropping at an annual rate of 1% in recent years. This exposes the actual cause of long-term weak consumer demand in the recent decade -- the government and enterprises took the lion's share in money allocation. The Gini coefficient is 0.4. Such a big income gap will be inevitably detrimental to the propensity to consume. Problems at medium-level are problems of the economic structure. The big income gaps exposed among regions, industries and between the towns and the countryside require adjustments by using the transfer payment policy of national fiscal, tax policy and monetary policy. The income gaps are manifested at three levels: macro, medium and micro. These problems cannot be solved by the market, but can only be solved by the government. The government should pay more attention to the distribution field, and issues in the field of production should be, to a greater extent, left to the market to solve.

4. Enterprises are responsible for the internal competition mechanism of the market; the government is responsible for the competition mechanism outside of the market.

There are two internal competition mechanisms in the market: the entity order and the trading order. The former refers to the enterprise property right system, and the latter is about the pricing system. The former answers the question of who are the players in the competition, and the latter is the answer to the question of how they compete. The internal competition mechanism of the market is more about the enterprise, and the relationships between competitors. The competition mechanism outside of the market is composed of two aspects: one is the ethical order, and the other is legal order. It is difficult for any one of these two aspects alone to give rise to an effective mechanism if we rely solely on the market, and so we need to rely on the nation and government to a large extent. One of Montesquieu's famous quotes is that a nation does not lie in its laws and regulations, but in its spirit of rule of law. During an economic transitional period, the spirit of legality is often the scarcest. There are many laws in China, the quality of which may not be superior, but we have time to improve them. The most terrible thing is that some legislators and law enforcement officers take the lead to disobey the law. This is clearly not a matter that can be resolved by the market, and it is necessary to rely on the government's self-reform.

In the moral order, a modern market economy is an economy of honesty and trustworthiness. Debit and credit, buying and selling, currency and contracts are all credit relationships, depending on the ability of the players to take responsibility for the society. However, during the transitional period, the moral mansion, the core of which is integrity, begins to tremble. It implies the state of moral anarchy, to cite James M. Buchanan. In order to redress the anarchy, first of all, we need to rely on the government to strengthen the rule of law, making people pay for any fraud and antisocial behaviors to the full extent, rather than relying on the blind and discrete market forces. The reason is that the market failure cannot play the role of resolving the above issues. To this end, we should advocate and implement ideas of rule of law. That is, any behavior that is not forbidden by law is permitted; any behavior that is not authorized by law should be prohibited; any behavior that is required by law must be done, while all duties and functions assigned by law are performed by the government. The 'invisible hand' should be freed according to the law and the over-riding right of the allocation of resources should be given to market, so as to tap the creativity of market entities and give full play to all sources of social wealth. We should curb the 'visible hand' by law, standardize government behaviors, reduce market distortions led by excessive intervention, and minimize the leeway for possible abuse of power which harms public interests.

The key to striking a balance between the government, or the 'visible hand', and the market, or the 'invisible hand' is to have a good understanding of functions and limitations of the 'two hands'. The government should get involved in what it should regulate, and let the market do what it is supposed to do. If the 'visible hand', the government, has a preference for short-term

18

races in economic expansion, it is hard to create a unified market and a leveled playing field; if the 'visible hand', or the government, undermines the pricing mechanism of resource products, then the basic signal or source information will be distorted, and an imbalanced industrial structure will also be inevitable. If the government cannot better perform its functions in the development of technology, and of the provision of talent resources, there will be little momentum for 'innovation', or the cost of innovation will be too high, which will become a bottleneck for China's innovation-driven development.

Therefore, the 'visible hand', the government, is an essential requirement to improve the modern market economy: First, to 'abolish' first and then to 'establish', which means that we should abolish market rules which are unfair and opaque, and then establish the negative list and the social credit system. Second, to 'delegate power' and 'strengthen regulation', which means that government should delegate powers in the pricing mechanism of resource products which should not be delegated or are poorly managed, and strengthen regulation where the market fails. Third, be 'clever' and 'flexible'. Being 'clever' means that we should have a clear understanding about the operating mechanism of the technology market and promote its development in a sound and rapid manner. Being 'flexible' means that we should do our best to pool all our resources of talent and let our people fully display their abilities. In the process of improving the market economy system, the transition to a 'strong' market economy requires the support of a 'strong' government, but the government should take advantage of its strength to master the timing of 'abolishing' and 'establishing' accurately, and take a resolute attitude towards 'delegating power' and 'strengthening regulation', and attach great importance to practical results of 'being clever and flexible'. If the 'visible hand' better performs its functions, it not only means that the 'invisible hand' can play a better role in the right direction, but the 'visible hand' can make greater progress in the transformation of government functions. We firmly believe that on the path of socialist market economy and with a sustainable and vigorous market and scientific and effective governance, we can certainly make China's transformation and upgrading of its economy a great success, and realize the brilliant Chinese dream.[1]

---

[1] Liu Wei. *Six Points of View on the Relationship between Government and Market.* China Times. June 5, 2014. Note: This article is out of the material collected by the China Times reporter, Shang Hao, derived from the speech by executive vice president of Peking University, professor Liu Wei, at the second session of the China Democratic National Construction "Urban Development Forum".

III. Structural Adjustment of the Economic New Normal

Carrying out economic restructuring and achieving the dynamic optimization of economic structure lays a foundation for a steadily growing economy and is essential to adapt to the 'new normal' of economic growth, while structural reform is extremely complex and critical. "**Making major headway in carrying out strategic adjustment of the economic structure is an irreversible and pressing task. International competition is always on time and speed. The country that acts fast can get a head start, gain advantage and initiative in terms of the competition; the country that acts slowly may lose chances and be left behind in the competition.**"[1] Just as Xi Jinping has stated, "The Chinese economy has entered a new stage of development. Its growth mode and structural readjustment are undergoing profound transformation. In this process, there will inevitably be one challenge after another. Efforts to meet these challenges will be accompanied by the throes of readjustments and other troubles in the development process, which will prove to be unavoidable. Rainbows mostly appear after wind and rain."[2] Thus we need to weigh the contents, the methods and subject of economic restructuring.

1. Adjusting economic structure will not be a smooth process, and there will inevitably be must be periods of turmoil. The practice of world economic development has proved that gross GDP in a country or a region is important, but what is more important, is the improvement of economic structure; the level of total factor productivity; and economic growth. Although it has achieved gross expansion, the Chinese economy has also accumulated obvious structural imbalances. It has moved into an accelerated period of structural adjustment, featuring a shift from imbalance of structure to improvement and rebalance of structure.

In terms of industrial structure, there is a degree of industrial overcapacity, mainly in processing and manufacturing industry, while service industry capacity is insufficient, manifested in inadequate medical services, school education and financing difficulty. This influences the improvement of living standards and enterprise operation. In terms of quality structure, the achievement assessment mechanism triggers competitive efforts to attract investments in different places, making the investment and export grow

---

[1] Xi Jinping Presided over a Forum on Economic Work in Guangdong Province. *People's Daily*, December 11, 2012.

[2] *Deepen Reform and Opening up and Work Together for a Better Asia Pacific*–President Xi Jinping's Speech at the APEC CEO Summit. Xinhuanet. October 8, 2013.

excessively, while the consumption ratio relatively declines. Considering regional structure, eastern coastal areas have grown rapidly, while some western areas lag behind. The 'urban maladies' in big cities, especially in megacities, are becoming more pronouced, while intrinsic character in middle-sized and small cities and small towns are relatively weak. Thus, in most cases improvement of economic structure is more important than overall economic activity.

On the issue of the economic development, we need to weigh the relationship between speed, gross economic activity and structure, and handle the relationship between quantity, quality and efficiency: all while applying dialectical scrutiny. Xi Jinping points out that: "The greatness in quantity is not equal to the strength in its quality; on the contrary, it may be an illusion of insubstantiality."[1] If we one-sidedly and simplistically regard increased production volume as the growth of our economy, or even "measure development solely by the GDP growth rate" and only pay attention to 'volume' and 'strength' of GDP rather than quality and efficiency, regardless of the cost in environmental resources, and violation of economic law and natural law, the result will not only be a 'bloated economy', but will also aggravate existing conflicts and bring about numerous risks.

For example, during the Opium War in 1840, the GDP of China was ahead of that of UK. But with an imbalanced economic structure, the products that made up China's GDP were mainly agricultural products and handicrafts. Cotton cloth was hand-loomed. Products for exports were tea, porcelain, silk, Tung oil and so on. Prior to 1840, the UK had been experiencing the Industrial Revolution for seventy years, since 1770, and had made progress in industrialization. Its GDP structure, with a high output of steel and iron and advanced equipment manufacturing technologies, moved in step with the development of science and technology. All the UK's cotton cloth was mechanically woven textile; this accounted for a proportion of the UK's export while other products for export were steam engine machinery. Their vehicles for transportation were steam ships and trains.

Although the GDP of China ranks the second in the world now, there still exist many problems in its economic structure. Compared with some developed countries, China's high technology products have accounted for a smaller proportion of GDP and have been on the low end of the value chain

---

[1] *A Series of Important Speeches by General Secretary Xi Jinping*. Beijing: Xuexi Publishing House. 2014.

globally. The industrial structure between secondary industry and service industry is irrational. Also, further adjustments are required in income distribution, and in the structure of urban, rural and regional development. In that respect, the priority and difficulty of our country's reform lie in structural adjustments.

As is known to all, every financial crisis brings a period of economic restructuring, and also a process for dynamic rebalancing, transforming and upgrading. Likewise, the economic transformation of any country will be accompanied by the disruptions of readjustment, and other troubles. Economic transformation cannot always run smoothly, for it is not an easy job to adjust structure and transform the growth model to realize an innovation-driven economy. To achieve all these, we still have a long arduous journey ahead during which it is inevitable we will experience 'throes' and 'twists and turns'.

At present, China's economic restructuring is based on the requirements of economic opening, technology development, and increase of total factor productivity, and is against the backdrop of an imbalanced economic structure. It is obvious that structural adjustment and optimization depend on investing in factor resources. In particular, the industrialization of capital accumulation is unsustainable in the long term, therefore sustainable and effective development can only be achieved by technology improvement, innovation in institutions and economic models and boosting the efficiency of institutions, technology and distribution of resources.

The strategy of sustainable development is not only to achieve the goals of technology-driven development, low resources consumption, less environmental pollution, and making full use of human resources, but also to realize the optimization of factor allocation efficiency. Such optimization, instead of simply shifting from a labor and capital factor-driven approach to one driven by innovation requires making full use of the market mechanism, especially to deepen the market system. Our government must transform to provide prerequisites for it, so as to provide institutional arrangements for realizing scientific and technological innovation-driven and intelligence-driven transformation, and massive entrepreneurship and innovation. Practice has proven that cultivation of a factor market is necessary in the factor driving model or it will certainly lead to factor price distortion.

No modernized country can realize industrialization without opening to the outside world. Resource factors should be allocated in a unified and open market, which indicates that economic opening-up is the basis of new industrialization. Opening can be a powerful tool to obtain new knowledge, conduct institutional innovations and improve technology. But it depends on various gaps in a country or enterprises within a certain business, especially the gap between demand and supply of skilled labor, technological absorptive capacity and payment of factors. It is imperative to specify the adjustment achieved by market prices or market mechanism: and that achieved by government institutional reform or exerting government functions, to overcome institutional inertia to restructuring.

For example, under a market economy, the market can address the problem of over-capacity, while the government must make efforts to promote energy saving and emission reduction to build a beautiful China. The problems of severe overcapacity, imbalance of enterprise competitiveness and industrial structure are the results of inadequate system and mechanism reform. The resolution to these complex problems depends on the innovation of efficiency-oriented marketing, and these problems can only be solved by pursuing efficiency-oriented innovation in the market institution and by shifting towards substantial market reform.

The problem of unbalanced income distribution cannot be addressed by relying solely on the market, for certain regulations and adjustments from the government are also necessary. The market's malfunction in these areas requires the government to exercise its fiscal policy, currency and tax policies to the fullest. In this process the government conducts the first distribution as the basis, the second distribution as a supplement and the arrangements of the other policies as improvements. The government, to better play its role in solving problems, should focus on coordinating government revenue, enterprises income and public income, including the problem of the high Gini coefficient among different strata and the widening gap between the rich and the poor, which will lead to social hierarchical system solidification.

2. The key to structural adjustment is to solve the problem of structural imbalance. Structural imbalance in China manifests itself mainly in two aspects, one of which is the imbalance among investment, consumption and exports structure. The economic structure of a country will be seriously unbalanced when the country overly relies on a certain driving force for its economic development. For example, China's economic development has long been over-reliant on exports and government investments, making it impossible for residents' consumption to play its part in the driving force to stimulate economic growth, which results in imbalanced industrial structure. The accumulated problems due to imbalanced structure have become increasingly difficult to solve as the economic scale enters middle income stage with returns to scale decreasing progressively. This also results in path dependence on increasing mechanism and interest distribution, that is, the coordinated development of structure is based on the original mechanism. Therefore the real problem of restructuring lies in how to find a growth mechanism derived from the imbalanced increase of structure to enable it in the context of a coordinated increase of structure. The criterion for this possibility is the motivation of prioritizing efficiency, and sustainable development. Through rectification of imbalanced structural mechanism, we can give full play to the fundamental role of consumption on growth, the important impetus function of investment on growth, and the supporting role of exports on growth. The other is the imbalance between the real economy and virtual economy. The imbalance in the current economic structure lies not only in industry but also in the spatial structure and even in the severe imbalance in development between the real economy and virtual economy, which means that 'the real economy has not been featured with purely 'real' and the virtual economy is overly inflated'. The problems of the real economy are mainly seen in three aspects. Firstly, instead of engaging in industry, many enterprises are attracted by the high profits of 'bubble territory'. Secondly, there is poor innovation ability in enterprises. Some so-called strategic emerging industries are actually carrying on traditional industry in the name of hi-tech industry. Thirdly, productivity and added value are low. Many entity enterprises are in loss as a result of being unable to absorb the pressure from increasing production factor costs.

The problems of an overly inflated virtual economy normally manifest themselves in four aspects. Firstly, real interest rates are high. The increasing interest rate and labor cost have made the real interest rates exceed the limitations of the real economy. It is a general issue that entity enterprises find it difficult and costly to obtain financing. Secondly, the exchange rate is high. The RMB exchange rate has continued to rise significantly and consequently, this has led export enterprises to suffer losses and even go bankrupt. Thirdly, the asset price is high. For a long time, asset prices, with real estate as the principal part, have increasingly pulled up the level of M2 and interest rate, curbing public consumption and restraining the strategy to expand domestic demand. Fourthly, the rate of debt is high. The debt of local governments and enterprises is in large scale and at high level. In terms of the structure, it mainly contains inverse yield curve public infrastructure projects and debt collateral which are mainly land assets with artificial high prices. The last challenge is to achieve the coordinated development of industrialization and urbanization.

Viewed from the perspective of economics, industrialization provides supply and urbanization influences mostly demands. Thus, they should develop in a coordinated way. The accelerated promotion of industrialization and urbanization drives high speed development of the Chinese economy. However, the advance of rapid industrialization and urbanization cannot be ignored in economic structural adjustment. The key to this problem is to take an efficient approach to industrialization or a new type of industrialization.

Also, in an economic catch-up period, urbanization can be the driving force as well as the major cause of structural imbalance. Urbanization is not only the growth mechanism derived from the 'unbalanced structural growth', but also a new route in the 'coordinated structural growth', with the prerequisite to adopt the efficient urbanization strategy.

Practice has constantly proved that the speed of dynamic balance of economy is dependent on that of structural adjustment. A fast structural adjustment means a rapid economic recovery. For example, the economy soon recovered after the 2008 financial crisis by a series of effective measures. They are; the debt reduction through the bankruptcy of the Lehman Corp; the reemergence of innovative enterprises represented by California; continuous innovative ability; and a sharp decline of exploitation cost of new shale gas in the traditional energy industry represented by Texas. The delayed structural adjustment in the EU made it hard to eliminate debt and, due to its slow structural adjustment, its economic recovery was slow. With its economy in a critical and difficult period, China takes enterprises as the principal part in its structural adjustment, and at the same time, makes the market play its decisive role and government better play its due role. Industrial structure is the result of the balance of market supply and demand. We should change the government's previous regulatory policy and the industrial support system of 'penalty kick' policy, since some unfair industrial support policies in most cases are the sources of enterprises' rent-seeking from the government.

A saying has it that, 'A watched flower never blooms, but an untended willow grows'. In practice, some industries, like photovoltaic, did not gain what they had expected, and it did not take long for them to turn from an emerging sector to an overcapacity one. By contrast some other industries, such as internet enterprises including Alibaba, Tencent, Baidu, and Jingdong, have made unexpected gains and rapid development.

3. The key of industrial structure is stock adjustment, increase of quantity and upgrade of quality. The impetus of traditional industry has been weak and emerging industries' impetus still lags behind, which resulted in a temporary shortage. The reason is largely related to the slowness of industrial structural adjustment. From the perspective of industrial structure, the capacity of traditional sectors has significantly surpassed demand and products prices have continued to decline. It is becoming tougher for some enterprises to operate. They are unwilling or even unable to invest. Consequently, it is imperative to solve the problem of overcapacity, merger and reorganization of enterprises.

Meanwhile, a new generation of information technology accelerates its integration with traditional industries. New technology, new products, new types of business, and new models emerged continuously. Features including intelligentization, digitization and servitization are becoming increasingly distinct. The route to structural adjustment is to expedite the transformation and upgrading of traditional industry and accelerate the development of emerging industry.

The new global industrial revolution provides a great opportunity for China's industrial transformation, technology promotion and upgrade of structure. In terms of scale, China's manufacturing has surpassed Japan, ranking the second in the world. However, from the perspective of economic structure, the proportion of advanced manufacturing, especially service-oriented manufacture, is still small. Trapped in the plight that our manufacturing is big in scale but not strong, we still have a long way to go before we achieve the dream of 'a great power of manufacture'.

In considering how to realize the structural adjustment, the main choices are: first, we will work to upgrade manufacturing, absorb overcapacity and encourage business acquisitions and reorganizations. With reference to the Belt and Road Initiative, we will intensify efforts to open even wider, and conduct industrial output. We will implement the 'Made in China 2025' plan and focus on ten critical fields, most of which are in strategic economic industry and advanced manufacturing industry. We should accelerate formulation of the '2025 Special Program' for each industry. Other basic sectors concerning national economy and the people's livelihood cannot be neglected, like steel and iron, petrochemical industry, nonferrous metal, building material, textile industry, light industry, food and so on, for these traditional industries need transforming and upgrading by advanced technology.

As is stated in the 'Made in China 2025' plan, intelligent manufacturing and research and development in digital design will increase to 84% by 2025. We will lift the efficiency and quality of R & D design by further promoting the information tools of analog simulation, 3D description, HD operation and big data. Efforts should be made to integrate electronic information technology into products and improve the quality, function and additional value of the product and to raise the quality and self sufficiency in particular of key components, components and parts, critical materials, so that OEM assembly will be transformed into self manufacturing. We should implement numerical control of manufacturing equipment and generalize high-grade CNC machine tool, intelligent industrial robot, 3D printing, production manufacturing and so on.

The second focus is to promote the development of service oriented manufacturing industry. Along with the deepening of the trends of information, network and intelligence, and the growing intensity of globalization, the division of labor in manufacturing has gradually been refined, cross-regional industrial convergence constantly been upgraded, and enterprises' integration of manufacture and service are on the rise. The general trend of global manufacturing is transforming from production-oriented to service-oriented manufacturing industry.

Service-oriented manufacturing industry, which is the key to breakthroughs in the low-end of the industrial chain stagnation as well as to securing competitive advantages, indicates the development direction of global manufacturing and new industrial revolution. At a macro level, it refers to the formation of service-oriented economy; at an intermediate level, it shows the transformation from manufacturing city to service-oriented city; at a micro level, it manifests the transformation from production-oriented enterprises into service-oriented enterprises. As is shown in *the Research Based on Global Service and Parts Management* from Deloitte, among the eighty manufacturing enterprises investigated, service income accounted for more than 25% of the average revenue; the service income of 19% manufacturing enterprises is more than 50% of their total revenue.

Also shown in *Research Based on Global Service and Parts Management* from Deloitte is that the level of service-oriented manufacturing industry in developed countries is clearly higher than that of countries in the process of industrialization. In the US, the number of manufacturing and service integrated enterprises accounts for 58% of the total manufacturing enterprises, with 51% in Finland, 40% in Netherlands, and 37% in Belgium; China's proportion of service-oriented manufacturing industry is relatively backward, and the number of enterprises that have realized service-oriented manufacturing accounts for only 2.2% of all the enterprises.

One method is to expand productive service industry by relying on manufacturing. For example, GE applies services to their daily operation management, and develops a modern service industry with high profits and with broad prospects including business finance, consumer finance, and information technology, by relying on manufacturing. GE Corp produces medical devices and at the same time provides services concerning finance and lease of medical device. Consequently, their business chain is extended and its competitiveness is improved accordingly. GE Corp has been the world's largest multi-service company and also the provider for high quality, hi-tech industry and consumer products.

Second, enterprises should become the providers of service and a set of solutions from the seller of manufactured goods. A typical example is IBM. The company can provide customers with a whole set of solutions in hardware, software, finance and services, by realizing the combination from hardware to software, finance and services to enhance its capability to satisfy customers' needs.

Third, enterprises should be transformed from manufacturers into service providers. For example, Li & Fung Group, which has neither factory nor manufacturing equipment, cooperates with about 7,500 suppliers from more than 40 countries. Once it gets its order, the company conducts industrial chain management and outsources every phase to the best manufacturer. For example, in making a dress, the lining may be produced in China's Taiwan Province but the zipper may be produced in Thailand, and the dress may be assembled in mainland China. In this way, the number of actual workers behind the 10 thousand Li & Fung Group staff reaches more than 1.5 million. At present, the business of Li & Fung Group reaches almost every corner of the world and the company cooperates with more than 300 multinational firms.

The no-border and virtual production mode not only guarantees the quality of the products, but controls the cost to the lowest level. In today's world, all the outstanding manufacturing enterprises are service oriented enterprises. The manufacturing service is the new source for increasing enterprise revenue, and the realization of product innovation is an ongoing process.

Third, develop the 'Internet Plus' action plan. China is at the crucial stage of industrialization and the Internet can be superimposed on any industry. In 'Internet Plus', new generation of information technology and platforms is used to advance the optimization of related industries; industrial development is planned and designed with a mindset oriented to the internet. As enterprises are the key actors in the Internet Plus, they should treat the internet with an open mind and increase their efforts to fulfill the goal of self transformation.

Internet Plus should be the combination of cyber-economy and real economy, and also the combination of Internet enterprises and real economy enterprises. The socialized, digitalized-networking industrial service requires the use of industrial networks to develop modern intelligent logistics and electronic commerce so as to greatly reduce manufacturing costs and conduct full life-cycle services. In this way, consumers can enjoy a hassle-free service and further stimulate consumption. Remote monitoring and online maintenance ensure long term and smooth operation. The socialized, digitalized-networking manufacturing supply chain and sales will adapt themselves to changes of new manufacturing mode to ensure rapid development of a productive service industry.

4. Rationalize the income distribution mechanism, and improve the income distribution structure. With certain amount of national income, the first distribution of national income is about how to coordinate the distribution relationship between the state and individuals, and substantially, how to deal with a rational proportion of accumulation to consumption. Government should play its role of regulation to the fullest to adjust citizen income distribution. The main factors that limited the expansion of urban-rural residents' demand for consumption are: first, the increase of disposable income of urban-rural residents lags behind overall economic growth with residents' income accounting for a low proportion of national income. Second, establishment of security systems is underdeveloped. Residents have a strong precautionary motivation and a lower marginal propensity to consume due to the inadequate basic public service provided by the government. Third, there is an apparent disparity of people's income distribution. The marginal propensity of consumption of high income groups decreases progressively, while the lower income groups are unable to increase their consumption, thus leading to a relative stagnation of the growth of the consuming volume.

In order to truly broaden the consuming demand of the citizens, we need to focus greater efforts on the strategy of fundamental solutions on the basis of providing temporary solutions, at the same time as implementing a series of effective consumption stimulus policies. We need to formulate and improve the institutional assurance base for the sustained consuming demand as follows: we will gradually increase the share of personal income in the distribution of national income, properly adjust the relation of national distribution, increase the share of resident's income and decrease the proportion of government's income, so as to enlarge consuming by increasing resident's income. We need to accelerate the progress of building a social security system, and advance the equalization of basic public services.

We will improve our social security system, and broaden its coverage and gradually promote the standard of social security. We will combine the reform of financial and taxation system with the transformation of government functions, pursue greater spending in fiscal on public services and goods, and dispel any further misgivings of the masses after expanding consuming. We will gradually narrow the income gap among our social members.

By adopting an economic means of tax revenue and transfer payment, we will adjust the income distribution structure among different stratums and regions, and between urban and rural areas. We will increase the income of medium-to-low earners who account the majority of the entire population, strengthen our assistance to those disadvantaged groups, and progressively expand the magnitude of middle-income class. At the same time, industrialization creates supply and urbanization generates demand. Therefore, we should pay special attention to the progress of growth in consumption demand through advancing the progress of urbanization, in a moderate way. We will accelerate reforms in the census register, finance, lands and social security systems, so as to promote the citizenization of rural migrant workers living and working in cities - especially in medium and small cities. We want, by allowing the rural migrant workers, who contribute greatly in the national modernization, to live and work in peace and contentment, to enable them to create a huge industrial capacity and at the same time to promote the sustained growth of effective demand.

Apart from the above, the government needs to adjust financial resources toward the economically less developed areas or poor areas through fiscal transfer payments, so as to change the situation of imbalances in regional development and strengthen the development capacity in less developed areas or poor areas. Not only should we pay attention to the initial distribution of national income, but also to its redistribution. The first distribution of national income needs to maintain the optimization of the income distribution structure of the state, enterprises and social consumption. The redistribution of national income should adjust the structure of national income distribution and remove the inappropriate part of the distribution structure through the redistribution of government finance to national income. Aimed both to protect low income and limit excessive income, we will adjust the residents' income distribution structure, and alleviate unfair social distribution. We will protect the income of low-income earners and the interests of disadvantaged groups, and raise taxes on high income earners. The focal point of these adjustments is to increase the income of the low-income earners so as to remit the unfairness in social distribution and narrow the gap between the rich and the poor. We should put equal emphasis on the fairness of residents' income distribution and on the equality of opportunities for individual development.

IV. Effective Implementation of the Innovation-driven Strategy

The new normal is the innovation-driven economy. The growth rate slows down, while the intelligent production, innovative manufacture, factor productivity and growth quality speed up. We should accelerate the transition from factor-driven and investment-driven growth to innovation-driven growth. The Fifth Plenary Session of the 18th CPC Central Committee stressed that China should highlight and implement the concepts of innovative development, coordinated development, green development, open development and shared development, and place innovation ahead of all other development concepts, in order to fulfill the goals of the 13th Five-Year Plan period, overcoming obstacles and sharpening its edge in development. Innovation-driven growth will be a key driving factor for the strategic restructuring of the economy. It will also be a basic support and key force in the overall plan for promoting all-round economic, political, cultural, social, and ecological progress. "We should stick to the innovation-driven development, centering on scientific and technological innovation, removing institutional obstacles as focal points and piloting reform in a systemic, integrated and coordinated way. While we should also promote coordinated innovation in science and technology, management, brand, industrial structure and model, speed up forming a new engine of our economic society to strongly support the construction of an innovation-oriented country."[1]

1. The new normal is the economy driven by innovation. The previous external and extensive development model is not sustainable, as it is driven by factors and investment. We need to transform the mode from excessive dependence on factor increase to deepening reform, promoting market expansion, market deepening and system innovation, so that it can yield system-wide dividends. Innovative capability and system arrangement must be put at the centre of the new normal in order to promote endogenous growth. Outwardly, the new normal is the change of pace in economic growth. Essentially, it is the transformation of the driving force of economic growth which will lead to industrial restructuring. Seen from the aspect of driving force for development, the constant rise of production costs, increasingly scarce resources as well as environment restraint and the weakened driving force of factors, determine that we should depend more on human capital quality as well as technological progress, and improve innovative ability. We should create a new economic growth point through an innovative drive to stimulate consumer demands.

Innovation-driven growth generates new competitive advantages and brings about a new driving force. Hence, we need to foster a new development driving force and speed up its pace of transformation. We should optimize factors such as workforce, capital, land, technology, and management. Firstly, we should stimulate the vitality of innovation and entrepreneurship, promote the massive entrepreneurship and innovation by all, and release new demand. Adam Smith believed the driving force of economic growth in human society is dependent on the improvement of labor productivity and market deepening, as well as the extension brought about by specialization of labor and profession. Specialization of labor improves the labor productivity, and thus promotes economic growth. Specialization and capital allocation, which contribute much to the improvement of labor productivity, will be naturally initiated and effectively achieved under the function of market forces. The government's mission is to maintain a stable legal system and market order, and provide institutional guarantees for economic growth. 'The father of GNP' - Kuznets - holds that economic growth mainly depends on the increase

---

[1] When presiding over the 12th leading group session of the Central Committee of the CPC on Comprehensively Deepening the Reform, Xi Jinping stressed that we need to grasp, serve and submit to the whole situation of reform, so that we can jointly improve the comprehensive deepening of reform. www.people.com.cn May 6, 2015.

of such factors as population, resources, and the transformation of economic structure from agricultural production in the leading role, to manufacturing industry playing the key role.

In his 'Diamond Model', Michael Porter, the founder of country competitiveness, analyzes the reason why a certain industry in one country will show strong international competitiveness. He points out that the difference between competitiveness of countries and regions lies in the divergence of superior factors of production, such as modern communication, information and highly educated human resources, and research. The reform of the market economy should attend to superior factors of production related to innovation activities, including competent personnel, technology, finance, education and brands. They need to be expanded and deepened in the market. To acquire persistent competitiveness, we must make industries that are based on primary factors of production, rise to superior factors of production and speed up their marketization. If we can make a breakthrough in this field, we can promote the substantial progress of innovation-driven growth and enable the shift of our growth mode. The creation and destruction is mainly achieved by competition of innovation rather than the competition of price. A high level of innovation will displace old technology but establish new production systems.

The new normal indicates that the growth model is shifting gear from a widespread model that emphasizes scale and speed, to a more intensive one emphasizing quality and efficiency, and from being driven by investment in production factors to being driven by innovation, which forms the basic logic of economic development. In this context, innovation-driven strategy becomes the inexhaustible impetus for industrial upgrading. Enterprise is not only the market entity, but also the innovation entity. The government should support innovative, as well as vital small and medium sized enterprises, and promote the upgrading of traditional industries; and form a new source of economic growth and industrial driving force under the new normal of economy - as soon as possible.

We should foster and develop strategic emerging industries, contrive an innovation chain serving the needs of strategic emerging industries, remove technological bottlenecks and secure key technology, so as to speed up the research, development and application of new technologies, products and production processes, strengthen innovation in integration of technologies and develop new business models; advanced technology should be applied to improve traditional industries. In key industries, we need to build a platform for technological innovation. We should speed up the transformation and application of scientific and technological achievements and improve innovation as well as the development ability of traditional industries; we need to emphasize the centrality of enterprises' technological innovation. We should establish a system of technological innovation in which enterprises play the leading role, the market directs the way, and enterprises, universities and research institutes work together. Innovative systems and mechanisms should be built to make enterprises lead the research of industrial technology. We should facilitate innovative factors such as technology and supply of competent personnel to R&D institutions of enterprises, and foster innovative enterprises.

We should implement an innovation-driven strategy and take steps to promote innovation to catch up with global advances. We should increase our capacity to make original innovations and to integrate innovation; and to make further innovation on the basis of absorbing fruits of overseas scientific and technological advances, and place greater emphasis on making innovation through collaboration. We need to carry out the transformation of scientific and technological findings and promote the integration of science and technology, as well as finance. We should strengthen the creation, utilization, protection and management of intellectual property rights, and intensify legal protection of innovation activities as well as achievements of science and technology so that it can ensure the realization of innovation in science and technology; we should establish sound norms for scientific research and strengthen education on scientific research integrity and scientific ethics. We need to build a relaxing and positive atmosphere and create an environment of innovation; we should speed up the construction of a national innovation system that is led by enterprises and guided by the market and that combines the efforts of enterprises, universities and research institutes. We should build a road towards endogenous growth driven by innovation and form a new pattern of innovation by the people and innovation by all.

To implement innovation, we need to create new supply and promote the rapid development of new technologies, industries, and formats of business. Based on innovation, we must develop mechanisms to promote innovation, drive more pioneering development on innovation and bring the first-mover advantages into full play. We need to foster new foreign economic advantages with technology, standard, brand, quality and service as the core. We should improve the added value and technology of labor-intensive products, create new advantages of capital intensive industries and technology intensive industries, and improve the status of China's industries in the global value chain.

In reality, innovation-driven strategy is essentially driven by talent. We should give full play to science and technology as the primary productive force and competent personnel as the primary resource, remove institutional barriers that impede the development of an innovation-driven strategy, and establish an favorable policy environment, as well as institutions which are most conducive to the optimization of innovation. We should realize the goal proposed by General Secretary Xi Jinping, "To carry out the innovation-driven strategy, the basic thing for us is to enhance our self-initiated innovation ability and the most urgent thing in this regard is to remove institutional barriers so as to unleash to the greater extent the huge potential of science and technology as the primary productive force."[1]

We need to deepen structural and institutional reforms, make breakthroughs in aspects such as government administration, taxation, finance, competent personnel, education, and equity incentive, and provide institutional innovation for innovation-driven development. For instance, we can deregulate market access for emerging industries and develop the system for innovative competent personnel and the corresponding educational system. We can implement a tax system of angel investment, promote innovation by commercial banks and financial services and create an equity intensive system for innovation by state-owned enterprises and public institutions. In this way, we can further promote massive entrepreneurship and innovation by all, build new driving forces and create strong new engines of China's economy. And we can create ecological innovation as well as entrepreneurship and form an innovative economy based on creation, circulation and application of knowledge.

2. The key lies in the innovation of institutional mechanisms

The Fifth Plenary Session of the 18th CPC Central Committee proposed that, "In pursuing innovative development, innovation should be placed at the heart of China's development and promoted it in every field, from theory

---

[1] Transition to Innovation-driven Growth (June 9, 2014). *The Governance of China*, Eng. ed. Foreign Languages Press. Oct 2014. p.133-134.

Note: This is the speech delivered by President Xi Jinping at the 17th General Assembly of the Members of the Chinese Academy of Sciences and the 12th General Assembly of the Members of the Chinese Academy of Engineering on June 10, 2014.

to institutions, science, technology, and culture. Innovation should permeate all work of the party and the country and become an inherent part of the society."[1] The present mechanism of government administration fails to meet the needs of innovation-driven development. It basically behaves in the following aspects: firstly, the ability of government to make and implement innovative policy needs to be improved. For instance, there are more 'penalty kick' policies promoting innovation, but fewer inclusive policies; there are more policies on the supply side, but fewer policies on the demand side; there are more direct subsidy policies, but fewer policies on society leading. The coordination of policies by government is inadequate. Secondly, the government still adopts a traditional mode of thinking in evaluating innovative activities via GDP, in its assessment of government and economic activities. The innovative and personnel value cannot be reflected by reform in science and technology through factor value. And the country cannot strive for success simultaneously from the aspects of economic development as well as social development. Thirdly, there are some problems in market mechanisms for transforming scientific and technological achievements. For instance, knowledge needs to be updated, management system of intangible assets should be improved, the institutions for finding, transforming, assessing, and benefit-allocating of scientific and technological achievements in market have not been soundly established, so improvement is required. Fourthly, society lacks an environment that is tolerant of inclusive and open entrepreneurship and innovation. The whole society is in want of an atmosphere respecting innovation and tolerating failures, and an environment encouraging innovation and the service system of entrepreneurship and innovation. For instance, there are few professional service institutions and competent personnel, insufficient openness as well as coordination among universities, scientific research institutions and enterprises and inadequate flow of innovative factors. Fifthly, services around social innovation need to be improved. For instance, public resources of the government are scattered, lacking a top-level design and overall planning. There are some problems in the scientific research investment and quitting mechanism especially around enterprises. Small and medium sized enterprises and young startups are underfunded by social capital. All these factors have a negative impact on the innovative mechanism and the vitality of enterprises and personnel.

Douglass Cecil North regards systemic factors as the source of economic

---

[1] Central Committee of the CPC: Recommendations for the 13th Five-Year Plan for Economic and Social Development. Xinhuanet. November 3, 2015.

growth, so he links economic growth with system changes. He believes that we should study the incentive structure behind the new growth that derived from systems and drives up economic growth. This incentive structure can reduce transaction costs so as to promote the property rights behind economic growth, including the innovation in the state system, government management methods, and the incentive mechanism of property rights, as well as enterprise organization. How should we deepen the market mechanism and establish the market culture of contracts, integrity and equality? How to strengthen the protection of intellectual property rights and encourage innovation and promote the capitalization of capital in rural areas and marketization of interest rate; how to take advanced technology from laboratories and apply them to the production line? How can the whole market system, which includes financing, scientific research, manufacturing and consumption, operate in light of a modern economic model? Furthermore, there are obstacles between capital and technology, technology and industries, industries and market, and domestic resources and foreign resources. And only through changes in the system can we remove these obstacles.

The practice of innovation-driven development indicates that innovative activities should conform to not only the law of scientific and technological activities but also to the internal requirements of the market economy, given the fact that enterprises take the lead in self-initiated innovation. We should enhance intellectual property protection to ensure the rights of innovators; we should create an open innovative environment to encourage innovation and entrepreneurship. Through institutional innovation, we can guarantee innovation in technology as well as the operating model of enterprises. Sustainable innovation needs help from sustainable innovation of enterprises, so innovation of technology, organization and the commercial model needs to be integrated, to ensure the launch of technological innovative activities with innovative achievements by system and organizations.

In reality, it is the mechanism or policy barrier rather than technology that hinders the sustainable development of the economy. Therefore, to enhance our self-initiated innovation capacity, the most urgent thing in this regard is to remove institutional barriers so as to unleash to the greatest extent the huge potential of science and technology as the primary productive force. Compared to the advantages of low costs, technological innovation has high added value and is not easily imitated, which results in its long-lasting and strongly competitive innovative advantages. We should achieve the organic unity and coordinated development of scientific and technological innovation, institutional innovation and open innovation. We should seek speed, sustainability as well as efficiency from scientific and technological innovation and focus more on quality and efficiency, so as to improve core competitiveness of all enterprises.

3. The method and model of innovation-driven strategy. Seen from the perspective of global emerging industries and their development of new models as well as new conditions, and as part of the wave of emerging new productive forces, the essential driving forces are technology, market and institution. The first factor is technology-driven strategy. It means that, with unprecedented new products and services, enterprises can create new requirements as well as market space, that is, using provision to create requirement. For example, after the birth of 3D printing technology, a start-up named Shapeways created '3D cloud printing mode' in 2007. After users upload a product design (or buy 3D design on the company's website), choose raw material and pay for it, Shapeways can print the finished product. Users can also exhibit and sell products online, and the website charges 3.5% of the profit as commission. The second factor is market-driven strategy. With new commercial models, enterprises can meet market requirements and conform to market competition through much lower costs, more convenient service and rapid response. For instance, in 2014, with (US)$568 million, Alibaba merged Sina Weibo and acquired 18% of its shares, and a new model of 'social network + commerce + third-party payment' is being developed. The third factor is system-driven strategy. It changes the relationship of interests among market entities through systematic adjustment or creation to provide huge development space for new models or new conditions of emerging industries. For example, the trade system of international carbon emissions gives rise to the global carbon trade market with a value of €140bn, and promotes the rapid development of new models and new conditions related to carbon trade, carbon finance, carbon audit and carbon intermediaries.

To establish an innovation-driven model, we need to do the following things: firstly, workforce factors and capital factors need to be upgraded. We should deepen the reform of higher education. Universities should integrate elite education with innovation, as well as with entrepreneurship education in an effort to build talents that include excellent insights and skills. Universities should improve the system of vocational skills training and cultivate many high standard skillful workers who can adapt to industrial upgrades and the development of emerging industries. We need to improve the multi-level capital market, promote the role of the capital market in capital flow, and support innovation as well as spread risk and optimize the configuration of labor elements as well as the element of capital. We should enhance the protection of intellectual property rights, protect the legitimate rights of innovators and improve the added value of intellectual property rights. We need to promote the reform of governmental management systems and establish a public service system which is conducive to innovation;

Secondly, we should promote the implementation of innovation-driven strategy in light of the industrial upgrading target to ensure the industrial chain leads the innovation chain and the innovation chain supports the industrial chain. We should remove institutional barriers impeding optimal configuration and integration, as well any that impede the interaction of industrial chain and innovation chain, to achieve innovative resource sharing. We should establish a mechanism in which industries as well as innovation elements are rationally distributed and optimally allocated upstream as well as downstream and all linkages can interact organically. Through the promotion of industrial innovation, we can create a sound industrial ecosystem and build an innovative service platform to promote the gathering as well as sharing of knowledge elements and innovation elements such as capital, talented personnel, scientific research, information, internet and data.

Thirdly, move forward in a coordinated way and concentrate on the key and common technology in the development in the industrial field. Targeting key industrial fields, through fiscal policies, tax revenue, finance and other methods, we should integrate the R&D system of kernel and common technology formed by existing scientific research institutions and enterprises and reform its management system and performance appraisal mechanism, so as to give full play to the advantages in research and development of those key and common technologies.

4. A sound ecological innovative environment is the basis of innovation. Innovation requires a suitable environment. The ecological environment is the key element to the cultivation of innovative entrepreneurs. Freedom, protection of property rights, rules of law and culture are of great importance to innovation. Innovation requires free thinking and protection by law. In the absence of strong protection of property rights and sound rules of law, there will still be arbitrage entrepreneurs, but the outcome of developing innovative ones is impossible.

Innovation needs freedom. It is impossible that you can innovate unless you take risks for your thought. Real innovation requires the strong protection of patent, or the motive power of innovation will be exhausted. A thorough analysis shows that all kinds of innovations are relative to opportunities and are an integral whole composed of research, trials, mistakes and repetitions. They are full of odd coincidences. Everyone can innovate. However, only a small group of people can achieve success and the probability is low. It lies in not only the innovative capacity of a person or a team, but also the innovative ecological environment. For example, what kind of resources can you use? What kind of personnel can you communicate with? Can you find relative resources and opportunities in every step you take when you innovate? Can other people give you enough feedback?

If we compare innovators to frogs, the innovative environment to a pond and success to reaching the other side of the pond: then, all kinds of exterior elements can be compared to the lotus leaves. When the frogs want to reach the other side of the pond, they must draw support from these lotus leaves. However, they never know what they will encounter when they jump on a particular lotus leaf, and they have no idea about what leaves may lie ahead. The only thing that is certain is that the closer and the shorter the distance between lotus leaves, the more likely they are to arrive at the other side of the pond. Given a constant degree of innovative capacity, the one who can draw more support from external elements has the greater possibility to succeed.

The creation of an innovative ecological environment calls for an innovative governance system. We should achieve innovation in government regulation, and the commercial environment as well as in innovation policy and focus on a 4-T environment which is relevant to an innovation-driven development, namely Tax, Trade, Technology and Talent. The reason for this is that technological innovation is about openness, freedom, persistent research and market competition rather than regulation. The top priority for the government is deregulation. As for the service function that can be achieved by the market mechanism or replaced by social institutions, the government should practice transformation and provide room for development as well as necessary support. The second thing the government should do is to refrain from intervention. As for the innovative activities that are guided by the market, the government should minimize its intervention on the choice of detailed program and enterprise innovation.

The third thing government should do is to move forward. The government should further strengthen coordination on different aspects and planning at the top level and focus on strategies, key points, the frontier and the foundation. The government should strengthen the innovation policy design, and change the arrangement of innovative policies on the supply side for its marginal utility is obviously diminishing. So it needs to implement a systematic plan and move forward in a coordinated way at a higher level. Speaking of innovative policy, the government should focus more on inclusive policy. Giving more is inferior to taking less. For example, we should implement the three inclusive policies, namely policies for weighted deduction of research and development expenses, recognition of hi-tech enterprises and advanced technology service enterprises; the innovative system aspeccts of government should have specific, stable definition, to ensure that there be rules for the elements of administration to follow. For example, every four to five years, the European Union will adjust the emission standard of automobiles and promote it throughout Europe and the public is informed five years ahead of schedule. All these measures force the auto industry to upgrade its technology.

Technological innovation is of utmost urgency and requires consistent efforts of the government. The government and society should keep the organic balance of overt achievements and covert achievements, translate the development model into sustainable development and allocate elements in response to innovation-driven development. The government should put more emphasis on the utilization of elements such as technology and regard technological innovation as the key benchmark of regions, industries and enterprises. To implement the innovation-driven strategy, we should respect technological innovation and the rule of industrialization of technological achievements, and establish an open, unified, fair and competitive market environment. We should establish a sound service system of scientific and technological innovation and industrial development, and a functional platform which supports innovation. We should build innovation parks with distinctive themes and platforms and build an innovative culture as well as the social environment that encourages innovation while tolerating well-intentioned failures. Furthermore, through institutional innovation, we should provide guarantees for innovation in enterprises' technology as well as their operating model, encourage more people to innovate and start up businesses, and create an open environment for innovation and entrepreneurship.

We should establish an low-cost, convenient, total-factor and open entrepreneur services organization through market-oriented mechanism, specialized service and capitalization approach. Technological intermediary services and technological finance are becoming increasingly important to the technological service industry. In economic structure, private small and medium-sized enterprises become the main body of innovation. In response to the needs of the establishment of an innovative ecological system, we should develop technological service industry and emphasize marketization, specialization and socialization. We should develop group innovation space, guide private enterprises and social capital to become involved in the establishment as well as the operation of business incubators, and improve the entrepreneurship incubator chain which consists of young science and technology entrepreneurship programs, and incubatory apparatus as well as entrepreneurship accelerators.

The angel investment system should be facilitated and an entrepreneurship investment fund should be set up. We should offer some preferential tax policies to support them. We should provide a public service facility which is low-cost as well as innovative and reduce the cost of enterprises; we should reduce the operating cost of innovative and entrepreneurial enterprises, and institute preferential policies of tax exemption relative to scientific and technological innovation. We should help scientific and technological innovators to reduce labor costs. For example, we can have a policy of subsidy of social insurance and low-cost dormitory. We can provide revenue subsidy policies for enterprises that employ local college graduates or attract talents. We should establish a market-oriented mechanism for technological innovation and make sure that technological research and development direction, route selection, resources and elements are optimally allocated in light of market orientation.

Chapter 2

Advance All-round and Deeper-level Reform

Reform and Opening up is a long-term and arduous cause, and people need to work on it generation after generation. We should carry out reform to improve the socialist market economy of China, and adhere to the basic state policy of opening up to the outside world. We must further reform in key sectors with greater political courage and vision, and forge ahead steadily in the direction determined by the 18th CPC National Congress.

— Main points of the speech at the second group study session of the Political Bureau of the 18th CPC Central Committee which General Secretary Xi Jinping presided over. (December 31, 2012)[1]

Since the 18th CPC National Congress, General Secretary Xi Jinping has made a series of remarks on comprehensively deepening reform and opening up, which are visionary, profound, rich in connotations and pertinent to the point. They are a new development and a breakthrough on reform, and opening up the theory of our party and provide fundamental guidelines for intensifying reform and opening up to a deeper level. It is of great significance in politics, theory and practice, to guide us to study and research General Secretary Xi Jinping's important speeches on reform and opening up.

I. Decisive Role of Reform and Opening Up in Determining the Destiny of Contemporary China

"Reform and opening up plays the decisive role in determining the destiny of contemporary China. It is also the key to realizing the Two Centenary Goals and the great rejuvenation of the Chinese nation. There are no bounds

---

[1] Reform and Opening up Is Always Ongoing and Will Never End (December 31, 2012). *The Governance of China*, Eng. ed. Foreign Languages Press. Oct 2014. p.119.

to practice and development, to freeing the people's minds, or to the reform and opening up effort. We will reach an impasse if we stall or go into reverse on our path; reform and opening up is always ongoing and will never end."[1]

Reform and opening up is of great significance to our party, to our people, to our nation and even to the international communist movement. General Secretary Xi Jinping has deemed reform and opening up as "the decisive role in determining the destiny of contemporary China and it is also the key to realizing the Two Centenary Goals and the great rejuvenation of the Chinese nation", which is appropriate, without exaggeration.

Reform and opening up is a new great revolution of the Chinese people led by our party in the new era. The reason why reform and opening up has been elevated to a 'revolutionary' level can be understood from the following three dimensions. The first dimension is self-improvement and development in the socialist system. Things are moving, changing and developing, which is the fundamental viewpoint of Marxism and holds true for the socialist system. Engels had addressed this point in his letter to Otto Von Boenigk as early as in 1890. He stated, "To my mind, the so called 'socialist society' is not anything immutable. Like all other social formations, it should be conceived in a state of constant flux and change." In the international communist movement, the rigid and closed developing model of socialism, in the USSR and Eastern Europe in particular, eventually led to the subversion and sabotage of the socialist system in these countries, as well as leading the setback and low-point in the international communist movement, which in turn confirmed the correctness of Engel's viewpoint. In the early days of the PRC, soon after its foundation, the CPC followed and indiscriminately copied the Soviet model of socialism construction under the 'one-sided' policy. Some fatal problems involving the whole nation had been created, such as 'being larger in size and having a higher degree of public ownership', 'equalitarianism and indiscriminate requisition of manpower, land, draught animals, farm tools and funds', and unilaterally pursuing 'purity' in relation to production. It even led to the 'Cultural Revolution', which weakened our national economy to the verge of collapse, and jeopardized the party, the country and the Chinese nation. The bitter historical facts taught a lesson to the CPC and the Chinese people, and later we changed our mode of learning from indiscriminately copying and mechanically imitating the Soviet Model, to reforming systems

---

[1] Explanatory Notes to the "Decision of the Central Committee of the CPC on Some Major Issues Concerning Comprehensively Continuing the Reform" (November 9,2013). *The Governance of China*, Eng. ed. Foreign Languages Press. Oct 2014. p. 77.

44

and institutions that are not suitable for our economic development or social realities. Hence, we started to explore socialism with Chinese characteristics, entering the great historical course of reform and opening up in accordance with our national conditions. This achieved self-improvement and led to the development of the socialist system which was then filled with new energy and vitality for further progress. It has proved that the practice of 35 years of reform and opening up has brought changes not only in the outlook of the CPC, Chinese people and the entire Chinese nation, but also in the historic destiny of Socialism and International Communist Movement. The second dimension is to liberate and develop social productivity. In the Preface to a *Contribution to the Critique of Political Economics*, Karl Marx stated that "In the social production of their existence, men inevitably enter into some relations which are independent of their will, namely, relations of production appropriate to a given stage in the development of their material forces of production. The totality of these relations of production constitutes the economic structure of society, the real foundation, on which arises a legal and political superstructure and to which correspond definite forms of social consciousness."[1] The basic conflicts of human society lie in the contradiction between productivity and production relations, and that between economic base and superstructure. Under different social and historical conditions, the two pairs of conflicts have different natures. Before socialist society, the two pairs of conflicts stood against each other, while in the socialist society they are compatible with each other. In different settings, the solutions differ accordingly. In the former society, a revolution conducted by one class served the purpose of overturning another one, while in the latter society, the ruling class consciously pushes ahead reforms by itself so as to liberate and develop productivity, by means of disposing of those parts of production relations and the superstructure that fail to accommodate corresponding productivity and the economic base. The cause of reform and opening up, led and pushed forward by our party, belongs to the latter practice. The third dimension is comprehensively intensifying reform to a deeper level, which means the reform is not conducted to repair minor faults by old systems and mechanisms, but to transform them all-round and to a deeper level. The economic base determines the superstructure. China's reform starts in the economic field and focuses on economic structural reform. However, the superstructure has an inverse effect on the economic base. Therefore, we must gradually extend the reform from the economic field to other areas,

---

[1] *Karl Marx and Friedrich Engels: Collected Works*, Vol.2, Eng. ed. Moscow: Progress Publishers. 1987, p. 263.

and further drive reform in systems of economy, politics, culture, society, and ecological progress as well as party building; so as to make the revolution deeper and more profound. Certainly, the reform of the economic system plays an important and leading role in that of other areas, as is expressed by the saying 'touching one part and affecting the whole'. Likewise, the speed of major reform in economic system determines the pace of reforms in other systems. As General Secretary Xi Jinping emphasized, "As we continue to reform comprehensively, we should keep our focus on economic reforms, and strive to make new breakthroughs in the reform of key fields, so that such breakthroughs will drive and stimulate reform in other areas."[1] In terms of the comprehensiveness and profundity of its contents and the difficulty of its implementation, this all-round and deeper-level reform is no less than a revolution.

Reform and opening up is a magic weapon that enables our party and people to keep pace with the times. Reform and opening up constitute the most salient feature of the new period. Since the Third Plenary Session of the 11th central Committee of CCP, we have been pushing forward reform and opening up from rural areas to cities, from economic fields to other fields and from the progressive reform to the reform of conquering harsh difficulties. Opening up has gone through a process from points to surfaces and from a shallow level to a deeper one, gradually impelling progress from the economic zones and coastal open cities, to cities along rivers and national borders, and from the eastern to the central and western regions. Melting into this tumultuous and irresistible tide, China has achieved rapid economic and social development, created miracles, and astonished the world with impressive accomplishments. First, productivity developed rapidly. Since the reform and opening up from 1978 to 2014, China's GDP has grown from Rmb364bn to Rmb63.65tr with an annual growth rate approaching to 10%, which is more than three times the world average. Second, China's overall national strength has developed substantially. China's GDP has risen to second place in the world by 2010. Moreover, China has become the world's largest exporter and possesses the largest foreign currency reserves. Through 30 years' reform and opening up, it has become an indisputable fact that China's overall national strength has greatly increased and the position and influence of our country have risen significantly in international politics. Third, the people's living standard has

---

[1] Align Our Thinking with the Guidelines of the Third Plenary Session of the 18th CPC Central Committee (November 12, 2013). *The Governance of China*, Eng. ed. Foreign Languages Press. Oct 2014. p. 105.

improved rapidly. Over the past three decades since the introduction of the reform and opening-up policy, we have provided 1.3 billion people with adequate food and clothing, and gradually marched towards a moderately prosperous society. Significant changes have been achieved in the per capita income. From 1978 to 2014, the urban per capita disposable income increased from Rmb343.4 to Rmb29,500, and rural per capita disposable income increased from Rmb133.6 to Rmb9,892. By and large, during the past thirty years, the driving force behind the improvement of the Chinese people's life, the advancement of our socialist country, the progress of our party, and the important international status we have attained is none other than our perseverance in carrying forward the reform and opening-up policy. As General Secretary Xi Jinping said, "What has helped our party inspire the people, unify them and pull their strength together over the past 35 years? What have we been relying on to stimulate the creativity and vitality of our people, realize rapid economic and social development and win a competitive advantage over capitalism? The answer has always been reform and opening up."[1]

Reform and opening up plays the decisive role in realizing the Two Centenary Goals and the great rejuvenation of the Chinese nation. As General Secretary Xi Jinping points out, "Without reform and opening up, China would not be what it is today, nor would it have the prospects for a brighter future."[2] The 18th National Congress of the CPC established a goal of building a moderately prosperous society in all respects by the centenary of the CPC (around 2020), and a further goal of building a prosperous, strong, democratic, culturally-advanced and harmonious modern socialist country by the centenary of the PRC (around 2050). Facing these glorious and arduous historical missions, we must continue reform, comprehensively striving for solutions to all kinds of problems and conflicts that challenge China's economic and social development, and work tirelessly to promote self-improvement and progress of socialism with Chinese characteristics. We should be keenly aware that our country was, and will be, confronted with extensive and profound changes domestically and internationally, and that China is still confronted with a series of prominent dilemmas and challenges in economic and social

---

[1] Explanatory Notes to the "Decision of the Central Committee of the CPC on Some Major Issues Concerning Comprehensively Continuing the Reform" (November 9, 2013). *The Governance of China*, Eng. ed. Foreign Languages Press. Oct 2014. p.97.

[2] Reform and Opening up Is Always Ongoing and Will Never End (December 31, 2012). *The Governance of China*, Eng. ed. Foreign Languages Press. Oct 2014. p. 75.

development, which poses a number of difficulties and problems on the path of development to realize the Two Centenary Goals. For example, the world economy is progressing slowly, and is still in the course of profound adjustment. International competition becomes more intensified; economic growth, particularly at home, has eased from high speed to medium-high speed. There is still much room for improvement in the socialist market economy. Unbalanced, uncoordinated and unsustainable development remains a prominent problem. Our capacity for scientific and technological innovation is far from sufficient. There remain issues such as unbalanced industrial structure and extensive development mode. We are confronting challenging tasks in deepening reform and development and transforming economic development mode. The development gap between urban and rural areas is still large. So are income disparities among individuals. Social conflicts have increased greatly, and many problems remain unresolved concerning people's vital interests in the areas of education, employment, social security, medical care and housing. Some people still live hard lives. The development of culture, economy and society cannot cater to the people's growing intellectual and cultural needs. The role of culture in improving the cultural and ethical quality of the whole nation needs to be enhanced. There is a lack of ethic standards and honest conduct in some fields of work. The education of socialist core values needs to be strengthened and the construction of cultural soft power demands great efforts. Water contamination, air pollution, and solid waste pollution stand out as major problems and seriously threaten people's work and life. Thus, the task of ecological progress is a demanding one. Formalism, bureaucratism, hedonism, and extravagance are serious and major problems. Corruption and other types of misconduct are likely to occur in some sectors, more frequently in some than in others, posing a serious challenge for us to combat corruption. There is no alternative but to continue reform and opening up, if we are to resolve all sorts of difficult problems that hinder our development, defuse risks and tackle challenges in all types of work.

Reform was pushed ahead by confronting new problems and was deepened by resolving problems. In a transitional period between the past and the future, General Secretary Xi Jinping emphasized, "Reform and opening up plays the decisive role in determining the destiny of contemporary China. It is also the key to realizing the Two Centenary Goals and the great rejuvenation of the Chinese nation. There are no bounds to practice and development, to freeing the people's minds, or to the reform and opening-up effort. We will reach an impasse if we stall or go into reverse on our path; reform and opening up is always ongoing and will never end."[1]

II. The Targets and Tasks of Reform

From the process of developing a more mature and well-defined system, we have walked half way on the path of socialism, in which the main historical mission is to establish the socialist system and carry out reform. Now, we have established a sound and solid foundation. In the second half, our main historical task is to improve and develop the socialist system with Chinese characteristics, and provide a set of more complete, more stable and more effective systems for the development of the party and nation, the wellbeing of the people, social harmony and stability, and the enduring prosperity and stability of the country.[2]

Comprehensively deepening reform, is to coordinate the reform of all fields. And the top priority is to establish a general goal as well as specific targets in all sectors. General Secretary Xi Jinping pointed out that in the past, we also initiated various objectives of reform. In general they were mostly targeted at specific areas. For example, in various earlier historical periods, the overall goals of political system reform were to consolidate the socialist system, to develop the productive forces of socialist society, to promote socialist democracy, and to mobilize the enthusiasm of the masses. In 1992, the party's 14th National Congress stipulated that China's economic reform should aim at establishing a socialist market economy. The Third Plenary Session of the 18th CPC Central Committee pointed out that the general goal is to continue the reform to a deeper level, and confirmed the sub-goals of deepening reform in the economic system, political system, cultural system, and social structural system; and of ecological environment management and the party building system under the command of the general goal.

With regard to the general goal, General Secretary Xi Jinping pointed out that to continue the reform comprehensively, we must improve and develop

---

[1] Explanatory Notes to the "Decision of the Central Committee of the CPC on Some Major Issues Concerning Comprehensively Continuing the Reform" (November 9, 2013). *The Governance of China*, Eng. ed. Foreign Languages Press. Oct 2014. p.77.

[2] The Speech at the Seminar Which Studies and Implements the Spirit of the Comprehensive Deepening of Reform in the Third Plenary Session of the 18th CPC Central Committee among Leading Officials at Provincial and Ministerial Level (February 17, 2014). *Excerpts of Xi Jinping's Remarks on the Overall Deepening of Reform*. Central Party Literature Press. 2014. p. 27.

the socialist system with Chinese characteristics and modernize our national governance system and capability. The general goal of continuing the reform comprehensively consists of two aspects: the fundamental guidance of reform (to improve and develop the socialist system with Chinese characteristics), and the basic approach to reform (to modernize our national governance system and capability). In this way, the two aspects are dialectically integrated, in guidance and approach. The experience of development of socialism with Chinese characteristics and the practice of reform and opening up over the past 30 years have fully proved that the prerequisite and guarantee for modernizing our national governance system and capability is to persistently improve and develop the socialist system with Chinese characteristics. To effectively respond to and cope with all kinds of conflicts and problems emerging in the practice of socialism with Chinese characteristics, and to accomplish new victories, we should make headway modernizing our national governance system and capacity.

Establishment of the general goal of continuing reform to a deeper level and in an all-round way is an objective requirement put forth during the process of pushing forward reform, which reflects our party's deep and systematic understanding of the reform and the development law that applies in socialist construction, and represents the new measures for the governance of China taken by the new Central Party Committee. In the history of the international communist movement, the classical Marxist authors failed to provide systematic answers for questions about how to develop and improve a socialist system appropriate to a country's conditions, and especially about how to effectively govern a new socialist society. Practices from Paris Commune to Soviet Union and to eastern European socialist countries, did not address these questions successfully. The CPC led the people in carrying on the arduous exploration to resolve these problems. Especially during the great historical course of reform and opening up, we have accumulated rich experience and achieved great success in improving the socialist system with Chinese characteristics, and our governance system and capacity. Even so, we should realize that compared against China's needs for social and economic development and our people's expectations, against today's increasingly intense international competition, and against the need to ensure permanent stability at home, we still have great scope to make our system more mature, with a sophisticated model. We have room to enhance our national governance system and capacity. System operation and governing capacity have increasingly become our 'short slab' or 'short leg'. Therefore, to address these problems, we have put forward the general goal of comprehensively continuing the reform, which has become a primary requirement for us to understand and to advance reform to a deeper level and in an all-round way. We must work hard to improve and develop socialism with Chinese characteristics, and establish a set of more complete, more stable and more effective systems for the development of the party and the nation, the wellbeing of the people, social harmony and stability, and the enduring prosperity and stability of the country. As General Secretary Xi Jinping pointed out, "This is a grand project. Neither piecemeal adjustment nor fragmented mending will do. It entails carrying out all-round and systematic reform, and integrating reforms in various fields to promote the overall modernization of our national governance system and capability."[1]

In terms of the sub-goals of deepening reform in all sectors, General Secretary Xi Jinping has made a systematic elaboration on the primary mission and major initiatives with regard to economy, politics, culture, society, ecological progress, national defense, and the army; and on opening up to the outside world. For instance, on deepening the economic structural reform - the central task of reform - we should adhere to the objective of a sound socialist market economy. We should strike a proper balance between the role of the government and that of the market as a key issue, and make the market play a decisive role in allocating resources, enabling the government to play its due role more effectively. As to deepening the political structural reform, we should uphold correct political guidance, and keep to the socialist path of making political progress with Chinese characteristics. To do so, we should ensure the unity of the leadership of the party, and the position of the people as masters of the country and law-based governance, so as to guarantee the fundamental position of the people. So doing, we will reach the goal of enhancing the vitality of the party and the country and keeping the people fully motivated, to expand socialist democracy and to promote socialist political progress. As to deepening reform in the cultural sector, we should take the path of socialism with Chinese characteristics, carry forward advanced socialist culture, greatly develop and enrich socialist culture, stimulate the cultural creativity of the whole nation and encourage the free flow of cultural inspiration from all sources. As to deepening social structural reform, we should promote social fairness and justice as well as the improvement of the people's lives as the

---

[1] The Speech at the Seminar Which Studies and Implements the Spirit of the Comprehensive Deepening of Reform in the Third Plenary Session of the 18th CPC Central Committee among Leading Officials at Provincial and Ministerial Level (February 17, 2014). *Excerpts of Xi Jinping's Remarks on the Overall Deepening of Reform*. Central Party Literature Press. 2014. p. 27.

starting point and ultimate goal. We should ensure that our development is for the people and by the people and that the fruits of development are shared among the people. We should make institutional arrangements more effective, regarding matters at the core of social reform, such as education, employment, income distribution, social security, medicine and public health, housing, food safety and safety in production. As to deepening the reform of ecological progress, we should pursue green development, remain committed to the basic state policy of resource conservation and environmental protection, and strike a balance between economic growth and environmental protection. We should improve the evaluation norms for economic and social development and the country's natural resource management. We should implement control of the amount and the application of energy consumption, of water consumption and of land for construction, and improve the ecological compensation mechanism in key ecological functional zones. As to deepening the reform of national defense and armed forces, we should strive to accomplish the goal of "building powerful armed forces that follow the command of the party, are able to win battles, and have fine conduct" under new circumstances. We should speed up military reform in key areas, further emancipate and develop fighting capacity, further liberate and enhance the vitality of the armed forces, and provide mechanisms and policy system security for achieving the goal of strengthening the military. We will build a new system of open economy by implementing a more proactive opening up strategy and improving the open economy so that it promotes mutual benefit and is diversified, balanced, secure and efficient. We should encourage coastal, inland and border areas to draw on each other's strengths in opening up; develop open areas that take the lead in global economic cooperation and competition; and establish leading zones for opening up that drive regional development.

All in all, reform and opening up is an in-depth and all-round social transformation. We must sincerely learn and research into a series of works by General Secretary Xi Jinping regarding top level design and overall planning, closely follow the guidance and strive for targets, and have a clear understanding about tasks and requirements. We should highlight core and key links, and at the same time focus on both the all-round progress and the coordination of all sectors. We should undertake a further study on the relationship between reforms in all fields, the compatibility of different targeted measures and the feasibility of approaches to reform. We should understand the significance of comprehensively continuing reform to make joint efforts in furthering reform to a deeper level, and wider opening up, in order to ensure meeting the targets and achieving the tasks of reform.

China (Shanghai) Pilot Free Trade Zone, located in Shanghai Pudong New Area District, is a regional free trade zone set in Shanghai by the Chinese government. (Xinhua News Agency)

III. Fundamental Issues and Drastic Mistakes

China is a big country. We cannot afford any drastic mistakes on issues of fundamental importance, as damage from such mistakes will be beyond remedy. Our position is that we must be both bold enough to explore and advance, and prudent in carefully planning our actions. We will keep to the correct direction and press ahead with reform and opening up. We will have the courage to crack the 'hard nuts,' navigate the uncharted waters and take on the deep-rooted problems that have accumulated over the years. We must not stop our pursuit of reform and opening up – not for one moment.[1]

A month before the opening of the Third Plenary Session of the 18th CPC Central Committee, General Secretary Xi Jinping made a speech on the 2003 APEC CEO Summit, and pointed out, "China is a big country. We cannot

---

[1] Work Together for a Better Asia Pacific (October 7, 2013). *The Governance of China*, Eng. ed. Foreign Languages Press. Oct 2014.p384.

afford any drastic mistake on issues of fundamental importance, as damage from such mistakes will be beyond remedy". The meaning and connotation of the statement is quite clear. French historian Alexis de Tocqueville once incisively claimed that "the goal of small countries is to realize free, rich and happy life for the people, while the goal of great powers is fated to create greatness and eternity and to take responsibilities and sufferings". China, with a population of 1.3 billion, is the only great power whose culture has never been appreciated like others among the world's Four Great Ancient Civilizations. China should assume the duties and responsibilities to continuously create 'greatness and eternity', all of which decide that we cannot afford the price of any drastic mistake, nor can the world.

What are the fundamental issues of importance? In a profound revolution, the direction and target, the theoretical guidance, and the starting point and ultimate goal of the reform and opening up are the issues of fundamental importance. What are drastic mistakes? Principled, fundamental and global mistakes are drastic mistakes. Reform and opening up concerns the self-improvement and development of China's socialist system, so we cannot afford any drastic mistake on issues of fundamental importance. In order to comprehensively deepen the reform, we are required to hold high the great banner of socialism with Chinese characteristics, to uphold the direction of reform towards the socialist market economy, and to put the promotion of social fairness, justice and improvement of people's lives as the starting point and ultimate goal. We should also further free our minds, continue to stimulate and develop productive forces, release and strengthen the vigor of the society, and eliminate defects in various systems and mechanisms so as to accomplish self-improvement and development of socialism with Chinese characteristics and strive to open up broader prospects for this great cause.

The direction decides the road and the road decides the destiny. Since China is a socialist country with Chinese characteristics, we must adhere to socialist direction and keep to the party's basic line, no matter what approaches we may adopt to drive reform and opening up. We should always combine the principle of taking economic development as the central task, with both the Four Cardinal Principles and the reform and opening-up policy, so as to achieve the organic unity of 'one central task, two basic points'. The Decision of the Third Plenary Session of the 18th CPC Central Committee pointed out clearly, "The success of reform and opening up has provided us with important experience for comprehensively deepening reform. We have to adhere to it in the long term. What is most important is to uphold the leadership of the party, adhere to the party's basic line, reject both the old and rigid closed-door policy and any attempt to abandon socialism and take an erroneous path, firmly keep to the road •of socialism with Chinese characteristics and ensure that our reform is in the right direction".

The great success of reform and opening up over the past 30 years can be ascribed to the practice of reform and opening up of a socialist nature and to the resolution to consolidate and develop socialism. Over the past 30 years, our party has been unswervingly adhering to the its basic line and to making efforts to realize the organic integration and dialectical unification of 'one central task, two basic points' while promoting the grand cause of socialism with Chinese characteristics. Moreover, our party has effectively withstood all risks, challenges and tests both at home and abroad, giving life and vitality to socialism with Chinese characteristics, as well as to the international communist movement. Though some big parties, and veteran parties, of other socialist countries in the world also promote 'reform' of the parties themselves, as well as their countries, their 'new thinking' deviates from socialist principles and direction, and their practice is bound to lead socialism to go astray and suffer setbacks and even failures. Their painful lesson is thought-provoking and must be taken as a warning. At present, some radical thoughts and ideological trends in society should indicate the need for continued attention and vigilance. For instance, some people take the political views and values of some western countries as the criterion by which to judge reform and opening up oriented towards western 'universal values' and political system. Some hostile forces and people with ulterior motives in this area make a spectacle, create public opinion and confuse public opinion. Those people, with all kinds of complex motives, 'predict' and anticipate the changes that China will make concerning some 'fundamental issues' and even hope for some subversion. In face of a complicated situation and numerous challenges, we should maintain our political composure, clarify the goals and directions of the reform and be aware of what we will reform and what we shall not. For example, the general goal of comprehensively deepening reform is to improve and develop socialism with Chinese characteristics and to promote the modernization of the national governance system and capacity. It is essential that we completely understand and grasp this. Of the two components of the general goal in the sentence immediately above, the former regulates the fundamental direction of all-round and deeper-level reform, while the latter specifics the clear direction as to how to improve and develop socialist system with Chinese characteristics. Our national governance system is to be improved and refined, but how to do it? The answer lies in our historical inheritance, cultural traditions, economic and social development level as well as the will of the Chinese people. These are the decisive factors, rather than a blind worship or a mechanical copy of any other country's institutional model. Otherwise, "none of the practical problems can be solved, and serious consequences will be brought about due to non-acclimatization. Just as an old saying goes, some set out to be tigers but end up as dogs—failure to achieve what one plans to get."[1] We must stay clear-minded about the direction of reform and the substantial issues concerning what to change and what to retain. We should "have courage to crack the 'hard nuts', navigate the uncharted waters and take on the deep-rooted problems that have accumulated over the years. We must not stop our pursuit of reform and opening up — not for one moment". Also, we should "be both bold enough to explore and advance, and be prudent in carefully planning our actions". Matters that must not be reformed include the basic line, basic principles, basic experience, and basic requirements of socialism with Chinese characteristics. They are not to be changed now, nor in the future. We should always keep to the correct direction of reform and opening up, and uphold and improve the party's leadership and the socialist system with Chinese characteristics. We should ensure we maintain the right tempo of reform in complicated situations and seek the right approaches to reform from varied opinions without swaying back and forth, relaxing our efforts or getting sidetracked.

While keeping firmly to socialist reform and opening up, we must always be vigilant against, and prevent, incorrect understanding or defective thinking from negating reform and opening up and socialism with the Chinese characteristics. During his inspection tour to the South in 1992, Deng Xiaoping mentioned that China should maintain vigilance against the 'Right' but primarily against the 'Left'. Leftist mistakes have brought many serious losses to the party's cause, and even almost completely ruined the Chinese revolution. Leftist bias has never disappeared in the history of our party. In the historical process of reform and opening up, there have always been various criticisms and negative voices against this cause. Some extremists deliberately distort and exaggerate the conflicts, difficulties and problems in the China's development course since reform and opening up.

---

[1] The Speech at the Seminar Which Studies and Implements the Spirit of the Comprehensive Deepening of Reform in the Third Plenary Session of the 18th CPC Central Committee among Leading Officials at Provincial and Ministerial Level (February 17, 2014). *Excerpts of Xi Jinping's Remarks on the Overall Deepening of Reform*. Central Party Literature Press. 2014. p. 22.

They condemn China's reform as shifting public ownership to private, and as transforming socialism to capitalism, denying the reform and opening-up policy and the path of socialism with Chinese characteristic. Instead, they propose to completely alter the process, to 'thoroughly set wrong things right again' as in the past; and to make China take the old path of implementing a rigid closed-door policy. Deng Xiaoping once said, "If we do not adhere to socialism, implement the policy of reform and opening up to the outside world, develop the economy and raise the people's living standards, we would find ourselves in a blind alley." At present, China's reform is sailing in uncharted waters and there are tough challenges. As noted by General Secretary Xi Jinping, "Having been pushed ahead for more than 30 years, China's reform has entered a deep-water zone. It can be said that the easy part of the job has been done to the satisfaction of all. What is left are tough bones that are hard to chew."[1] At this time, it is extremely important that we press ahead without letting up, and "We will reach an impasse if we stall or go into reverse on our path". If we hesitate and become indecisive, waver in our faith and even give up reform, all our previous gains in the 35 years of reform and opening up may be totally ruined. Reform and opening up accord with the aspirations of the party membership and the people, and keep up with the trend of the times. Only through reform and opening up can we properly develop China, socialism and Marxism.

In short, as long as there is no drastic mistake, China will be able to maintain a good momentum for reform and opening up and national rejuvenation. The Chinese Dream will certainly come true.

IV. Methodology Adopted for Reform and Opening up

We should take the pulse of reform from the complex outcomes, in the light of the inherent laws of comprehensively deepening the reform and, especially, pay attention to some major relationships during the process of reform. We should also cope well with the relationship between freeing up the mind and seeking truth from facts, between promoting all-round progress and making breakthroughs in key areas, between making top-level design and "wading across the river by feeling for the stone", and between holding courage and staying prudent.[2]

[1] Push Ahead with Reform Despite More Difficulties (February 7, 2014). *The Governance of China*, Eng. ed. Foreign Languages Press. Oct 2014. p. 113.

[2] The Speech by Xi Jinping at an Investigation Tour of Reform and Development Work in Hubei (from July 21 to 23, 2013). *Excerpts of Xi Jinping's Remarks on the Overall Deepening of Reform*. Central Party Literature Press. 2014. p. 37.

The issue of approaches is like a bridge or a boat crossing a river. Reform and opening up is a brand-new cause that has never been pursued before, so we should adopt a correct methodology. From the in-depth exploration and the inherent laws of reform and opening up, General Secretary Xi Jinping acutely revealed some of the major relationships in deepening the reform comprehensively, and made some new methodological explorations in the approaches to reform and opening up. In particular, he proposed that we should pay attention to both wading across the river by feeling for the stones, and to top-level design, to promoting an all-round progress and making breakthroughs in key areas, and to courageous exploration and steady advancement.

We should not only free our minds but also seek truth from facts, for the thought is the forerunner of action. The main theme throughout 30 years of reform and opening up is emancipating the mind. There are no bounds to practice and development or to freeing up the people's minds. Though we have accomplished a lot during the past 30 years of reform and opening up, we still need new thoughts for guidance with the emancipation of the mind as the leading principle. Without great ideological emancipation, there would be no major reform initiatives and great achievements in reform. To free up the mind is to eradicate backward understanding so that we can become more practical and realistic rather than unrealistic or overwhelmed with wild fantasies. It requires us to promote the development of reform based on China's national realities and conditions. We should always bear in mind the people's interests and expectations, and we must dare to explore and be down to earth to constantly promote theoretical and practical innovation, and to effectively resolve various risks and challenges on the way forward. We should continually push forward reform and opening up so as to keep ahead of the times.

We should promote both all-round progress and breakthroughs at key points. Reform and opening up is an in-depth and all-round social transformation and is a systematic project. Every reform will have great impact on others, and all reforms support each other and interact positively. Therefore, "It should be pushed forward in an all-round way with all kinds of reforms well coordinated."[1] If the overall situation is not handled well and the overall promotion is not made, many concrete reforms are too difficult

---

[1] Part of the speech at the second group study session of the Political Bureau of the 18th CPC Central Committee (December 31, 2012). *Excerpts of Xi Jinping's Remarks on the Overall Deepening of Reform*. Central Party Literature Press. 2014.p. 35.

to conduct. Therefore, we must promote reforms in the context of the overall situation, and intensively study the relevance of the reforms in various fields and the correlation among various reform initiatives, to make sure that "they can work well with each other on policy orientation, facilitate each other in the process of implementation, and complement each other in the effectiveness of reform."[1] However, the whole advancement of reform does not mean making equal efforts in every field and having no key focus of work. We must ensure the unification of the central task and the two points, as well as that of the whole advancement and of key breakthroughs. In the process of comprehensively promoting reform, we should clearly recognize the principal conflict and its main aspects, and learn to set priorities. With greater political courage and vision, we should strive to make breakthroughs in key sectors and key parts of reform so as to promote the all-round advancement and deeper-level development of reform and opening up.

We should consider both the whole and individual parts. The whole is composed of every single part, and each belongs to the whole. Without the whole, there wouldn't be any part to depend on, and vice versa. Therefore, we can't replace the whole with any part or only consider the whole while ignoring the parts. As to the reform measures, we must develop a holistic view and act in the overall interests of the country. Every plan for reform should be made in accordance with the overall situation. Meanwhile, we should also take the specific situation of each part into account and act accordingly to conduct reform. Considering the interests that the reform may affect, we should not only aim at serving the overall, holistic and long-term interests of the people, but also the sectional, private and immediate interests of the people. In all, we should appropriately handle the relationship between the whole and parts.

We should both 'wade across the river by feeling for the stones' and conduct the top-level design. China's reform and opening up is a great innovative cause that has never before been pursued, for which we have no ready-made answers or experience to learn from, so we have to advance cautiously; like, 'wading across the river by feeling for the stones.' General Secretary Xi Jinping once said that "wading across the river by feeling for the stones is a reform method with Chinese characteristics and in line with the prevailing conditions in China. Wading across the river by feeling for

---

[1] Part of the speech at the second group study session of the Third Plenary Session of the 18th CPC Central Committee (November 12, 2013) *Excerpts of Xi Jinping's Remarks on the Overall Deepening of Reform.* Central Party Literature Press. 2014.p. 44-45.

the stones, we can identify the laws that apply."[1] The path of socialism with Chinese characteristic has been explored through 'wading across the river by feeling for the stones.' This gradual reform can help us avoid social unrest caused by unknown situations or improper measures, and provides a guarantee to steadily advance the reform and achieve the goal smoothly. However, with the deepening of reform and opening up, complexity and difficulty have been increasing day by day. Against this backdrop, we need to keep wading across the river by feeling for the stones and still encourage bold experiments and breakthroughs. At the same time, we need to strengthen our macroscopic thinking and top-level design, and make sure that the reform is systematic, integrated and coordinated, and strive to make real progress in deepening the reform in an all-round way. The Belt and Road Initiative proposed by General Secretary Xi Jinping is a marvelous work out of the top-level design.

We must push reform forward boldly and steadily. At present, our country's reform has entered a deep-water zone with tough challenges. The reform has been impeded by the barriers of old notions, the fences erected by interest groups, and the inertia of operating systems. The arduousness, complexity and risks of reform have become more noticeable. "The inherent difficulty of reform entails extraordinary courage, and only persistent efforts befit this commendable cause." General Secretary Xi Jinping required that even knowing that it is hard to solve, we should have courage and backbone, dare to face tough choices, to crack hard nuts and chart a path through the treacherous river, and advance reform continuously to a higher level. Meanwhile, General Secretary Xi Jinping has tirelessly told the whole party that "Reform is a gradual process. We should make bold breakthroughs while steadily advancing step by step."[2] Confronted with the arduousness and complexity of comprehensive reform, we must keep a positive and steady pace, based on practice, seriously explore the laws of reform, and be prudent in carefully planning our action so as to ensure the attainment of the goals of the reform.

We should accelerate development through reform, maintain stability

---

[1] Part of the speech at the second group study session of the Political Bureau of the 18th CPC Central Committee (December 31, 2012). *Excerpts of Xi Jinping's Remarks on the Overall Deepening of Reform.* Central Party Literature Press. 2014.p. 34.

[2] The Speech at the Seminar Which Studies and Implements the Spirit of the Comprehensive Deepening of Reform in the Third Plenary Session of the 18th CPC Central Committee among Leading Officials at Provincial and Ministerial Level (February 17, 2014). *Excerpts of Xi Jinping's Remarks on the Overall Deepening of Reform.* Central Party Literature Press. 2014.p.151.

through development and promote reform and development through social stability. Reform, development and stability are important points in the construction of China's socialist modernization. To properly handle the relationship of the three and achieve their unity are important guiding principles for the overall situation of China's drive for socialist modernization. Only development will make a difference, and it is the basic purpose of reform, development and stability and the key to solve the economic and social problems. Stability is the critical task; it is a prerequisite of, and fundamental to, reform and development. Reform is the great ability providing a strong driving force for development and stability. Relying on each other, supporting each other, taking advantage of each other, these three form a relation in a closed loop. To properly handle the relationship among the three, we should take into full consideration the momentum of reform, the speed of development, and the capacity of the general public to sustain change. Further, we should coordinate the three to promote and facilitate each other so as to ensure that the people can live and work in peace with happiness and that our country can maintain social and political stability and realize enduring peace and stability.

V. The Principal Position of the People to Advance Reform

Reform and opening up is a cause involving billions of Chinese people. We must respect the people's pioneering spirit and advance this cause under the leadership of the party. Reform and opening up put into effect the requirements of the people and the proposals of the party. The people are the makers of history and the practitioners of reform and opening up. Therefore, we must adhere to the principles of position of the people as masters of the country and the leadership of the party, and closely rely on the people to push forward reform and opening up.[1]

The people constitute the main force of reform. We should adhere to and respect their position as masters of the country, give free rein to their creativity, and promote reform with the close support of the people. We have to follow this basic principle to deepen reform comprehensively.

General Secretary Xi Jinping pointed out that "The fundamental reason why our reform and opening up has won the people's wholehearted support

---

[1] Part of the speech at the second group study session of the Political Bureau of the 18th CPC Central Committee (December 31, 2012). *Excerpts of Xi Jinping's Remarks on the Overall Deepening of Reform.* Central Party Literature Press. 2014.p. 138.

and vigorous participation all along lies in the fact that from the very beginning we let the cause strike deep roots among the people."[1] Looking back on the process of reform and opening up over the past 30 years, we have witnessed a series of reforms from the exploration of big contracts to the overall spread of contract system with remuneration linked to output, from emerging township enterprise to prevailing private economy, and from the expansion of the enterprises' decision-making power to state-run enterprise reform. From the whole process, we can discover that it is the people's great creativity and wisdom that contribute to each breakthrough and innovation concerning knowledge and practice, to each emergence and development of new things and to the creation and accumulation of reform experience in multiple fields of many aspects. The willing support and active participation of the people is the source of power leading to the accomplishments of reform. The valuable experiences of our reform and opening up lie in our practices of putting people first, respecting their principal position in the country, giving free rein to their creativity, and promoting reform with the close support of the people.

As extensive and profound changes are taking place domestically and internationally, China faces a series of prominent dilemmas and challenges, and there are quite a number of problems and difficulties on its path of development. To solve these problems, the key lies in deepening reform. However, "having been pushed ahead for more than 30 years, China's reform has entered a deep-water zone. It can be said that the easy part of the job has been done to the satisfaction of all. What is left are tough bones that are hard to chew."[2] Facing the difficulties and obstacles on the road of reform, only the close support of the people as well as their endorsement and participation can lead us to victory by conquering challenges one after another.

As General Secretary Xi Jinping has said again and again in addresses to the press, the people's aspiration for a better life is our goal, so "We should focus on serving the people and make realizing, safeguarding and developing the fundamental interests of the overwhelming majority of the people our starting point and goal."[3] While conducting the all-round and deeper-level

---

[1] Align our Thinking with the Guidelines of the Third Plenary Session of the 18th CPC Central Committee (November 12, 2013). *The Governance of China*, Eng. ed. Foreign Languages Press. Oct2014.p.109

[2] Push Ahead with Reform Despite More Difficulties (Feb.7, 2014). *The Governance of China*, Eng. ed. Foreign Languages Press. Oct 2014. p.113.

[3] Enhance Publicity and Theoretical Work. *The Governance of China*, Eng. ed. Foreign Languages Press. Oct 2014. p.172-173.

reform, we should stick to the principle above and take people's satisfaction as the basic standard against which the reform is measured. To push forward any key reform, we must have the major issues concerning the reform examined and addressed from the people's standpoint, while formulating guidelines and measures based on the people's interests. We must always worry about the people's security and kept their wellbeing at heart, understand the people's thoughts, hopes, sorrows and worries in a timely and accurate way, and make efforts to resolve the problems that most concern the people in relation to their most direct and practical interests. Changes should be made in areas that the masses look forward to the most, and to the constraints and the most prominent issues of economic and social development. We should adhere to the shared development concept so that the whole society can experience the real achievements of reform and development and the people can get real fruits and naturally gain a stronger sense of benefit. At the same time, we should appropriately handle the relationship among the fundamental interests of the majority of the people, the common interests of the masses at this stage and the special interests of different groups so as "to make all the Chinese who live in our great country in this great age share the opportunity to pursue excellence, realize our dreams, and develop ourselves along with our country."[1]

The people are the creators of material wealth and spiritual wealth, and they are the main body and the decisive force in reforming the society, so we must adhere to the principal position of the people. Dating back to 1944, comrade Mao Zedong has pointed out in *The United Front of Cultural Work* that our cultural workers must "link themselves with the masses, not divorce themselves from the masses. In order to do so, they must act in accordance with the needs and wishes of the masses. All work done for the masses must start from their needs and not from the desire of any individual. ... There are two principles here: one is the actual needs of the masses rather than what we fancy they need, and the other is the wishes of the masses who can make up their own minds instead of we making up their minds for them."[2] We make plans, decisions and do things out of an impulsive rush, with a closed mind, or by relying on the masses, to get close to them, mobilize their initiatives and pool their wisdoms. Different choices lead to completely different results. We should take the masses' proposals, because on the one hand, we gain their

---

[1] Addre*ss to the First Session of the 12th National People's Congress (March 17, 2013). The Governance of China*, Eng. ed. Foreign Languages Press. Oct 2014. p.42.

[2] The United Front in Cultural Work (October 30, 1944). *Selected Works of Mao Zedong*, Vol.III, Eng. ed. 2006. p. P236-237

support by adopting their proposals, and on the other hand, even if different opinions emerge, we can rely on the masses to persuade. Conversely, if the government works out decisions from its own point of view, on the one hand, we may find that the people may not willingly support them. On the other hand we will find it difficult to convince the people, even through experts' evaluation and persuasion, which may incur a reverse response. Therefore, the party members and officials must develop a sound attitude towards the people and firmly stand by the people. We must take maintaining close ties with the people and finding out what the people think and want as our basic work method and style, as well as the basic content and form of the work of the party and government. Reform and opening up is the common cause of all the people, who are the source of strength, and most often the people from the grassroots come up with solutions to many problems. Party members and officials must earnestly seek advice, needs and comments on administration from the people, instead of paying lip service or working behind closed doors, not to mention acting out of fancies and whims. As a saying goes, 'the roc soars lithely not because of the lightness of one of its feathers; the steed funs fast not because of the strength of one of its legs.' Only by mobilizing the masses and relying on them can we achieve success in reform. As General Secretary Xi Jinping stated, "We should fully mobilize their enthusiasm, initiative and creativity, bring their wisdom and strength to the cause of reform, and work with them to move the cause forward."[1]

---

[1] Align our Thinking with the Guidelines of the Third Plenary Session of the 18th CPC Central Committee (November 12, 2013). *The Governance of China*, Eng. ed. Foreign Languages Press. Oct, 2014.p.110.

Chapter 3

Develop a Law-based Country

Comprehensively implementing the Constitution is the primary task and groundwork for developing a law-based socialist country. The Constitution is the fundamental law of the state and the general program for managing state affairs; enjoying supreme legal status, legal authority and legal validity, it is fundamental and consistent, and is of overall and long-term importance. ...No organization or individual is privileged to act beyond the Constitution or the law. All acts in violation of the Constitution or the law must be investigated.

— from Xi Jinping's Speech at the Meeting of the People from All Walks of Life in Beijing to Commemorate the 30th Anniversary of the Promulgation and Implementation of the Current Constitution (December 4, 2012).

Since the 18th National Congress of the CPC, General Secretary Xi Jinping has published a series of important works on the rule of law in China. During the Fourth Plenary Session of the 18th National Congress, the CPC for the first time made an important decision with the theme of the rule of law, which performed critical deployments to comprehensively promote the rule of law, whereby the CPC launched the most significant campaign for the rule of law with the most far-reaching influence since the founding of the PRC. General Secretary Xi Jinping's important talks on the rule of law are highly comprehensive and profound, covering all aspects of the rule of law. They provide direct answers to many perplexing problems on the rule of law in the society today and have corrected a number of misunderstandings, thereby serving as a beacon for the smooth advancement of the rule of law along the right path. Studying these important talks by General Secretary Xi Jinping provides excellent guidance to deepening our understanding of the party's new strategy of law-based governance.

I. The Rule of Law: the Basic Way of Governance

General Secretary Xi Jinping's strategic decision to elevate law-based governance to the basic strategies and approaches to governance is fully compatible with the scientific view on the law of development of human society. More than 2000 years ago, the ancient Greek philosopher Plato divided political systems into two categories of 'ruled by law' and 'not ruled by law,' each being subdivided into autocracy (monarchy), oligarchy (aristocracy) and democracy and thus arrived at six political systems. Of the six political systems, Plato believes that "a tyranny is the most wretched form of government, and the rule of a king is the happiest." When bound by positive regulations or laws, the monarchy is the best of all; when uncurbed by law, it becomes tyranny, the most merciless and insufferable of all.[1] Though we may disagree with Plato on his views of monarchy, aristocracy and democracy, we can discern his advocacy of rule of law. It seems to Plato that the degree of centralization of powers is variable but the rule of law is absolute. In a word, 'rule of law' is the cardinal truth. In this era, the rule of law should naturally be the basis of a modern state, an indispensable and unshakable cornerstone of the national governance system and the modernization of capacity for governance.

1. Rule of law is indispensable for deepening reforms

The comprehensive advancement of the rule of law is an integral part of the 'Four-Pronged Comprehensive Strategy.' At the opening ceremony of a seminar of provincial or ministerial-level leading officials on the implementation of the guiding principles of Fourth Plenary Session of the 18th CPC Central Committee and the comprehensive advancement of the rule of law, organized by the Party School of the Central Committee of CPC, Xi Jinping has pointed out that comprehensively building a moderately prosperous society in all respects is our strategic goal. Meanwhile our three strategic measures are; to drive reform to a deeper level comprehensively; to implement the comprehensive rule of law; and to exercise strict discipline in running the party, respectively. These 'Four-Pronged Comprehensive Strategies' are mutually complementary and beneficial, creating improved synergy. To accurately grasp the spiritual nature of the comprehensive rule of law, we need to put it against the backdrop of our strategic planning of 'Four-Pronged Comprehensive Strategies.' Specifically, we need to have a thorough understanding of the relationship between 'comprehensive rule of law' and

---

[1] Plato. (2002). *Republic*. http://www.idph.net/conteudos/ebooks/republic.pdf. P437.

'comprehensive deepening of reform.' After the strategic deployment of 'driving reform to a deeper level' was issued during the Third Plenary Session of the National Security Commission, the strategic deployment of 'comprehensive rule of law' was subsequently approved at the Fourth Plenary Session. This amply proves that reform and rule of law are both sides of a coin, both wings of a bird, or both wheels of a bicycle. They are the two basic approaches to the strategic target of completing the building of a moderately prosperous society in all respects. However, in practice today, some comrades still hold erroneous beliefs regarding the relationship between these two elements, that is, that reform and rule of law are fundamentally contradictory to each other, for reform itself entails breaking the confines of law. This conception is wrong, for reform and rule of law are a dialectic unity. During the Second Meeting of the Central Leading Group for Comprehensively Continuing the Reform on February 28, 2014, Xi stressed that all major reforms should have a legal basis. He said that we should attach great importance to the application of law-based thinking and approaches during the whole process of reform, build on the guidance and promotion of rule of law, strengthen the alignment and complementary aspects of related legislative efforts, and ensure that reforms be advanced on the track of law. Good rule of law itself leaves much room for flexible regulations and innovation. At this critical stage of reform, we can authorize the reform entities through legislation so that they can give full play to the proactive innovation of reforms without breaking basic standards of activities. Even when faced with major institutional obstacles, as long as we conduct scientific evaluation and democratic procedures, we can still unleash reforms through timely revisions of laws. In this way, we can coordinate our legislative work with our decisions on reform to ensure that all of our major reforms have a legal basis, and that legislative work is carried out proactively to meet the needs of reform, economic development, and social progress. Practices that are proven effective should be promptly enacted into laws. By contrast, immature practices that need to be piloted should be authorized for trial through legal procedures. We should promptly modify or abolish laws and regulations that do not conform to the needs of reform. The guarantee of the rule of law is indispensable for comprehensively deepening reforms.

2. Economic development is inseparable from the rule of law

It is pointed out in the resolution of the Fourth Plenary Session of the 18th CPC Central Committee that in essence, the socialist market economy is a law-based economy. To ensure the decisive role of the market in resource allocation and better promote the role of the government, we must improve the legal system of the socialist market economy with basic orientations to protecting property rights, guaranteeing contracts, coordinating markets, and safeguarding equal exchange, fair competition and effective supervision. Without the rule of law, there would be no rules to follow in market transactions, and market competition would lead to a vicious circle. The scandals of tainted milk powder and recycled cooking oil are essentially a logical result of the profit-oriented market competition. So it is in the Chinese society today, so had it been in the Western society. Marx pointed out in *Capital* that "... enumerated multiple methods of adulteration. He named 6 for sugar, 9 for olive oil, 10 for butter, 12 for salt, 19 for milk, 20 for bread, 23 for brandy, 24 for meat, 28 for chocolate, 30 for wine, 32 for coffee." "...he had to eat daily in his bread a certain quantity of human perspiration mixed with the discharge of abscesses, cobwebs, dead cockroaches and putrid German yeast, not to mention alum, sand and other agreeable mineral ingredients." "It did not, however, prevent them, during 10 years, from spinning silk 10 hours a day out of the blood of little children who had to be placed upon stools for the performance of their work."[1] History has proven long ago that in the era of market economy, without prevention, and without legal restrictions on basic standards, market competitions are prone to become gates to hell. The only way to address the potential aftermaths of market competition is to enhance the rule of law so that the market economy will develop healthily under the constraint and guidance of law.

3. Social governance is inseparable from the rule of law

During the fourth group study session of the Political Bureau of the Party Central Committee held on February 23, 2013, General Secretary Xi Jinping pointed out that we should promote the socialist rule of law, encourage all the people to obey the law, solve problems with the law and develop a positive atmosphere that honors compliance. We should adhere to the combination of legal education with legal practice, carry forward law-based governance extensively and enhance the application of law in social governance. Once a rural society, China is now in the process of rapid urbanization. The agricultural production model and the rural way of life that were inherited throughout several millennia have contributed to the making of an 'acquaintance community' whereas the industrial production model and the urban way of life have led to a 'strangers' community.' The former is necessarily organized upon powers and relations while the latter

---

[1] Marx, Karl. (2012) *Capital, Volume One: A Critique of Political Economy*. Translated by Samuel Moore & Edward Aveling. New York: Dover Publications. p. 275.

is inevitably ruled by law and contracts. In other words, an acquaintance community can be governed with imperial edicts, a strangers' community has to be ruled by law. In the acquaintance community in which everybody is related to each other, mutual familiarity enables the community to curb one's behaviors with imperial edicts, family rules and folk customs. However, once this social fabric is torn, the explosion of social mobility alienates one from another, hence the society is rife with the soaring ethical risks of 'hit-and-run' mentality. With fast-growing deregulation, the law as the basic standard for governance has risen to be the critical stabilizer of the society. The process of urbanization in China is irreversible. So is the process of law-based governance in China. With respect to the application of law to social governance, it was amply explained in the decision at the Fourth Plenary Session of the 18th CPC Central Committee that we should strengthen the awareness of rules, promote the spirit of agreement, deepen the law-based governance by the local authorities, organizations and industries, and support the self-governance and management of all social entities. We should promote the active role of social norms that comprise resident codes of conduct, industry rules and regulations, and charters of organizations in social governance, enhance the active role of public groups and social organizations in building a law-based society, and help industry associations and guilds to provide industry self-discipline and professional services. The modernization of social governance is inseparable from the rule of law.

Many journalists from different media were reporting about the first case held at the First Circuit Court of the Supreme People's Court.(Xinhua News Agency)

4. The development of democracy is inseparable from the rule of law

It is pointed out in the resolution of the Fourth Plenary Session of the 18th CPC Central Committee that clearly defined systems, standards, and procedures are the fundamental guarantee of socialist democracy. Democracy and the rule of law comprise a pair of twins, but each has its unique character. It can be concluded from Gustave Le Bon's discussion on the relationship between democracy and rule of law that without the support of democracy, the constitutional government would become the champion of an 'evil' legal system[1]. The constitutional government is the fruit of a revolution of democracy. However, without the restrictions of the Constitution, democracy is usually vulnerable to ephemeral impulses that even result in tyranny. Law-based governance results from the processes of democratic mediations. However, once the rule of law is built, it determines the rules and the basic standard of games of democracy. History shows that in the paradoxical myth of priority for democracy or law, the latter should indeed precede the former. The authoritarian dictatorship of Napoleon Bonaparte eventually brought about the immortal *Code Civil des France* in 1804. The long-standing dominance of the People's Action Party did not prevent Singapore from growing into a country truly ruled by law. Therefore it is possible that the initial establishment of law-based governance can be advanced by the conscious actions of the core politicians of the state. Once the basic standard of rule by law is set, the potential chaos resulting from trade-offs of democracy will be greatly reduced. In countries devoid of rule by law, democracy spread in such an unrestrained manner like floods breaking through dams, leading to catastrophic aftermaths. Since the 16th CPC National Congress, we concluded positive and negative lessons from history and stressed the leadership by the CPC and the organic unity between the people being the masters of the country; and the rule of China by law. This is a correct judgment based on keen insights into the inherent relationship between democracy and law.

5. National harmony is inseparable from the rule of law

During the Second CPC Central Committee Symposium on Xinjiang Issues in 2014, General Secretary Xi Jinping proposed the strategy of "ruling Xinjiang by law, stabilizing Xinjiang with unity and developing Xinjiang with

---

[1] Le Bon, Gustave. *The Psychology of Revolution*. Translated by Tong Dezhi & Liu Xunlian. Guangzhou: Guangdong People's Publishing House. 2012. p. 20.

long-standing efforts." During the 6th CPC Central Committee Symposium on Tibet Issues, General Secretary Xi Jinping proposed the strategy of "ruling Tibet by law, invigorating Tibet by making Tibetans rich, and developing Tibet with long-standing efforts." Xinjiang and Tibet are the forefronts of anti-separatist activities and anti-terrorism efforts. How to practice good governance there and safeguard the unity of the state and national harmony? This is thus a key challenge that deserves careful reflection by the whole party and the whole country. The talks by General Secretary Xi Jinping clearly accorded top priority to the rule by law, which reflects his profound understanding of the basic and strategic role of rule by law in safeguarding national harmony. Every country in the world has its own untouchable basic standards. Fixing these principles in the form of laws constitutes the basic standard of rule by law of the country. To such a 'worldly state' as China, safeguarding national unity and opposing separatist activities conform to the supreme interest of the nation and the state. Anybody that dares to touch or violate this basic standard will suffer severe legal punishments. With no leeway for its basic standards, a country under rule of law must defend the dignity of law with utmost resoluteness and preclude any words or behaviors that dare to challenge this unchallengeable certitude. Before gaining independence in 1964, Singapore witnessed two severe ethnical clashes between the Malays and Chinese, causing hundreds of casualties. Since independence, the government of Singapore adopted various means of curbing the harm of ethnical or religious factors on national unity, including harsh legal penalties. For example, in 1990, the Maintenance of Religious Harmony Act was issued by the government of Singapore to delimit the spheres of religious activities and give the Minister of Internal Affairs the mandate to make restraining orders. The Minister may "make a restraining order against any priest, monk, pastor, imam, elder, office-bearer or any other person who is in a position of authority in any religious group or institution..." who has "committed or is attempting to commit any of the following acts: (a) causing feelings of enmity, hatred, ill-will or hostility between different religious groups; (b) carrying out activities to promote a political cause, or a cause of any political party while, or under the guise of, propagating or practising any religious belief; (c) carrying out subversive activities under the guise of propagating or practising any religious belief; or (d) exciting disaffection against the President or the Government of Singapore while, or under the guise of, propagating or practising any religious belief," restraining the said person's words and behaviors. The local court can also punish offenders. Under the heavy pressure of law, the ethnic and religious factors of Singapore are strictly limited within the rule of law. For more than two decades, no one has dared challenge this law in Singapore. The government has basically achieved ethnic and religious harmony. The history and personal stories can serve as mirrors for reflection. In the same vein, the anti-separatist activities in China are inseparable from the basic role of the law.

6. Combating corruption and promoting integrity is inseparable from the rule of law

At the Second Plenary Session of the 18th Central Discipline Inspection Commission held on January 22, 2013, General Secretary Xi Jinping pointed out that we should strengthen national legislation against corruption, step up the construction of anti-corruption rules and regulations within the party, deepen the reform in areas and procedures that are prone to corruption, and ensure that government agencies exercise their powers in accordance with legal mandates and procedures. To strengthen the restriction and supervision of the operation of power, we should keep power within the confines of systemic checks, develop a disciplinary mechanism in which no one dares to become corrupt, a preventive mechanism in which no one can become corrupt, and a guarantee system in which no one is prone to corruption. It was reiterated in the Fifth Plenary Session of the 18th CPC Central Committee that we should rule the party by law in a comprehensive and strict manner, deepen the party integrity initiative and restraints against corruption, strengthen the achievements of campaigns against corruption, and seek to build a mechanism in which no one dares to be, can be, or even wants to become corrupt. History shows that the unique geopolitical structure has contributed to a strong tradition of administrative centralization since ancient times in China. To effectively curb the abuse of administrative centralization, Chinese society has naturally developed the counterpart system of imperial censorship. For over two millennia, the imperial censorship system had remained one of the pillars of the Chinese system with its basic function remaining constant - as a dedicated supervisory body affiliated with the supreme ruler. It was independent of the administrative system and exercised strong supervision over the latter. Aside from being the top official of the Censorship Office, the supervisory censors were usually given low ranks and few administrative powers. However, they enjoyed such high discretion and powers in terms of supervision and impeachment that even Prime Ministers were afraid of them. In a sense, the Control Yuan of Taiwan (China); the Corrupt Practices Investigation Bureau (CPIB) of Singapore; the Independent Commission Against Corruption (ICAC) of Hong Kong; and the Central Commission for Discipline Inspection System of China's mainland are modern versions of this censorship tradition. However, these inherited traditions should undergo rigid legal transformations in the era of law. In a sense, CPIB and ICAC's successful transformation helped build the top two clean societies in Asia. However powerful in their discretion while performing tasks, both CIPB and ICAC have acted in strict compliance with legal procedures and contents without the least departure from those principles. In particular, they are also powerfully restrained by prosecutorial and judicial functions. These mark a fundamental distinction between these modern systems and the traditional censorship system acting upon 'gossips and hearsay' in the ancient ruled-by-man tradition. They are also far superior to the secret police system such as secret police (*jin yi wei*) of the Ming Dynasty. The world has witnessed the current remarkable progress in China's anti-corruption struggles. If there is any possible room for further improvement, that would be the expectation that the application of law in anti-corruption efforts will be further enhanced. Struggles against corruption beyond the curbs of law will not stand up to scrutiny in the modern society and their failures are doomed.

II. The Organic Integration of the Leadership of the party and the Law-based Governance

During the seminar of provincial or ministerial-level leading officials on the implementation of the guiding principles of Fourth Plenary Session of the 18th CPC Central Committee and the comprehensive advancement of the rule of law, General Secretary Xi Jinping once again expounded the core issue of the relationship between party's leadership and law-based governance. He pointed out that as the core leadership of the socialist cause with Chinese characteristics, the CPC plays the role of central control and coordination. The socialist rule of law should be based on party's leadership while the latter also depends on the former.

Whether law-based governance requires adherence to party's leadership is a key issue in building rule of law in China and plays a major role in the formation of social consensus. To understand the issue correctly, we need to introduce the theory of systems science. In his book *Republic*, the ancient Greek philosopher Plato wrote that "or that [the best-ordered State] which most nearly approaches to the condition of the individual - as in the body, when but a finger of one of us is hurt, the whole frame, drawn towards the soul as a center and forming one kingdom under the ruling power therein, feels the hurt and sympathizes all together with the part affected, and we say that the man has a pain in his finger; and the same expression is used about any other part of the body, which has a sensation of pain at suffering or of pleasure at the alleviation of suffering."[1] Using the simplest language, Plato expounded the theory of systems science. According to this theory, each life system is a common destiny with the integral whole composed of different elements in a hierarchy. It also states that the goal of development of each social system is to evolve into an advanced quasi-life system. Within the social 'common destiny', society is composed of discrete elements in a hierarchy that constitutes an integral whole in which they work on the basis of division of labor and face the common destiny.

If this argument is valid, then it is easy to understand that it can be compared to the human body working under the command of the brain. However, when the body is injured, the signal will be relayed to the brain through the neural system so that the brain will give due attention and work out a solution. In the same vein, the society also has its own 'brain,' 'body' and 'neural system', or the legal system, which connects the former two. In this sense, a society with the rule of law is just like a person without the neural system — one cannot feel when or where an injury happens and how serious it is. The grievous aftermath that results would be simply beyond our imagination. Moreover, the systems science holds that an advanced system of life is an organic whole in which each subsystem has its own capacity for 'self-organization.' When one goes to sleep, one never worries if the heart and breathing might stop, because the capacity for 'self-organization' of the heart and lung subsystems enables them to operate automatically on their own rhythms. In spite of being the most advanced system of supervision, the brain cannot give orders to the heart and the lungs at every moment. In a sense, the rule of law is manifested in the self-organization capacity of subsystems of the society.

Let us further elaborate on this issue by taking the relationship between party's leadership and rule of law. Needless to say, some people in the society have been trumpeting 'judicial independence' in China as the ultimate indicator of law-based governance. In fact, we prefer 'independent judiciary' rather than 'judicial independence.' This is by no means a word game, for the word 'judicial' in 'judicial independence' is a modifier denoting the concept of independence of the subject whereas the word 'judiciary' in 'independent judiciary' is a word of action that denotes functional independence. Hereby

---

[1] Plato. (2002). *Republic*. http://www.idph.net/conteudos/ebooks/republic.pdf. p. 320.

lies the fundamental difference between the two. From the perspective of systems science, the 'party's leadership' can be compared to the 'brain system' of a country or a society, for it embodies the soul and the will thereof. 'Independent judiciary' can be compared to the liver and kidney system of a country and a society, which is responsible for the 'removal of waste products of metabolism', or the mediation of social conflicts and disputes. Obviously, the liver and kidney system cannot exist while being independent of the body, and therefore sheer 'judicial independence' is an inherent fallacy. Even the so-called 'judicial independence' in the Western society is inherently a verbal expression of the concept of functional independence. However, given the exclusive capacity of the liver and kidneys for removing waste products of metabolism, even the brain cannot take their place and fulfill their duties, or else it would be poisoned by toxins. Therefore we can see that a real law-based society must effectively ward off the interference of political power in regular judicial activities, especially in certain case investigations. During the Conference on Politics and Law of the CPC Central Committee on January 7, 2014, General Secretary Xi Jinping stressed that we should handle the relationship between adherence to the party's leadership properly and ensure the exercise of power by the judicial bodies legally, independently and unbiasedly. Party organizations and leaders of all levels should support all agencies of the political and legal system in their operation based on individual responsibility and coordination in compliance with the Constitution and laws. The decisions of the Fourth Plenary Session of the 18th CPC Central Committee also unequivocally require that party and government organizations and leaders of all levels should support the Court and the Procuratorate in their exercise of power legally and independently. We should establish a system for recording and reporting leaders' interference in judicial activities and specific cases and holding them accountable. No leader in party organizations and governments of any level should order the judicial body to act beyond their legal responsibilities and against judicial justice. No judicial body should comply with demands of leaders of party organizations and governments that illegally interfere with judicial activities. It is thus expressed very clearly that the party's leadership has shown maximum respect for the functional independence of the judicial system.

Meanwhile, the functional independence of the judiciary does not deny the leadership of the party's leadership. Let's return to the human body analogy. If a person develops a fatty liver, the brain must give orders to diet and exercise regularly and, if necessary, take some medicine. Then what if the person knows about a tumor in his liver or kidney? The brain will probably make a critical decision to undergo a surgical operation at the right time. During the third and fourth plenary sessions of the 18th CPC Central Committee, careful strategic deployments were made in judicial reforms. The range of coverage and the influence of reform measures on the old system were unprecedented over scores of years. In a sense, the importance and level of difficulty of this judicial reform makes it comparable to a surgical operation on the judicial system. This surgical reform is obviously not initiated by the judicial system itself, and must rely on the strong political will of the political core as well as the excellent political consciousness of being accountable to the history and the people. Without the strong leadership of the party, all reforms, including judicial reform, could become a mirage, like the moon in water or flowers in the mirror. Of course, whether through diet, medicine or surgical operations, the ultimate goal of the brain's so-called 'interference' in the operation of the liver and kidneys is to help them to regain their independent functions for self-organization. Once they are fully recovered, the brain will make no further intervention, nor can it interfere with their independent operation. This is the scientific relationship between the control system and subsystems in systems science. It can also be used to help us understand the organic unity between the party's leadership and the rule of law.

III. The Synergy between the Rule of Law and the Rule of Virtue

It is pointed out in the Fourth Plenary Session of the 18th CPC Central Committee that we must persist in a joint commitment to the rule of law and the rule of virtue. Effective national and social governance demands a combination of law and morality. We need to lay emphasis on both the rule of law and the rule of virtue. It is imperative that we vigorously promote our core socialist values; carry forward traditional Chinese virtues; and cultivate social morality, professional ethics, family values, and the moral integrity of individuals. We should not only highlight the normative function of law but also value the educational function of virtue. The rule of law gives expression to moral values and the law better promotes the cultivation of morality. We must draw on virtue as a means of nurturing the rule of law and strengthen the role of morality as a pillar of the law-based culture, so that law and virtue promote each other, and the rule of law and the rule of virtue reinforce each other.

Whether rule of law should be combined with rule of virtue is a topic of controversy in academic circles in China. Some point out that while China's rule of law is a sign of progress, rule of virtue may give leeway to rule by man. This issue requires a comprehensive and dialectical perspective. In terms of restriction of power, the rule of law is indeed a cage for powers. At the Second Plenary Session of the 18th Central Discipline Inspection Commission held on January 22, 2013, General Secretary Xi Jinping pointed out that we should "strengthen the restriction and supervision of the operation of power, we should keep power within the confines of systemic checks." This statement by General Secretary Xi Jinping was so impressive that it soon caught on and became a classic remark on the rule of law and confines of power. In fact, keeping power within the confines of systemic checks has become a universal consensus in both China and the West. In *Essays on Freedom and Power* by Lord Acton, a 19th-century British historian, there is such a famous quote, "Power tends to corrupt, and absolute power corrupts absolutely." Realizing the risk of power and restricting it with the principles of democracy and law are indeed a laudable leap forward in the history of social development. In this regard, China still has a long way to go and needs to learn a great deal from other countries.

However, is keeping power within the confines of systemic checks alone enough? Just think about it. What do people usually cage in confines to protect their own security? They are probably two things – beasts in the zoo, and criminals in prison. We cage them because of their potential for harming us. But even when we cage them, dare we approach them? Can we expect them to serve us the people? Certainly not. However, we expect the power to serve us. Ultimately, the power is neither a beast nor a criminal, and thus should not be treated as our enemy. If the power were a latent foe, even when we caged it within the confines of the system, we would win half the battle and lose the other half. For 'keeping power within the confines of systemic checks' is half the story of rule of law, the other half being caging those good people with powers within the confines of systemic checks.

Then what is 'power'? Here is a quote from Mencius: there are two *ways* (*Tao*), the constant being routine while the changeable being power. It is good practice to follow the constant and curb the changeable. It is recorded in *Biography of Gong Yang in Spring and Autumn* (*chunqiu gongyang zhuan*) that: "What is 'power'? Power restores the routine and ushers in virtue." The relationship between the constant and the changeable and between the routine and the power reminds us of the one between law and power. Power lies in changes. The nature of power lies in the necessary room for discretion. However a society tries to curb and regulate powers with the institution, such room for discretion cannot be eliminated. This is one of the truths of power. The popular TV drama *House of Cards* may not be depicting the reality, but the political ecology that it reflects shows that even in a self-proclaimed law-based democracy such as the United States, the elite still have enormous room for discretion in exercising power. It thus can be seen that however sound the institution of a society is, given the permanent room for discretion, it should always resort to meritocracy. The rule of law should not only keep power within the confines of systemic checks, but also ensure that the necessary room for discretion should be reserved for the good people. The confines of systemic checks can prevent powers from deviating into great evil. But when powers are in the hands of good people, they not only ward off petty grievances but also serve the good of the people.

This issue touches upon the difference in political ideology between China and the West. The political ideology of the West centers upon skepticism, with the premise that all politicians are evil. The sentence that follows the famous quote of Lord Acton goes like this, "Great men are almost always bad men." However, the political ideology of China centers upon rule by virtue and benevolent governance, with the premise that politicians are virtuous people. Just as Confucius put it, "He who exercises government by means of his virtue may be compared to the north polar star, which keeps its place and all the stars turn towards it." These two ideologies bloom and prosper separately in the two ends of the Eurasian continent. With their separate historical origins and justifications of reason, they each help the West and China build political mansions that stand erect for thousands of years. Despite the fact that China is actively learning from the political ideologies of the West and fending off the abuse of power by learning to build the confines of systemic checks, Chinese people should never lose heart in their own political traditions and sway from one extreme to the other. However powerful the mechanism of checks with law and democracy, it can never deny the value of the moral consciousness of rulers. That is the fundamental reason why General Secretary Xi Jinping, while promoting the rule of law, still reiterates that we should "adhere to the supreme status of the people's interests, closely rely on the people, and serve the people heart and soul." During his inspection in Shandong in November 2013, General Secretary Xi Jinping pointed out that a nation cannot thrive without virtue, and a person cannot stand erect without virtue, either. We must strengthen the ideological and moral construction of the whole society, inspire people to develop positive moral will and sensibility, cultivate proper moral judgment and responsibility, enhance the capability for ethical practices, in particular the capability for conscious practice, guide people in their pursuit of a lifestyle that stresses, respects and observes moral values, and forge a positive attitude towards kindness. As long as generations of the Chinese nation pursue lofty moral standards, there is forever hope for our nation. In a sense, the rule of law and rule of virtue are to governance what both wings are to the bird or what both wheels are to a carriage. The core of a system lies in skepticism while the core of morality lies in trust. A good society should be a core of trust in a shell of skepticism. In this sense, 'law' indeed should go hand in hand with 'virtue,' creating synergy between rule of law and rule of virtue. In terms of the rule of law, Chinese civilization and Western civilization should be, as Gottfried Wilhelm Leibniz put it, "good if those two strengths can combine and draw upon each other, and enlighten each other."[1]

IV. The Legal Mentality and the Basic-standard Mentality in Governance

Since the 18th National Congress of the CPC, Comrade Xi has reiterated that we should always adhere to the basic-standard mentality, face up to conflicts instead of trying to conceal problems, and work for the best but prepare for the worst. Only in this way can we be always prepared for risks and contingencies and have a grip on the initiative. The new leaders of the CPC Central Committee such as Li Keqiang and Zhang Gaoli have also stressed adherence to the basic-standard mentality on various occasions. Subsequently, leaders of ministries of the CPC Central Committee and officials at all levels of the government recognized and underscored the importance of such mentality for their own work. The basic-standard mentality reminds us of the other mentality that has been stressed by the CPC Central Committee since the party's 18th National Congress – the legal mentality. The report of the 18th CPC National Congress points out that we must improve leading officials' capacity for applying the legal mentality and approaches to deepening reform, promoting development, resolving conflicts, and maintaining stability. So what is the basic-standard mentality? What is the legal mentality? What is the relationship between the two?

From the perspective of governance, the legal mentality and the basic-standard mentality are two different yet interacting modes of thinking. The legal mentality is the mainstream thinking mode of governance for leaders,

---

[1] Gottfried Wilhelm Leibniz. *Novissima Sinica*. Translated by Yang Baojun. Zhengzhou: Elephant Press. 2005. p. 2.

covering the three fields of reform, development and stability in today's society; the basic-standard mentality is one of the key thinking modes of governance by leaders, with a majority of its content incorporated in legal mentality but also has its unique denotations and connotations. For example, the basic standards for economic development and the rate of unemployment in specific periods, the certain basic standards of morality and discipline above the law for party officials. But generally, the majority of the content of basic-standard mentality is indeed incorporated by the legal mentality. Let's interpret the denotation of basic-standard mentality from the perspective of law and try to unveil its legal attributes.

1. The rigid basic-standard mentality

The basic standard of the law is a rigid and decisive line, the ultimate line of defense for the security of lives and possessions of a society. Once the law is made, the basic standard is set, nobody can break it under any excuse. It was written in China's Constitution that "All state organs, the armed forces, all political parties and public organizations and all enterprises and institutions must abide by the Constitution and the law. All acts in violation of the Constitution and the law must be investigated. No organization or individual is privileged to act beyond the Constitution or the law. For the purposes of law enforcement, the certainty and rigidity of this basic standard requires not only passive compliance but also proactive law enforcement."

This is the rigid basic-standard mentality of law-based governance. It has been proven with evidence that the more rigid this basic standard is, the greater deterring effect to criminals, and hence the lower costs of social management. By contrast, the less rigid this basic standard is, the greater becomes the opportunism mentality of criminals, and hence the higher costs of social management. From curbing violence to preventing corruption, from social management to the construction of a clean government, the rigid basic-standard mentality is an untouchable, unbreakable and indispensable 'high-voltage power cable' of the society. Any room for the discretion of power should be strictly limited within the sphere of compliance, and any deviation incurs severe punishment by law.

2. The basic-standard mentality of fairness

During the Central Economic Working Conference at the end of 2013, General Secretary Xi Jinping stressed that we must steadfastly follow the strategy of adhering to basic standards, highlighting some issues of focus, improving the institution and guiding public opinion; we should coordinate education, employment, income distribution, social security, medicine, housing, food safety and the safety of industrial production, and take concrete measures to improve people's standard of living. At the Fifth Plenary Session of the 18th CPC Central Committee, the concept of shared development was raised, requiring all people to participate in development, devote themselves to development, and share the fruits of development. It also requires steadfast adherence to basic standards, highlighting some issues of focus, improving the institution, guiding public anticipations, stressing equal opportunities, ensuring basic standard of living, and realizing a moderately prosperous society in all respects for all people. General Secretary Xi Jinping's speech and the decision of the CPC Central Committee show us clearly the perspective of how we look at people's standard of living and the equality of basic standards. As is known to all, recent years have witnessed a series of public security incidents targeting innocent civilians all over China.

In either killing sprees on school campuses or arsons on buses, criminals that deprived innocent people of their lives deserve the most severe punishment and the most vehement criticism. However, reflections on a law-based society should go beyond the phenomena per se. In the animal world, killings of herbivores by predatory animals are irrelevant to morality or law, for the supreme law of animals is survival. Life requires rules and regulations, but survival requires all means available. Being a kind of animal, human beings also have animal instincts that can lead us to kill each other for the sake of survival. However, human society differs from the animal society in that a basic standard has been accepted in the former—the part above it is called 'life' while the part below is called 'survival.' The part above belongs to the human society while the part below is categorized as the animal society. Just as is depicted by the film *Back to 1942* (2012) directed by Feng Xiaogang, the basic standard of living was completely shattered by a great famine that hit Henan Province in the year 1942. Under such circumstances, neither landlords with any storage of foodstuff or farming hands without a grain at home could protect their own lives or possessions in the whirls of chaos, because when the basic standard was broken, human society instantly reverted to animal society. In today's society where difference has become an indisputable reality but everybody lives above the basic standard, such a society can still maintain stability, and happiness that varies from person to person is largely determined by themselves. However, once someone falls below the basic standard into the state of subsistence, the happiness index of the whole society would probably be determined by the most unhappy people.

In a differentiated society, given the legal protection of individual rights of private property and rights of inheritance, the so-called propositions of 'justice at the starting point', or levelling the playing field, and 'justice of results' are in fact hard to prove. The most important justice worthy of pursuit in a differentiated society is the justice of basic standards, i.e., an irrevocable firm pledge to all members of the society that everyone can make a basic living with dignity. Only in this way can we prevent members of the society from losing heart in crisis and victimizing the society in desperation. As Maslow's pyramid of needs shows, survival and security are the most basic of human needs which in fact are the most basic standards for everyone. This ultimate standard ensures absolute fairness for everyone. In a differentiated society, though people differ in identity and wealth, they are equal in terms of the respect and protection of life. An ordinary commuter travelling in crowded subway trains may find a millionaire driving his luxury limousine acceptable, but would never accept it if the latter runs his car recklessly into pedestrians without getting punished. Such is the basic-standard mentality of fairness in a differentiated society. Once this basic standard of fairness is broken, the society would be plagued by turmoil and ultimately subverted.

The rule of law must guard this basic standard of fairness for society. However, this basic standard will not stay constant, but rather be adjusted in response to changes in times and conditions. As the old saying goes, 'When the river rises, the boat floats high.' If a society is finally free from such problems as subsistence and survival, then where should we set the basic standard of the society? In his speech at the Central Economic Working Conference at the end of 2013, General Secretary Xi Jinping has pointed out the direction for our efforts, and a good government should try their best to mobilize public resources and safeguard this basic standard of fairness for the society. It certainly needs to be noted that safeguarding this basic standard does not encourage loiterers to be parasitic on society, for the fairness of basic standards should be complemented by the fairness of opportunities. The value of the former lies in maintaining stability while the value of the latter lies in stimulating development. Ultimately, an unstable society cannot develop, and a society that does not develop eventually cannot remain stable. Therefore the perspective of fairness in a good society is like the letter T upside down – the horizontal stroke at the bottom represents the fairness of basic standards while the vertical stroke represents the fairness of opportunities. With basic standards and opportunities, there will be no real regret in life, and there will be no true failure in the society.

3. Mentality of reversed transmission by the basic standards

While talking with non-communist party personages on Sept. 17, 2013, Comrade Xi Jinping pointed out that reforms result from reversed transmission of problems but are deepened in constantly finding solutions. On Nov., 12, 2013, *Decision of the Central Committee of the CPC on Some Major Issues Concerning Comprehensively Continuing the Reform* was approved at the Third Plenary Session of the 18th CPC Central Committee, and resounded like a trumpet summoning all to comprehensively advance reform to a deeper level. In a sense, this comprehensive and profound reform resulted from reversed transmission by problems, just like the epic reform and opening up that started in 1978. Back in 1978, the turmoil of the Cultural Revolution had just ended in China, with the national economy towards the verge of collapse, and all fields were plagued with grave problems. The fate of China and the fate of the CPC were both upon the verge of death. One step backward, and China would have slipped into an apocalyptical abyss of history. Thus the Chinese people, unwilling to yield to doom and destruction, made a desperate attempt for development under the leadership of the CPC Central Committee centering upon Comrade Deng Xiaoping. The reversed transmission effect transformed problems into initiatives towards reform, leading to the successful establishment of the socialist market economy system. After three decades of arduous efforts, China has become the No. 2 economy of the world. The predicament of life-and-death did not deter the courage of the Chinese and the CPC, but rather gave rise to the initiative of reform. The same mentality that led to the reform and opening up in 1978 is once again driving reform to a deeper level. We call this the mentality of reversed transmission by the basic standards.

The mentality of reversed transmission by the basic standards is prevalent in all walks of life. A company cannot run well without the reversed transmission of the market mentality, for the market is the basic standard for the survival of a company; an army cannot be combative without the reversed transmission of the battlefield, and thus the battlefield is the basic standard of the army. In the same vein, good governance cannot be achieved without the reversed transmission of the legal mentality, and rule of law is the basic standard of the government. Rule of law stems from the will of the people, so a government that opposes the will of the people will eventually be dumped ruthlessly into the trash bin of history, just as will be companies that oppose the market rules, and armies that oppose the laws of the battlefield. Therefore companies must conscientiously follow the rules of the market and strive to produce goods that are popular on the market, if they seek survival; armies must consciously follow the laws of the battlefield in their drills, to develop real combative capacity, if they seek victory in the battlefield. In the same vein, if the government seeks to avoid being eliminated by the will of the people, it must conscientiously follow the requirements for rule of law, apply legal mentality and approaches to deepening reform, promoting development, resolving conflicts, and maintaining stability.

A conscientious government should respect the basic standard of rule of law. In fact, the reversed transmission by the basic standard of the will of the people may take many forms, the rule of law just being one of them. Such reversed transmission is inherently a constructive or systemic action. If a government rejects such reversed transmission from the rule of law, the will of the people would be realized through revolutions of violence, which in turn would still constitute reversed transmission to the government. However, this kind of transmission is destructive in nature. The regular cycle of dynasties in ancient China that was epitomized in such quotes as 'it rose robustly and fell abruptly' and 'the water that bears the boat is the same that swallows it up' is such destructive reversed transmission. Once the regular cycle of dynasties was applied, society had to pay a heavy price of total destruction. During the peasant uprising at the end of Qin Dynasty, "Xiang Yu led his troops to conquer the capital of Xianyang with a massacre, killing Ziying, the Qin king who surrendered, setting the Qin palaces on fire that did not extinguish until three months later, and trooping east with all the loots of goods, treasures and women." (from *Records of Xiang Yu, The Chronicles*). During the peasant uprising in the twilight of Tang Dynasty, Huang Chao twice conquered the capital of Chang'an, "allowing his soldiers to slaughter so wantonly that blood pooled into rivers, and hence the expression of 'bathing the city in blood.'" (Vol. 254, *History as a Mirror (Zi Zhi Tong Jian)*). By 2 AD, the total population of China in West Han Dynasty was 59.59 million, but by 57 AD of East Han Dynasty, a bloody civil war that lasted scores of years left China with a population only somewhat over 21 million. It was recorded that thousands of miles of fields were left barren, and nine households out of ten were exterminated. This was the horrible force of destructive reversed transmission by the regular cycle of dynasties. Only a profound understanding of its terrible destructive force can ultimately lead to the voluntary transmission of the institution. In this sense, the mentality of reversed transmission by the basic standards of rule of law is a real solution to the myth of the regular cycle of dynasties.

Therefore, the mentality of reversed transmission by the basic standards is dynamic in nature. Given the appalling aftermaths of breaking the basic standards, people must try their best to exceed basic standards instead of lingering upon their margins or even deliberately walking upon the tightrope. As the saying goes, if you often walk along the river, how can you avoid wetting your shoes? Walking upon the tightrope of basic standards, one is likely to fall off any time, incurring horrible aftermaths. Therefore the basic standard can be transfused into the starting line or the source of power for a conscientious government or official in their active pursuit of achievements through reversed transmission; for an unconscientious government or official, by contrast, the basic standard may well become the line that leads to their downfall. It is the mentality of reversed transmission by the basic standards of rule of law that defines the basic standard and drives up the awareness through reversed transmission. Therein lie the true elements of General Secretary Xi Jinping's statement of "working for the best while preparing for the worst."

Respecting the rigid basic standard, safeguarding its fairness, and complying with its reversed transmission - these constitute the basic-standard mentality in the landscape of rule of law. Only by firmly upholding the basic-standard mentality can modern officials and leaders be truly prepared against risks, stay calm in case of emergency, and have a firm hold of the initiative. Only in this way can they truly enhance their capacity for driving reform to a deeper level, resolving conflicts, promoting development and maintaining stability, thereby making their contributions to building a moderately prosperous society in all respects.

Chapter 4

Promote Deliberative Democracy

" S ocialist deliberative democracy is a unique form and a distinctive strength of China's socialist democracy. It is an important embodiment of the party's mass line in the political field. It was stated at the 18th CPC National Congress that as China's socialist democracy progresses, we need to improve the institutions and mechanisms for deliberative democracy and promote its broad-based, multi-level, and institutionalized development. It was stressed at the Third Plenary Session of the 18th CPC Central Committee that with a focus on the major issues concerning economic and social development and the practical issues that affect people's immediate interests, the party should lead extensive deliberations throughout the whole of society and ensure that deliberations are conducted both before decisions are made and during their implementation. These important statements and plans have shown what the way forward will be for China's socialist deliberative democracy.

— Xi Jinping's keynote speech at the conference to celebrate the CPPCC's 65th anniversary, *People's Daily*, September 22, 2014.

'Deliberation' is a familiar word; 'democracy' is a word more familiar to us. When 'deliberation' and 'democracy' are combined, however, a 'new concept', namely 'deliberative democracy' is formulated, yet people find it 'fresh' and not easy to understand. Recently, the term 'deliberative democracy' has been emerging intensively and frequently, and has been interpreted variously. Since 1978 when the policy of reform and opening up to the outside world was implemented, people have been holding diversified views on deliberative democracy. Some note the discrepancy between paces of economic development (faster) and political development (slower). Some take the role of democratic parties as 'a decorative vase', deliberation among political parties standing as 'a show, full of empty rhetoric', and the united front and political participation for nothing but 'going through the motions'. All these voices are still very audible on certain occasions, because some people are still likely to 'repeat the past' and turn a blind eye and a deaf ear to objective reality. All these phenomena oblige us to interpret the scientific connotation, spiritual essence and practical measures of socialist deliberative democracy in a timely, thorough and accurate way. Theoretically and practically, we find it necessary and urgent to foster and intensify confidence in the construction of socialist democracy with Chinese characteristics.

I. Deliberation and Democracy

What is 'socialist deliberative democracy'? President Xi Jinping defined it precisely as, "socialist deliberative democracy is a unique form and a distinctive strength of China's socialist democracy. It is an important embodiment of the party's mass line in the political field." Fact is stranger than fiction. In the 'global village' where humans coexist, numerous examples show that some people pretend to be holding a 'democracy' banner or flaunt their 'deliberative democracy'. President Xi's concept of 'deliberative democracy', based on the precise and rigorous logical reasoning, is a complete scientific category. The modifier 'socialist' cannot be 'omitted', so it cannot be simplified as 'deliberative democracy'. 'Socialist deliberative democracy' profoundly reveals and manifests the essential socialist attribute and nature of deliberative democracy.

It has been president Xi Jinping's logical approach and methodology to stress the characteristics and essence of scientific categorisation. When we study the important speeches made by President Xi Jinping, we not only earnestly learn from the speeches' main contents and key thoughts, but also deeply comprehend the scientific thinking methods embedded in his speeches. It is important to grasp President Xi's scientific thinking method, in order to completely and accurately understand the spiritual essence of the speeches made by the President. Since the 18th National Congress of the CPC, Xi Jinping has been insisting the party "uphold and develop socialism with Chinese characteristics", and he also stressed in a straightforward way that "Socialism with Chinese characteristics is socialism rather than anything else. The basic principles of scientific socialism must not be abandoned; otherwise it is not socialism."[1] Socialist deliberative democracy is closely

---

[1] Xi Jinping's Speech at the Seminar of the Members and Alternate Members of the Newly-elected Central Committee of the CPC for Implementing the Guiding Principles of the 18th CPC National Congress. *People's Daily*. January 6, 2013

associated with the basic system of socialism. The word 'socialist' plays an indispensible part in 'socialist deliberative democracy', for it indicates the nature of our deliberative democracy.

The conference to celebrate the CPPCC's 65th anniversary was held in Beijing on September 21, 2014. (Xinhua News Agency)

1. Socialist deliberative democracy: a unique form and a distinctive strength of China's socialist democracy

"The people's democracy is the very life of socialism." "The position of people as masters of the country is the essence and core of socialist democracy." In a nutshell, adherence to people's democracy and the position of people as masters of the country ensures that the people can maintain their dominant position and that the country's power belongs to the people. The over-90-years' history of the CPC since it was founded in 1921, more than 60 years' development of the PRC since it was founded in 1949, and the achievements in reform and opening up and the socialist modernization over the past 30 years, all repeat the same fact that "the very purpose of the CPC's leadership of the people in developing people's democracy is to guarantee and support their position as masters of the country." "Guaranteeing and supporting the position of the people as masters of the country" is neither a 'slogan' nor 'lip service'. We must ensure its implementation in both the country's political and social activities, and guarantee the people's right to effectively manage state affairs, economic and cultural undertakings, and social affairs, in accordance with the law.

"Only the wearer of the shoes knows if they fit or not." Xi Jinping's remark is concise, comprehensive, thought-provoking yet easy to understand. As the saying goes, 'we don't need the same shoes, for each of us needs one pair that fits best. Approaches to governance may diverge, but converge in the interests of the people.' Only the people are best qualified for judging if the development path they have chosen fits for their country or not. In the world, each country and their people are entitled to equal dignity. Therefore, Xi Jinping reiterates our steady refrain that, "We stand for ... all countries, irrespective of size, strength and wealth, are equal. The right of the people to independently choose their development paths should be respected, interference in the internal affairs of other countries opposed and international fairness and justice maintained."[1] He also pointed out clearly, "The criterion of selecting the ideology is based on whether it can address historical problems that confront the country." The same applies regarding what type of democracy to choose, what path to follow and what doctrine to apply. ComradeXi Jinping's metaphor of 'shoes', simple but profound and powerful, is rich in philosophy. It is stated in plain words that have great appeal. This vivid metaphor conveys our firm confidence in continuously upholding and developing socialism with Chinese characteristics.

Xi Jinping stated frankly, "The reason why the political system of socialism with Chinese characteristics is feasible, dynamic and efficient is that it has been grown in the soil of Chinese society. The political system of socialism with Chinese characteristics, which was, and is, growing in the soil of Chinese society, must be deeply rooted in the soil of Chinese society for its thriving in the future."[2] Similarly, "guaranteeing and supporting the position of people as masters" as the basic requirement and content has to be implemented in corresponding forms and measures. Reality indicates there are a variety of approaches to democracy, so we should not follow any stereotype. "Further, we must recognize that there is no such a thing as a standard model that is universally acceptable." For this reason, it is extremely unreasonable, even irrational for one country to arbitrarily criticize or groundlessly rebuke the path of development and political system that other countries choose, or to impose its own approach to democracy on other countries.

---

[1] Xi Jinping. Part of the Speech at Moscow State Institute of International Relations. *People's Daily. March 24, 2013.*

[2] Xi Jinping. Part of the Speech at the Conference to Celebrate the 60th Anniversary of the National People's Congress. People's Daily. September 6, 2014.

The position of people as masters of the country is congruent with the rights that people duly enjoy. Election and ballots are tangible means of democracy. They are so evidently present in people's life that they intuitively take 'direct election' and 'public voting' for the standard by which to measure the process of democracy. Election and voting, which are indeed the key ways and means to practice democracy, are not the whole case. Whether the people enjoy democratic rights or not depends on "whether they have the right to vote in elections, as well as whether they have the right to constantly participate in everyday political activities." These two perspectives interrelate with and promote one another. The former is more 'obvious', while the latter is more 'profound'. "Socialist democracy requires not just a complete set of institutions and procedures, but also full participation." Based on this, Xi Jinping further explained the position of people as masters of the country with the following: it must be substantially and practically fulfilled through the exercise of the governance of the country by the party, through works of the party and government organizations at all levels in all sectors, and through the realization and development of the people's own interests.

In brief, "in light of the realities of each country, to guarantee and support the position of the people as the masters of the country", it is paramount that people's elected representatives participate in the management of state affairs and social activities, and it is equally important that the people participate in such activities through systems and methods other than election. In real life, we cannot take 'voting', mechanically and partially as the only way to democracy, or even as the 'best' one. Xi Jinping remarked frankly with great insight, "If the people merely have the right to vote but no right of extensive participation, in other words, if they are only awakened at election time but go into hibernation afterwards, then this kind of democracy will only be a formalistic one."

The experience with people's democracy in China shows that in such a vast and populous socialist country, extensive deliberation under the leadership of the CPC on major issues concerning the economy and the people's quality of life embodies the unity of democracy and centralism. Chinese socialist democracy takes two important forms, in one of which, the people exercise their right to vote in elections, and in the other, people from all sectors of society undertake extensive deliberations for reaching consensus on certain issues before major decisions are made. In China, these two forms do not cancel one another out, nor do they deny each other; they are complementary. They constitute institutional features and strengths of Chinese socialist democracy.

Xi Jinping stressed repeatedly, "The leadership of the CPC is the most essential feature of socialism with Chinese characteristics". China, the most populous developing country in the world, would fail to make progress and accomplish nothing in any cause without the core strength of the CPC's leadership. Both history and reality have constantly proved, and will prove completely, this incontrovertible scientific judgment. Both history and reality have proved, and will prove, that deliberative democracy has been integrated into the whole process of China's socialist democracy. The Chinese socialist deliberative democracy not only upholds the leadership of the CPC, but also gives expression to the positive role of all sides; it not only upholds the people's principal position in the country, but also implements the leadership system and organizational principle of democratic centralism; and it not only adheres to the principle of people's democracy, but also promotes unity and harmony. Therefore, the Chinese socialist system of deliberative democracy diversifies the forms and expands the channels of democracy, and enriches the connotation of democracy.

2. Socialist deliberative democracy is an important embodiment of the party's mass line in the political field

A song has it that "The common people are the earth, the common people are the sky, and they are forever the party's care. The common people are the mountains, the common people are the sea, and they are the lifespring of the party." As the vanguard of Chinese working class as well as Chinese people and Chinese nation, the party's tenet is to serve the people, heart and soul. This tenet is the basic requirement to uphold Marxist historical materialism. The people are the makers of history; the people are the driving force of historical progress. The people of all ethnic groups under the leadership of the CPC founded the PRC, and they are the masters of the country. The Constitution of the PRC stipulates that all power of the state belongs to the people, and all state organs and employees must rely on their support, keep in close touch with them, listen to their opinions and suggestions, accept their oversight, and work hard to serve them. Therefore, anytime and anywhere, China must closely rely on the people in governing the country and managing society.

Following Marxist historical materialism, the CPC implements mass line in its work. Mass line is the CPC's key achievement in theoretical innovation and practice by integrating basic principles of Marxism and Chinese concrete realities. The party systematically applied the Marxism-Leninism's principle of the people being the creators of history to its all activities and formed its basic work route of mass line. Mass line is "the basic work route to achieve the party's ideological line, political line and organizational line."[1] Historical experience shows that mass line is in accordance with 'seeking truth from facts' and 'keeping the initiative in our own hands', which is the very soul of Mao Zedong's thoughts.

The party's mass line cannot be randomly simplified as 'from the masses, to the masses'. *Constitution of the CPC* stipulates, "The party follows the mass line in its work, doing everything for the masses, relying on them in every task, carrying out the principle of 'from the masses, to the masses' and translating its correct views into action by the masses of their accord."[2] It is an organic integral of three parts: value endowment (doing everything for the masses, relying on them in every task), practice approach (from the masses to the masses) and goal orientation (translating its correct views into action by the masses of their own accord). Xi Jinping reiterated at the Working Conference of the party's Mass line Education and Practice, "Mass line is the lifeline and basic work route of our party." "Both history and reality show us that keeping close links with the masses is the embodiment of the party's nature and tenet, the distinctive sign that distinguishes the CPC from other political parties, and the main reason for the party's development and growth. Whether or not the party can maintain its close ties with the masses determines the success or failure of the cause of the party."[3]

Xi Jinping pointed out, "Serving the people wholeheartedly and always representing the fundamental interests of the greatest possible majority of the people are the important preconditions and foundation for the implementation and development of deliberative democracy." Since the moment it was founded, the CPC stated clearly that the CPC has no special interests of its own outside of the interests of the working class and the greatest possible majority of the people. The CPC and the state it leads represent the fundamental interests of the greatest possible majority of the people, and all of their theories, lines, principles, policies, and work plans should come from the people and should be formulated and implemented for the people's interests. With this as our major political premise, we have the obligation and

---

[1] *Selection of Important Documents on all the Plenary Sessions of the Central Committee of the Party's National Congress Since the Third Plenary Session of the 11th Central Committee of the CPC (the second half).* Central Documents Press. 1997. p. 47.

[2] *Document Compilation of the 14th CPC National Congress.* People's Publishing House. 1992. p. 94.

[3] Xi Jinping. A Speech at the Working Conference of the Party's Mass Line Education and Practice. *People's Daily.* August 5, 2013.

ability to listen extensively to the people from all sectors of society for their comments and suggestions.

Experience has persuasively shown that we, under the CPC's unified leadership, are able to extensively listen to recommendations and suggestions, and accept criticism and oversight through various forms of deliberation, which reflects the unique strength of Chinese socialist deliberative democracy. Meanwhile, we are able to reach 'five possible goals' and fulfill 'five tasks effectively'. They are as follows: we are able to reach the broadest possible consensus on all decisions we make and on all our work, ensuring that factional rivalry and even bitter disagreement between parties and between interest groups can be avoided. We are able to have all the demands, on matters affecting the interests of all sides, heard before decisions are made so that political forces do not remain fixed in their own opinions or reject others with different views for the sake of their own interests. We are able to put in place broad-based mechanisms for recognizing and correcting errors so that decisions are not made without a clear understanding of the circumstances, or on the basis of belief in one's own blind pretension. We are able to build mechanisms for ensuing people's participation in administration and governance at all levels in order to effectively enable people's voices to be heard and their opinions to be incorporated in decision-making and governance. We are able to pool the wisdom and strength of the whole society to advance reform and development, effectively overcoming any problems with our decisions and work not being carried out for lack of consensus.

Socialist deliberative democracy is an important reflection of the party's mass line in the political field. It comprehensively shows that we should carry out the party's mass line in all work of the state, keeping close ties with the masses, listening to the voices of the people, responding to the expectations of the people, and constantly solving the most direct and practical problems that most concern the people, so as to pool the wisdom and strength of the vast majority of the people.

We are about to enter into the important historical period of the 13th Five-Year Plan for Economic and Social Development (the 13th Five-Year Plan). This is a decisive period to achieving the goal of making Chinese society moderately prosperous in all respects, which is the first of the Two Centenary Goals set by the CPC. In order to ensure that Chinese society becomes moderately prosperous in all respects within the set time frame, and to promote the sustainable and healthy development of economy and society, we must follow a series of important and basic principles in accordance with the situations of our country. Among them, first of all is 'upholding the people's principal position in the country.' *Central Committee of the CPC: Recommendations for the 13th Five-Year Plan for Economic and Social Development* (*Recommendations* for short) points out, "The people are the fundamental force that drives development, and realizing, safeguarding, and developing the fundamental interests of the largest possible majority of people is the fundamental purpose of development. We should adhere to a people-centered notion of development, make improving their wellbeing and promoting individuals' well-rounded development the starting point and ultimate goal of development." Hereby, the Central Committee proposed clearly that we should "develop the people's democracy, safeguard social equity and justice, protect the rights of the people to participate and develop on an equal footing, and give full rein to their enthusiasm, initiative, and creativity." Currently, we should inspire more citizens' orderly participation in political affairs at all levels and in all fields, and develop a more extensive, more complete and more robust people's democracy. We should further expand the people's democracy, strengthen the democratic system, enrich democratic forms and broaden democratic channels.

Completing the building of a moderately prosperous society in all respects, and achieving the Two Centenary Goals are central to the vital interests of billions of people and to the great rejuvenation of the Chinese nation. Hence, *Recommendations* points out emphatically that we should "motivate people to work together". "We should give full rein to democracy, implement the party's mass line, become better able to communicate with and organize the people, strengthen deliberation on major economic and social development issues as well as on issues that affect the vital interests of the people, protect all of their interests in accordance with the law, and inspire within every Chinese person a sense of contribution to their country's development." In practice, we should create new institutions, mechanisms, and approaches in our work with the public, and "properly handle problems among the people, so that, to the greatest possible extent, we can develop consensus and pool strength throughout China for the advancement of reform and development and the promotion of social harmony and stability."[1]

Socialist deliberative democracy is "a unique form and a distinctive strength of China's socialist democracy. Politically, it is an important

---

[1] *Central Committee of the CPC: Recommendations for the 13th Five-Year Plan for Economic and Social Development. People's Daily.* November 4,2015.

embodiment of the party's mass line". This statement has withstood the test of history and the test of practice. History and practice have convincingly shown that "socialist deliberative democracy is deeply rooted in China. It has its rich resources and is full of vitality. It is the great creation of the CPC and the Chinese people."[1]

II. Down-to-earth Democracy

1. Socialist deliberative democracy is not a matter of doing things for the sake of appearances; it must be carried out in a down-to-earth manner.

As Xi Jinping stated, "Democracy is not an ornament to be used for decoration; it is to be used to solve the problems that the people want to solve."[2] The CPC has always been practicing what it advocates and doing solid work. Neither engaging in formalism nor doing superficial writing is the intrinsic requirement of the party's ideological line. Socialist deliberative democracy should not be written on the paper, or shouted by mouth, nor hung on the wall. Instead, it should be applied to social life in a down-to-earth manner. In view of its development progress, "socialist democracy requires not just a complete set of institutions and procedures, but also full participation." The participation by billions of people, especially, their 'full' participation, has its basic requirements, that is, the position of the people as masters of the country must be given concrete and practical expression through the exercise of state power by the CPC and its governance of the country, in all aspects of the work of the party and government organizations at all levels, and through the realization and development of the people's own interests.

Further, real-world and difficult situations at home and abroad objectively require socialist deliberative democracy to be 'down-to-earth'. It cannot, even, is not allowed to, be a matter of doing things for show. From a domestic perspective, in the process of reform and opening up, the pattern of interests has undergone drastic changes and resulted in a new situation; new and old social problems are interwoven with one another; and notions and systems in market economy are diversified. From an international perspective, the competitive game of different political development paths

---

[1] Xi Jinping. Socialist Deliberative Democracy Takes Roots in China with Vitality. *People's Daily*. October 28, 2014.

[2] Xi Jinping. The Speech at the Conference to Celebrate the CPPCC's 65th Anniversary. *People's Daily*. September 22, 2014.

across the world presents new challenges. Thus, it is of great and far-reaching significance to carry out socialist deliberative democracy in a 'down-to-earth' manner for the following five purposes. It is conducive to attracting more citizens to participate in a orderly way in political life and to better realizing people's rights of being the masters of the country; to improve skills in scientific and democratic decision-making and accelerate the modernization of national governance system and capacity; to resolve conflicts and facilitate social harmony and stability; to maintain close ties between the party and the people and consolidate and enlarge the party's governing basis; to give full play to the advantages of our country's political system, and reinforce our confidence in the path, theories and system of socialism with Chinese characteristics.

'Democracy is not an ornament' drives the point home. It is the requirement for the development of socialist deliberative democracy, as well as the objective evaluation on the construction of socialist democracy with Chinese characteristics. Some ridicule those participatory parties as 'vases', while others simplify political consultation with Chinese characteristics as 'beckoning, raising hands, clapping, and waving', which is utter formalism and quite contrary to the reality. Frankly speaking, socialist deliberative democracy still needs to be improved and perfected in its development. However, it is even more necessary for us to affirm its achievements and to acknowledge its substantial contributions. 'Democracy is not an ornament to be used for decoration; it is to be used to solve the problems that the people want to solve.' This is a scientific conclusion.

Party consultation is a distinctive strength of socialist democracy with Chinese characteristics, which plays an indispensable role in the work of the party and the country. On the eve of the founding of the PRC, the first plenary session of the CPPCC was held. Representing the will of the people of all ethnic groups in China and performing the functions of the National People's Congress, that session adopted the *Common Program of the CPPCC* – a provisional kind of Constitution; the *Organizing Law of the CPPCC*; and the *Organizing Law of the Central People's Government of the People's Republic of China*. It adopted major resolutions on the capital, the national flag, the national anthem, and the calendar system of the PRC. In addition, the session elected the National Committee of the CPPCC and the Central People's Government Council of the PRC, and proclaimed the founding of the PRC. All these are the landmark achievements of democratic consultation, demonstrating significant and 'down-to-earth' contributions to the founding of the PRC made by the CPPCC.

Party consultation is another important part of the national governance system. Since the PRC was founded, the CPC has conducted extensive and in-depth consultation with the democratic parties on both domestic and foreign affairs, such as socialist transformation of capitalist industry and commerce, and the movement to resist US aggression and aid Korea (Korean War, 1950-1953). The CPC did not take actions until they reached a consensus, which was advocated and supported by all sectors of the society. At the initial stage of reform and opening up, in order to mobilize the business sector and motivate their enthusiasm to participate in economic construction, comrade Deng Xiaoping invited five leaders of the China Democratic National Construction Association, and All-China Federation of Industry and Commerce, to have an informal discussion. Their meeting called 'Five Seniors' Hotpot Feast' became a much-told story. Ji Fang, 92-year-old chairman of the Chinese Peasants and Workers Democratic Party, Hu Juewen, chairman of the Central Committee of the China Democratic National Construction Association, Hu Ziang, chairman of the All-China Federation of Industry and Commerce, jointly put forward *Proposals on the Promotion and Development of Chinese Medicine*, which was highly approved by the Central Committee of the CPC. The so-called 'Three Seniors' Proposal' is another much-told story in the history of multi-party cooperation.

Since the beginning of the 21st century, the central committees of the democratic parties participated in investigation of and proposals for revitalizing the old industrial bases in Northeast region, developing the Western Taiwan Straits Economic Zone, and establishing the Central Plains Economic Zone, which have become the significant strategies to drive our country's regional development. Since the 18th National Congress of the CPC, the central committees of democratic parties put forward many practical and efficient opinions and suggestions on issues such as promoting the coordinated development of Beijing, Tianjin and Hebei, and coping with the haze pollution. By means of party consultation and deliberation, the CPC set up an institutionalized platform for opinions, communication and consultation, widely pooling the wisdom and strength of all sectors of society, and boosting the scientific and democratic development of national governance decisions.

The great practice of building socialism with Chinese characteristics provides a broad stage for further stimulating and giving full play to the characteristics and advantages of each participatory party, and promoting multi-party cooperation and socialist deliberative democracy, so as to pool strengths and join hands to build a moderately prosperous society in all respects. The achievements of socialist deliberative democracy are highly valued by the party and the country, which have been transformed into policies and guidelines and put into practice. The ample and substantial fruits of investigation, participation in state affairs, and political consultation have been adopted and absorbed by the party, the government and the departments concerned.

When looking back to history and summarizing experiences of both past and present, we can clearly see that the diversified approaches and channels of socialist deliberative democracy have made tangible contributions of historic significance to rejuvenating and developing the economy, consolidating the newly founded people's government, giving impetus to social reforms, advancing the socialist revolution and development, building a moderately prosperous society in all respects, and constantly advancing socialist modernization. In the new historical development epochs and stages, the Party Central Committee with Comerade Xi Jinping as its core accurately understands the nature and position of the CPPCC, gives full play to its role as a main channel for deliberative democracy, and builds institutions regarding political consultation, democratic oversight, and participation in the deliberation and administration of state affairs, with the focus on the themes of unity and democracy. The CPPCC, along with the socialist deliberative democracy, has developed while carrying forward its fine traditions, and has kept making innovations throughout its development. It has concentrated on the central task of economic development, served the overall interests of the country, and made new positive contributions by developing consensus, drawing together people's energies, and making proposals on comprehensively deepening reform. All these are indisputable and obvious to all as solid facts.

In the light of dialectical materialism and historical materialism, we should recognize that socialist deliberative democracy has made significant 'down-to-earth' progress; meanwhile we should be aware that the deliberative democracy construction is a process requiring constant development. There are new problems, new challenges and new tasks under new circumstances, so in the new historical developmental epoch and new historical developmental stage, we should "support and encourage the exploration and innovation in deliberative democracy construction", respect people's initiatives, and attach importance to extracting and summarizing hands-on experience which can be developed into institutional norms in timely fashion. Efforts can be made in the following three aspects: We should strengthen leadership and organizational coordination, encourage exploration and innovation, implement extensive consultation by means of diversified mechanisms, channels and methods, and set up and perfect multiple consultative processes, including proposals, meetings, informal discussions, seminars, hearings, public notices, assessments, consulting, networks and public opinion polling. We should reinforce the construction of new think-tanks, establish and improve policy-making consulting system. We should advance theoretical research on deliberative democracy to constantly enrich and develop the theoretical system of socialist deliberative democracy.

2. We should establish a system of deliberative democracy with reasonable procedures while staying all-inclusive.

Xi Jinping stated that socialist deliberative democracy must be put into practice in all respects, and 'across the country at all levels'. It profoundly reveals that socialist deliberative democracy is a 'systematic engineering' composed of many elements, and emphasizes the significance and necessity of building a system of socialist deliberative democracy that is all-inclusive, with reasonable procedures.

As regards this issue, Xi Jinping, General Secretary of the CPC, put forward requirements clearly. They are to: expand the consultation channels of the organs of state power, committees of the Chinese People's Political Consultative Conference, political parties, and community-level and social organizations; conduct intensive deliberation on issues relating to legislation, administration, democracy, political participation and social problems; give full play to the important role of the united front in deliberative democracy; make the Chinese People's Political Consultative Conference serve as a major channel for conducting deliberative democracy; improve the systems of the CPPCC, standardize the contents and procedures for consultation, enrich the forms of deliberative democracy, and more actively carry out consultations on particular topics with specialists and representatives from all sectors of society and with the relevant government departments on the handling of proposals, to improve the intensity and effectiveness of the consultations.[1]

---

[1] Xi Jinping. Explanatory Notes to the"Decision of the Central Committee of the CPC on Some Major Issues Concerning Comprehensively Continuing the Reform." *People's Daily*. November 16, 2013.

The reason we lay emphasis on the CPPCC deliberative democracy and its requirements is that the CPPCC deliberative democracy is an important component of socialist deliberative democracy. Soon after *Opinions of the Central Committee of the CPC on Strengthening the Construction of Socialist Deliberative Democracy* was promulgated, on June 25, 2015, Xinhua News Agency published the full text of *Implementation Opinions on Strengthening the Construction of the CPPCC Deliberative Democracy* issued by the general office of the CPC Central Committee. The CPPCC deliberative democracy is an important democratic form. Under the leadership of the CPC, the political parties and groups, people of all ethnic groups and people from all walks of life have joined the CPPCC, perform their functions of political consultation, democratic oversight, and political participation in state affairs, and carry out extensive consultation and build consensus before and during decision-making with focusing on the major issues of reform, development and stability and the practical problems affecting the people's vital interests. The CPPCC functions on the basis of the China's Constitution, the CPPCC Charter, and relevant policies. It is guaranteed by the system of multiparty cooperation and political consultation under the leadership of the CPC and assumes the functions of deliberation, oversight, participation, and cooperation. It has become an important platform for political parties and groups, people of all ethnic groups and people from all walks of life to promote democracy, to participate in state affairs, to unite and cooperate. It is an institutional arrangement with distinctive Chinese characteristics suitable for China's national conditions. For a long time, the CPPCC, as an important channel for deliberative democracy, has played the role of an organization specializing in deliberation, and has made significant contributions to extensively soliciting advice and opinions, gathering consensus, making the decision-making of the party and the country scientific and democratic, better realizing the position of the people as the masters of the country, resolving conflicts and promoting social harmony and stability: so as to constantly advance the modernization of the national governance system and governance capacity.

Looking into the basic elements of socialist deliberative democracy system, we will find out that the logical framework of '3+3+1' is being built step by step in deepening the reform of the political system. The first '3' refers to the deliberation of political parties, government and the

CPPCC. The second '3' means the deliberation of the National People's Congress, people's organizations and community-level organizations. The last '1' is the deliberation of social organizations. It is worth careful study and understanding that, concerning the contents of the framework of '3+3+1', each implies a different focus of work. The first '3' is strengthening emphatically, and the second '3' is developing actively, while the last '1' is exploring gradually, which does not merely show differences in expressions, but embodies dialectical thinking of stratification and classification. In practice, the purpose of building and perfecting the logical system of '3+3+1' is to give full play to the advantages of deliberative channels and to adequately integrate them, so as to develop and improve the system of socialist deliberative democracy. What needs to be emphasized is that various forms of deliberation must determine the contents of their deliberation and methods in accordance with their respective characteristics and actual demands, enabling the people to enjoy the rights to know, participate, express and supervise, and participate jointly in democratic consultation via different democratic channels.

Based on the present levels of people's practice and understanding, in building the system of socialist deliberative democracy we need both to pay attention to the basic ways and channels of the framework of '3+3+1'. In accordance with reality and in line with the requirements of being scientific and reasonable, standardized and orderly, simple and convenient, and democratic and centralized, we need to formulate deliberation plans, clarify topics and contents for deliberation, determine members of deliberation, carry out deliberation activities and lay emphasis on the feedbacks on the deliberation achievements, so as to ensure the deliberation activities are orderly, practical and efficient.

It is necessary to point out that emphasis on 'in all respects' and 'across the country', essentially means that we need to firmly hold the view of putting the people ahead in the priority list for socialist deliberative democracy. We need to redouble our efforts in developing deliberative democracy at the community level, with a focus on conducting deliberations among the masses. All decisions that affect people's immediate interests must be made on the basis of opinions fully solicited from the people, as well as deliberations conducted with them through various means, on different levels, and from different sectors. We should improve the system by which community-level organizations maintain contact with the people, strengthen deliberation on community affairs, make a good job of two-way communication of information from the top-down to the bottom-up, and make sure the people manage their own affairs properly in accordance with the law. We should make the exercise of power more open and standardized, and increase transparency in the operations of the party, the government, and the judiciary, as well as in the administration of other fields. We should ensure that the people oversee the exercise of power and that it happens in broad daylight.

The *Central Committee of the CPC: Recommendations for the 13th Five-Year Plan for Economic and Social Development* was adopted at the Fifth Plenary Session of the 18th Central Committee of the CPC On October 29, 2015. *Recommendations* proposes, "We need to consolidate and expand the broadest possible patriotic united front; implement party policies on intellectuals, ethnic groups, religion, and work related to overseas Chinese; give full rein to the role of all other political parties, federations of industry and commerce, and public figures without party affiliation; substantially increase the people's awareness of the importance of ethnic unity and progress; and guide regions in adapting to China's socialist society. We need to foster harmony among political parties, ethnicities, religions, social strata, and Chinese both at home and abroad, consolidate unity among Chinese people of all ethnic groups, and strengthen unity among all the sons and daughters of China whether at home or overseas."[1] This functions as guiding principles for us to build a moderately prosperous society in all respects during the decisive period of the 13th Five-Year Plan, give full play to the important role of the united front in deliberative democracy, and achieve the Two Centenary Goals and the great rejuvenation of the Chinese nation.

3. Real deliberation requires deliberation both before and during the process of decision-making.

Xi Jinping stressed, "When we talk about deliberation, we mean real deliberation. Real deliberation requires deliberation both before and during the process of decision-making. It requires that decisions are made and work is adjusted on the basis of opinions and suggestions from all sectors. It also requires that institutions are in place to ensure that the results of deliberations are implemented, so that our decisions and work both better reflect public will and are more suitable to real-life conditions."[2] Implementing people's

---

[1] *Central Committee of the CPC: Recommendations for the 13th Five-Year Plan for Economic and Social Development. People's Daily.* November 4, 2015.

[2] Xi Jinping. The Speech at the Conference to Celebrate the CPPCC's 65th Anniversary. *People's Daily.* September 22, 2014.

democracy and ensuring the position of the people as the masters of the country require us to conduct extensive deliberation among people from all sectors of society in the governance of China. Extensive deliberation is the fine tradition of the CPC. Ranging from 'state affairs' to 'trifles', deliberation is indispensable. Therefore, Mao Zedong once said, "the relations between all aspects of the state need deliberation." He also said frankly and humorously that, "As you are familiar with the nature of our government – to do things through deliberation with the people, we may call it a deliberative government." Remarks of Mao Zedong are both witty and profound, and reveal the truth that the people's government is for the people. As a 'deliberative government', how to conduct deliberation is a 'question'. In consequence, Zhou Enlai clearly pointed out that "the spirit of deliberation is not in the final voting; it is mainly in the deliberations and repeated discussions that happen before a decision is made." With the passage of time, a lot of things may have changed, while the CPC's notions on deliberation before decision-making have been passed down from generation to generation, involving aspects such as; 'we should do things through deliberation with the people,' 'we should mainly conduct deliberations and repeated discussions before a decision is made,' and 'real deliberation requires deliberation both before and during the process of decision-making'.

Xi Jinping said, "The process of holding extensive deliberations among the people is the process of promoting democracy and drawing on collective wisdom, the process of unifying people's thinking and building consensus, the process of scientific and democratic decision-making, and the process of ensuring the position of the people as masters of the country. It is only in this way that we can have solid foundations for our country's governance and for social governance; it is only in this way that we are able to draw together powerful strength." For a long time, the CPC has been conducting deliberations, through various mechanisms, channels, and methods, on the major issues of reform, development, and stability, and especially on the issues that have a bearing on people's immediate interests. We need to respect the wishes of the majority of the people, and at the same time take into account the reasonable demands of those who are in minority. We should extensively solicit opinions and pool wisdom from society, expand consensus, and bolster cooperative strength.

The practice of socialist deliberative democracy vividly depicts the logical locus of 'to do things through deliberations' and 'to do things through effective deliberations'. Deliberation is not only of significance and necessity, but also of possibility and effectiveness. It shows that under China's socialist system, deliberations help effectively when a problem crops up, and matters involving many people are discussed by all those involved; to reach consensus on the wishes and needs of the whole of society is the essence of people's democracy. 'To conduct effective deliberation' means in the construction of socialism with Chinese characteristics, we can, and are able to, conduct deliberations on problems, by which we get things done to the utmost. We will make the 'people's government' a 'deliberative government'. The key of deliberation lies in repeated deliberations when we find and address issues. In a nutshell, the more numerous and in-depth deliberations we hold, the better the result can be.

It is worth noting that in practice, when we conduct deliberations on different contents, we need to take into consideration the scope of deliberation. That is to say, on matters that have a bearing on the interests of people of all our ethnic groups, deliberations will be held extensively throughout the whole of society; on matters that concern the interests of people in one specific area, deliberations will be held among the local people there; on matters that affect the interests of certain groups of people, deliberations will be held among those groups; and on matters that concern the interests of people at the community level, deliberations will be held within the community.

History and reality tell us repeatedly that "the process of holding extensive deliberations among the people is the process of promoting democracy and drawing on collective wisdom, the process of unifying people's thinking and building consensus, the process of scientific and democratic decision-making, and the process of ensuring the position of the people as masters of the country. It is only in this way that we can have solid foundations for our country's governance and for social governance; it is only in this way that we are able to draw together powerful strength."[1]

"Real deliberation requires deliberation both before and during the process of decision-making" indicates that there are two possibilities when conducting deliberation, one is real deliberation; the other is false deliberation. While "real deliberation requires deliberation both before and during the process of decision-making", false deliberation is likely to take place after decision-making. The emphasis on deliberation before and during decision-

---

[1] Xi Jinping. The Speech at the Conference to Celebrate the CPPCC's 65th Anniversary. *People's Daily*. September 22, 2014.

making is both profound and simple. As everyone understands, if deliberation is only carried out after decision-making, it is just like 'a Monday morning quarterback' or 'belated wisdom' – it is repellent 'formalism' and 'obscurantist policy' which does not respect the people but deceives the people.

Practice has proved that it is the important experience of deliberation among political parties that, on major policies and issues affecting the interests of the people, before and during the process of decision-making, they carry out extensive deliberation and make their efforts to build consensus to avoid making subversive mistakes in major issues. The party and the country conduct deliberations with democratic parties before establishing major policies and guidelines, and listen earnestly to suggestions from non-communist parties; while democratic parties prepare their opinions and suggestions from their particular perspectives, on major policies and issues affecting the interests of the people, demonstrating their participatory parties' advantages and functions. Furthermore, extensive deliberation before and during the process of decision-making is the process during which the party listens extensively to the suggestions of democratic parties; at the same time, it is the process by which democratic parties get to know and accept the party's political views and constantly enhance their confidence in the road, theory and system of socialism with Chinese characteristics.

'Real deliberation' before and during decision-making should be guaranteed by institutional construction. In recent years, the Central Committee has promulgated a series of documents on deliberative democracy, to make it more institutionalized, normalized and proceduralized. As for strengthening the deliberation among political parties, it is stipulated clearly that General Secretary of the CPC holds deliberative forums four time a year at regular intervals, conducting deliberations with the central committees of democratic parties and the representatives of the people without party affiliation, on the issues of economic development proposals, semi-annual economic work, Central Plenary documents, and Central Economic Work Conference documents. The forums enrich the contents and broaden the channels of socialist deliberative democracy to promote its broad-based, multi-level and institutionalized development.

III. Negations of 'Imported' Deliberative Democracy

As a saying goes, 'there is nowhere but Greece'. Once 'deliberative democracy' is mentioned, some people cannot help thinking about Greece, or they take some western scholars such as Rawls and Habermas as its 'initiators'. We have to know that during the process of human social development, countries in the world have developed diversified and varied democratic content and forms. We need to understand deliberative democracy in other countries, but we cannot simply and crudely conclude that our 'deliberative democracy' was invented by western countries, or that China's deliberative democracy was 'originated' from the West and 'transplanted' to China. In that interpretation, 'deliberative democracy' is 'imported'. Is this indeed the case?

Socialist deliberative democracy is the great creation of the CPC and the Chinese people with a unique form and the distinctive strength of China's socialist democracy. It is an important embodiment of the party's mass line in the political field. Socialist deliberative democracy is different from western deliberative democracy in theory and connotation. They have great differences in theoretical origins, institutional basis, political practice and cultural background. Socialist deliberative democracy finds its roots in Chinese history and culture, took its shape through the Chinese people's revolutionary struggle in modern times, and developed in the practice of socialism with Chinese characteristics. It is the important guarantee of the state's prosperity and strength, national rejuvenation and people's wellbeing.

Xi Jinping, General Secretary of the CPC, once summarized the major contents of socialist deliberative democracy, highlighting its Chinese characteristics, Chinese styles and Chinese manners. Socialist deliberative democracy is "a unique, particular and original form of Chinese socialist democracy. It derives from our nation's long-established inclusive political culture, in which we believe that all under heaven belongs to the people and we can seek common ground while putting aside differences. It derives from China's political evolution in modern times, from the long-term practical experience built as the CPC led the people through the course of revolution, development and reform. It derives from the great innovations made in our political institutions by all political parties, people's organizations, ethnic groups, and people from all social strata and different backgrounds after the PRC was founded. It derives from the continuous innovations in China's political system since the policy of reform and opening up was carried out. Hence, General Secretary Xi Jinping summarized strategically and concisely that socialist deliberative democracy "has firm cultural, theoretical, practical, and institutional foundations". All these reflect that fundamentally, our socialist deliberative democracy is not in any way copied or 'imported' from the western world.

1. Profound cultural foundation

China is a country that boasts thousands of years' cultural tradition, both extensive and profound. It not only contains the thoughts, theories, and institutional practice concerning political deliberation, but also embodies the cultural spirit and value orientation pertinent to deliberative democracy. Generally speaking, it includes the people-oriented thought, values, and spirit of harmony, expressed as 'the whole world as one community,' 'fully inclusive and equitable,' and 'seeking common ground while putting aside differences'. Other relevant notions, as 'the people are the basis of the country, and government serves the people', 'encouraging the people to advise, and listen to the people's suggestions', 'harmony in diversity', 'valuing justice above material gains', 'peaceful co-existence' and 'expostulation', have played a significant role in defining China's long-standing and well-established tradition of political deliberation.

2. Scientific theoretical foundation

Socialist deliberative democracy is the great creation and latest achievement of the basic tenets of Marxism, integrated with the actual conditions in China. It is the key content of the theoretical system of socialism with Chinese characteristics, and boasts a unique and firm theoretical foundation. It mainly consists of the following elements.

The first is the party theory, state theory, and democratic political theory in Marxism. Marxism puts forward the view that the proletarian party adhering to the leadership should unite other workers' parties, and contract an alliance with other democratic parties, the view on the origin and nature of the country, on proletariats seizing the power, and on how to apply the proletariat regime, and the view that though bourgeois revolution achieved the political democracy, it is based on private property, and in nature is false democracy for a minority of the people. All these views provide significant theoretical guidance for the construction of socialist deliberative democracy.

The second is the party's theory concerning the united front. The united front, as one of the 'three treasures', is important for the CPC to achieve victories in revolution, development, and reform and opening up. The essence of the united front is to unite with all available forces, and mobilize all positive forces to the utmost, which lies at the core and is a valuable experience of the CPC in its governance of China. Socialist deliberative democracy both adheres to the principle of people's democracy, and carries out the requirements of unity and harmony. It is a flexible application and creative development of the theory of the united front.

The third is the CPC's mass line theory. The CPC has been unswerving in upholding mass line, representing the fundamental interests of the greatest possible majority of the people, relying closely on the people in governing the country and managing society, listening extensively to the opinions and suggestions from all sectors of the people, and accepting their oversight. At a new historical starting point, the CPC highlights that socialist deliberative democracy is an important reflection of the party's mass line in the political field. Deliberation with the people and for the people reveals the value orientation of socialist deliberative democracy.

3. Solid practice foundation

Socialist deliberative democracy is deeply rooted in the vast territory of China. It is the inevitable result of the great practice of the Chinese people under the leadership of the CPC in their long-term struggle for revolution, development and reform, and in their exploration of a path for political development of socialism with Chinese characteristics. During the New Democratic Revolution Period, the CPC effectively implemented deliberative democracy in the construction of the 'three-three' democratic regime model, which was the initial stage of China's deliberative democracy. On April 30, 1948, the eve of May Day, in order to mobilize the people of all sectors of the country to achieve the glorious mission of building a new China, the CPC issued a commemorative 'May Day' slogan of great historical significance. It called upon democratic parties, people without party affiliation, and community leaders to hold the CPPCC promptly, which received a positive response from all sectors of the society, and started a prelude to the victory of the foundation of the new China, holding deliberative democracy deliberation with the people. In September, 1949, the first plenary session of the CPPCC was held for the establishment of the PRC and officially established the system of multiparty cooperation and political consultation under the leadership of the CPC, marking the nationwide implementation of deliberative democracy – a new democratic pattern in China.

It is worth noting that the CPPCC at this period played a 'special' role and had 'double' attributes. On the one hand, it was the organizational form of the people's democratic united front. On the other hand, it was the organizational form of the central state political power, a substitute of the National People's Congress – an organization of supreme state power. This is the CPPCC's special nature and historical function under the historical conditions at that time. In September, 1954, the first National People's Congress was held, marking the system by which the people's congress became the national fundamental political system. The CPPCC was no longer the substitute of the People's Congress. Then, the CPPCC had two 'prospects': one was to withdraw from the historical stage because it no longer played the roles of the People's Congress. While the other was to be kept as an organizational form of the people's democratic united front, although it didn't serve the function of the People's Congress any longer. The wise Chinese people and the CPC chose the latter, keeping the CPPCC. History has proved that this choice is correct. This choice of far-reaching significance opened up the road marking two forms of practice in terms of the people's democracy with Chinese characteristics.

Since the policy of reform and opening up was implemented, socialist deliberative democracy has been developing while inheriting, and improving, its traditions. The 13th National Congress of the CPC put forward the concept of building the 'system of social consultation and dialogue'. In 2007, *White Paper on China's Political Party System* firstly proposed the concepts of 'democratic election' and 'deliberative democracy'. The 18th National Congress of the CPC and the Third Plenary Session of the 18th CPC Central Committee put forward the strategic deployment of improving the system of socialist deliberative democracy, and promoting wide, multi-tiered and institutionalized deliberative democracy. Until now, China has gradually constructed the consultative channels that suit China's national conditions. Deliberative democracy has expanded its coverage from deliberation between political parties to social deliberation, from deliberation in the political field to the social and living areas, and from the state-level to the local and community-level.

4. Systemic foundation of institution

China has built its socialist deliberative democracy to be a relatively complete institutional system, protected by the Constitution, supported by the basic political system, and guided by the party's policies and guidelines.

Firstly, the Constitution, China's fundamental law, provides legal protection for the development and improvement of socialist deliberative democracy. From a legal perspective, it stresses the vital function and significance of upholding and developing the CPPCC, the united front and political consultation system.

Secondly, the basic political system and a series of important documents issued, are an important support to consolidate and develop socialist deliberative democracy. China has formed the deliberative democracy system with Chinese characteristics composed of state-level political deliberation, social deliberation between state and society, and society-level citizen deliberation. The process in brief is as follows. The deliberative government, founded in September 1949, marked the formal establishment of the multi-party cooperation system under the leadership of the CPC. At the end of 1989, the Central Committee of the CPC formulated the *Opinions on Sticking to and Improving the System of Multi-party Cooperation and Political Consultation under the Leadership of the CPC*, institutionalizing the multi-party cooperation system. In 1997, the 15th National Congress of the CPC brought it into the three basic programs of the primary stage of socialism. In 2005, the Central Committee of the CPC published the *Opinions on Further Strengthening the System of Multi-party Cooperation and Political Consultation under the Leadership of the CPC*, reiterating and intensifying this system. In 2012, the 18th National Congress of the CPC made an important decision to establish deliberative democracy as a major form of people's democracy through the congress of party representatives, so as to improve the system of socialist deliberative democracy. After the 18th National Congress of the CPC, the Central Committee of the CPC consecutively promulgated the *Opinions on Strengthening the Construction of Socialist Deliberative Democracy*, and *Opinions on Strengthening the Implementation of the People's Political Consultative Conference on the Construction of Deliberative Democracy*, providing theoretical and practical guidance for the construction of socialist deliberative democracy under the new circumstances.

Finally, a series of policies and guidelines of the CPC are the essential basis of the construction of socialist deliberative democracy. Currently, we have formulated clear requirements to improve the system of socialist deliberative democracy and promote its broad-based, multi-level, and institutionalized development, in terms of guiding thought, basic principles, measures, deliberative channels, procedures, and guarantees. They are the guides to actions and principles to follow to promote socialist deliberative democracy, and should be sincerely implemented in practice.

IV. 'Multi-Party Cooperation' instead of 'Multi-Party System' in Contemporary China

At the first sight, the two concepts of 'multi-party cooperation' and 'multi-party system' are 'similar', for both have a 'multi-party' modifier. Actually, they have a world of difference between them, especially in their nature. Across the world, each country has its respective national conditions. To choose a political system is to choose what development road to follow, which should be each country's independent choice. Similarly, in contemporary China, it is the Chinese people's independent choice to implement 'multi-party cooperation' instead of 'multi-party system'. It is the political system of socialism with Chinese characteristics, and also a basic political system in contemporary China. It is a great creation of the Marxist theory of political parties, the United Front Theory, and the theory of socialist democratic politics integrated with China's concrete practice. Meanwhile, an in-depth analysis of the nature of the 'multi-party system' in the West enables us to clarify that the 'multi-party system' does not suit China's national conditions, and then consolidate our confidence in following the political development road of socialism with Chinese characteristics. Indeed, we should not either exaggerate, or criticize the countries that implement 'multi-party system'. What matters is that 'multi-party cooperation' is not 'multi-party system', and 'one-party rule' is not 'one-party dictatorship'. The relations between the CPC and democratic parties are quite different from those between 'the party in power' and 'the party out of power', or between 'the party in power' and 'the opposition party'. Concerning these major theoretical issues, no 'sloppy' or 'vague' thinking whatsoever is permissible, even in the slightest.

That China cannot implement a 'multi-party system' is the choice of the people and also the choice of history. As Xi Jinping pointed out, "What political system to build in China has been a historical task that the Chinese people were faced [with] in modern times. To solve this historical task, the Chinese people have had a hard exploration."[1] The past is not easily forgotten. In modern Chinese history, a fair number of people conceived of the capitalist 'multi-party system' as the way to save the nation. After the Revolution of 1911, they followed the example of this western system, and hence political parties sprang up overnight, and at one point the number of parties reached more than 300. But at last, they all came to an end hastily,

---

[1] Xi Jinping. The Speech at the Conference to Celebrate the CPPCC's 65th Anniversary. *People's Daily*. September 22, 2014.

failing to change the backward situation of the Chinese nation. After the Chinese People's War of Resistance against Japanese Aggression (1937-1945), some people proposed 'a third way', under the banner of 'multi-party system'. However, the Kuo-min-tang with its autocratic dictatorship shattered the illusion of these people. History has proved time and again that 'multi-party system' does not work in China, which is the bitter experience at the cost of blood and life.

Xi Jinping made the following clear-cut judgments with his superb dialectical thinking, which are worth our earnest study and understanding. "Designing and developing a national political system, we should attach great importance to the organic unity of history and reality, theory and practice, and form and substance. We should insist on proceeding from China's national conditions and from the reality. We should grasp the long-term historical heritage, the development road we have followed, the accumulated political experience, the formulated political principles, and the realistic request to solve the realistic problems. We should not cut off history, and build a 'flying-peak' political system only based on imagination." He further stated, "The functions of political system are to regulate political relations, build political order, promote national development, and maintain national stability. It is out of the question to make abstract judgments by breaking away from the specific social and political conditions, to follow the same pattern and to be attributed to one standard." He stressed, "With regard to political system, we should not simply think whatever we do not have while other countries have is in deficiency, and then we are eager to bring it back. Or we should not simply think whatever we have while other countries do not have is redundant, and then we are eager to get rid of it. Both views are simplified and one-sided, so neither is correct."[1]

"The tasty orange, grown in southern China, would turn sour once it is grown in the north". China cannot copy the political system of other countries, because it would not fit us, it might even lead to catastrophic consequences, and it might even ruin the future of our country. Regardless of China's national conditions, it did not, does not and will not work to copy the development model of other countries. In a word, "a system, only rooted in its own national soil to absorb nutrients, is reliable and effective." "The political system of socialism with Chinese characteristics which was, and is,

---

[1] Xi Jinping. The Speech at the Conference to Celebrate the CPPCC's 65th Anniversary. *People's Daily.* September 22, 2014.

growing in the soil of Chinese society, must be deeply rooted in the soil of Chinese society for its prosperity in the future."[1] All these classical sayings should be kept in mind.

It should be shown clearly that 'multi-party cooperation' is only the shortened form of 'multi-party cooperation and political consultation under the leadership of the CPC'. It must be completely and clearly understood that, in particular, 'under the leadership of the CPC' cannot be omitted, though the complete name is much longer than the brief one. Xi Jinping clearly stated, "The leadership by the CPC is the common choice of the Chinese people, including the democratic parties, people's organizations, ethnic groups, social strata, and people from all sectors of society. It is the most essential feature of socialism with Chinese characteristics, and it provides the fundamental guarantee for the development and progress of the CPPCC."[1] In a word, the leadership by the CPC is the prime prerequisite and fundamental guarantee, and the core content of multi-party cooperation. The leadership by the CPC and multi-party cooperation, and the governance by the CPC and multi-party participation in politics are distinct features of the political party system of socialism with Chinese characteristics.

1. The implementation of the system of multi-party cooperation and political consultation under the leadership of the CPC is a requirement of the nature of socialist democracy. In the relations between different political parties, the CPC is in the leading position. This leadership is the correct choice of the Chinese people and democratic parties in their long-term practice of revolution, construction and reform, which suits China's national conditions. In contemporary China, no other political party can replace the CPC and become the core of leadership of 1.3 billion people. Democratic parties have a clear understanding of the importance, necessity, and practical significance of being under the leadership of the CPC, and an aspiration for sincere cooperation and common endeavor under the leadership of the CPC.

In the relations between political parties and state power, the CPC is the ruling party, and democratic parties participate in and deliberate on state affairs. The CPC's leadership is the choice of history, endowed and defined clearly by the Constitution. The actual role played by democratic parties in

---

[1] Xi Jinping. The Speech at the Conference to Celebrate the CPPCC's 65th Anniversary. *People's Daily*. September 22, 2014.

China's historical and contemporary political life determines their position as participant parties. Democratic parties, as the political alliances of socialist working people, builders of socialism and patriots who support socialism with whom they maintain ties, participate in the exercise of state power and the administration of state affairs under the leadership of the CPC, which is a major indication of people's democracy. It is different from a 'one-party system', 'two-party system' or 'multi-party system'. In China, the status and rights of democratic parties as participant parties are protected by laws. Democratic parties maintain wide and close cooperation with the CPC in participating in the exercise of state power and being responsible for the people. Members of democratic parties and some personages without party affiliation hold an appropriate number of posts in state organs at all levels. They also hold some leading posts in the People's Congress, governments, courts and procuratorates at all levels.

In relations between political parties and society, democratic parties in cooperation with the CPC jointly perform the function of social administration. In contemporary China, the CPC rules the country and performs the function of social administration. But with the deeper development of a market-oriented economy, social structure has been differentiated and reorganized, creating a variety of new social strata and groups. Democratic parties have historical, natural and close connections with many emerging social strata. In this way, the CPC representing the overwhelming majority of the people, and democratic parties and personages without party affiliation who represent some social strata and groups, jointly commit themselves to the cause of socialist construction. The system of multi-party cooperation and political consultation under the leadership of the CPC is conducive to giving play to the political advantages of democratic parties in maintaining ties with different social strata and groups, so as to cooperate with and assist the governing party to perform the function of social administration.

2. The implementation of the system of multi-party cooperation and political consultation under the leadership of the CPC facilitates the democratization of the state's political life. This basic political system is a key form to ensure the position of the people as masters of the country. It facilitates democratic parties and personages without party affiliation to participate extensively in state and social administration, makes decision-making democratic and scientific, and provides crucial guarantees for carrying forward socialist democracy and realizing democracy in state political life.

The system of multi-party cooperation and political consultation under the leadership of the CPC is an important practice of democratic consultation. As participating parties, democratic parties participate in the consultation on fundamental state policies and perform democratic oversight of state affairs. They cooperate with the CPC in each field to promote democratization in the state political life.

The implementation of the system of multi-party cooperation and political consultation under the leadership of the CPC plays an important role in maintaining social stability. History and reality have both proved that to push forward modernization in the largest developing country of the world, it is imperative to have the CPC as the strong core of leadership. Meanwhile, the change of the objective situations such as social transformation and interest diversification, requires more effective democratic involvement. Multi-party cooperation is conducive to developing channels for the expression of multiplicity of interests, mobilizing far-ranging social and political resources, settling and mitigating various conflicts involving interests, promoting social stability, fully arousing the enthusiasm and creativity of the people with whom democratic parties and personages without party affiliation maintain ties, duly handling disagreements among the people and coordinating diverse interest relationships.

3. The implementation of the system of multi-party cooperation and political consultation under the leadership of the CPC helps strengthen and improve the leadership of the CPC.

Mutual supervision among political parties, and especially, the oversight of democratic parties and personages without party affiliation over the CPC, enables the ruling party to listen to different opinions and criticisms at any time, so as to better accept the people's desires and demands, overcome and rectify bad practices such as bureaucracy and abuse of power for personal gains, and correct errors promptly. The supervising function of democratic parties is an important mechanism for the ruling party to guard against corruption. To strengthen and improve the leadership of the CPC, it is imperative for the CPC to improve its governing style, and establish and perfect the supervision mechanism of people's democracy that suits China's national conditions, so that the CPC and state organs can work better with the people's supervision. Certainly, the mutual supervision between the CPC and democratic parties is based on the Four Cardinal Principles, political supervision by putting forward criticisms, opinions, and suggestions, and by means of investigation and discussion. This is an important means of multi-party cooperation, whose purposes are to be better committed to the common cause and to achieve the common goal instead of undermining the opposite side. This mutual supervision is active, well-meaning and beneficent, completely different from that in Western countries where different parties fight against and cheat on each other. As Xi Jinping said, "We must uphold and improve the system of multi-party cooperation and political consultation under the leadership of the CPC, strengthen cooperation and coordination of various social forces, and feasibly guard against conflicts and in-fighting between parties." In a word, "we should adhere to the core of leadership of the CPC, coordinate leading forces from different sectors, improve the CPC's level of scientific governance, democratic governance and governance according to law, ensure effective governance of the country by the people under the leadership of the CPC, and feasibly guard against the state of disunity for lack of the leadership."[1]

---

[1] Xi Jinping. The Speech at the Conference to Celebrate the 60th Anniversary of the National People's Congress. *People's Daily*. September 6, 2014.

Chapter 5

Shape the Chinese Spirit

Our party has been consistently putting ideological building on the top agenda of the party building. We lay emphasis on the notion that 'the revolutionary ideal is higher than the sky', indicating the dialectics by which spirit can be transformed into material, and vice versa. We must not slacken any effort in ideal and belief in education, moral and ethical improvement, and ideological work. We must cultivate and disseminate the core socialist values to pool China's strength through the Chinese spirit, keeping pace with the times.

— A Speech stressed by Xi Jinping when he presided over the 20th group study session of the Political Bureau of the 18th CPC Central Committee (January 23, 2015)

Socialism with Chinese characteristics is the New Norm of socialism in all-round economic and social development, a key aspect of which is to develop socialist culture. Since the 18th CPC National Congress, Xi Jinping has been attaching great importance to promoting advanced culture and cultural and ethical progress. He put forward, in order to realize the Chinese dream of the rejuvenation of the Chinese nation, we should be greatly abundant not only in material wealth, but also in spiritual wealth. We must promote cultural and ethical progress with perseverance and consistency, intensify the exploration and interpretation of the excellent traditional Chinese culture, and achieve the creative transformation and innovative development of traditional Chinese virtues, providing firm ideological guarantees, powerful spiritual strength and rich moral nourishment for people of all ethnic groups to keep forging ahead. Only when the people hold to faith, can we enable the nation to stay hopeful and the country to grow powerful.

I. Ideological Progress: One of the Party's Top Priorities

Xi Jinping stated in the speech at a national meeting on publicity and theoretical work in 2013 (hereinafter shortened as August 19th Speech), "Economic development is the party's central task, and ideological progress is one of its top priorities." In this claim, Xi Jinping put ideological progress on a par with economic development, and stressed that ideological progress is more than important, but "one of top priorities", which reveals the core issue of socialist cultural advancement.

1. Ideological progress is one of the party's top priorities.

History and reality have told us that whether we can do well in ideological work is crucial for the party's future and fate, for the country's long-term stability, and for national cohesion and central force. A country should not only have hard power but also soft power, and it should not only feasibly accomplish the central task and provide a solid material foundation for ideological progress but also substantially accomplish ideological progress and provide forceful guarantees for the central task. We should neither neglect ideological progress because of the central task, nor make ideological progress away from the central task. Negligence of ideological progress would lead to endless trouble. There are profound lessons in this respect. Concerning the political disturbance that happened in Beijing in 1989, comrade Deng Xiaoping pointed out clearly that it was the consequence of errors in the political and ideological work within the party. Concerning international affairs, Deng said in a speech delivered in 1992, "The Soviet Union, once a strong country, collapsed in a few months. If China did not learn from this lesson, without noticing the symptoms of a trend, as Mikhail Gorbachev did not notice the 'new thinking' when it emerged, consequences would be disastrous."[1]

We should adhere to materialistic dialectics, and have a profound understanding of the decisive role of the economic base to the superstructure. Meanwhile we should thoroughly understand the reaction of the superstructure to the economic base. If we neglect ideological progress, we deny this reaction. Evidence has shown that if a country develops well, it is easy to carry out ideological progress and publicity and theoretical work. On the other hand, only with ideological progress and publicity and theoretical

---

[1] Wu Songying. *Record of Deng Xiaoping's Speeches in the South of China*. People's Publishing House. 2012. p. 66-67.

work done well, can a country develop well. Ideological progress is one part of promoting cultural and ethical progress. Only by promoting material, cultural and ethical progress, can we enhance the cause of Chinese socialism.

2. Ideological progress is confronted with unprecedented challenges and difficulties.

With regards to the actual status of ideological progress, Xi Jinping said, with his farsightedness, in his speech on August 19, 2013, "We are new to a battle with many new historic features. We are facing unprecedented challenges and difficulties. Therefore, we must continue to enhance and intensify the underlying trend of thought in our country, advocate the themes of the times, popularize positive energy, and encourage the whole country to strive as one for progress."

What does this mean by, "facing unprecedented challenges and difficulties"? This claim is based on the complex conditions in the current ideological sphere of China. China's reform has entered a deep water zone, and various social contradictions are intensified, driven by interest demands. People's value orientations present the tendency of 'independence, selectivity, variability and diversity.' Meanwhile, the hostile forces of the West have never stopped their efforts to achieve China's westernization, and their differentiation initiatives with cultural and ideological spheres as the key realm of their long-term penetration. Against this backdrop, together with the technical features of the network era, diversified interest demands, values and cultural pursuits, and even individual emotional release, all are transmitted and disseminated rapidly on the internet. Those who harbor grudges against the CPC, the basic system of socialism, and the achievements in building socialism with Chinese characteristics, may sabotage by means of slander, rumor-mongering and stigmatization through websites. The erroneous ideological trends represented by nihilism and neoliberalism are extremely obstinate, and spread unchecked from time to time. Concerning ideological leadership, there exists the problem of 'weakness and slackness' in varying degrees.

3. We must consolidate Marxism as the guiding ideology in China.

All sorts of problems point to the state of the ideological leadership, so does the primary solution. Xi Jinping stressed, "Our publicity and theoretical work aims to consolidate Marxism as the guiding ideology in China, and cement the shared ideological basis of the whole party and the people. Both party members and officials must hold a firm belief in Marxism and communism, make unremitting and pragmatic efforts to realize the party's basic program at the present stage, take every step needed for progress and pass the baton dutifully to our successors."

It is the 'relay race' of the CPC members, generation after generation to solve the problem of China's social development path and achieve the great rejuvenation of the Chinese nation under the guidance of Marxism. Marxism is our 'baton'. Xi Jinping sharply criticized a phenomenon, "Among the party members and officials, a lack of faith is a problem that needs attaching great importance to. Some even take criticizing and ridiculing Marxism as a 'fashion' or a 'gimmick.'"[1]

Therefore, Xi Jinping pays special attention to these officials – the "key minority". Officials, especially high-ranking ones, should master the basic theories of Marxism as their special skill and diligently study and learn their essence. Marxism must be a required course in party schools, executive leadership academies, academies of social sciences, institutes of higher learning and seminars for theoretical studies. These places should serve as the centers for studying, researching and disseminating Marxism. Officials should observe and solve problems from the Marxist stand, viewpoint and method, and become firm in their ideals and convictions.

4. We should stick to the principles of unity, stability and encouragement with a focus on positive publicity.

Above all, when it comes to major issues, including those of political principles, we must take the initiative. "The initiative" means we should maintain political sensitivity, have an insight into the situation, and help officials and the people draw a line between right and wrong and acquire a clear understanding in this regard. Especially we should absolutely say no to the political values dispersed by the western hostile forces, and to those who benefit from, but meanwhile undermine, the CPC's governance. Officials are in no way allowed to cherish the reputation of so-called 'enlightened gentleman', abandoning political principles. The departments concerned with publicity and theoretical work should play their part well, try their best, and improve their work, starting with their leaders and leading bodies.

---

[1] Central Commission for Discipline Inspection of the CPC; Party Literature Research Centre of the CPC Central Committee: *Excerpts of Xi Jinping's Exposition on the Construction of the Party Conduct and of an Honest and Clean Government and on the Struggle against Corruption.* Central Literature Publishing House& China Lianzheng Publishing House. 2015. p.17.

Secondly, we should both accumulate experience and become skillful at innovation in the fields of ideas, methodologies and grassroots work. In the current society featuring dynamic thoughts, concept collisions, daily progress of new technologies and new media such as the internet, only by sizing up the situation, making the best use of the circumstances, bringing forth new ideas and vehicles, and improving methods and styles, can we promote ideological, cultural and ethical progress with energy and vitality. The key to success lies in raising the quality and level of our publicity and theoretical work. We should have the proper timing, tempo and efficiency, make this work more attractive and influential, inform the people about what they love to hear, read and watch, and let positive publicity play its role in encouraging and inspiring the people.

We are reasonably confident that so long as the whole party devotes themselves to ideological progress – an extremely important work – we will achieve the Xi Jinping's outlook for 2015, "Faithful people, hopeful nation and powerful country."

II. Standing Firm in the Global Mingling and Clashing of Cultures

In the age of the Nation-state, culture is bound to have national attributes. In the era of globalization initiated by western modernity, the relationship between Chinese culture and western culture, as well as world culture, is an inescapable issue to confront. How to cope with it properly is important for promoting China's cultural development. In the relationship between western and Chinese cultures, what is the basic orientation of Chinese culture? Xi Jinping pointed out that to cultivate and disseminate core socialist values, we must draw on roots in traditional Chinese culture. Standing on the high ground of the history and sizing up the situation, Xi Jinping initially put forward the proposition of "the extensive, profound and outstanding traditional Chinese culture is the foundation for us to stand firm upon in the global mingling and clashing of cultures." Looking back on the history of relations between Chinese culture and western culture, we can say that Xi Jinping's proposition reverses the declining tendency of Chinese culture in modern times, so it is of extraordinary significance.

1. Chinese culture has been nourishing the Chinese nation.

The Chinese nation boasts a 5000-year history of civilization, and it has created a long-standing and well-established ancient culture. Why has the Chinese civilization never suffered from essential collapse while other ancient civilizations declined one after another? Xi Jinping has addressed this question in a series of his speeches. He said, "In the historical changes of the past thousands of years, the path of Chinese development has not always been smooth. It has undergone numerous difficulties and hardships, but we finally survived and made it. One of the key reasons is that the Chinese people, from generation to generation, have cultivated and developed the extensive, profound and outstanding Chinese culture with unique characteristics, which has provided formidable spiritual support for the Chinese nation to overcome difficulties and ensured the lineage, development and growth of the Chinese nation."[1] In the first place, Chinese culture has equipped the Chinese nation with the spirit of innovation. Our ancestors said that "Although Zhou was an ancient state, the ordinance which lighted on it was new", that, "As heaven maintains vigor through movements, a gentle man should constantly strive for self-perfection." and that, "If you can one day renovate yourself, do so from day to day. Let there be daily renovation." Hence it is safe to say the spirit of innovation has been the most distinct gift of the Chinese nation. In the course of more than 5000 years of development, the Chinese nation has created a highly advanced civilization. Our forefathers invented papermaking technology, gunpowder, the art of printing, and the compass. They also accomplished innumerable and remarkable achievements in a variety of fields such as astronomy, mathematics, medicine and agriculture, contributing countless scientific and technological innovations to the world and meanwhile exerting great influence on the progress of world civilization, so that China has long been in the list of world powers.

Secondly, Chinese culture is characterized by flexibility. In the course of more than 5000 years of development, the Chinese nation created an extensive, profound and outstanding culture. When Chinese culture holds fast to itself, the Chinese people realized long ago that "civilizations would become richer and more colorful with exchanges and mutual learning." During the long-term process of evolution, Chinese civilization absorbed abundant nourishment from its exchanges with other civilizations, and has made great contributions to the progress of human civilization. Vivid examples show exchanges and mutual learning between Chinese civilization and other civilizations, and they go as follows: China worked on the Silk Road leading to the Western Regions; large numbers of envoys from other

---

[1] Xi Jinping. A Speech at the Forum on Literature and Art Work (2014). *People's daily*. October 15, 2015.

countries were sent to China during the Sui and Tang dynasties; Xuanzang, the Tang monk, went on a pilgrimage to the west for Buddhist scriptures; and Zheng He, the famous navigator of China's Ming Dynasty, made seven expeditions to the Western Seas. As for various civilizations created by human beings, such as Chinese civilization, Greek civilization, Roman civilization, Egyptian civilization, Mesopotamian civilization, and Indian civilization in ancient times, or Asian civilization, African civilization, European civilization, American civilization and Oceania civilization at present, we should adopt the attitude of exchanges and mutual learning, so as to absorb their beneficial elements. By means of cultural exchanges and mutual learning, and with confidence in Chinese culture, the Chinese people's ideals and goals, and their values and inner world, are going to keep the same tempo with the times as society and history move forward, while they are deeply rooted in the soil of the splendid traditional Chinese culture.

2. The Chinese people are making the utmost efforts to achieve rejuvenation of the Chinese culture.

On account of the long-established ancient civilization it boasted, China ran ahead of the West in many aspects. Hence, in the relations between Chinese and western cultures, there once emerged a tendency of 'westward spread of Chinese culture' in the 18th century, with Chinese culture regarded as model civilization. However, in the 19th century, the West, driven by the industrial revolution, started its process of globalization. In 1840, the Opium War between China and the United Kingdom broke out. China was defeated on its own territory and forced to open up to the West. Facing the powerful western industrial civilization, people of insight in modern China chose to focus on and learn from the West. From the late 19th century to the early 20th century, no matter if we like it or not, traditional Chinese culture suffered a declining tendency. From the perspective of radical changes over one hundred years, we reach a conclusion after dialectic analysis of the decline of traditional Chinese culture: its positive significance is that the decline led to the modern development of Chinese civilization, while the negative influence is that the decline greatly damaged the Chinese people's confidence in Chinese culture.

Since the Opium War, after 170 years' exploration, as the world's second largest economy, China has achieved its rejuvenation, taking up over one-third of the world economy. China has been developing fast and the days when the Chinese nation was ridden roughshod over are gone forever. Currently, China has raised its international status and expanded its international influence, which demonstrates the respect won by the Chinese people striving over one hundred years.

From the perspective of cultural significance, China's rejuvenation marks the end of Chinese culture's decline. Chinese culture has stood on its own feet in the forests of world cultures. The age of 'there is nowhere but the West' is gone, and the Chinese should have a new cultural self-awareness.

3. The road of socialism with Chinese characteristics was determined by the Chinese historical inheritance and cultural tradition.

When he pondered on the historical path of the development road of China, Xi Jinping applied Marxist dialectics to his rational reflection on the Chinese ideological and cultural history in the past one hundred years. He affirmed the positive significance of western advanced culture to China's modernization and, meanwhile, he pointed out the other side under the surface. That is, although the outstanding traditional Chinese culture was once on the defensive, it never abandoned its tradition. Instead, it has been constantly rectifying the partiality of western culture, and opening up its own development path for China.

From the perspective of the relationship between culture and national development, Xi Jinping said, the traditional Chinese culture is our deepest cultural soft power and it is also the rich cultural soil in which the road of socialism with Chinese characteristics is deeply rooted. Each country and nation differs in their historical tradition, cultural accumulation, and basic national conditions, so their roads of development are bound to be with their own characteristics. For thousands of years, the Chinese nation has been taking a different development road of civilization from those in other countries and nations. The road of socialism with Chinese characteristics we opened up was not taken by chance, while it was determined by China's historical inheritance and cultural tradition.

What does it mean that, "the road of socialism with Chinese characteristics was determined by China's historical inheritance and cultural tradition"? Outwardly, the New Culture Movement in the early 20th century led to abandoning the dominant position of traditional Chinese culture and, meanwhile, openly absorbing western culture. However, during China's development, the potential influence of the outstanding traditional Chinese culture, along with its refusal of various westernization demands, has become the major theme of reality.

Xi Jinping pointed out, when looking back to the modern history of China, in order to save the nation from peril and achieve national rejuvenation, the Chinese people, and people with lofty ideals, persevered in seeking the model of political system that suited national conditions. Before the Revolution of 1911, the Taiping Rebellion, the Westernization Movement, the Hundred Days' Reform, the Boxer Uprising and the Late Qing Reform - all failed. After the Revolution of 1911, China tried constitutional monarchy, restoration of a dethroned monarch, a parliamentary system, multi-party system, and presidential system. Various political forces and their representatives came on stage one after another. However, none of them worked out the solution. Only the revolution led by the CPC fundamentally changed China's tragic fate of domestic strife, foreign aggression and being trampled upon at will in modern times. The revolution led by the CPC was squarely based on China's national conditions, and was an outcome of integrating Marxism with the outstanding traditional Chinese culture. In essence, Xi Jinping revealed that the Chinese revolution in the 20th century featured a high cultural self-awareness, under the guidance of which, the Chinese people correctly sought for China's road. The cultural significance of China's road lies in the reflection on westernization.

Nowadays, China is developing rapidly, but we have not yet completely realized the Chinese Dream of achieving the great rejuvenation of the Chinese nation. Neither have we fulfilled the task of comprehensively deepening reform. Therefore, to maintain China's development road with Chinese characteristics still requires our historical awareness. As Xi Jinping said, China is a country of over 9.6 million square kilometers of land with 56 ethnic groups. Whose model can we follow? Who can tell us what we should do? It does not work to copy political systems from other countries, which are unaccustomed to the climate of a new place. We will set out to be tigers but end up as dogs. In this way, we will ruin our country's future. Only the system which is deeply rooted in our country's soil and takes in its abundant nourishment, can be reliable and effective. We have to know that 'our country's soil' essentially refers to the outstanding traditional Chinese culture.

When taking into account Chinese history and the development road in China, do we have any reasons to doubt that Chinese culture is the foundation for us to stand firm upon in the global mingling and clashing of cultures? No.

III. Building the Core Socialist Values: A Significant Aspect of a Nation's Governing System and Capacity

In 2013, the Third Plenary Session of the 18th Central Committee of the CPC put forward the concept of 'modernizing the country's governance system and capacity', attracting lots of attention and giving rise to heated discussions in society. One tendency is to interpret it in reference to modern western political ideas, neglecting the Chinese historical and cultural background, deliberately or inadvertently. Xi Jinping emphasized the Chinese historical and cultural backgrounds and rectified certain partialities in his speech delivered on February 24, 2014.

1. Traditional Chinese political philosophy verifies Xi Jinping's proposal of 'Two Relations'.

Why is building the core socialist values a significant aspect of the national governance system and governance capacity? Xi Jinping said that to build core socialist values is connected with a country's social harmony and stability, as well as its long-term peace and order, namely the 'Two Relations', which has been verified by traditional Chinese political philosophy, above all by that in the Qin and Han dynasties.

In the history of China the Warring States Period, featuring constant chaotic warfare (476BC-221BC) was put to an end by the State of Qin which extinguished six states. In light of the Qin's way, which was to take the world with violence, the early rulers of the Han Dynasty (202BC-220 AD) had blind faith in the governing style of 'getting the world on horseback', disdaining to build values by applying the Confucian classics such as *Book of Odes and Book of History*. Until the reign of Emperor Wu (156 BC-87 BC) of the Han Dynasty, in order to achieve long-term national governance, Dong Zhongshu (917BC-104BC), a renowned scholar, took the Zhou and Qin dynasties as examples, saying that Zhou lost the world because of 'its complete loss of *Tao*'. So did Qin. He stated, "Nowadays there are different schools of thought with varied opinions. Different philosophers adopt different approaches, and have different pursuits and expectations. All these lead to the consequence that the imperial court fails to establish a fixed and uniform legal system. If the legal system changes frequently, the officials at lower levels and the plain folks are frustrated and don't know what to comply with. Therefore, I am holding such a humble view that anything that is out of the Six Liberal Arts and any doctrines and schools of thought that are different from those of Confucianism should not be allowed to publicize and disseminate, forbidding them to co-develop with Confucian thoughts. If the heretical thoughts are extinguished, national policies and guidelines can be established universally and the legal system will be formulated, with which people will know what to comply consistently." To be briefer, he meant that if there were no universal *Tao* in the society, namely values, the people would not know what to observe. To solve this problem required the uniform interpretation and promotion of *Tao*, making "heretical thoughts extinguish", then the people would know how to behave. This is Dong Zhongshu's well-known proposal: "to pay supreme tribute to Confucianism while banning all other schools of thought."[1]

Dong Zhongshu's suggestion was adopted by Emperor Wu of Han, solving the problem of governing by doing nothing in social governance. Meanwhile, it got over the rigid style of merely relying on political reign while neglecting to cultivate the people's ideology, and established the positive effect of building values on social stability and national governance and confirmed the core appeal for social values.

History has been proving that the Confucian values used to have positive significance for China's social governance, and even for the continuation of Chinese civilization. Helmut Schmidt, former German Chancellor, said in a recent dialogue with Chinese scholars that, besides China there were a couple of ancient civilizations 3000 years ago, such as Egypt, Iran, Greek, and Rome. Those civilizations have vanished, while China still exists and has achieved rejuvenation beyond our anticipation. He noticed that in the Chinese history of civilization, Confucianism covers almost half of its process.

Under the impact of the modern world trends, the cultural pattern of 'honoring Confucianism exclusively' faded away gradually in the late 19th century, while National rejuvenation and the revolution in pursuit of socialism became the major theme of China in the 20th century. A conspicuous fact is that although Confucian thoughts were criticized in the revolutionary process, when revolution was changing the old system and setting up the new one, the CPC inherited the tradition of attaching importance to building values and ensured the co-development of system revolution, and the transformation of humans with their raised moral standards. Maurice Meisner, a famous American scholar, wrote, "For the study of Chinese Communist ideology, it is a matter of special importance to understand the relationship between values

---

[1] *History of the Han Dynasty: Biography of Dong Zhongshu*

and goals and to understand how the former are made 'meaningful' in terms of the latter." He holds the view that one of the biggest and most significant features of the Maoist version of Marxism was "the recognition that economic development and the existence of 'socialist relations of production' do not by themselves automatically guarantee the future realization of communist goals. Communism cannot be achieved, it constantly has been emphasized, unless Marxist goals are consciously pursued, embryonic forms of communist social organization implemented, and the proper social values popularized and internalized *in the process*, and for the purpose, of creating the material prerequisite for the future communist society."[1]

It is fair to say that comrade Xi Jinping's argument inherited both the fine tradition of Chinese culture and the fine historic tradition of the CPC itself, consistent with the objective law of social governance.

2. The core values should be conducive to the modernization of a nation's governing system and capacity.

Society has always been developing throughout history. It is far from enough to acknowledge in a general way the significance of the core values in the national governance system and capacity. The Third Plenary Session of the 18th CPC Central Committee brought forward the notion of 'the modernization of the national governance system and capacity', leading to the consideration of how to build core values suitable for 'the modernization of the national governance system and capacity'.

On another occasion, Xi Jinping said, "to modernize our national governance system and capacity, we should foster and promote the core socialist values and the relevant system, and accelerate the building of a value system that fully reflects the characteristics of China, the Chinese nation and the times. We should delve deeper into and better elucidate China's excellent traditional culture, and make greater efforts to innovate and develop traditional Chinese virtues, promoting a cultural spirit that transcends time and national boundaries, and has eternal attraction and contemporary value. We should also present to the world China's contemporary creative cultural products that carry both our excellent traditional culture and contemporary spirit and that are based in China and oriented towards the outside world."[2]

---

[1] Maurice Meisner. *Marxism, Maosim and Utopianism*. China Remin University Press.2005, p.104.

[2] The Speech at a Provincial-level Officials' Seminar on Studying and Implementing the Decisions of the Third Plenary Session of the 18th CPC Central Committee on Continuing Reform. *People's Daily*. February 18, 2014.

That is to say, the core socialist values must modernize themselves in order to suit the modernization of the national governance system and capacity.

As for the inevitability of the modernization of the national governance system and capacity, Xi Jinping stated that a country's governance system and capacity are the major barometers of its system and that system's governing efficiency. The two are complementary. By and large, our governance system and capacity are good and have unique advantages, suitable for our national conditions and development needs. Nevertheless, our national governance system and capacity still have much room for improvement, and we should exert greater efforts to enhance our national governance capacity. It means that modernization should be realized in the "much room for improvement". Only with such improvement, can we say we have realized the modernization of our national governance system and capacity.

In the ideological system of Communists, the principles of democracy, which serves as a value category, are entirely in accordance with the value orientation of proletariats and the people. It reveals the requirements of democracy to take the majority as the starting point. Accordingly, the Third Plenary Session of the 18th Central Committee of the CPC highlighted maintaining the principal position of the people and developing socialist democracy, and stressed the principle of ensuring the position of people as the masters of the country as the foundation of a country's governance. It is imperative to make the design of the social fundamental system and the operation of the basic social institutions conducive to improving the democratic system and to diversifying democratic forms. Hence, what suits the democratic demands in the modernization of the national governance system and capacity is the core Socialist values, which can be condensed into 24 Chinese characters including 'minzhu' (Chinese characters for democracy) in support of the modernization of a national system system with incorporation of modern values and ideology.

Indeed, the origins of the concepts such as democracy and liberty have a closer relation with western culture. 'Democracy' originated from the Greek 'demos', meaning the people. In western culture, the realization of democratic rights is closely linked to the free choices of individuals. The core socialist values affirm democracy and liberty, proving that its modernization is in agreement with the law of cultural development. Xi Jinping, taking account of a cultural spirit "that transcends time and national boundaries, and has eternal attraction and contemporary value", pointed out the requirement of "carrying forth both our excellent traditional culture and contemporary spirit, and being based in China and oriented towards the outside world." It means we should absorb categories widely accepted by the world civilization such as democracy and liberty, if our values are built to promote the underlying trend of the modern times and to be oriented to the outside world. However, China should not fall subject to foreign forces at their will because of this absorption, but instead it should insist on its own interpretation of democracy and liberty within the framework of socialism with Chinese characteristics.

IV. Saying 'No' to De-Sinicization

When inspecting Beijing Normal University on Dec. 9, 2014, Xi Jinping talked about the problem of scoring out classic poetry in textbooks and put forward the remark, "De-Sinicization is very pathetic". About one month later, at the Forum on Literature and Art work, Xi further stated clearly, "Strengthening cultural awareness and confidence is included within the practice of the confidence in our road, theories and system. If we take whatever from foreign countries as the exalted, the appreciable and the best to model after, aim to achieve overseas awards as our ultimate goal, ape others at every step, and are wild about '**De-ing**', such as 'De-thoughts', 'De-values', 'De-history', 'De-Sinicization', and 'De-mainstream', all these will absolutely lead us to nowhere."[1] It shows that Xi Jinping has penetrated the façade of the current global trend that there exists a cultural risk – following the lead of western culture, and taking great pride in 'De-Sinicization'. If things continue this way, the plots of westernization and differentiation will be achieved easily. In consequence, the Chinese Dream of achieving the great rejuvenation of the Chinese nation will be ruined.

1. We should face up to the impact of western culture on traditional Chinese culture.

Frankly speaking, since the policy of reform and opening up to the outside world was implemented, western cultural products have swarmed into China, having unprecedented impact on traditional Chinese culture. An essay from *The New York Times*, an American newspaper, on February 25, 2002 wrote:

"In the last few years, China's major cities have sprouted American stores and restaurants at prodigious rates, including Starbucks, PriceSmart, Pizza

---

[1] Xi Jinping. A Speech at the Forum on Literature and Art Work (2014). *People's Daily*. October 15, 2015.

Hut, McDonald's and Esprit clothing outlets. New housing compounds bear names like Orange County and Manhattan Gardens. A high-end Buick is a sought-after luxury car, a replacement for last year's Audi." "Europeans may be wont to view every Big Mac as a terrifying sign of American cultural imperialism, but Chinese have mostly welcomed the invasion - indeed they have internalized it."

Ten years has passed, but this tendency is by no means slowing down. Among the buildings in China, it is nothing new to mention some of them as 'Broadway in China', 'Hollywood in China', 'Thames in China' and 'Paris of the East'. It seems that without getting associated with the West, they were worthless.

In addition, another problem is the overemphasis on English at the cost of Chinese language. Due to the existing social institutions, from children in kindergartens to young and middle-aged professionals, all without exception study English assiduously leading to the emergence of an enormous English training industry, while their Chinese language capabilities degrade day by day. Even worse, in a country with Chinese language as its mother tongue, if an academic conference is held domestically but entitled 'international XX', English must be used as the working language. Against this backdrop, scoring out the ancient Chinese poetry is indeed an inevitable consequence of the wide-spreading 'De-Sinicization'

2. The collapse of vernacular culture is a tragedy for a nation.

How are we to understand the phenomenon of 'De-Sinicization' in the global era? Actually, the first to generalize and describe globalization should be Karl Marx and Friedrich Engels. They pointed out in *Manifesto of the Communist Party*, "The bourgeoisie has, through its exploitation of the world market, given a cosmopolitan character to production and consumption in every country. To the great chagrin of reactionaries, it has drawn from under the feet of industry the national ground on which it stood. All old-established national industries have been destroyed or are daily being destroyed. They are dislodged by new industries, whose introduction becomes a life and death question for all civilized nations, by industries that no longer work up indigenous raw material, but raw material drawn from the remotest zones; industries whose products are consumed, not only at home, but in every quarter of the globe. In place of old local and national seclusion and self-sufficiency, we have intercourse in every direction, universal inter-dependence of nations.

And as in material, so also in intellectual production. The intellectual creations of individual nations become common property. National one-sidedness and narrow-mindedness become more and more impossible, and from the numerous national and local literatures, there arises a world literature." "The bourgeoisie, by the rapid improvement of all instruments of production, by the immensely facilitated means of communication, draws all, even the most barbarian, nations into civilization. The cheap prices of commodities are the heavy artillery with which it forces the barbarians' intensely obstinate hatred of foreigners to capitulate. It compels all nations, on pain of extinction, to adopt the bourgeois mode of production; it compels them to introduce what it calls civilization into their midst, i.e., to become bourgeois themselves. In one word, it creates a world after its own image."[1]

That is to say, it is not a blessing for a nation that its culture is destroyed, neither is it neutral for a nation, but a tragedy for a nation, imposed on it by the western bourgeois. It would lead to the result that this nation is more apt to be enslaved and exploited by the West. In modern history, an ideological trend emerged of 'wholesale westernization'– in nature 'De-Sinicization'. One representative is Hu Shi, who said, "We have to acknowledge we are inferior to others in almost every aspect, from physical machinery, to political system, and to morality, knowledge, literature, music and arts, and even health."[2] Hence, we have to be 'hell-bent' on the western civilization.

3. Only by holding back 'De-Sinicization', can China achieve its great rejuvenation.

So to speak, without the revolution led by the CPC that in a practical way held back the promotion of 'De-Sinicization', it is impossible for China to achieve its rejuvenation. China today is closer to the goal of achieving rejuvenation of the Chinese nation than at any other period in its history. China is more confident and more competent to attain this goal, so it is more necessary to restrain 'De-Sinicization' than anytime before.

To the rejuvenation of the Chinese nation, the world cannot stay indifferent any longer. In 2009, Martin Jacques, a British scholar, published his new book *When China Rules the World*, causing a great stir in both the United Kingdom and the United States. "In the first half of the twenty-first century, Jacques speculates, Western rule will give way to a fragmented global order,

---

[1] *Karl Marx and Friedrich Engels: Collected Works*, Vol.2. People's Publishing House. 1972.p. 254-255.

[2] Hu Shi. An Introduction to My Thoughts. *Collected Works of Hu Shi*. Vol. 3. Anhui Education Press. 2003. p.667.

with multiple currency zones (dollar-, euro-, and renminbi-denominated) and spheres of economic/military influence (an American sphere in Europe, southwest Asia, and perhaps South Asia, and a Chinese sphere in East Asia and Africa), each dominated by its own cultural traditions (Euro-American, Confucian, and so on). But in the second half of the century, he predicts, numbers will tell; China will rule and the world will be Easternized. All over the world, people will forget the glories of the Euro-American past. They will learn Mandarin, not English, celebrate Zheng He, not Columbus, read Confucius instead of Plato, and marvel at Chinese Renaissance men such as Shen Kuo rather than Italians such as Leonardo."[1] To criticize 'De-Sinicization' is in nature to criticize 'wholesale westernization', and to break away from the western discourse hegemony, demonstrating the awareness of, and confidence in, 'Chinese characteristics'.

---

1 Ian Morris. *Why the West Rules-for Now*. London: PROFILE BOOKS LTD. 2010.
  Available on http://www.doc88.com/p-9982181840436.html

Chapter 6

Improve People's Livelihood

O ur people have an ardent love for life. They wish to have better education, more stable jobs, more income, greater social security, better medical and health care, improved housing conditions and a better environment. They want their children to have sound growth, have good jobs and lead a more enjoyable life. To meet their desire for a happy life is our mission.

— Part of a speech highlighted by Xi Jinping at the press conference by members of the Standing Committee of the Political Bureau of the 18th CPC Central Committee, *People's Daily*. Nov. 16, 2012.

Xi Jinping, General Secretary of the CPC Central Committee, puts special focus on improving people's livelihood and social construction. He has stressed the significance of people's livelihood many times. The improvement of people's livelihood involves many aspects. Employment is a fundamental one, so we should make great efforts to increase job opportunities. Income is a prominent one, so we should work hard to make the increase of labor remuneration keep pace with productivity improvement. Education is a long-term aspect, so we should strive to provide the education that satisfies the people. Social security is an inclusive aspect, so we should build a more equitable and sustainable social security system. Eliminating poverty is an urgent issue, so we should pay extra attention to people in straitened circumstances. The whole party must remain clear-minded, stay true to our principles, effectively avert, manage and respond to risks to our national security, and take up, cope with and resolve challenges to our social stability. We must follow the general trend of social development, respond to social voices and public concern, bring forth new ideas in social governance system and improve the level of social governance.

I. Outlook on People's Livelihood

Since the 18th CPC National Congress, General SecretaryXi Jinping, has expounded his 'outlook on people's livelihood' repeatedly, and put forward that the focus of people's livelihood lies in pooling the strength of the people for their pursuit of a happy life. On April 8, 2013, when inspecting Hainan province, Xi Jinping stressed that improving people's life means we must focus on the most direct and realistic issues of interest that concern the people most, working hard on them one by one and year after year and forging ahead with perseverance. People's livelihood refers to the people's lives, concerning their immediate interests that they most care about. It serves as the foundation of people's happiness and social harmony. [1]

People's livelihood is closely related to popular support that determines the fortune of a nation. The biggest challenge in governing a country is the issue of people's livelihood. Improving people's life is the biggest political task of the ruling party, and also concerns its most important political achievement. Officials at all levels must firmly establish the concept of political achievements oriented to people's livelihood and do a good job of attending to people's livelihood, with perseverance, to guarantee and improve people's lives. This is the basic requirement of the party's tenet of serving the people heart and soul, and the concrete embodiment of its governing concept of being built for public interests and exercising governance for the people. "We should make the improvement of the people's lives both the starting point and ultimate goal of all our work." We should make it our biggest achievement to do well in the improvement of people's livelihood and to make the people satisfied. We should share the people's sorrow and joy, do beneficial and practical things for the people, and help them solve problems. We should listen to the people's voices and evaluations, ensuring the people to have a greater 'sense of gain' in reform and development.

1. 'People's livelihood' is 'national economy', which is the foundation of the people at peace and a country in prosperity.

It has been a dream of the Chinese people since ancient times that the country is prosperous and the people live in peace. "With regard to the way of governance, nothing is more important than making the people live in peace; while the way to make people at peace lies in understanding

---

[1] Speed up the Construction of an International Tourism Island, Compose a Beautiful Chapter in Hainan, China. *People's Daily*. April 11, 2013.

their sufferings." Only by improving people's livelihood and solving the problems in their lives, can we achieve long-term peace and stability. The issue of people's livelihood is attracts unprecedented importance at present. It not only involves the people's fundamental interests, but also concerns the overall situation of national reform and development. The better this issue is addressed, the better the social economy develops. Therefore, we must ensure 'all people can benefit from the fruits of development'. *Recommendations for the 13th Five-Year Plan for Economic and Social Development* further stresses the concept of sharing, "We should ensure that development is for the people, that it is reliant on the people, and that its fruits are shared by the people. We should improve our institutions to ensure the people have a greater sense of gain as they contribute to and share in development."[1]

At present, the quality of people's life has experienced a general improvement, and people are free from worries about daily necessities. However, the rapid advance of marketization constantly amplifies all kinds of livelihood issues. The particular characteristics of market regulation, such as spontaneity, blindness and delay, make people both enjoy the happiness brought about by the rapid growth of the economy, and face a large number of new risks and uncertainties, which are continuously internalized into new bread-and-butter issues. For example, people are discontented with their jobs, and they have new higher requirements concerning the issues of educational equality, medical treatment, social security, and uneven distribution. We have to acknowledge that people's livelihood is, after all, a dynamic process with sustainable development, the intensity and extension of which will expand and upgrade constantly as the society develops and advances. The variety and complexity of demands of people's livelihood, in turn, make the government's task in effective supply more difficult. Hence, it has always been an important duty on the shoulders of the party and government to care for livelihood issues, which is the foundation and guarantee of social harmony. We can never be 'best' in the improvement of people's livelihood, but we can make it 'better'. On May 14, 2013, when inspecting Tianjin, Xi Jinping proposed that ensuring and improving people's wellbeing is a permanent job with continuous new starts, but without a end-point.

We should persevere in improving people's wellbeing, adept at transforming the work of improving people's livelihood into the 'engine' of

---

[1] *Central Committee of the CPC: Recommendations for the 13th Five-Year Plan for Economic and Social Development. Wen Hui Bao.*November 4, 2015.

economic development. Some local governments regard 'people's livelihood' as a 'burden' at work, holding the view that people's livelihood only means input and expenditure. They fail to understand the relationship between people's livelihood and development, making them contradictory to each other. Actually, if we think differently from another perspective, we can see the other side of the problem. According to the rationale of materialistic dialectics, people's livelihood and development have a positive interaction. Under China's 'new norm' condition, people's livelihood projects and engineering is another point of growth, both increasing investment and fuelling consumption. It is a new impetus with a multiplier effect. Meanwhile, coping with people's livelihood well is conducive to unifying the people and motivating the vitality of social startups, creativity and innovation. To this end, local governments at all levels should on one hand continuously increase the supply of public products and services; and enlarge their input in education, medical treatment and public health, and security housing. On the other hand, they should endeavor to boost public business and mass innovation, incubating and fostering new power for economic and social development.

2. People's livelihood is connected with people's wellbeing, which is the source of the progress of human civilization.

The pursuit of joy and happiness is the eternal theme of human society. It is also the ultimate goal for the government to pursue when they introduce public policies. David Hume, a Scottish philosopher once said, "The great end of all human industry is the attainment of happiness." What each pursues may differ in thousands of ways, but the ultimate goal that human beings strive for, in simple terms, is exactly the pursuit of happiness. The goal for the party and government to drive the development of the society should be the people's happiness as well. The ultimate purpose of economic growth is to benefit the public, as are 'good governance' and cultural development. Throughout almost the entire span of human history, it is not difficult to discover that people's happiness is not only an important aspect of a harmonious society but also the source of human civilization and the foundation for social harmony.

GDP, listed as one of the 'great inventions' by western economists, functions as a key criterion to evaluate the social development of countries worldwide. However, it cannot reflect the total real information regarding the status of a national people's livelihood. Neither can it offer complete information about public welfare. When GDP reaches a certain level, what determines the state of people's happiness is no longer the growth of material wealth, but other non-economic factors. GNH (Gross National Happiness) has received emphasis recently, becoming an important reference indicator to measure a country's stability and its people's happiness. GNH helps not only to monitor economic and social operation, but also to understand people's satisfaction with their lives. It serves as a 'barometer' of social operation and state of public life.

At present, there still exists a controversy around GNH, for happiness is a subjective assessment of people's satisfaction with life, and indeed it is hard to seek out objective measurements. As Leo Tolstoy once said, "All happy families resemble one another, each unhappy family is unhappy in its own way." The resemblance is that happiness, as a benign pleasure, is the ultimate goal of people's pursuit. Jigme Singye Wangchuck, King of Bhutan, was the first one to apply GNH in practice. He believed that government administration should be aimed at the attainment of happiness, focusing on the balanced development between the material and and the spiritual. Accordingly, in 1970, the Bhutan government treated economic growth, good governance, cultural development and environmental protection as four pillars of its national development. Today, GNH is gradually gaining recognition worldwide. For example, in 2008, Nicolas Sarkozy, French president, organized a panel of over 20 world-renowned experts, including Joseph E. Stiglitz, and Amartya Kumar Sen, two Nobel Laureates in economics, to conduct research entitled 'Happiness and Measuring Economic Progress'. This research suggests that reforms should be implemented in national economic accounting methods, GNH be listed into indicators measuring economic performance, and indicators such as subjective feeling of wellbeing, quality of life and distribution of income be applied to measure economic development.

Currently, a number of local governments in China have put forward an urban development strategy with 'happiness' as the ultimate goal. Social development should be in agreement with ensuring people can enjoy a happy life, which shows the progress in the governance concept. Certainly, local governments should not take building 'a happy city' as a show, follow suit, and fail to solve problems fundamentally. In order to make the people happy, building a happy city must be oriented to people's well-being. A happy city is not only a livable and workable place, but also one that can achieve full coverage in people's livelihood services.

The people can live and work in peace and contentment; meanwhile, the elderly can be looked after properly, the young can enjoy proper education, the poor and those in need can get help. In this way, people will attain their genuine 'happy life'.

On December 16, 2015, Feng Xinxing (front right in the picture), a low-income villager from Tangxia village, Wangqiao Town, Dongxiang County in Jiangxi province, together with other villagers was harvesting taros on the farms of Jiangxi Lvmu Agriculture Development Company Limited. This agricultural company adopts a cooperative pattern of 'company+cooperatives+farms+farmers' to plant over 1500 mu taro flowers, a well-known local product, by which it helps about 800 low-income families to alleviate their poverty. (Xinhua News Agency)

II. The Bottom Line of People's Livelihood

On Dec. 13, 2013, at the Central Economic Work Conference, Xi Jinping said we must do well in guaranteeing and improving people's livelihood, "we must continue to hold the bottom line, highlight the key points, perfect the system, guide public opinion, and plan as a whole in education, employment, income distribution, social security, medicine and health, housing, food safety, and safe production, substantially accomplishing various tasks in the improvement of people's livelihood."[1] On many other occasions, he

---

[1] The Central Economic Work Conference was held in Beijing. *People's Daily*. The front page. December 13, 2013.

repeatedly mentioned the livelihood work and the issue of holding the bottom line. We should accomplish the work of people's livelihood well in line with the principle of "holding the bottom line, highlighting the key points, perfecting the system and guiding public opinions." We must clarify the key point of the social security policies, so as to define the direction for comprehensively deepening the reform of people's livelihood. At the decisive stage to achieve the goal of building a moderately prosperous society in all respects during the 13th Five-Year Plan period, we should make sure that basic living needs are met, focus on key areas, improve systems and guide expectations. At the same time, we need to emphasize equal opportunity, guarantee basic living standards, and ensure that all our people enjoy moderate prosperity together."[1]

When paying close attention, and attaching great importance, to people's livelihood, and constantly guaranteeing and improving it, we must have a clear understanding of the most immediate and practical interests of the people's top concern, and know who needs help the most. We must solve their problems one by one, and forge ahead, with perseverance, year by year. The party officials must know in timely and accurately fashion what the people think of, hope for, worry about, and are concerned about, and do the mass work honestly, deeply, meticulously and thoroughly. Then, how can we best accomplish the work concerning people's livelihood? What counts is to hold the bottom line, namely 'social policies must be integrated'. It means that good social policies must be inclusive, everlasting and effective. 'Inclusive' means each should benefit from the achievements of development. People are different in their gifts, abilities, performance and opportunity, but the society should offer them basic livelihood protection. 'Everlasting' means the supply level of social welfare should be tailored to the practical development level. We should do our best and do it according to our abilities. We shouldn't make social welfare beyond our ability, but should avoid getting deep in debts and losing the trust of the people. 'Effective' means the supply of social security and social welfare should help formulate the mechanism to encourage people 'to live a better life through diligent work'. We should not practice egalitarianism and reward the lazy by punishing the diligent. Instead, we should maintain the vitality of society through establishment of the mechanism of fair competition.

---

[1] *Central Committee of the CPC: Recommendations for the 13th Five-Year Plan for Economic and Social Development. Wen Hui Bao*, November 4, 2015.

1. Holding the bottom line reflects the determination of the party and government to shoulder their responsibility for people's livelihood.

The 'bottom line' means that the government shoulders inescapable responsibilities, and must strive to match up to them. We all know how important a goalkeeper is in a football match. A good goalkeeper can be worth half of a football team. The task of a goalkeeper is to hold the gate (his bottom line). Once the line is broken, the game is a failure. Holding a bottom line stresses that we should stay on the alert and have a sense of responsibility at all times. We should have the awareness of crises and prevent any that are possible from arising. With regards to people's livelihood, holding the bottom line means to safeguard the minimum social equity, ensure the common people to live and work in peace and contentment, and provide the most basic needs for residents by means of a series of government social policies. For example, a number of issues, such as the subsistence security system which ensures the low-income group to have adequate food and clothing, the medical security system, and the compulsory education system, need to be dealt with by institutional guarantee and financial support. All these basic requirements belong to the inclusive livelihood rights and interests.

2. Holding the bottom line requires the joint efforts of all social powers to contribute to the improvement of people's livelihood.

In reality, giving play to the decisive role of the market in resource allocation is not incompatible with sticking to the bottom line in equity. The key lies in whether we can proceed from the weakest link of the market mechanism in resource allocation, 'preparing from the worst', and effectively resolve the problem of market failure. The teachers' fiscal subsidy mechanism should be established in the poor and remote areas. The Central Economic Working Conference repeatedly highlighted that large-scale enterprises should fulfill their social responsibility and increase the share allocated to labor elements, so they might participate in the distribution of wealth. The urban and rural insurance system for serious illness should raise its operational efficiency to be as good as a commercial insurance management system. The bottom line equity in these fields, such as education, income distribution, and social security, cannot do without strong national coordination, nor can it do without the multi-participation of enterprises, society and individuals. In fighting poverty, we need to "improve mechanisms for coordinating poverty reduction efforts between the western and eastern regions as well as mechanisms for party and government agencies, the military, people's organizations, and SOEs to support targeted poor areas. We should encourage enterprises and social organizations as well as individuals to pledge contributions to poverty reduction efforts."[1] For enterprises, establishing a staff welfare system is the effective human resource investment to enhance staff cohesion, as well as an effective supplement and response to the bottom line thinking. For individuals, they should cultivate sound values under the guidance of the social bottom line equity, getting rich by working hard instead of making a huge fortune overnight through speculation, against the law.

3. Holding the bottom line means making the low-income groups feel 'assured' of their life.

Holding the bottom line means to ensure a steady rise of people's living standard, especially that of the low-income groups. In order to increase support for low-income groups, in recent years, we have taken a series of measures, such as raising in succession minimum wages, basic pension and subsistence allowance standard, increasing the income of low- and middle-income groups, and lifting the threshold of personal income tax. Certainly, the minimum living standard of urban and rural areas should be adjusted in a timely way according to the local economic development level and financial positions, to ensure the basic living needs of the masses. We will take the treatment level of endowment insurance as an example. In recent years, enterprise retirees have enjoyed pension increases ten times in succession. At the same time there is a 10% increase in the risk of institutional sustainability. Experience from Germany shows that pension level should be linked to the consumer price index (CPI) to maintain purchasing power. Meanwhile, it should be linked to the social development level (like GDP growth rate), enabling all the citizens to enjoy the achievements of economic development. The bottom-line thinking is neither a rash advance nor the withdrawal of state responsibility. Instead, it is a moderate promotion based on institutional rationality.

4. Highlighting the key points means focusing on solving the urgent problems of people's livelihood.

Highlighting the key points means to grasp the most urgent problems of people's livelihood, for examples, paying attention to the stability

---

[1] *Central Committee of the CPC: Recommendations for the 13th Five-Year Plan for Economic and Social Development.Wen Hui Bao*. November 4, 2015.

and expansion of employment, doing a good job in youth employment with college graduates as the focus, and "increasing assistance for those who face difficulties in obtaining employment."[1] We need to perfect the employment service system, improve employment service capacity, treat well and support the development of small and micro enterprises, intensify the social responsibilities of large enterprises, continue to strengthen the construction and management of indemnificatory housing, and accelerate the transformation of shanty towns. Highlighting the key points makes clear that, under circumstances of limited financial resources, we need to solve the prominent problems, which are top concerns of the people and related to the people's wellbeing. General Secretary Xi Jinping said, "We should pay close attention to people in straitened circumstances, and extend care to them with respect and love", which reminds officials at all levels to care for the special groups. In late December 2012, General Secretary Xi Jinping, soon after he assumed office, regardless of the temperature of minus ten degrees Celsius, went to Fuping County, Hebei province, for a visit to people in straitened circumstances and an inspection of poverty-alleviation and development work. He stressed, "It is the essential requirement of socialism to eradicate poverty, improve the people's livelihood and achieve common prosperity."[2]

5. To perfect the system is to enable the system 'dividends' to benefit more people.

The bottom-line thinking requires us to constantly perfect system design. Specifically, in the field of people's livelihood, we need to continuously strengthen the responsibility for national institutional improvement and financial accountability, and shoulder three great responsibilities for transfer payment, public services and industrial strength. We will take the retirement pension system as an example. In 2012, we launched a pilot project on social endowment insurance system, and attempted to carry it forward for urban residents nationwide. However, because of the low basic level of endowment insurance, problems such as transfer to different places and connection inconvenience still make some people unsettled. How to perfect the system and make the system 'dividends' benefit more people is a direction for us to aspire to. In regard of services for the elderly and disabled, we need both to

---

[1] *Central Committee of the CPC: Recommendations for the 13th Five-Year Plan for Economic and Social Development. Wen Hui Bao.* November 4, 2015.

[2] Eliminate Poverty and Accelerate Development in Impoverished Areas. *People's Daily.* December 31, 2012.

offer subsidies to those in need by sticking to the bottom-line equity, and to 'strive for the best results' from a perspective in the long run, supporting and offering subsidies to the activities such as services for the elderly and nursing care for the disabled. In the process of system design, we need both to expand total government investment, and structurally to make clear the responsibility system of fiscal at all levels (central and local). We need to continuously perfect income guarantee systems, such as the subsistence security system and social insurance, and to further develop a series of public service systems such as compulsory education equity in underdeveloped areas, for example old revolutionary bases, areas with concentrations of ethnic minorities, border areas, and contiguous poor areas.

III. Promotion of Equity and Justice and Improvement of People's Living Standards

On July 23, 2013, when in Wuhan he presided over a forum of principals from some provinces and cities, Xi Jinping said we needed to achieve social fairness and justice and guarantee various rights and interests of the people by means of institutional arrangement. On the basis of joint efforts of all the people and continuous development of economic society, we need to safeguard rights and interests of the people by means of institutional arrangements and ensure all the people can enjoy rights and fulfill obligations equally according to law.[1] In *Recommendations for the 13th Five-Year Plan*, the Central Committee of the CPC stresses in particular the principal status of the people, and sets a requirement to "develop the people's democracy, safeguard social equity and justice, protect the rights of the people to participate and develop on an equal footing, and give full rein to their enthusiasm, initiative and creativity."[2]

The development and progress of human society, from a certain perspective, is reflected in the changes of two relations. The first is the relation between man and nature, that is, the issue of economic development. The second is the relation between individuals, namely, the issue of social equity and justice. The relation between man and nature mainly concerns human survival, the core of which is how to make conditions of existence increasingly better, in other words, how to enable people to live a happy life.

---

[1] Xi Jinping's Speech at the Forum in Wuhan with Heads of Some Provinces and Cities. *People's Daily*. July 25, 2013.

[2] *Central Committee of the CPC: Recommendations for the 13th Five-Year Plan for Economic and Social Development*. *Wen Hui Bao*. November 4, 2015

Conditions of existence are the bases for human development as well as for all social activities, which is the basic principle of Marxism that economic base determines superstructure. We must liberate and develop social productivity in order to improve the people's conditions of existence. As productivity develops, there is more and more wealth, giving rise to the problem of uneven possession of wealth, that is to say, the issue of social equity and justice. The greater is the accumulation of wealth, the more prominent is the equity problem. At all times and all over the world, the great turbulences, even changes of dynasties, in history, mostly resulted from serious conflicts associated with social inequity and a big gap between the wealthy and the poor, and escalating conflicts resulted in social revolutions.

1. Promoting equity and justice is an active response to increasingly strong social voices.

As China develops further and the people's living standards improve continually, public awareness of equity, of democracy and of rights and interests have been steadily enhanced, and hence people's resentment at injustice becomes more pronounced. For example, some get rich overnight by exploiting an advantage or through dishonest practices. Some get extremely rapid promotion due to prominent family background. Because of incomplete policies and systems, residents of different identities are treated differently in income, medical treatment, education and pension for the aged. Some suffer from unfair treatments. China's luxury consumption ranks second in the world, but still a large number of people live below the poverty line. In the past, awareness of unjust events and phenomena spread slowly, exerting little influence. Nowadays, the rapid development of the internet and mobile phones enables each individual to be a 'journalist'. Once an unjust event happens, knowledge of it will be spread rapidly. In addition, some people, when noticing unjust phenomena, are likely to be charged with with irrational and extreme emotions and deliberately hype or overstate the degree of inequity. 'Unfair things lead to unsettled minds, which result in irritability'. The issue of equity and justice becomes the focal point of many social conflicts, arousing people's top concern.

The issue of equity and justice, if not dealt with well, will not only reduce public confidence in reform and opening up but also undermine social harmony and stability. Therefore, *Recommendations for the 13th Five-Year Plan* puts forward, "We should make the social security system fairer and more sustainable. We need to ensure the social safety net essentially covers all people entitled by law. We should keep the social security system in actuarial balance, improve its funding mechanisms, and define the responsibilities of the government, enterprises, and individuals in this regard."[1] If we cannot bring practical benefits to the people and create a fairer social environment, we cannot keep the development sustainable. Then the reform we are carrying out will be meaningless. The issue of equity and justice is a big problem our party is confronted with. It concerns whether the party can stay in power permanently. We are still facing a tough test when dealing with this issue. Xi Jinping attached great importance to this issue. He saw through clearly that it is an issue related to the party's rise and fall. Hence, he warned the whole party, "This problem, if not resolved in good time, will reduce public confidence in our reform and opening up, and undermine social harmony and stability." In the *Report to the 18th CPC National Congress*, it is stressed that "We must establish in due course a system for guaranteeing fairness in society featuring, among other things, equal rights, equal opportunities and fair rules for all, and foster a fair social environment and ensure people's equal right to participation in governance and to development."[2] On the road to pursuing equity and justice, China must hold up the banner of reform.

2. The pursuit of equity and justice is a basic requirement of Marxism as well as the reflection of reform.

With regard to this old but often renewed topic of equity and justice, human beings have never stopped reflecting on and pursuing it tirelessly. From Plato to Aristotle, and then to early utopian socialism, ideologists have depicted a picture of society without exploitation and oppression but with equity and justice. However, because of historical limitations, they failed to find a route leading to their ideal society. Karl Marx and Friedrich Engels, based on the analysis of fundamental contradictions of capitalism, created the theory of scientific socialism by applying historical materialism and the doctrine of surplus value, making socialism a real social movement. Although capitalist mode of production created a large amount of social wealth, its system would inherently cause polarization between the rich and the poor. Therefore, it should be changed. Marx visualized an ideal society in the future which, whether at the lower stage of communism with distribution in accordance with labor; or at the advanced stage of communism with distribution

---

[1] *Central Committee of the CPC: Recommendations for the 13th Five-Year Plan for Economic and Social Development. Wen Hui Bao.* November 4, 2015.

[2] *Firmly March on the Path of Socialism with Chinese Characteristics and Strive to Complete the Building of a Moderately Prosperous Society in All Respects.* People's Publishing House. 2012.p.14-15.

according to one's needs; is based on the fundamental principles of equity and justice as well as human emancipation.

Reform is the self-improvement and development of the socialist system. On the basis of the reform and development achievements, we must attach importance to the requirements to improve social equity and justice and enhance people's living standards. In recent years, with the advance of reform in social fields, with regard to the people's livelihood construction, we have accomplished remarkable achievements. However, we must see, at the existing level of development, there are still many phenomena of violations of equity and justice. For example, there are wide income gaps between different occupations and different regions. In some places, violent law enforcement in the process of land expropriation and house demolition gives rise to tense relations between officials and the masses. Other serious issues such as environmental pollution, food safety, excessive-priced housing, difficulty of getting medical service, and high cost of getting medical treatment, mirror the social problems concerning justice. As China develops further and the people's living standards improve continually, public awareness of equity, democracy and of rights and interests has been steadily enhanced, and hence people's resentment at injustice becomes stronger. Deng Xiaoping was particularly concerned about the issue of equity and justice in his old age, stressing "How to make a population of 1.2 billion wealthy? How to distribute the wealth after they become rich? Both are big problems. They are the issues we should work on. It is more difficult to resolve these problems than to develop the country [to make it] stronger." If we cannot create a fairer social environment after China has developed well, or if the development leads to more injustice, reform will be meaningless. So to speak, promoting equity and justice is a serious problem that humans will not avoid or bypass.

3. We need to constantly explore the way to achieve equity and justice in practice.

At the initial stage of reform and opening up, our party realized the relation between equity and efficiency. Which is more important, 'to make the cake bigger' or 'to cut the cake fairly'? It is hard to decide, after all, for both of them are indispensable. At the initial stage of reform and opening up, under the pressure of development, people preferred efficiency, attaching more importance to make 'the cake' bigger, while after they get rich, they have more expectations for justice, which is inevitable. How to deal with it? It was pointed out in the *Decision of the Central Committee of the CPC on Some*

Major Issues Concerning Comprehensively Deepening the Reform at the Third Plenary Session of the 18th CPC Central Committee that, 'To deepen the reform comprehensively, we must put the promotion of social fairness, justice and improvement of people's lives as the starting point and ultimate goal.' If we fail to bring tangible benefits to the people and to create a fairer social environment, and even bring about more social injustice, reform will be meaningless and will not be sustainable. We must deepen reform, perfect the system, intensify supervision, and take comprehensive measures to form a feasible and orderly income-distribution structure, making the development achievements benefit all people more fairly.

How to correctly handle the relationship between justice and efficiency is a difficulty that each country is bound to encounter in its development. To address it well is conducive to both economic development and social harmony and stability. This issue, if not handled well, will bring about difficulties for economic development. Even if the economy may endure for a certain period, it cannot last long. Even worse, serious social chaos may take place. In general, China has done a good job on this issue in recent years. In particular, at the beginning of reform and opening up, the national economic and social development both improved efficiency and underscored fairness, and hence it greatly mobilized the initiative and creativity of the people, and liberated productivity to an unprecedented extent. Nowadays, we have gradually shaken off poverty and backwardness, and developed to be the world's second largest economy with per-capita income reaching the level of medium-developed countries. However, the large population and the wide gap between the urban and rural areas as well as that between different regions result in discrepancies of regional development.

4. We must guarantee the improvement of equity and justice by means of comprehensively deepening the reform.

The realization of social equity and justice is determined by a variety of factors, the most important of which is the level of economic and social development. At different levels of development and in different historical periods, people of different social status differ in their understanding of, and their demands for, social equity and justice. There exist phenomena of equity and justice violations at our present stage, most of which are consequential problems during the development process that can be solved through constant development by means of institutional arrangement, legal regulation and policy support. The improvement of social equity and justice must start from the fundamental interests of the majority of people. We must treat and deal with this issue from the perspectives of social development, overall social situation and concern about all the people. We must take economic development as the central task, promote sustained and sound growth and 'make the cake bigger,' thereby laying a more solid material foundation for greater social fairness and justice. Meanwhile, we must cut 'the cake' fairly by establishing a just and reasonable income-distribution system, striving to increase the proportion of residents' income in national income and of labor remuneration in primary distribution so as to achieve the residents' income growth at the same pace with economic development and labor remuneration growth at the same pace as labor productivity. We should accelerate the establishment of a reasonable and orderly national income-distribution structure, and practically narrow down income distribution gaps.

Proceeding from our national conditions, we must fundamentally rely on institutions to guarantee the improvement of social equity and justice. We should make great efforts to be innovative in institutional arrangements so as to eradicate social injustice and inequality caused by man-made factors, and ensure the people's equal rights to participate in governance and self-development. General Secretary Xi Jinping said, "We should take social fairness and justice and the living standards of the people as a mirror to examine our systems, mechanisms, policies and regulations in all respects, and introduce reforms accordingly by focusing on areas where the problems of injustice and inequality are most prevalent."[1] As for problems caused by unsound institutional arrangements, timely measures should be taken to better reflect the principle of fairness and justice in our socialist society and better realize, maintain and develop the fundamental interests of our people. On the basis of the joint efforts of all people and of economic and social development, we must accelerate building the institutions that may best guarantee social fairness and justice, and gradually establish a system to guarantee social justice by taking rights equity, opportunity equity and rule equity as major contents. We should strive to create a fair social environment and ensure our people's rights to equal participation and development. The core of building institutions is to reasonably address the issue of power disposition, improve the legal foundation to be beneficial to equity and justice, and avoid social injustice caused by abuse of rights. We need to transform government functions through reform, eliminate monopoly, break

---

[1] Xi Jinping. Align Our Thinking with the Guidelines of the Third Plenary Session of the 18th CPC Central Committee. *People's Daily*. January 1, 2014.

up any kind of special interest group, and offer each individual the equal opportunity to fulfill their dreams by their own efforts. We should provide rural residents, over half of the population, with freedom of migration through reform, and eradicate the injustice in social stratification caused by an unreasonable household registration system.

IV. Participation of Citizens and Social Organizations in Social Governance

On March 5, 2014, Xi Jinping stressed at the deliberation session of the Shanghai delegation at the Second Session of the 12th National People's Congress, that the key to strengthening and innovating social governance is institutional innovation with the people at the core. We must adhere to being people-oriented when solving social conflicts and problems, and firmly establish the concept of social governance for the people, in order to achieve the goal of serving people, being close to people, loving people and being favorable to people.[1] We must investigate and survey at grassroots level, satisfy the people's increasing needs, adapt ourselves to the situation that people's democratic and legal awareness has been enhanced, and attract each citizen to participate in social governance, so as to effectively solve all kinds of social conflicts and problems. In the *Recommendations for the 13th Five-Year Plan*, it is clearly stated, "We should further refine social governance and establish a structure of social governance which is exercised by the people and for the people. We should improve mechanisms for expressing, coordinating, and protecting interests, and guide people in exercising their rights, expressing their demands, and resolving their disputes in accordance with the law. We should make sure that communities provide better services and that there is positive interaction between government governance on the one hand and social regulation and resident self-governance on the other."[2]

There is currently a variety of social affairs issues. Practice has proved that the government, if it attempts to take on everything, cannot work well, and goes nowhere. Therefore, how to solve this problem? The best way is to attract citizens and social organizations to participate in social governance, and achieve the effective and integrated use of social resources by means of social coordination and public participation. On a world scale, modern social

---

[1] Xi Jinping. Advance the Development of Shanghai Free Trade Zone, Strengthen and Innovate the Social Governance of Megacities. *People's Daily*. March 6, 2014.

[2] *Central Committee of the CPC: Recommendations for the 13th Five-Year Plan for Economic and Social Development. Wen Hui Bao*. November 4, 2015.

governance is the collaborative governance in which, under the structure of normative public governance, citizens participate by interacting positively with the government. At present, our social organizations are developing rapidly, playing a significant role in maintaining social stability, providing public services and promoting the development of science, education, culture and health, and have become an important participant in social governance. Certainly, social organizations are at the initial stage in their development, hence improvements are still needed in quantity, scale and capacity. It is hard for them to give full play to their coordinative function in social governance. Therefore, government at different levels should conscientiously mobilize social organizations and general citizens to participate positively, and promote the capacity of social self-governance and public service.

1. Social organizations should adapt themselves to the current trend of social development, transform the old mindset and dare to take actions.

In modern society, social organizations, as an important force independent of government and market, play an irreplaceable role in rectifying the excessive concentration of government power and the tendency to a monopoly of market power. Our social organizations have been developing to certain extent in recent years; however, compared with those in western countries, they are far from sufficient. Each 10,000 people only have 3.2 social organizations, taking up 1/16 of that in the USA, 1/31 of Japan and 1/34 of France. In particular, the social organizations of some industries that society has urgent need of, such as science and technology, public interest and charity, urban and rural community services, need to speed up their development. Local governments are taking measures to actively foster and promote the growth of social organizations. Citizens and social organizations themselves should take initiatives to fulfill the function of social governance transferred by government. Besides carrying out more and better social service programs authorized by the government as contracts, they should exert subjective initiatives to shoulder the responsibility for social governance as a main force. They should fulfill the function of social governance transferred by the government, so as to accelerate the transformation and concession of governmental functions and realize the model of modern collaborative governance. For example, the senior citizen associations will gradually fulfill the community's function of serving the elderly. The associations for the disabled will gradually assume the role to serve the disabled. The youth and adolescence organizations will play a pioneering role, leading a new trend as volunteers.

2. Social organizations should strengthen their progress, normalize their internal governance and constantly promote their capacity.

Social organizations, as the undertakers of public services, should continuously perfect their internal governance, strengthen their organizational capacity and constantly improve the competitiveness of their own development. Many places have set out their strategic plan, aimed for long-term goals, and strengthened standardization management of social organizations so as to promote their sound development. For example, since 2002, Shanghai has formulated in succession a series of regulations. They are *Interim Measures for the Administration of the Industry Associations in Shanghai, Opinions on Further Promoting the Participation of Non-governmental Organizations in the Community Construction and Administration, Guiding Opinions on Further Strengthening the Construction of Social Organizations in Shanghai,* and *Guiding Opinions on Encouraging the Public Welfare Social Organizations to Participate in the Community Livelihood Service.* On the one hand, we should actively foster and encourage social organizations to participate in social governance. On the other hand, we should formulate and improve related laws, regulations and policies to support and guide their legal and orderly participation in social governance. We should strengthen and improve government supervision, establish information publication and an evaluation system of social organizations, and perfect and integrate a withdrawal mechanism, in order to ensure the organizations can carry out activities in accordance with standards. Social organizations must comply with requirements for clearly-stated status of legally-responsible persons, and have a complete internal governance structure, as well as their standardized management operation, enact regulations for their internal governance, implement democratic election, democratic decision-making, democratic management and democratic supervision, promote the specialization and professionalization of their teams, and improve their credibility and service capability.

3. Social organizations should offer specialized services, optimize social resource allocation, and realize social collaborative governance.

A basic way for social organizations to participate in social governance is to offer more specialized social services, which has a direct bearing on their survival and development. It is the basic requirement for them to offer public welfare services and non-profit services in modern society, in particular during the period of social transition. They should fulfill the service function and substantially represent and safeguard the legal interests and common interests of specific groups and members. At the same time, they can give full play to their advantages in mechanism, resources and talents to fulfill those public services that the government and market mechanism cannot offer, and play a supplementary role in the fields that the government and market are unable or unwilling to be involved in. For instance, urban communities may have access to plenty of undeveloped resources, unused facilities, and idle funds of residents. The government usually has no time to deal with the integration and distribution of these resources, while individuals are not powerful enough, so social organizations can put their capacity to good use, and their specialized services can meet the needs of community residents. Apart from their needs for life services and cultural recreation, with the improvement of living standards, residents increasingly put forward more sophisticated requirements. For instance, community residents require more specialized services in education (early childhood education), health (professional nursing), and law (elderly real estate disputes), and social organizations are characterized with wide coverage and flexibility, offering more meticulous and attentive services. By means of accepting commissions and participating in bidding, social organizations can undertake functions of social management and public services. Practice has proved that social organizations enjoy unique advantages in satisfying the needs of special groups and vulnerable groups and in resolving a variety of social problems. We should give full play to the advantages of all kinds of social organizations, which helps to develop the effective collaboration of government, market and social organizations, effectively distribute social resources, strengthen social coordination, defuse social conflicts, and meet the needs of society in an all-around way through specialized social services.

Chapter 7

Pursue Ecological Progress

Ecological progress is of vital importance to the wellbeing of the people and the future of the nation. It is an important element in the Chinese dream of the great rejuvenation of the Chinese nation. "We want both clean waters and green mountains as well as golden and silver mountains. And if we have to choose between the two, we would rather choose the former over the latter. In essence, clean waters and green mountains are golden and silver mountains."

— *A Series of Important Speeches by General Secretary Xi Jinping*. Beijing: Xuexi Publishing House. (the version of People's Publishing House). 2014. P.120.

I. Ecological Progress Boosts National Civilization

Xi Jinping stated that "Ecological progress boosts our national civilization, while ecological deterioration causes civilization declination." when he presided over the sixth group study session of the Political Bureau of the Central Committee of the CPC in May, 2013. This remark reveals the keen relationship between ecological environment and human civilization, and reflects the CPC's profound understandings on laws of nature, of the development of human civilization, and of economic and social development. Also, it shows the objective laws in the development of human civilization, embodies the very importance of ecological construction, and has enriched and developed the Marxist outlook on ecosystems.

Chinese civilization boasts a long-standing history of more than five thousand years with a rich accumulation of wisdom on the ecosystem. At one point in history, Confucians proposed that, "The benevolent regards all creatures as a whole"; Taoists claimed that "Man is an integral part of nature",

"The way (tao) accords to nature", and "Heaven, Earth and I came into being at the same time, and all things and I became an integral whole"; other classic verses went as 'Never shoot at birds in spring, for the infants are expecting their mothers' return'; and there are other familial precepts such as 'While taking a mouthful of congee or rice, or using any bit of resource, you should bear in mind that it is not easy to come by'. All of these sayings embody profound wisdom of ancient Chinese philosophers about the relationship between man and nature, and they still resonate with us in the depth of our hearts. The ecological environment is the natural precondition and material foundation for the existence and development of human civilization, without which there would not have been the formation and continuation of human civilization. Ecological environment has great influence on, and places constraints on, the historical process and development level of human civilization. From a historical perspective, the ebb of some ancient civilisations was closely related to the destruction of their eco-environment. Examples include the civilization of ancient Babylon, the Harappa civilization of ancient India, and the ancient Maya civilization of Central America that all thrived with dense forestation and rich water resources in a good natural environment, but all declined due to damaged ecological balance. In *Dialectics of Nature*, Engels wrote that "The people who, in Mesopotamia, Greece, Asia Minor and elsewhere, destroyed the forests to obtain cultivated land, never dreamed that by removing along with the forests the collecting centres and reservoirs of moisture they were laying the basis for the present forlorn state of those countries." "Let us not, however flatter ourselves overmuch on account of our human victories over nature. For each such victory nature takes its revenge on us."

The natural environment that human beings live in is the basis and precondition for the incubation, formation and development of human society. Throughout history, mankind has been living in the nature's grace, which provides abundant raw materials and living materials for human activities in much the same way that a loving mother raises her children, which is called 'the virtue of nature'. In the ancient times, people stood in awe of nature and searched for basic living necessities under the sky. Nature nurtures living beings and human beings, and enables mankind to make it to the top of the biological chain, like the most brilliant pearl on the earth. Since the Industrial Civilization, the belief that 'Mankind is the master of the world' has alienated the relationship between human and nature, and human beings have harbored an unprecedented passion for transforming and exploiting nature as if launching a greedy and relentless war against it. As productivity advances in an unparalleled manner, it at the same time changes the ecosystem and the environment at an unprecedented speed and to an unimaginable extent. In consequence, the damaged eco-environment has brought about catastrophic influence on human being themselves and their life. Many countries repeat the practice of, 'pollute first and remedy later'. During this process, water and soil are contaminated, and they are still beyond remedy to the present day. Among the countries, Britain took a lead in industrialization and London had long been the infamous 'City of Fog'. At the end of 19th century, the photochemical smog in London resulted in thousands of death in a short period of time. Then in the 1930s, the shocking Smog Incident in Meuse Valley broke out in Belgium. Later in the 1940s, the photochemical smog caused by exhaust gas emitted by millions of vehicles in Los Angles, U.S. led to numerous illness and death.

In China, over thirty years' rapid development, the accumulated ecological and environmental problems have surfaced more frequently and have reached a peak. The relationship between economic development and environmental protection is not addressed properly in some places and regions where, in wild pursuit of treasure, people fail to suppress their heated passion to demand foods from mountains, lakes and prairies by relentlessly exploiting various natural resources, deforesting to reclaim lands, cultivating grasslands abusively, and enclosing lakes for croplands. Soil fertility degrades greatly because of desertification from abusive cultivation of grasslands. Sandstorms can be constantly seen in cities, screening the sky, blocking the sun, and floating overhead like ghosts. Among the 74 cities monitored according to the new air quality measurements, only 4.1% of them stood up to the standard. Across the country, extensive and longstanding haze comes about frequently. Land-reclamation from lakes continuously shrinks water storage area, weakens the lakes' natural capacity to hold or regulate flood, and degrades the ecosystem around the lakes. The problem of scarcity of water resources is hanging over about two-thirds of small and medium-sized cities in China. The pollution of rivers and ground water has become quite severe. The area of arable land nationwide has dwindled close to the red bottom line of 1.8 billion *mu*, among which 150 million *mu* have been polluted, more than 40% have degraded, and moreover some of them are seriously contaminated with heavy metals. Deforestation and reclamation for croplands have greatly reduced forest coverage and accelerate global warming. Forests that used to be the lungs of the earth are weakening day by day. Large-scale water and soil erosion has caused more and more natural disasters such as floods and mud slides, swallowing our homes up...... In one event after another, ecological tragedy comes around us repeatedly. According to some statistics, it is estimated that the damage resulting from environmental pollution all over the country, including diseases caused by air pollution and loss from deforestation, may amount to 5% to 6% of our GDP in total. The degraded eco-environment is breeding a variety of diseases such as asthma, tracheitis, hypertension, and cancer that are on the rise, seriously threatening human health and making mankind more vulnerable. Human beings are trying their utmost to develop the so-called industrial civilization, while at the same time they have triggered divorcing of man from nature.

Human civilization and the eco-environment are interdependent and interrelated as an integral whole. Harmonious coexistence and mutual development with a dynamic ecosystem is not only the necessity for man's life and spirit, but also the cornerstone for the continuation of human civilization. In December 2014, Xi Jinping reiterated at the Standing Committee Conference of the Political Bureau of the Central Committee, "We must put the problem in the perspective of historical development of the Chinese nation. We should leave to our future generations a beautiful homeland. The pen of history will keep a record of the positive power of the contemporary Chinese people. "

The picture above is the Bauhinia scenic spot in Jinchang City, a live example for a unique urban construction of 'a city amidst sceneries' and 'sceneries all over a city', demonstrating the Jinchang Municipality's idea of an integral ecosystem of mountains, waters, woods, fields and lakes.

II. Clean Waters and Green Mountains Are Golden and Silver Mountains

In September 2013, Xi Jinping pointed out that "we shall never sacrifice eco-environment for temporary economic development." While he was answering questions from students at Nazarbayev University in Kazakhstan, he also said, "We want both clean waters and green mountains as well as golden and silver mountains. And if we have to choose between the two, we would rather choose the former over the latter. In essence, clean waters and green mountains are golden and silver mountains."

General Secretary Xi Jinping has reiterated the notion of 'Two Mountains' on a couple of occasions when he either took part in a Political Bureau group study, or had a discussion with NPC representatives, or conducted researches deep into grassroots and countryside, or even had state visits abroad, since the 18th CPC National Congress, vividly illustrating the dialectical relationship between economic development and eco-environmental protection and firmly interpreting and disseminating this governance ideology. Xi Jinping has made an in-depth analysis of the 'Two Mountains', and he said, "We have been through three phases in understanding the relationship between clean waters and green mountains, and golden and silver mountains. At first, we exchanged the former for the latter, while seldom or even never considered the sustainability of the environment and only took blindly from nature various resources. During the second phase, we want both a mountain of material treasure and a sound natural system with clear water and green mountains, when the conflict between economic development and scarce resources along with deteriorating natural environment becomes more conspicuous and people come to realize that a good natural environment is fundament for our survival and development. Metaphorically, at least by keeping a green mountain, we can get plenty of firewood for living. When we enter the third phase, we come to understand that lucid waters and lush mountains can bring to us mountains after mountains of material treasure like gold and silver, they themselves are indeed the material treasure and they can yield to us even more treasures continuously. We can turn the ecological advantage into the economic advantage and integrate them into an organic one in harmonious existence, which is the highest phase among the three." General Secretary Xi Jinping's strategic idea that, "To protect the ecological environment is to protect productive forces, and to promote ecological progress is to advance productivity," profoundly reveals the inner relationship of eco-environment and productivity. We should develop productivity while promoting ecological progress and protecting the environment, and vice versa, to realize a synchronized and coordinated advancement of both productivity and ecological progress.

General Secretary Xi Jinping's knowledge about the relationship between the Two Mountains does not arise on a whim, but has been acquired and accumulated from more than ten years' experience. In 1999, Xi Jinping conducted research in Changting, Fujian. Later, the water and soil erosion problem in Changting was enlisted as one of the 'Serving the People' programs by Fujian province and lasted for ten years. As an important habitation for the Hakka, Changting used to boast picturesque sceneries with clear waters, green mountains, dense forests and fertile lands where people lived and worked in peace and with contentment. However, in modern times, it has been experiencing deforestation which was worsened to the extent that that Changqing became one of the regions in China suffering the most from water and soil erosion. In 1985, the area of water and soil erosion in Changting reached 1.462 million *mu*, accounting for 31.5% of the whole county, which rendered a scene of 'bare mountains, muddy waters, infertile lands and impoverished residents'. Without a sound natural system with clear waters and green mountains, where can we find a mountain of material treasure with gold and silver? When he worked in Fujian province, Xi Jinping exerted himself to resolve water and soil erosion in Changting. He went to the county five times, visited farmers, explored real situations and endeavored to seek solutions. With more than ten years' continuous efforts, Changting has treated the problem land of 1.628 million *mu*, saved 988 thousand *mu* from the water and soil erosion problem, and also increased forest coverage from 59.8% in 1986 to 79.4% at the present, realizing a historic transformation from a desertified mountainous area to an oasis and then to an ecologically pleasant homeland. The example of Changting reflects Xi Jinping's acute understanding on ecosystem. In August, 2005, Xi Jinping, who worked then as General Secretary of Zhejiang province, visited Anji county for research, initiated the important statement that "clean waters and green mountains are golden and silver mountains". He proposed that "If we could transform these eco-environmental advantages into eco-economic advantages in eco-agriculture, eco-industry and eco-tourism, we are transforming the natural resources into a mountain of material treasures." On March 3, 2006, comrade Xi Jinping elaborated on the dialectical unification of these Two Mountains again in his article 'A View of Two Mountains on Ecology and Environment' published in the column of 'Zhijiang Xinyu' in Zhejiang Daily newspaper.

As time passes, the idea that 'clean waters and green mountains are golden and silver mountains' has been brought into effect as a general approach in Zhejiang province, and transformed into a vivid picture in the real world. Everywhere in Zhejiang, people make full use of their beautiful mountains and rivers, and at the same enjoy the economic development and its corresponding dividends yielded by virtue of the landscapes and natural resources.

The Yu village in Anji county, once inspected by General Secretary Xi Jinping, taking the opportunity of an overall planning exercise by the Tianhuang Ping Tourist Center, has developed its own plans in three areas, namely eco-tourism, eco-inhabitancy and eco-industry, and set a reasonable lay-out for the space of villagers' life, production and development.

Pan Chunlin, a villager who used to be a tractor driver in a quarry, said, "As I can tell, since 2005, the village officials have been guiding us to learn from the outside, and encouraging us to develop a leisure activity economy such as farm tourism." In expectation of a better life, Pan Chunlin invested all his belongings into this business and built up his 'Chunlin Villa' for farm stays. With 10 years' efforts, he has grown the villa to be the biggest one in Yu village and won the titles of honor as 'Hundred Excellent Enterprises in Municipal Services' and 'Beautiful Farm Tourism Model' in Anji county.

The change of Pan Chunlin is a miniature of the transformative development of Yu village. From 'selling stones' to 'selling sceneries', villagers in Yu have put an end to the simple and extensive production mode. Though both means of living are dependent on the mountains around them, the villagers now gain pleasure from their harmonious co-existence with nature, and at the same time get a keen awareness of the value of nature, which is quite different from the past.

Sheng Xiaomei, another villager in Yu, set up Yesheng Bamboo and Wooden Crafts in the planned eco-friendly industrial area in the village. Here are 32 enterprises among which 25 produce bamboo crafts. They all draw on the local resources of bamboos yielded by 6000 *mu* mountains, and enjoy the benefits to the full. Also a villager in Yu, Hu Jiaxing took the advantage of the increasingly lucid river, and started his own business by organizing tourists to appreciate lotus while drifting along the river. It is very popular in summer, attracting numerous tourists. Seeing more and more tourists coming, villager Yu Jinbao decided to set up an eco-friendly fruit planting and picking garden instead of making a living away from his hometown... By 2014, the per capita disposable personal income of Yu villagers reached to Rmb27667 almost five times their income at the end of 2004.

The green mountains and clear rivers attract more and more investors. Now, The Lotus Mountain scenic area, with funding by investors from other areas, receives nearly 100,000 visitors every year; The 'JinXi Hall Holiday Inn', invested in by Shanghai travelling merchants, is under construction... Up to the end of 2014, Yu village has established 3 tourism scenic spots and 14 hotels for farm stays with 410 beds.

The villagers changed the environment, and the environment changed these villagers' life in return. 64-year-old villager Hong Yuexian witnessed and keenly experienced the changes, and then said, "Now, there are no quarrels among neighbors any more, and no need to bother at all. We are all busy. You see, soon after a visitor litters a cigarette stub, one of us will pick it up and throw it into a dustbin......." The picturesque Yu village with old ginkgo trees and peacefully gurgling rivers around is a vivid illustration of the scientific argument of 'Two Mountains'.

In March 2015, the Political Bureau of the CPC Central Committee first proposed the concept of 'greenization' in its meeting, adding another item to 'New Four Modernizations' proposed by the 18th CPC Central Committee - 'New Industrialization, Urbanization, Informatization and Agriculture Modernization'. It is a natural result of the economic and social development of China and an outcome from the high level of attention paid by central government leaders, providing a practical path and theoretical spur to ecological progress. Then, what is 'greenization'? In terms of the economy, it is a way of production, namely 'an industrial structure and production model featuring high technology, low resource consumption and little pollution'. It is also a style of life, 'A transition of living and consuming mode from extravagance, waste and unreasonable consumption to a thrifty, green, low-carbon, civilized and healthy lifestyle, far distant from extravagance and unreasonable consumption.' Meanwhile, 'greenization' is also an outlook on value. We should integrate ecological progress into core socialist values, and cultivate a new social atmosphere in which everyone values ecological progress at all times and in all matters. We should highlight 'greenization' of production, lifestyles and values, and make the Two Mountains of natural resources and material assets bring forth the best from each other.

Nowadays, we have reached a consensus on the development theory of 'Two Mountains'–'clean waters and green mountains are golden and silver mountains'. In May 2015, there was issued *Opinions of the Central Committee of the CPC and the State Council on Accelerating the Promotion of Ecological Progress*. China is marching towards a new era with ecological progress under the important guidance of the notion of 'Two Mountains'.

III. The Ecological Red Line

On May 24th, 2013, General Secretary of the CPC Central Committee Xi Jinping stressed one more time that we should delimit and enforce the ecological red line and fully understand its importance when he presided over the sixth group study session of the Political Bureau of the CPC Central Committee. Any violations regarding environmental protection will be punished. The third plenary session of the 18th CPC Central Committee made setting ecological red lines a prime task and set as a top priority, reforming the regulation system for ecological progress and environmental protection and promoting the institutional construction of ecological civilization.

In recent years, the current situation on resource and environment is becoming grimmer with the fast development of industrialization and urbanization. In spite of increasing efforts in environmental protection and construction, in general, the pressure for scarce resources that curbs development is still on the rise, and the problem of environmental pollution is going from bad to worse. Deterioration of the eco-system is still severe, the ecological problem is becomiing more complicated, and the worsened situation has not been reversed. Problems also exit in spatial planning, such as overlapping of protection zones, unreasonable layouts, inefficiency in ecological protection, lack of holistic awareness and loosened control. Up to this time, a spatial framework has not yet been formulated for national and regional ecological security and for coordinated economic and social development.

Against this backdrop, to make more efforts in ecological conservation, the State Council issued *Suggestions of the State Council on Strengthening Major Activities of Environmental Protection* (Number 35 [2011]), and stipulated that the environmental protection authority should draw red lines for ecological conservation in regions with key ecological functions, and in terrestrial and marine eco-sensitive and fragile regions. For the first time, the concept of 'the red line for ecological conservation' was encoded in the State Council document, with specified tasks. This strategy is meant to construct and reinforce a national structure for ecological security, to curb the deterioration of ecosystem and environment, maintain a balance between population and resources, and coordinate economic and social benefits and ecological benefits. Setting red lines for permanent protection of the ecosystem reflects our scientific regulation to standardize ecological protection zones, and demonstrates policy orientation and our resolution to enforce the construction of national ecological security.

So, what is the ecological red line? What are the important connotations of the notion? The red line for ecological reservation refers to the minimal space in need of strict protection and the maximum or the minimum parameters of such space that functions to maintain national and regional ecological security and the sustainability of economic and social development; to safeguard people's health, to enhance ecological function and to improve environmental quality. Specifically, it includes the basic line for ecological function, the bottom line for environmental quality and security and the upper line for natural resource utilization in terms of efficiency. They are simplified as red lines of ecological function, environmental quality and resource efficiency. Among them, the red line of ecological function refers to the minimal space for ecological conservation in key ecological function zones, and eco-sensitive and fragile regions, and it is crucial to maintain the natural ecological system and safeguard national and regional ecological security. The red line of environmental quality refers to the minimal degree of environmental regulation that must be strictly implemented to ensure the basic needs of the living environment and people's health. The red line of resource efficiency is the highest or the lowest standard in safe and efficient use of resources in terms of energy, water and soil to promote resource and energy conservation.

Hereby, we need to illustrate the notions of ecosystem, resources, and environment, and the inter-relationship among them. Ecologically, the word 'ecosystem', short for the term 'natural ecological system', refers to the integral whole of all living creatures and their interaction with the environment through energy flow and material circulation in a certain time and space. The main body of an ecological system is the creatures, including plants, animals and microorganisms. That which surrounds the creatures in an ecosystem, namely the conditions the creatures are dependent on for survival, is called 'environment' in ecology. The resources that we often talk about refer to the things in the environment consumed by creatures, such as food, light, nutriment (for plants) and important space. We can conclude that creatures and environment are constituent elements for an ecosystem, while resource is part of the environment, so none of them can include or represent the whole ecosystem. Hence, when we mention 'resource conservation' or 'environmental protection', we cannot use either to cover the complete notion of 'ecological conservation'. Because the ecosystem, as an organic integration, consists of creatures, environment and resources, when we talk about 'ecological conservation', we have to consider 'resource conservation', 'environmental protection' and 'animal protection' at the same time. This is the reason why the '*Decision*' makes it clear that we have to delimit a red line for ecological conservation instead of for 'resource conservation' or 'environmental protection'.

Up until the present, we have set red lines with strict constraints in two basic national policies, one at a time, regarding family planning and resource conservation (protection of croplands, water and energy). In fact, these red lines represent the top-level design for ecological progress and sustainable development. China should establish a red line regulation system based on three basic national policies concerning 'population-resources-environment', with the ecological red line as one part of the system. The nature of setting up ecological red lines is fostering bottom-line thinking.

Within only a couple of decades, China has completed industrialization and urbanization which took developed countries hundreds of years, so the corresponding environmental problems that gradually surfaced in developed countries during past two hundred years emerged in a short period of time in our country, in the form of problematic structures, concentrated in style and with complicated features. Rome was not built in one day, and likewise we should not expect immediate success. To reverse the difficult environmental situation is to fight a protracted war that calls for our long and arduous efforts. Therefore, we must adapt ourselves to the new norm by strictly observing ecological red lines by way of bottom-line thinking. Institutionally, we should strictly observe the red lines to gradually restore the overdrawn resources, to enlarge the green ecological areas of forests, lakes and wetlands and to improve water conservation and environmental capacity. In practice, to set ecological red lines is hard, but to strictly implement them is even harder. To rehabilitate the eco-environment with real effects, the red line should be set as a 'high-voltage line' to guarantee not only that it can be set up, but also that it can be can be strictly carried out as a hard restriction and a task of necessity; these being the red lines of population, croplands and water resources in operation.

To consolidate the concept of the ecological red line, we should strengthen publicity of, and education on, ecological civilization. In particular, we should integrate them into the contents of official education and training to help officials at all levels cultivate awareness of the ecological red line, usher in the concept of ecological conservation during their decision making process, implement it in every sector of work concerning oversight of environmental influence, and play a leading role and set a good example in green development, clean production and low-carbon living. Meanwhile, we should strengthen public awareness of thrifty life, environmental protection and ecological conservation, and nurture a good atmosphere in which people know the existence of the red line, take part in its establishment, supervise its implementation and secure its function.

In addition, we should adjust the performance evaluation system scientifically. We should improve the economic and social development evaluation system by integrating into it all indicators such as resource consumption, environmental damage and ecological benefits, and make it a prime guidance and a strict regulation to promote ecological progress. Moreover, in different functional zones, we should implement different evaluation systems and follow different guidance. In areas under the ecological red line, we should place the emphasis of performance evaluation on the delivery of green GDP, integral enhancement of environmental capacity and improvement of the ecological environment. At the same time, we should highlight ecological achievements in terms of the appointment or promotion of officials, and enable good officials to come not only from areas with high productivity but also from places where ecological progress is well achieved.

IV. 'A Major Political Issue: Eco-Environmental Protection'

General Secretary Xi Jinping addressed the 18th Standing Committee Conference of the Political Bureau of the Central Committee, thus; "If we still follow the extensive approach to development, even if the GDP doubles, how serious the pollution would be then? I am afraid that the resource environment can hardly bear it at that time. What will it become if the people feel unhappy and have strong negative reaction even although the economy is improved? In conclusion, the construction of ecological civilization, protection of ecological environment and promotion of green and low-carbon lifestyle are not only economic issues but also political ones."

While actively promoting economic development, we have to realize that environment is both an important resource and a public product. Hence the air, water and soil in cities can be regarded as public products with political features, so, the question of how to explore and make use of the environment and resources also concerns fairness and justice. In recent years environmental pollution in big cities is escalating due to the high density of population and high intensity of economic activities, leading to numerous economic losses and detriment to people's health. It is becoming an important factor triggering social crises. May 5, 2015, saw publication of *Opinions on Accelerating the Promotion of Ecological Progress* that was previously deliberated and approved by the CPC Central Committee and the State Council. The *Opinions* highlights that group events caused by environmental pollution and the 'NIMBY' (not in my back yard) tendency due to project site selection problems have appeared frequently on the Internet and newspapers in recent years, arousing a great deal of attention from the masses and leading to a strong reaction in society. In the past few years, there have been many such cases centred on environmental pollution. Beginning in 2007, we can find the following group events, drawing much more public attention than usual: in June 2007, a large number of locals in Xiamen City, Fujian province, rallied against a PX project by walking together in a large group which resulted in the project's relocation; in 2008, citizens of Shanghai also demonstrated by walking together against the construction of Maglev; in November 2009, a massive group protest was staged against the construction of waste incineration plant in Fanyu, Guangdong province; in August 2011, there was another massive protest against a PX project in Dalian, Liaoning province; in April 2012, severe pollution by a PC project led to another group rally in Tianjin; there was an incident in Shifang and one in Qidong respectively at the beginning and the end of July, 2012; in May 2014, another group protest occurred against the construction of waste incineration plant in Yuhang, Hangzhou province; in April 2015, a large group of people gathered to protest against a coal coking plant because of the leaking of condensed gas in WeiRmb, Sichuan province.

Through analyzing these cases, we may find that these group events are usually caused by environmental pollution and are based on people's collective appeal for public attention. In contrast to other group events, these involved a very large number of people (according to the '*Report on the Rule of Law*' released by Chinese Academy of Social Sciences: environmental pollution is a major cause for big events involving more than ten thousand people), and usually led to a protest that had a significant influence, in which the government showed a lack of capability to respond and properly control the event. Invariably and ultimately, they were concluded by the local government's announcing the cancellation of projects soon after the event, resulting in an awkward situation where 'one place's event attracts massive attention from its neighboring areas and even involves criticisms nationwide'. These problems urge us to reflect on the following questions: How serious could the pollution be, caused by one of these projects? Did the local government prioritize economic development but neglect environmental protection? Was the evaluation for the environmental influence of these projects complete? Was the decision of the government transparent? Why did the local governments seek solutions after the outbreak of protests instead of enabling the public to participate in these projects initially? Were these public behaviors all rational and legal? Why did such events always involve radical behaviors such as 'breaking, smashing and grabbing'? How should the government respond to such sudden incidents? Will the government lose its credibility if it stops every project after the occurrence of of such an event?

As a big developing country, China has entered a sensitive period confronting many environment problems, when the economy develops rapidly while the environment is severely polluted. Meanwhile, conflicts in society are accumulating, with people's greatly increased environmental awareness and stronger desire to protect their environmental rights, according to law. The rapid progress of urbanization and intensive accumulation of conflicts both urge the government to improve its efficiency in resolving problems. In addition, when addressing the problems, the government quite often finds itself unable to adapt to spontaneous situations, lacking precautions and preparations in terms of system, knowledge and practice. With a tradition of prioritizing the economy but ignoring the ecosystem, some local governments lower the threshold of environmental protection when inviting business and attracting investment, to enhance their performance in their official career, while burying hidden hazards affecting people's health. Once these hazards cross a psychological bottom line, group events are likely to occur. Moreover, an inadequate approach to dealing with the event after it has occurred, inadequate recognition of people's great desires to guard their environmental rights according to law, and insufficient communication by the governments with the mass are major factors which aggravate the situation and escalate conflicts.

The outbreak of group events on environmental pollution can be regarded as a release of social emotions accumulated for a long time against the backdrop of rapid urbanization. This release reflects multiple problems, ranging from shortcomings of institutions and mechanisms in addressing environmental problems, a lack of government credibility in people's minds, poor communications between the government and the people, local governments' dilemma of priority choice between GDP and living environment and that between efficiency and people's will, and the long-term institutional problems of multi-participation in scientific decision-making; and problems of evaluating social risks. If these problems cannot be resolved at source and the people's appeal cannot be responded to reasonably, large-scale group events will be likely to break out, leading to serious impacts on our stable social life and political ecosystem.

Protection and improvement of the eco-environment is related to the growth of a state's comprehensive national strength. Practice has proved that economic development without environmental protection is as bad as, 'getting all the fish while draining the pond', while environmental protection without economic advancement is as impossible as, 'seeking fish in a tree.' Economic development determines people's living standard, while the ecological environment determines people's living conditions. It is inadvisable either to give priority to productivity while neglecting environmental protection, or to put emphasis on environmental protection while ignoring economic development.

As an old saying goes, one prospers in worries and hardships, but perishes in ease and comfort. We must hold the environment in respect and place the environmental protection in an important position in social development. As water can either carry or sink a boat, we must keep in mind the relationship among the ecological environment, political stabilization and economic development, and give a priority to the environmental protection in social development. In practice, we can learn a lesson from our ancestors in a Chinese legend as Gun and Yu: Gun blocked the river to control flood, but failed, while his son Yu guided people to dredge channels of the river to combat floods, and succeeded. We should always stay conscientious about our duty as citizens of China to protect our environment and integrate that duty into our daily political life. Only when we make more efforts in ecological conservation and environmental protection, can we achieve the social and political stability, and in return, a stable social and political life will be more conducive to creating a more harmonious and beautiful ecological environment for us!

Chapter 8

Exercise Strict Self-Governance in Every Respect by the Party

The party should supervise its own conduct so as to run it well; it should operate under strict discipline so as to govern it well. To such a party with 85 million party members and governing a country with 1.3 billion population for a long time, the CPC cannot afford to relax its efforts, for even a second, in supervising and governing itself. If the party cannot supervise its own conduct and run itself with strict discipline, and if the pressing problems of major concern to the people cannot be resolved, our party will sooner or later lose its qualification to govern, and will unavoidably be consigned to history. This is no intimidation.

— Part of *The Speech at the National Conference on Organizational Work* (June 28, 2013)

We are confronted with a complex and volatile international situation and arduous domestic tasks of continuing reform and development in China. To fulfil the various goals and tasks set by the 18th CPC National Congress and carry out great undertakings with many new and historic features, the emphasis should be placed on our party and our officials. 'It takes good iron to make good products.' Therefore, Comrade Xi Jinping proposed a series of new thoughts, new ideas and new requirements as to how to exercise strict self-governance. He stressed that "it should be substantial rather than abstract, sincere rather than perfunctory, in disciplining the party strictly." All these important statements pin down the direction for the grand new mission of pushing ahead party building in an all-around way, at a new historical starting point.

I. The Party's Great Emphasis on Exercising Strict Self-Governance

In response to new situations and new tasks, exercising strict self-governance in every aspect is a major strategic plan and also a general requirement set by the CPC Central Committee to enhance and improve the party's leadership and to press ahead with the new task of party building. Promoting the exercise of strict self-govenance in every respect is of great significance to a great undertaking with many new historic features, and to the achievement of the great rejuvenation of the Chinese Dream.

1. Exercising strict self-governance is a good tradition and important experience of the party. Ever since its founding in 1921, the CPC has upheld the principles of strengthening party building, strictly observing the party's discipline, and operating under strict discipline. The *Constitution of the CPC*, confirmed by the 2nd National Congress of the CPC, deliberately set up the party discipline and listed nine conditions for nullifying one's party membership, for example, absence without reason for a meeting, twice in succession, non-payment of party membership dues for three months, or no service for the party for four successive weeks. The 2nd CPC National Congress stipulated seven requirements for party members, and pinned down the nature of the party; that it should be the most revolutionary party among the proletariat, and that it would organize the masses to fight for the interests of the proletariat. During the Agrarian Revolution, the party held a meeting in Gu Tian in December 1929 and brought forth the issue of theoretical building of the party for the first time. The meeting prescribed very specific standards for party members, such as holding no erroneous political views, keeping loyalty to the party, staying courageous enough to brave death, making no attempts to make a sudden fortune, not taking any opium or getting involved in gambling, and so on. During the War of Resistance against Japanese Aggression, at the Sixth Plenary Session of the 6th CPC Central Committee in 1938, Mao Zedong also required that Communist Party members should play an exemplary role in every sector of work; such as, fighting heroically, following commands, observing regulations, doing political work, maintaining internal unity, working hard but asking for little remuneration, seeking truth from facts, being visionary, and intensifying study. In October 1939, Mao Zedong summarized the experience and lessons of the Chinese revolution in *Introducing the Communist* (*The Communist* was an internal party Journal from 1939 to 1941) that, "our eighteen years of experience have taught us that the united front, armed struggle and party building are the Chinese Communist Party's three 'magic weapons'." From 1941 to 1944, our party carried out the Yan'an Rectification Movement and created an effective means of addressing major problems of the party collectively through rectification. Before the founding of the People's Republic China, Mao Zedong proposed the 'two musts' in the Report to the Second Plenary Session of the 7th CPC Central Committee, which state, "our comrades must remain modest and prudent, neither conceited nor rash, in our practices; and our comrades must remain hardworking despite difficulties in our working experiences". After the establishment of the People's Republic China, the CPC became the governing party in China, and then the situations, the tasks, the position and function of the party underwent fundamental changes. During the struggle against the 'Three Evils' in the early days of the People's Republic China, we executed Liu Qingshan and Zhang Zishan – two corrupt officials, which demonstrated the determination of our party to operate under strict discipline and to uproot all evils, and at the same time achieved good results in deterring the corrupt, upholding integrity and eliminating evils. After the 'Cultural Revolution', our party summarized its lessons and stated more clearly the means of exercising strict party discipline and self-governance. At the beginning of reform and opening up, some proposed to relax control over both enterprises and party discipline. Comrade Chen Yun made a clear instruction, "There is no such a thing as 'deregulation' in party principles and discipline. Without good party Conduct, reform and opening up would be impossible. No matter when the party operates as an underground party or as a governing party, the party members should always abide by party discipline." Exercising strict party discipline was formally put forward at the 13th CPC National Congress in 1987 as the basic guideline of strengthening party building in the new era. In 1992, under a requirement of the 14th CPC National Congress, 'practicing self-governance' was formally written, for the first time, into the General Program of Constitution of the CPC. Over the past 90 years, we have grown from a small and weak party into the largest governing party of socialist countries in the world, and we have successfully led the Chinese people in achieving one victory after another on the path of revolution, construction and reform, the key to which lies in the fact that the party practices self-governance and is strict with its members, and that it constantly enhances its creativity, cohesion and combat effectiveness, and maintains its progressive nature and integrity, providing a solid and fundamental foundation for the success of our socialist undertakings.

2. Exercising strict self-governance is a response to the objective requirements of new situations and new challenges. In the decisive stage of building a moderately prosperous society in all respects, our party shoulders a glorious and grand historical mission, and confronts various challenges and risks that arise from both home and abroad, but most fundamentally from the party. From an international perspective, we can see that the world is undergoing a period of great reform and major adjustments with complex and profound changes. On the one hand, peace and development remain the themes of our times. As the trends of global multi-polarity, economic globalization and IT application in society are deepening, and scientific and technological innovation continue to accomplish a great deal, interdependence among countries has reached an unprecedented level. On the other hand, the deep impact of the global financial crisis will be felt for a considerable time to come, growth in developed countries' economies is sluggish, protectionism is gaining ground, hegemony, power politics and neo-interventionism is on the rise, terrorist activities remain rampant, and regional turbulence occurs frequently. Judging from the relationship between China and the world, through many years of rapid development, China's comprehensive national strength and international status have been growing and our influence continues to expand. Hence, on the one hand, these accomplishments have strengthened China's capability of promoting world peace and development, but on the other hand, they also aroused some countries' suspicion and vigilance against our country, resulting in these countries' intensified efforts to constrain and deter our development. Even worse, some countries take a hostile stance against us. From a domestic perspective, we can find that after 30 years of reform and opening up, people's material and cultural living standards have been greatly improved and urban and rural areas have changed tremendously. However, the basic fact that China is still in the primary stage of socialism and will long remain so, has not been changed; nor has the fact that China is the world's largest developing country. Unbalanced, uncoordinated and unsustainable development remains a big problem, and the development gaps between urban and rural areas and between regions are still large, and so too are income disparities. In particular, China's reform is sailing in uncharted waters with tough challenges, and the barriers set up by old notions and interest groups seriously restrict the reform process. In the ideological field, the tendency of local pluralism, diversity and variation is becoming increasingly obvious. Mainstream ideology and diversified social trends of thought coexist and interact with each other. All these difficulties are posing severe challenges to our party. Viewing from the party itself, we are in a great undertaking with many new historical features, undergoing tests of the times. In view of the need to manage changes in domestic and international conditions, and to accomplish its historic mission, there is still considerable room for our party to improve its art of leadership, governing capacity and organization, and the quality, competence, and practices of its members and officials, and there are many pressing issues within the party that need to be addressed. A small number of party members and officials waver in respect of the party's ideals and convictions and are not fully aware of its purpose. Muddling along and accomplishing nothing at all, as well as extravagance and waste, among some party members are serious problems. Some community-level party organizations are weak and lax, and fail to play the role of a fighting fortress. Some party members have diminished vanguard consciousness and weakened sense of organizational discipline, and have failed to play an exemplary role. There are also other prominent problems of misconduct among some party members and officials, such as being divorced from the people, showing no concerns for problems encountered by the people, or even oppressing the people or infringing upon the people's interests. Formalism, bureaucratism, hedonism and extravagance are prevalent, especially the problem of extravagance and waste. Some sectors are often prone to corruption and other types of misconduct. Not only do some appalling incidents happen at times, but misconduct and corruption problems that directly affect the people's livelihood have also become more pronounced, with many examples. Why should there be such problems? As General Secretary Xi Jinping pointed out, over the years, some localities and departments are lax in discipline and poorly organized; unhealthy practices have advantages over righteousness; hidden rules in the party and society are prevailing; the political ecosystem and social environment are contaminated. All these problems are rooted in the fact that the party discipline is not strictly operated. Some places and units seem to supervise their own conduct and exercise party discipline, but they are not strict enough, or show the necessary capability. If the situation is allowed to run rampant, it will be a threat to our party. General Secretary Xi Jinping once pointed out that, "If the party cannot supervise its own conduct and run itself with strict discipline, and if the pressing problems of major concern to the people cannot be resolved, our party will sooner or later lose its qualification to govern, and will unavoidably be consigned to history. This is no intimidation." Hereby, the 'Two Centenary Goals' and the 'Chinese Dream' of the great rejuvenation of the Chinese nation will be out of the question. Therefore, to govern the country well we must first run the party well, and to run the party well we must run it strictly. We should also constantly improve our self-purification, self-improvement, self-innovation, and self-enhancement, and assemble invincible power - as the 'good iron' - to accomplish brilliant achievements of historical significance.

3. Exercising strict self-governance is an inevitable conclusion drawn from lessons of the Communist Party of the Soviet Union. In the late 1980s and early 1990s, some of the long-term governing parties in the socialist countries collapsed one by one. There are various reasons, but the most essential one lies in the lesson that the governing parties in those countries had ignored their own party building, turned lax in discipline, and succumbed to decay and degeneration, resulting in its disintegration. Take the Soviet Union as an example. The Communist Party of the Soviet Union did not submit while confronting aggression from 14 countries and the German Fascist attacks, but marched with songs of triumph, and had created a gigantic economic miracle. Why, however, did such an accomplished party collapse instantly like 'an edifice crashing down' without the stimulus of any invasion or internal violence? The causes are manifold, but without any doubt, one of the most important reasons lay in its failure in supervising its own conduct and exercising strict discipline. For example, under the disguise of 'democratization' and 'openness', starting from the Communist Party Central Plenary Session in February, 1990 through the 28th Congress of the Communist Party of the Soviet Union to the Plenary Session of the Central Committee in July, 1991, Gorbachev made fundamental changes to the guiding ideology of the party, surrendered the dominant position of Marxist doctrines, and recognized pluralism in the guiding ideology. These changes were responsible for great commotions among party members and officials, for the loss of the party's cohesiveness and professional capability. Soon after the '8.19' event, the Communist Party of the Soviet Union collapsed, resulting from the loss of the principal position of Marxism-Leninism as its guiding ideology, which in turn was an inevitable result of the fact that the Communist Party of the Soviet Union allowed the development of such ideological trends as anti-communism and anti-socialism. As to 'democratization of political life within the party', in practice it was Gorbachev's abandonment of the organizational principle of democratic centralism, leading to two immediate consequences, namely, factionalization and federalization of the Communist Party of the Soviet Union. For lack of effective rules and organizational discipline, there frequently occurred various conflicts among different branches of the party, which greatly affected the fighting capacity of the party and its unity, tearing the party apart. As for the separation between the party and government, the Communist Party of Soviet Union made undue emphases, jeopardized its own governance, and finally lost its leadership of the country. The 19th Congress of the Communist Party of the Soviet Union raised a proposal that, 'all powers belong to the Soviet Union, the country'. From that point the Soviet Congress had lost control and had become the platform for power struggles among different branches, and the country was devoid of power: there was a 'power vacuum'. Due to the loss of support from the communist party, the administration system of the Soviet Union soon descended into total chaos. All in all, as General Secretary Xi Jinping summarized, "Before the collapse of the Soviet Union, under the guise of the so-called 'openness' and 'democracy', the Soviet Communist Party deserted the principle of democratic centralism, allowed party members to publicize opinions different from the organization's decisions, and called for the implementation of autonomy within the party at all levels. Some of the Soviet Communist Party members, even some leading officials, turned to become the vanguard in negating the history of Communist Party of the Soviet Union and socialism, trumpeting to disseminate western ideology. Accordingly, the ideological confusions in the Soviet Communist Party transformed to organizational ones. In the end, such a big and veteran party with a long-standing history of more than 90 years and with its governance of the country for over 70 years, just collapsed violently and instantly." To draw lessons from the failure of governance of Soviet Communist Party and to avoid repeating its frustrations, we should exercise our strict party discipline in all respects. The following remarks made by Lenin bear particular significance for our party. He said, "No matter when it is in the past or at present, our strength lies in our sober analysis of the bitterest failure…… If the past experience cannot bring to light the errors of our old methods, then we will never learn new approaches to tackle our own tasks."

The sixth plenary session of the 18th CPC Central Committee was held from October 24 to 27, 2016 in Beijing (Xinhua News Agency)

II. The Party's Strictness in Exercising Self-Governance in Every Respect

To adhere to the principle of exercising strict self-governance in every respect, we must emphasize 'every respect' and 'strict'. We should implement it throughout the whole process of party building so as to bring into effect strict theoretical education, strict official management, strict party conduct, strict organization construction and strict system enforcement.

1. We should remain strict in theoretical education and have firm faith in communism.

As a Chinese saying goes, "For a tree to grow tall, a strong and solid root is essential; for a river to reach far, an unimpeded source is necessary." As for the party members and officials, theoretical degradation is the most serious problem. If their 'ultimate switch' is not tightened, they cannot properly handle the relationship between public and personal interests, and may not have healthy outlooks on right or wrong, on justice and benefit, and on power and career. Hence, a variety of misconducts as well as derailed and erroneous behaviors may surface as a natural consequence. "A slight degree of slackness in thought will result in desultoriness in action to a large extent." Therefore, we must give priority to theoretical party building, strengthen education on ideals and conviction, and lay a solid intellectual foundation for exercising strict party discipline.

Ideals and conviction are the spiritual banner for struggles and for the unity of the nation, ethnic groups and political parties. Since the 18th CPC National Congress, General Secretary Xi Jinping has paid great attention to ideals and conviction, and pointed out that it has always been the foundation for the lifeline and pursuit of all Communists, to have full confidence in ideals of, and firm faith in, communism. Belief in Marxism and faith in socialism and communism are the political soul of Communists, enabling them to withstand all tests. Put figuratively, the ideals and convictions of Communists are the marrow of their faith. Without, or with weak, ideals or convictions, they would be deprived of their marrow and suffer from 'lack of backbone.' At present, we must attach great importance to the absence of ideals and conviction; or to wavering in ideals and conviction among some party members and officials. For instance, some are skeptical about communism, considering it a fantasy that will never come true; some do not believe in Marxism-Leninism but in ghosts and gods, and seek spiritual solace in feudal superstitions, showing intense interest in fortune-telling, worship of Buddha and 'god's advice' for solving their problems; some have little sense of principle, justice, and right and wrong, and perform their duties in a muddle-headed manner; some even yearn for Western social systems and values, losing their confidence in the future of socialism; and others adopt an equivocal attitude towards political provocations against the leadership of the CPC, the path of socialism with Chinese characteristics and other matters of principle. They passively avoid relevant arguments without the courage to express their opinions, or even deliberately deliver ambiguous messages. Facts have repeatedly proved that the most dangerous moment is when one wavers in, or begins to show doubt about, one's ideals and convictions. This has been proven true by the cases of some party members and officials who acted improperly due to lack of ideals, and confused faith.

Comrade Xi Jinping pointed out that whether an official is qualified or not is judged primarily by whether he is firm in his ideals and convictions. No matter how competent an official is, he cannot be regarded as the sort of good official that we need, if he does not hold fast to his ideals and convictions, does not believe in Marxism, nor in socialism with Chinese characteristics. Xi Jinping stressed that a party member devoid of ideals lacks an essential quality – as does one who engages in empty talk about lofty ideals without doing anything. In other words, we should be both forward-looking and down-to-earth. If the communists lose sight of ambitious goals, we would lose direction and might become utilitarianists and pragmatists. Once we have firm ideals and convictions, we will stand high and see far, with a generous mind, and we can follow the correct political direction and uphold the communists' political integrity. However, when we intend to underscore the communists' and officials' ideals and conviction, we should not simply pay lip service by shouting out the communist slogans or 'rushing into the communist society', but instead, we should make unremitting and pragmatic efforts to fulfill the party's basic program at the present stage – build socialism with Chinese characteristics, and adopt a down-to earth attitude to fulfill our present duty.

In order to stay firm in ideals and convictions and to build 'diamond-hard bodies', we must equip ourselves with various scientific theories and master Marxism systematically. The ideals and conviction should be founded on the bases of correct understanding about, and scientific mastery over the truthfulness of, Marxism and the inevitability of socialism and communism. General Secretary Xi Jinping stressed that faced with complex domestic and international situations and shouldering a heavy governance mission, we cannot conquer risks or difficulties; or move forward continually, if we lack powerful support from theoretical thinking. Officials at all levels of the party should meticulously study and research into the classical Marxist works, and earnestly learn Marxist philosophy, especially historical materialism.

Communists and leading officials at large should learn the fundamental theories of Marxism, especially the theoretical system of socialism with Chinese characteristics, and enhance their ability to work more systematically and with greater foresight and creativity, so as to keep up with the times, follow the law of development, and be innovative in our leadership and policy-making. Marxism must be a required course in party schools, executive leadership academies, academies of social sciences, institutes of higher learning and groups for theoretical studies. These places should serve as the centers for studying, researching and disseminating Marxism. We should guide party members and officials to learn theories of Marxism to enhance their theoretical qualification and moral outlook and to make continuous progress in their ability to apply Marxism to resolving practical problems. In particular, party schools should have proper orientation in this regard. Learning at party schools, officials should put in first place cultivation of firm ideals and convictions as well as improving the level of ideology and politics. They should sincerely and diligently study Marxism-Leninism, Mao Zedong Thought, especially Deng Xiaoping Theory, the important thought of the Three Represents, the Scientific Outlook on Development, and a series of important speeches by Comerade Xi Jinping. New and young officials in particular should work hard to study Marxist theory, learn to observe and solve problems from the Marxist standpoint, viewpoint and method, become firm in their ideals and convictions, improve their ability in dialectical analysis, and act with sincerity and persistence as well as honesty and prudence. He emphasized that it is quite necessary for officials to study in party schools to broaden their vision and update their minds with more knowledge, but it would be improper for them to act as presumptuous guests rather than learners. At the same time, party schools should intensify their efforts in fostering an all-pervading atmosphere of theoretical learning.

2. We should remain strict in official management, and especially with the 'key few'.

General Secretary Xi Jinping stressed that to supervise its own conduct, the primary work of the party is to manage its officials well; and that running the party with strict discipline lies in strictly disciplining the officials. We should endeavor more to train and select good officials who are willing to serve the people wholeheartedly, and implement the principle of exercising strict discipline throughout the whole process of building a contingent of officials. We should remain strict in educating, managing and supervising officials and enable every one of them to understand thoroughly that to be an official, one needs to toil more and be more strict with oneself. Otherwise, if one does not possess such mental preparation or awareness, he or she is ineligible for the post.

The first issue of personnel management is the criterion for official selection. What is the criterion of good officials who are required by the party and the people in the new era? At the National Conference on Organizational Work, General Secretary Xi Jinping concisely summarized the criterion into twenty Chinese characters concerning five aspects– literally in Chinese, they are *xin nian jian ding, wei min fu wu, qin zheng wu shi, gan yu dan dang, qing zheng lian jie*. To put them into English, they mean: good officials must be firm in their ideals and conviction, willing to serve the people, diligent in work, ready to take on responsibilities, honest and upright. To select good officials, we must stick to four principles. First, we should stick to the principle that the party should supervise the performance of officials, ensure leadership over officials and respond to the question of 'for whom to select officials'; Second, we should stick to the principle that the party should appoint officials on their merits and select them from all over the country to put into practice the principle that the party is founded for the public good, and thus address the question of 'how to select officials'; Third, we should stick to the principles that the party should select officials on the basis of both moral integrity and professional competence with priority given to the former, and make sure that officials have firm political orientation and good conduct, and thus we address the question of 'whom to select'; Fourth, we should stick to the principle that the party should value officials' performance as well as the approval by the mass, and test them in practice, and thus we address the question of 'what standards to apply'. To realize these four principles, we must integrate the leadership of the party and the full play of democracy, and reinforce the leading and supervising roles of party committees. We should make right decisions on such key issues as adopting what democratic method from many, correctly analyzing and treating recommendation results and official appointments, instead of using votes and scores as the sole standard, so as to find in good time, and reasonably use, good officials. To do so, we can conduct the following practices. Firstly, we should take loyalty, integrity and responsibility as the key guidance and major standards, and select those who have firm ideals and conviction, care for the people, and are honest and upright. We should never appoint as officials those who are wavering in convictions, divorced from the people or deceiving the party; Secondly, we should select those who are upright, law-abiding, disciplined, and earnest in governance at work. We should never appoint those who violate the law and discipline, abuse their power for personal gains, and are morally corrupted; Thirdly, we should select officials who uphold principles, are responsible and have the moral fiber to denounce and rectify violations of party discipline. We should never appoint those who seek for personal interests through trickery, tackle their responsibilities in a perfunctory manner or struggle for merits but shift the blame on to others.

Good officials do not emerge spontaneously. To become a good official, both personal efforts and organizational training by the party are necessary. We must pay more attention to the education and training of millions of officials at all levels, especially those working in important and key positions. We should educate and guide party members and officials to stand firm in the ideals and conviction of the party, strengthen morality, regulate their behavior in the exercise of power, cultivate fine conduct, conscientiously fulfill their duties prescribed by the *Constitution of the CPC* and work in accordance with strict rules and regulations of the party. We also need to strengthen the training of officials in practical circumstances to facilitate their progress through expanding channels and seeking more platforms. We should guide officials to go to the grassroots to see real situations and communicate with the people, and thus help them make a solid foundation for their work. We should step up efforts of officials at all levels to communicate across different sectors, fields, and regions of work, and make them experience something difficult, urgent, important or complicated. We should systematically arrange for new and outstanding officials to work at the grassroots, in tough conditions. Moreover, we should improve institutions and policies to cultivate and select new outstanding officials, further broaden the sources, optimize structures and upgrade working methods so as to improve the quality of party officials.

In reality, some officials act improperly due to relaxed requirements on themselves, and this is also closely related to inadequate management and loopholes in our management system. Therefore, we should focus on officials' daily management and supervision, further improve relevant measures, and strengthen supervision by organizations, public opinion and the masses to make sure that officials are subject to restrictions either in or after working hours.

General Secretary Xi Jinping emphasized that the exercise of power without supervision will definitely lead to corruption. This is an axiomatic law. It is not an easy process to train officials, so measures should be adopted to better manage and supervise them and keep them on the alert 'as if they were treading on thin ice or standing on the edge of an abyss.' As to the emerging and potential problems among some officials, we should give them timely reminders rather than turn a blind eye or even please or protect them in an effort to prevent minor flaws from becoming serious menace. We should strengthen the supervision over officials concerning the following issues: their observance of rules, especially political rules, implementation of democratic centralism, improvement of their work style, fulfillment of their work requirements and resolution of their own problems. We must strengthen oversight of officials of a higher level over those of a lower level within party organizations and also intensify mutual oversight among leaders.

Since the 18th CPC National Congress, we have made a regulation on officials' taking a part-time job (or full-employment) at enterprises. In 2014, we had cleaned up 63,000 people who assumed leading positions, with part-time jobs at enterprises, including 229 provincial-level officials. We have laid down rules of administration for those officials whose spouse or children have emigrated to foreign countries, and stipulated that 'naked officials' should not hold important or key positions in party or government organs. Also in 2014, we deposed more than 3,200 'naked officials' at or above the deputy county or division level. We should improve the reporting system of leading officials on their personal matters. In the same year, we randomly inspected more than 60,000 officials' individual cases nationwide, and accordingly cancelled the promotion qualifications of those problematic officials and gave penalties to those involved in the worst cases. Since 2015, the ratio of random inspection has increased to 10%, and every newly appointed official above the county or division level has been inspected after their promotion. Moreover, we began to lay down regulations about officials' spouses, their children and their children's spouses on their conduct of doing business or running enterprises, and we arranged special programs to oversee the officials' policy implementation. The aim of these measures is to bring into effect the principle of strict official management and carry it throughout the regulation of institutions and all sectors of officials' work.

General Secretary Xi Jinping pointed out that to implement strict management well, it is crucial for the leading bodies and leading officials to take the lead. Only when they set good examples, can the those at lower levels keep up and do the same. Officials at all levels, especially leading officials, should act in line with the requirements of 'Three Stricts and Three Earnests', diligently learn and sincerely practice the spirit of Jiao Yulu (1922 -1964, party secretary of Lankao county, Henan Province, devoted all his life to the cause of the party), and work hard to behave like Jiao Yulu, our party's good official. Party organizations at all levels should clearly and firmly recognize the achievements of, and reward, those officials who achieved a lot at work; should educate and help those who fail to protect the people's interests; should support and encourage the officials who act for the public good, dedicate themselves to work and are ready to take on responsibilities. Those who incur serious damages to the cause of the party and the people due to dereliction of duty or malpractice, should be punished accordingly and severely.

3. We should remain strict in party conduct, and uphold integrity all through the party.

The new CPC Central Committee with Comerade Xi Jinping at its core put party conduct improvement as a starting point of, and a breakthrough in, work to exercise strict self-governance all through the party and in all respects. Since the 18th CPC National Congress, we have worked out 'Eight Codes of Conduct' to improve our work style and maintain close ties with the people, have carried out an extensive program throughout the party to heighten awareness of, and implement, the party's mass line with the focus on serving the people and staying pragmatic and honest, and have launched a special education program on 'Three Stricts and Three Earnests' among leading officials, at and above the county level. All these allowed the people to witness substantial results and changes in party conduct, and thus won extensive approval and sincere support from the people.

General Secretary Xi Jinping pointed out that the issue of working style is in no sense a small one. If misconduct is not corrected but allowed to run rampant, it will build an invisible wall between our party and the people. As a result, our party will lose its base, lifeblood and strength. 'Hedonism and extravagance lead to decline and demise.' The farther we stay away from misconduct, the closer the people will approach us. The party has always emphasized that party conduct is vital for the survival of the party. Through a thorough review of history in China and elsewhere, we can see many examples of loss of lives and bankruptcy of administration due to misconduct. Therefore, we must take those as great warning and set strictest standards and measures to crack down on misconduct. It is undeniable that under the backdrop of developing a socialist market economy, the rule of commodity exchange would have permeated into the inner-party life, which is outwith the people's will. Party members and officials are overwhelmed with various temptations in society. Just like the proverbial slow-boiled frog, some party members and officials are unconsciously seduced into the traps. Despite years' promotion of good party conduct, some problems have not been resolved but instead have become intensified. Tackling misconduct is like cutting chives: while you cut them off, they grow up later, batch after batch. The root of the problem is the underestimation of conduct recurring and persisting, and the failure to resolve problems with tenacity and patience as well as a lack of a feasible system that can control problems over a long period and that can consolidate the basis of this operation. Therefore, it is impossible to accomplish the whole task at one stroke, and we cannot promote party conduct in temporary phases, like a passing gust of wind. Our efforts in this regard must be constant, and we must have long-term plans and establish new and strict rules in improving conduct to achieve solid results and prevent them from rebounding.

At present, the 'four forms of decadence' represent the majority of conduct problems within the party. General Secretary Xi Jinping stated that formalism, bureaucratism, hedonism and extravagance are the problems that the public hates the most. They are of the most pressing concern to the people, and they are at the root of the greatest damage to the relations between the party and the people and between officials and the people. Once the 'four forms of decadence' are resolved, there will be a sounder base for treating other problems. He also stressed that to solve the 'four forms of decadence,' we must set an accurate focus, locate the 'acupoints,' and firmly grasp the vitals. In fighting formalism, we should focus on promoting down-to-earth work and improving officials' approach to theoretical study, meetings and official documents, and working practices. And officials must spare themselves no effort in promoting concrete measures, and in achieving solid results through a down-to-earth approach. In fighting bureaucratism, we should focus on solving the problems of isolation from the people and failure to protect their interests. We must be resolute in correcting problems such as perfunctory performance of duties, evading and shirking responsibilities, and infringing upon the people's interests. In fighting hedonism, we should focus on overcoming indulgence in pleasure and privileges, and guide them in keeping to the 'two musts,' in upholding political integrity, and in preserving a spirit of high principles and hard work. In fighting extravagance, we should focus on putting an end to unhealthy practices such as self-indulgence, luxury and dissipation. We should guide the party in leading a simple life, in being strict with their spending, and in doing everything in a no-frills manner.

The Program of Mass Line Education and Practice was launched in June 2013 and has been unfolded in two sessions from the top down, and ended in October 2014. In this program, the Political Bureau set an example, learning from the experience of the Yan'an Rectification Movement, with the current requirements for studying and practicing the party's mass line clearly defined as 'examine oneself in the mirror, straighten one's clothes and hat, take a bath, and treat one's disease.' The whole party from top down had launched full-scale examinations, overhauls and clean-ups to eliminate defects and misconduct from the party. These measures have effectively addressed the four prominent problems, namely: formalism, bureaucratism, hedonism and extravagance. In addition, the tendency of isolation from the people has been clearly reversed, and party conduct, government conduct and social conduct have been greatly improved.

Facts have proved that misconduct is apt to recur and persist, so it should be constantly addressed. It is impossible to accomplish the whole task at one stroke, and we cannot promote party conduct in temporary phases, like a passing gust of wind. The practice of combating 'four forms of decadence' has also proved that nothing can be accomplished unless we take a serious, pragmatic and strict approach. Currently, on the surface, the 'four forms of decadence' have been pushed back to some extent, but they are deep-rooted and difficult to eradicate. A single light stroke after the suppression may result in its quick rebound, so how to prevent it from happening is still an arduous mission. 'Promoting good party conduct is always high on our agenda and will never end.' We should promote good party conduct with strong determination, 'leave marks when we tread on stones or grasp iron,' work long and hard without letup till we achieve final success. We will fall short of our aims if this program tails off and we become lax in the later stages. We should improve and strictly implement all regulations concerning conduct, enhance oversight of enforcement, set the 'four forms of decadence' as a key point to check the discipline of the party, establish sound and effective institutions and mechanisms, and voluntarily accept public assessment and supervision by the whole of society.

As General Secretary Xi Jinping requires, leading officials at all levels should be strict in self-development, the exercise of power and self-governance; be earnest in making plans, opening up new undertakings and upholding personal integrity. 'Three Stricts and Three Earnests' is the cardinal practice, the key to success and basic ethical principle of party members and officials, especially leading officials at all levels. Moreover, it is a new requirement for party members and officials, and a new starting point to reinforce cultivation of good conduct. As an extended and deepened practice of Program of Mass Line Education and Practice, and as an important measure of reinforcing the party's theoretical and political education, the special program of 'Three Stricts and Three Earnests' plays a key role in eliminating vulgar interests and resisting unhealthy practices and evil influences, upholding integrity and honesty and achieving the greatest possible success in improving party conduct.

"If you fail to attend to trifling matters, your virtue will be affected." Officials at all levels need to start from themselves and with small matters, take the lead in keeping to the right way, uphold integrity and endeavor to foster a better environment for the government. We should keep a close watch on new changes and problems in the field of our work style and promptly follow up relevant countermeasures without being insensitive to emerging situations or procrastinate in addressing problems so as to resolve conflicts in time. Those who violate the law must be resolutely corrected and punished. We should develop our work further in addressing the 'four forms of decadence,' and make headway in improving our approaches to ideology, working practice, leadership and life style as well as to theoretical study, meetings and official documents. We should strengthen the work of addressing causes that deters, stops, and discourages officials from being infected with unhealthy practices and evil influences so as to uphold integrity all through the party.

4. We should remain strict in the construction of party organizations, and keep them robust all the time.

Lenin said, "In the struggle to seize power, the proletariat had no other weapon but the organization." General Secretary Xi Jinping emphasized, "We should strengthen party organization and carry out its work in places with more complex conditions or weaker foundations, ensuring large-scale coverage of the work and consolidating our social foundations to prevent 'Cask Effect'." Therefore, the enforcement of strict discipline must be practiced and reflected in party organizations.

Party members are organizational cells of the party. The demands of governing the party with strict discipline must be implemented in the management of party members. On January 28, 2003, General Secretary Xi Jinping presided over a meeting of the Political Bureau of the CPC Central Committee. He researched into and worked out arrangements for the development and management of party members under new conditions, and set up general requirements for "controlling quantity, optimizing structure, improving quality as well as performing duties". We need to control the quantity of the party members. We should strengthen overall guidance in the work of recruiting new party members, formulate and implement recruitment plans, and keep a moderate amount of party members. We must be strict in the recruitment work, set political standards as the priority of work, and never allow those with impure motives or those seeking profits by taking advantage of being a party member to join our party, so as to guarantee the quality of party members from the start of work. Also, we need to optimize the structure of party organizations. We should make more efforts to recruit party members from workers, continue to conduct the job among farmers and attach importance to recruiting party members from among young workers, farmers and intellectuals. We should strengthen daily education and routine work, and impose restrictions on organizational activities within the party. It is an ideal for us to see that our party members can usually conduct themselves in an exemplary fashion, act resolutely while undertaking crucial work and brave dangers in crisis, setting a good example for the people. We need to clear the outlet of the organization, treat problematic members of the party in a timely way and accordingly, we should expel unqualified ones from our organization, nullify ineffective ones and tackle corrupted ones and violators of party discipline or state laws in accordance with the law.

Community-level party organizations are the foundation for all the work of the party and its governance capability. To carry out the policy of governing the party with strict discipline, we must do solid work to develop community-level party organizations, lay a sound foundation, and improve their systems. Under the new circumstances, there emerged a new situation and a new problem that organizations at the upper level are sound and complete, while those at the lower level, the community level, are weak and in need of improvement. If we want to have a larger coverage over communities for the establishment of party organizations, we should place more stress on cooperation with farmers' cooperatives, rural-urban fringe zones, gathering places of migrating population, industrial parks and so on, so that we can work out a new pattern of urban-rural integration in community-level party building. We should tackle feeble and lax community-level party organizations as an urgent task. To substantially strengthen community-level party organizations, we should draw on experience of state-owned enterprises in the construction of party organizations and on opinions and methods of social organizations in party building, to amend the *Regulations on the CPC*

Rural Grassroots Organizations Work so as to further regulate and standardize duty orientation, work requirements and activity style of community-level or grassroots organizations. We must establish rigorous regulations for the work of community-level organizations and make efforts to make the practice of serving the mass and engaging in the mass' work more institutionalized, more regular and ever-lasting. We should shift the focus of party organizations' work to serving the national development, the peoples' happiness and wellbeing, the masses and the party members, and cater to the requirements of serving the mass in terms of its leadership, working approach and activity style. With both sincere concern and strict requirements, we should be giving more understanding, trust, attention and care to officials at community-level while intensifying their education and training and advocating exemplary models, with the hope that they will work diligently and happily with honor and the aspiration to serve the people even better. Officials at all levels should pay attention to community-level party organizations, care for them, support them, increase investments, enhance the competence of their leaders, and ensure that they can be more resourceful and capable to serve the mass.

Intra-party political activities function as the major platform for the party to educate and manage its members and to cultivate their party spirit. To exercise strict self-governance, we must take these activities seriously. However, under the impact of various factors, regulations on intra-party political activities have not been fully implemented in some localities, leading to a tendency of being vulgar, entertainment-oriented, professionalized and arbitrary. Meanwhile, decentralization, individualism and the 'nice guy' mentality prevail among party members, and some of them, with a blurred judgment of right or wrong, do not even know what intra-party political activities are actually for. The Program of Mass Line Education and Practice is in essence a healthy and serious activity conducted within our party, widely tempering and baptizing party members for their spiritual pursuit and sense of party awareness. If we want to promote it further, we should continue to improve and implement various regulations on our political activities, and to promote them sincerely and strictly throughout the party. How can we conduct intra-party political activities under strict discipline? General Secretary Xi Jinping stressed that we should adhere to and fully utilize the 'four crucial weapons' - democratic centralism, criticism and self-criticism among party members, strict enforcement of regulations on political activities and strengthening solidarity and unity of the party. First, democratic centralism must be faithfully implemented. We should carry forward democracy in our party, foster a better atmosphere for democratic discussions, and encourage party members to speak the truth, allowing the collision and arguments of different ideas while properly using centralism, instead of discussing without making any decisions or making decisions without implementing them. We must strictly follow procedures, regulations and collective will, resolutely oppose and prevent arbitrary will of individuals or of the minority. Second, we should make good use of the weapon of criticism and self-criticism. The quality of intra-party political activities largely depends on how well this weapon is applied. We should use it courageously, frequently, fully and effectively, make it a habit, a kind of awareness and a duty of party members, and make it more flexible and productive at work. Positive and healthy ideological activities need to be carried out in the party to help party members and officials to learn right from wrong, tell truth from falsehood, firmly uphold the truth, correct mistakes, unify the will and strengthen solidarity. We should take party branch meetings as a crucial platform to solve leading groups' own problems, with leaders taking the lead, and enable them to accept advice with wide-open posture, hold positive and healthy theoretical arguments and truly improve the quality of democratic meetings. Third, we must exercise intra-party organizational activities with strict discipline to enhance the political, principled and militant character of party members, and make sure that all such kinds of activity are oriented to addressing real problems. Fourth, we should value the genuine unity of the party based on principles and party awareness, but resolutely fight against or correct a false façade of all getting on well with others on the surface, while rivaling or erecting barriers against each other behind the scenes.

5. We should remain strict in system enforcement, and exercise strict self-governance through party laws and regulations.

Before assuming the post of General Secretary, Comrade Xi Jinping had clearly pointed out that to deal with the issue of exercising strict self-governance, "The fundamental approach is building systems by strictly conforming to the law that applies for developing a governing party. Hereby, we should continue to strengthen intra-party activities and development institutions in a more rigorous and scientific way. We should establish both tangible institutions and procedural regulations. We should explicitly prescribe not only how to act but also how to punish in case of violation of provisions, and reduce the discretion space in the implementation of regulations so as to promote party building in a more scientific, institutionalized and standardized way." Since the 18th CPC National Congress, in light of the Program of Mass Line

Education and Practice, improving party conduct, upholding integrity while combating corruption, General Secretary Xi Jinping delivered a series of speeches on supervising and governing the party via institutions, and revealed that this practice is vital for the survival of the party. He stressed that we should strengthen the construction of party rules and regulations, improve the systems and mechanisms for their formulation, and correspondingly create a complete system of institutions within the party. We should apply these rules and regulations to the full implementation of the principle that the party supervises its own conduct, exercise strict discipline, and encourage party members and officials to take the lead in acting in accordance with state laws and party regulations. He points out that, "We should integrate the requirements of the Central Committee, actual needs, and fresh experiences to develop new systems that are appropriate to the current situation, to upgrade the existing systems and to abolish those that are not." Xi Jinping believes that, "Any newly-developed or improved system must be easy to implement, be coherent with the established laws, and function within the existing legal framework. Attention must be given to formulating supporting measures to match the new systems. Besides, we should apply revolutionary spirit and law-based approach, integrate the requirements of the Central Committee, people's expectations, actual needs and fresh experiences in an effort to develop a complete system of institutions that provide for rigid institutional constraints and strict systematic execution. With these practices, we may make it possible that the party work style is standardized, normalized and persistent", and may prevent our institutions from becoming a façade - like a scarecrow.

General Secretary Xi Jinping emphasized that the vitality of laws and regulations rest with the implementation of them, which in turn depends on taking real actions and performing with strict discipline. Efforts should be made to promote the awareness of laws, regulations and disciplines among the party's members and officials by carrying out publicity and education in the party, so as to create a fine environment of respecting, observing and guarding the laws and regulations. We should ensure that all people are equal before the law and regulations, and the enforcement of such rules allows no privilege or exception. We should intensify our efforts in implementing regulations, making rigid systems and prohibitions exert power and authority, and ensuring they are fit to resolve real problems. We should strengthen the exercise of the supervision and inspection institutions, exerting pressure and pushing forward their implementation. We must discipline violators seriously, making no exceptions for the powerful, not indulging minor offenses and not letting violators go, even if they are legion. The CPC should guard against 'broken windows theory,' referring to the idea that petty crimes need to be stopped to prevent more serious crime. Since the 18th CPC National Congress, the 'cage' of the party laws and regulations has been woven more closely and tightly. The *Regulations of the CPC on Formulation of Party Laws* and the *Rules of the CPCon Archives of Party Laws and Documents* were newly issued as an important move in using laws to regulate power. We intensively dealt with the party regulations and regulatory documents formulated since 1978, 40% of which were abolished or publicized regarding their invalidity. More than 20 new regulations on clean government were introduced, ranging from major matters such as the selection and appointment of officials, official receptions and department conference expenditure, to small matters like banning cigarette smoking in public, sending greeting cards, and purchasing fireworks. We have achieved remarkable results through formulating and strictly enforcing regulations and systems.

III. The Party Members' and Officials' Exemplary Role in Observing Rules and Disciplines

General Secretary Xi Jinping has repeatedly stressed that party organizations at all levels, and all party members, especially the party's leading officials, must abide by party rules and act in accordance with party discipline. At the Fifth Plenary Session of the 18th CPC Central Committee, he focused on the major issue of strict party rules and discipline, and also emphasized one more time that we should reinforce regulation construction and put observing rules and discipline in a more prominent position. Since the 18th CPC National Congress, we placed observing strict rules as an important measure for exercising strict self-governance. The rigidness of rule constraints has been more pronounced through intensified discipline reinforcement and strict execution. Indeed, we should realize that these results are only temporary at a certain stage, so we must persevere in efforts of regulation formulation and compliance, and make it as a high-tension line of deterrence so as to foster a lively situation in which party members stay true to party rules and discipline.

The *Guidelines of the CPC on Integrity and Self-discipline* (*Guidelines*, in brief, for later reference) and *Regulations of the CPC on the Penalty for Rule Violation* (*Regulations*, in brief), newly approved by the Political Bureau of the CPC Central Committee, are important fruits of the practice of the guiding principles of the 18th CPC National Congress and the spirit of a series of important speeches delivered by General Secretary Xi Jinping. They are also important achievements in strengthening the construction of the party laws and regulations, as well as fundamental measures to strengthen party building and exercise strict party discipline. Party members, especially leading officials, should conscientiously pursue high standards of integrity and self-discipline, stay away from regulation red lines by strictly observing party discipline, serve an exemplary role, and take a lead in fostering a good environment for the party in which rule and disciplines are respected, observed and safeguarded.

1. To exercise strict self-governance of the party relies on strict rules and discipline.

No political party can run without discipline or rules, and they are a must for all parties. In Britain where the earliest modern political party in the world emerged, all parties have strict rules and discipline. For example, as early as in 1903 in Britain, the Labor Party made it clear that its party members should promote the interests of the party and should not to contradict the 'vows' they made to the party. Besides, many political parties in Europe and the United States have a parliamentary supervisor, the so-called 'party whip', whose main responsibility is to urge the party members to comply with the rules of the party and to take disciplinary measures against members who violate the rules. Historical experience has proved that there is no such a political party without discipline in the world, not to mention a Marxist party. With lax discipline or rules, any political party is doomed to decline and even to collapse. An important lesson from the failure of the Communist Party of the Soviet Union is that they abandoned the principle of democratic centralism and strict discipline of the party.

Our party is a Marxist party, the organization of which relies on revolutionary ideals and strict discipline. This has always been our party's fine tradition and unique advantage. Under the new historical circumstances, our party must depend on strict rules and discipline to unite and lead the people in realizing the 'Two Centenary Goals'. Certainly, the party's rules and discipline have not emerged only recently. But why have the CPC Central Committee and General Secretary Xi Jinping been highlighting this issue since the 18th CPC National Congress? Because for a period of time, we have not been strict enough in governing the party; some party members nurtured wrong understandings and misconceptions regarding party rules and discipline. They took them for granted, regarding them as a façade, and even worse, some of them recklessly breached party rules and discipline. If this tendency cannot be reversed in timely and effective fashion, a big problem will develop for our party. Therefore, General Secretary Xi Jinping stressed, "The party must supervise its own conduct and run itself with strict disciplines." Our party, with more than 88million members, should make it a higher priority that party members will strictly conform to party rules and disciplines, so that our party can maintain its status as a governing party in running a big developing country with a population of over 1.3 billion.

2. The priority of the party's self-governance is to stay true to strict political rules and discipline of the party.

The party has both written and unwritten rules and discipline. Some of the fine traditions and routines are formed during long term practice. Though some of them are not in a written form, they are still party discipline that must be followed by party members and officials. Among the written documents, there is the *Constitution of the CPC*, two Guidelines, more than twenty Regulations and many other rules, standards, measures and specifications. The CPC *Constitution* is the party's 'fundamental law' with general rules by which all comrades of the party must abide. The newly amended *Guidelines of the CPC on Integrity and Self-discipline* and *Regulations of the CPC on the Penalty for Rule Violation* are specified rules of the CPC *Constitution* and should also be observed by all party members. Among all types of rules of the party, the most important, fundamental and critical ones are political rules and discipline. The party's organizational discipline, regulations of work and mass line rules are reflections of the party's political discipline in different aspects and in different sectors of work. Any type of violation will undermine our governing foundation and sabotage our political discipline. On the contrary, if we can stay true to our political rules and discipline, sober in political awareness and firm in political conviction, we may avoid doing anything in violation of party rules and discipline. Therefore, to abide by the party's political rules and discipline is the important foundation for observing all other rules of the party.

The essence of observing the party's political discipline is to adhere to the party's leadership, basic theory, basic line, basic program, basic experience and basic requirements, keep in line with the party Central Committee, and conscientiously safeguard its authority. The party's political rules and discipline are not abstract but concrete, and to align with the CPC Central Committee is not an empty slogan but a major political principle. Oriented to outstanding problems of discipline violation at the present stage, the *Regulations of the CPC on the Penalty for Rule Violation* underscore political rules and discipline, and specify penalties over any opposition against the party's leadership, basic theory, basic line, basic program, basic experience and basic requirements. We should always put priority on strictly observing political rules and discipline, and sincerely abide by political rules of the *Regulations of the CPC on the Penalty for Rule Violation* in an effort to promote the strict enforcement of other rules or discipline.

3. To observe rules and discipline is a test of party spirit for members and officials of the party.

The party's rules and discipline are behavioral yardsticks for party organizations and members, while the national laws and regulations are basic rules for all Chinese citizens. The nature and purpose of the party have determined that the party's rules and discipline are supposed to be stricter than our national laws and regulations. Whoever breaches the national law must have already violated the party's regulations. Therefore, to help party members and officials avoid ending up as criminals, but consistently stay as good comrades, we should prioritize the enforcement of party rules and discipline, and tackle small problems as early as possible to stop them from developing into big disasters. The observance of discipline is an important test of party spirit and loyalty for party members and officials. Leading officials of party members should play an exemplary role in practicing honesty and self-discipline, and voluntarily maintain the authority of the discipline. Also, they should act as a sensible promoter, take the lead in learning, promoting, and elaborating the *Guidelines* and *Regulations* as well as various other rules of the party, raise the consciousness of observing these rules, and always bear them in mind. We should always be strict with ourselves, improve our own conduct, resolutely discard the idea of 'privileged party member', work and exercise authority under strict discipline, do what we ask others to do and never do what we ask others not to do, and subject ourselves to the supervision and restraint of party organizations and party members, playing a leading role in observing the party's rules and discipline. We should perform our duties with loyalty, operate under strict party discipline, take the lead in enforcing discipline and upholding integrity, and seriously tackle problems and the violations of rules and discipline, even in our own working units. We should not evade or shirk responsibilities, or behave only like 'nice guys', but instead we should perform as discipline guardians to ensure the strict exercise of all rules and laws of the party.

IV. Understanding regarding 'Make Party Building Our Biggest Achievement'

At the concluding conference of the Program of Mass Line Education and Practice held in October 2014, General Secretary Xi Jinping emphasized, "Party committees at all levels and in all departments should have a clear understanding of job performance, always examine situations from the perspective of a governing party and with a consideration of how to consolidate the ruling status of our party, and make party building our biggest achievement." He pointed out, "If our party is weakened, disintegrated or collapsed, what's the point of other achievements?" The succinct statement of "make party building our biggest achievement" reveals the important position of the work of party building in new situations, and brings to light its practical and far-reaching significance, receiving active responses from party members and officials. However, some comrades have some doubts in their mind, for example; 'Isn't it contradictory to our repeated principle that development is the top priority', or 'whether we should only attach importance to party building rather than development', and so on. The answer is definite: NO. Then, what is the relation between these two principles? How can we correctly understand and properly handle it?

1. The key to development lies in promoting party building, which is a sure requirement of the principle that 'development is the top priority'. The victory of the independence and liberation of the Chinese nation has been achieved under the leadership of the CPC; the success of settling the problem of food and clothing of over 1.3 billion Chinese people and essentially completing the building of a moderately prosperous society in all respects is also accomplished under the party's leadership. All the historical experiences in modern times have come to the basic conclusion that without the CPC, the birth of new China, the formation of socialism with Chinese characteristics, and the modernization of socialism would have been impossible. With the practice of contemporary China and the features of the times, the party is going to lead the people in carrying out the great undertaking with many new historical characteristics, withstand and overcome various risks and challenges. Among them, a primary and essential task is to advance party building, a basic prerequisite and fundamental guarantee for the attainment of the 'Two Centenary Goals'. If our party is weakened, disintegrated, or even collapsed, the great cause of socialism with Chinese characteristics will come to an end, and the accomplishments of national prosperity and rejuvenation as well as the people's happiness and wellbeing will be groundless. As Comrade

Deng Xiaoping pointed out, without leadership by the party, a big country like China would be torn by strife and incapable of accomplishing anything. And likewise, with degraded atmosphere, disintegrated teams and distracted minds, we may gain temporary achievements, but they are definitely not what we want. At the same time, leading officials at all levels should be aware that outstanding performance in a mis-directed development will not receive natural political recognition. If we do advance the economy greatly, but corruption grows worse, people may harbor an even stronger sense of deprivation against us. Deng Xiaoping, as early as in the 1980s, warned the whole party that, "If standards of social conduct are deteriorating, what's the use of achieving economic development? Worse, deteriorating social standards will in turn lead to a qualitative change in the economy, eventually producing a society in which embezzlement, theft and bribery run rampant." In this sense, it is essential to promote party building if we want further development, so party building will be the greatest achievement of development. Research by politics of development also shows that a powerful political party plays a crucial role for the stability and development of modern developing countries. The success of our modernization and the creation of 'Chinese miracles' are all achieved under the leadership of the CPC. It is a natural conclusion from the experiences of modern Chinese history that the key to resolving Chinese problems lies in the party. Therefore, party committees at all levels must have the following consciousness: it is our task to do a good job in party building, and if not, it will be our dereliction or malpractice of duty. We must concentrate on party building, take it as the greatest achievement of our party so as to provide a solid political guarantee for the realization of the 'Two Centenary Goals'.

2. Development is also a must to party building, for the requirement for development is an implication of the statement: 'make party building our greatest achievement'. The frustrating and humiliating experiences of China since modern times tell us that the weak is prone to be bullied, and that a nation can never stand firmer and stronger among the world's nations without self-improvement. Development is of primary importance to China as a key to addressing all of our problems. Thanks to our development strategy, it only took China a few decades to travel a journey that took developed countries several centuries to cover. Eventually, we should proceed with the journey of development to realize the 'Two Centenary Goals' and the Chinese dream of the great rejuvenation of the Chinese nation. At present, China as the largest developing country in the world, is still in the primary stage of socialism, and will remain so for a long time to come, so taking economic development as the central task is vital to national renewal, and development is still the most important matter for our party, to govern the country well and rejuvenate the nation. Only by promoting sustainable and sound economic development can we lay a solid material foundation for enhancing the country's prosperity and strength, improving the people's wellbeing and ensuring social harmony and stability. Party building has been long connected with its political lines, serving the historical mission of the party and its central task. At present, party building must be oriented to the realization of the 'Two Centenary Goals' as its fundamental direction, so we must focus our work closely on development, that is the most important thing for our party to govern the country well and rejuvenate the nation, and endeavor to transform the advantage and fruits of party building into the competitive edge and achievements of our national development, making party building more aligned to the requirements of socialist modernization. Only when party building is oriented to serving the overall situation of the party and the state, can we secure the foundation for, and ultimate attainment of, the great practice of socialism with Chinese characteristics, and thus broaden our stage for development and obtain the source of vitality. Hence, party committees at all levels and in all departments must take development as the most important thing for our party to govern the country well and rejuvenate the nation, and pursue development wholeheartedly so as to promote the coordinated, sustainable and overall development of economic, political, cultural, social and ecological progress, consolidating the foundation for party building and the governing status of the party.

We should organically integrate party building with development, truly concentrate on party building and pay full attention to development. Party building is the support and guarantee of development, while development is the foundation for and ultimate attainment of the advancement of party building. They complement each other and form an integral and organic whole. However, for a long time, some party committees, leading party members' groups and party officials have not been able to understand or handle their relationships well. In their view, development is a crucial and solid task, but party building is virtual and ignorable and does not require much attention. Currently, it is prevalent among them to believe that more importance is attached to development rather than party building, resulting in an unbalanced relationship between party building and development. Over time, the problem of 'four forms of decadence' tends to pile up, hidden rules prevail and the political ecosystem deteriorates. The root cause lies in the fact that party building has not yet been well conducted and the requirement of exercising strict discipline has not yet been sincerely implemented. Party committees at all levels should correctly understand the relationship between party building and development so that they would no longer judge the performance of officials merely by GDP growth rate, or conduct 'Party building solely for the sake of party building'. Instead, they should continue to plan, implement and assess party building along with the central work of development. They should adopt a concrete and profound approach to promoting party building in all types of work, in all areas and in all sectors, and make sure that equal emphasis and mutual reinforcement are put on them simultaneously.

Party committees at all levels must shoulder the responsibility of exercising strict discipline, and implement it throughout their work. In his speech to the concluding conference of the Program of Mass Line Education and Practice, General Secretary Xi Jinping expounded thoroughly on how to supervise our party's conduct and exercise strict discipline in all respects, and he also brought forth clear requirements in this regard. In this speech, he initiated the description of 'three NOs', corresponding to the lesson we draw from history and reality, and especially from this program. He said that if there is no clear prescription of duty, no genuine fulfillment of work and no accountability system for performance, it is impossible for us to govern the party strictly. Therefore, to exercise strict self-governance of the party, we must better understand the importance of the accountability system and heighten our awareness and sense of responsibility for this task. Soon after, General Secretary Xi Jinping raised 'three questions' with regard to the same issue, strict party self-governance. He pointed out that party committees at all levels, through years of efforts, have completed the construction of a system of institutions accountable for the responsibilities of party building. Under this system, a party committee supervises its secretary who in turn is responsible for the work of party building in his field, and this operation goes on hierarchically throughout all sectors of work in the party. "Nonetheless, have the party committees (leading party member's groups) at all levels and in all departments been dedicated to promoting party building? Have their secretaries been taking the lead in exercising strict discipline the party? Have the members of the party committees performed their duty in this regard at their work?" General Secretary Xi Jinping thought that some localities and departments might not have met those standards, and could not give satisfactory answers to the three questions mentioned above. These three thought provoking questions, hit the nail on the head – sharply locating "three misunderstandings" regarding responsibility for party discipline enforcement. First, some leading officials think that, compared with development, party building is more intangible and it is not easy for them to attain outstanding accomplishments. Second, they think they don't need to bother too much but just organize a couple of meetings every year. Third, some of them think that we are endeavoring to develop socialist market economy, so there exists a dilemma for exercising strict party discipline: on the one hand, if the discipline is not strict enough, some people will cross the 'red line' and lots of others will follow suit, making punishment impossible; on the other hand, if the discipline is too strict, officials may be fettered by stringent rules, weakening their vitality at work, making them fail to accomplish a lot and even affecting their votes. All these are misconceptions. Therefore, party committees (leading party members' groups) at all levels and in all departments should have a clear understanding of job performance, put consolidating the party's governing status first, and take supervising and governing the party as a significant political responsibility. In practice, party committees at all levels should assume and fulfill the responsibility for exercising strict party discipline. They should adhere to the principle of planning, implementing and assessing party building simultaneously with the central work of development. They should adopt a concrete approach to deepening party building in all types of work, in all areas and in all sectors, with equal emphasis on development so as to guard against 'a firm hand on one type of work, but a soft hand on the other'. Our performance appraisal of the head of party committees (leading party members' groups) at all levels and in all departments, especially party secretaries, is firstly targeted at the effectiveness of party building in order to encourage them to be strict with discipline enforcement. In addition, the performance appraisal system for other members and leading officials should include more assessment indicators in this regard, so as to boost their responsibility for exercising strict party discipline in their field and make it possible that our party can truly operate under strict discipline in all sectors of work.

Chapter Follow-up Questions and References

Chapter 1

Questions:

1. What is the new normal in economic development?
2. How do you understand supply-side structural reform?

References:

1. *Xi Jinping: The Governance of China*. Beijing: Foreign Languages Press. 2014.
2. Publicity Department of the CPC Central Committee: *A Series of Important Speeches by General Secretary Xi Jinping* (2016). Beijing: Xuexi Publishing House, People's Publishing House. 2016.
3. *Central Committee of the CPC: Recommendations for the 13th Five-Year Plan for Economic and Social Development. Xinhua News Agency.* November 3, 2015.
4. Liu Wei. *Six Points of View on the Relationship between Government and Market.* China Times. June 5, 2014.
5. *A Renewed Definition of Informationization with Internet+: A Research Report on 'Internet+' (Part A, Part B)*. Guangming Daily. October 16, 2015.

Chapter 2

Questions:

1. Why does reform and opening up play a decisive role in determining the destiny of contemporary China?
2. What are your understandings on the targets and tasks of an all-around and deeper-level reform?

References:

1. *Xi Jinping: The Governance of China.* Beijing: Foreign Languages Press. 2014.
2. *Excerpts of Xi Jinping's Remarks on the Overall Deepening of Reform.* Beijing: Central Party Literature Press. 2014.

Chapter 3

Questions:

1. How do you interpret that the leadership of the CPC is the soul of rule of law for socialism with Chinese characteristics?
2. Why is the rule of law working as the basic means of governance in China?

References:

1. *Xi Jinping: The Governance of China.* Beijing: Foreign Languages Press. 2014.
2. *Guidance Book to 'Decision of the Central Committee of the CPC on Some Major Issues Concerning Comprehensively Promoting Rule of Law'.* Beijing: People's Publishing House. 2014.

Chapter 4

Questions:

1. What is the socialist deliberative democracy?
2. Why can't China implement a 'Multi-Party System'?

References:

1. Xi Jinping: *The Speech at the Conference to Celebrate the CPPCC's 65th Anniversary. People's Daily.* September 22, 2014.
2. Xi Jinping: *The Speech at the Conference to Celebrate the 60th Anniversary of the National People's Congress. China Daily.* September 6, 2014.
3. *Central Committee of the CPC: Recommendations for the 13th Five-Year Plan for Economic and Social Development.* Xinhua News Agency. November 3, 2015.

Chapter 5

Questions:

1. Why is ideological progress one of the Party's top priorities?
2. Why is building core socialist values functioning as a significant aspect of a nation's governing system and capacity?

References:

1. Xi Jinping. *A Speech at the Forum on Literature and Art Work (2014). People's Daily*. October 15, 2015.
2. Central Commission for Discipline Inspection of the CPC, Party Literature Research Centre of the CPC Central Committee: *Excerpts of Xi Jinping's Exposition on the Construction of the Party Conduct and of an Honest and Clean Government and on the Struggle against Corruption*. Central Literature Publishing House, China Lianzheng Publishing House. 2015.

Chapter 6

Questions:

1. Why do the CPC and the Chinese Government pay special attention to people's livelihood?
2. How do you understand equity and justice during the process of reform?

References:

1. Party Literature Research Centre of the CPC Central Committee: *Excerpts of Important Speeches by General Secretary Xi Jinping*. Beijing: Party Building Books Publishing House, Central Literature Publishing House. 2016.
2. *Central Committee of the CPC: Recommendations for the 13th Five-Year Plan for Economic and Social Development*. Xinhua News Agency. November 3, 2015.
3. Luo Huide: *Experiences and Implications of Foreign Governing Parties on Solving Livelihood Problems. Journal of The Party School of Tianjin Committee of The CPC*. 2012 (1).

Chapter 7

Questions:

1. Why is it of great necessity to promote socialist ecological progress?

2. Why is setting ecological red lines reckoned as a prime task and a top priority to promote the institutional construction of ecological civilization?

References:

1. *Opinions of the Central Committee of the CPC and the State Council on Accelerating the Promotion of Ecological Progress.* Beijing: People's Publishing House. 2015.

2. *For the Ever-Growing of the Chinese Nation: Records on General Secretary Xi Jinping's Activites in Support of the Construction of Ecological Civilization.* Beijing: Xinhuanet. March 9, 2015.

Chapter 8

Questions:

1. Why does the CPC especially stress exercising strict self-governance in every respect?

2. What are the proofs of 'strictness' in exercising strict self-governance in every respect by the CPC?

References:

1. Publicity Department of the CPC Central Committee: *A Series of Important Speeches by General Secretary Xi Jinping* (2016). Beijing: Xuexi Publishing House, People's Publishing House. 2016.

2. Party Literature Research Centre of the CPC Central Committee: *Excerpts of Xi Jinping's Remarks on Exercising Strict Self-Governance in Every Respect.* Beijing: Central Party Literature Press. 2016.

3. Central Commission for Discipline Inspection of the CPC, Party Literature Research Centre of the CPC Central Committee: *Excerpts of Xi Jinping's Exposition on the Construction of the Party Conduct and of an Honest and Clean Government and on the Struggle against Corruption.* Central Literature Publishing House, China Lianzheng Publishing House. 2015.

责任编辑:洪　琼
版式设计:顾杰珍

图书在版编目(CIP)数据

中国治理新方略/冯俊　主编. —北京:人民出版社,2017.2
(中国故事丛书/冯俊主编)
ISBN 978－7－01－017286－6

I.①中… Ⅱ.①冯… Ⅲ.①社会主义法制-建设-研究-中国　Ⅳ.①D920.0

中国版本图书馆 CIP 数据核字(2017)第 015355 号

中国治理新方略

ZHONGGUO ZHILI XINFANGLÜE

冯　俊　主编

人民出版社 出版发行
(100706　北京市东城区隆福寺街 99 号)

北京汇林印务有限公司印刷　新华书店经销

2017 年 2 月第 1 版　2017 年 2 月北京第 1 次印刷
开本:710 毫米×1000 毫米 1/16　印张:26
字数:410 千字　印数:0,001-5,000 册

ISBN 978－7－01－017286－6　定价:64.00 元

邮购地址 100706　北京市东城区隆福寺街 99 号
人民东方图书销售中心　电话 (010)65250042　65289539

《中国治理新方略》一书的英文部分由蔡君梅（Cai Junmei）翻译